PROGRAMS FOR ACTION
IN THE SIXTIES

Goals
for
Americans

comprising

U.S.

*The Report of the President's
Commission on National Goals*

and

*Chapters Submitted for the
Consideration of the Commission*

A Spectrum Book
Prentice-Hall, Inc.

Administered by
The American Assembly
Columbia University

Third Printing—April 1961

HENRY M. WRISTON, *Chairman*
President, The American Assembly, Columbia University; President, Brown University, 1937-55.

FRANK PACE, JR., *Vice Chairman*
Chairman of the Board, General Dynamics Corporation; Secretary of the Army, 1950-53.

ERWIN D. CANHAM
Editor-in-Chief, *Christian Science Monitor;* President, United States Chamber of Commerce, 1959-60.

JAMES B. CONANT
Ambassador to the Federal Republic of Germany, 1955-57; President, Harvard University, 1933-53.

COLGATE W. DARDEN, JR.
Governor, Commonwealth of Virginia, 1942-46; Member of Congress, 1933-37, 1939-41; President, University of Virginia, 1947-59.

CRAWFORD H. GREENEWALT
President, E. I. du Pont de Nemours & Company.

ALFRED M. GRUENTHER, General, U.S.A. (ret.)
President, American Red Cross; Supreme Allied Commander in Europe, 1953-56.

LEARNED HAND
Retired Judge, U. S. Court of Appeals for the Second Circuit. *Served until October 1, 1960.*

CLARK KERR
President, University of California.

JAMES R. KILLIAN, JR.
Chairman of the Corporation, Massachusetts Institute of Technology; Special Assistant to the President of the United States for Science and Technology, 1957-59.

GEORGE MEANY
President, AFL-CIO.

Members of the Commission

Preface

Goals for Americans—the Report of the President's Commission on National Goals and the essays accompanying it—is designed to encourage informed discussion by the American public. The book will also provide a basis for deliberations by regional, state and municipal sessions of The American Assembly as well as by civic groups, classes and other discussion meetings.

President Eisenhower requested that the Commission be administered by The American Assembly, Columbia University, because of its status as a non-partisan educational institution and its established practices for encouraging wide consideration of public issues. The Assembly, founded by President Eisenhower in 1950 when he was President of Columbia, takes no official stand itself on any of the topics it presents.

Private financing and fiscal management of the Commission were provided under the auspices of the Assembly. The Commission wishes to record its gratitude to the following foundations, which gave financial support: Carnegie Corporation of New York, Maurice and Laura Falk Foundation, The Ford Foundation, Johnson Foundation (Racine), Richardson Foundation, The Rockefeller Foundation, Alfred P. Sloan Foundation, U. S. Steel Foundation. The foundations are not responsible for the views stated in the Report or in the chapters.

A special word of gratitude is due to President Grayson Kirk and the Trustees of Columbia University for waiving the normal administrative charges for Assembly projects.

The Commission is appreciative of the efforts of members of the White House staff, who have assisted in every possible way without seeking to influence the Commission's work.

In devising methods to assure the widest possible circulation of the Report, the Commission has had the valuable, and unpaid, assistance of Messrs. Harold Brown, Merle Colby, Douglas Larsen, and Albert Zack. The Advertising Council will conduct a public service campaign to assist in wide circulation of the Report and essays.

Contents

ACCOMPANYING CHAPTERS
BY INDIVIDUAL AUTHORS

THE ROLE OF GOVERNMENT

THE WORLD WE SEEK

Letter of Transmittal

THE PRESIDENT'S COMMISSION ON NATIONAL GOALS

administered by

THE AMERICAN ASSEMBLY, COLUMBIA UNIVERSITY
New York 27, New York

November 16, 1960

Dear Mr. President:

We transmit herewith the Report of the President's Commission on National Goals. It is in compliance with your request to "develop a broad outline of coordinated national policies and programs" and to "set up a series of goals in various areas of national activity."

We have respected your desire that our efforts be non-partisan, and have no connection with the government. All financial support has come from private sources, with the sole exception of unfurnished offices temporarily available for our small staff. The only participation of government officials has been to supply requested data.

We asked the counsel of approximately 100 people expert in various topics, and invited 14 men and women of acknowledged competence to write essays for our consideration. The response was generous, many accepting the assignment at considerable personal sacrifice. We desire to record our deep gratitude to them. We have also drawn upon excellent work and reports in relevant fields, by many groups and institutions.

However, the Report expresses views that reflect solely our own judgment, sometimes in accord with and other times at variance from those of the several authors. This judgment was arrived at during long hours at the conference table, and members of the Commission participated actively in drafting the Report.

We do not expect our recommendations to command unanimous acceptance. Rather it is our hope that they will evoke active discussion. Under the democratic process this is the path to a national consensus. The Report and the accompanying chapters will be published in cloth and paper bound editions. We hope the volume will have wide circulation.

Our work would have been impossible without the assistance of a brilliant staff. Mr. William Bundy, the Staff Director, Mr. Hugh Calkins, his Deputy, Mr. Guy Coriden, Jr., Miss Barbara Donald, and Mr. Hubert Kay, together with Miss Blanche Moore and Mrs. Margaret Keefe, have given themselves unsparingly to this task. They have had the loyal and effective support of the officers and staff of The American Assembly, especially Mr. Peter Grenquist, Mrs. Olive Haycox, and Mrs. Sylva Sinanian.

Judge Learned Hand participated in the early meetings which established the procedures and policies of the Commission. His wisdom and cooperative temper made his participation extremely valuable. To our great regret, because of ill health he was forced to withdraw from active participation before the Report of the Commission was drafted.

We express our gratitude for the opportunity which you opened to us by our appointment.

Respectfully,

Erwin D. Canham
James B. Conant
Colgate W. Darden, Jr.
Crawford H. Greenewalt
Alfred M. Gruenther
Clark Kerr
James R. Killian, Jr.
George Meany
Frank Pace, Jr., *Vice Chairman*
Henry M. Wriston, *Chairman*

The President,
The White House

The Commission Report

INTRODUCTION

The paramount goal of the United States was set long ago. It is to guard the rights of the individual, to ensure his development, and to enlarge his opportunity. It is set forth in the Declaration of Independence drafted by Thomas Jefferson and adopted by the Continental Congress on July 4, 1776. The goals we here identify are within the framework of the original plan and are calculated to bring to fruition the dreams of the men who laid the foundation of this country.

They stated their convictions quite simply:

"We hold these truths to be self-evident, that all men are created equal, that they are endowed by their Creator with certain unalienable Rights, that among these are Life, Liberty, and the pursuit of Happiness. That to secure these rights, Governments are instituted among Men, deriving their just powers from the consent of the governed."

It was a mighty vision. In the echo of those fateful words can be heard the onrolling thunder of a new age. It was an even broader and bolder declaration than those who made it knew. Its soaring vision enabled our society to meet the trials of emerging nationhood. It placed the young republic securely behind the principle that every human being is of infinite worth. In time it led the nation out of the morass of human slavery. It inspires us still in the struggle against injustice.

To make this vision a reality, a framework of self-government was established nationally and in each state. It rested upon two fundamental principles—the election of representatives from among competing candidates, and the constitutional limitation of power of those elected.

The way to preserve freedom is to live it. Our enduring aim is to build a nation and help build a world in which every human being shall be free to develop his capacities to the fullest. We must rededicate ourselves to this principle and thereby strengthen its appeal to a world in political, social, economic, and technological revolution.

In the 1960's every American is summoned to extraordinary personal responsibility, sustained effort, and sacrifice. For the nation is in grave danger, threatened by the rulers of one-third of mankind, for whom the state is everything, the individual significant only as he serves

1

the state. These rulers seek the "peace" of a Communist-oriented world, in which freedom is suppressed and the individual permanently subordinated. Supporting their aim are the Soviet Union's great and swiftly growing strength, the industrial and military progress and potential of Red China, a great capacity for political organization and propaganda, and the specious appeal of Communist doctrine to peoples eager for rapid escape from poverty.

Meanwhile, weapons of cataclysmic power have come into existence. A major nuclear conflict would be a world catastrophe; violence even in or between small nations could involve the great powers and spark the holocaust.

The Sino-Soviet threat and modern weapons present great dangers; we have equally great opportunities. With the increase of knowledge and material resources, we have achieved a standard of individual realization new to history. We can continue to improve our own way of life, and at the same time help in the progress of vast numbers in the world whose lives are blighted by chronic sickness, hunger, and illiteracy.

Since 1946, foreign rule has ended for more than one billion people in Asia and Africa. Much of their yearning for independence, for respect, and for abundance has been inspired by Western and especially American example. Nevertheless, historic resentments, inadequate economies, inexperience in self-government, and excessive expectations offer fertile ground for Communist persuasion and conquest. This restless tide of events defines the magnitude of our problems and the scope of our opportunity.

* * * * * * * * * *

To preserve and enlarge our own liberties, to meet a deadly menace, and to extend the area of freedom throughout the world: these are high and difficult goals. Yet our past performance justifies confidence that they can be achieved if every American will accept personal responsibility for them.

This Report identifies goals and sets forth programs. It is directed to the citizens of this country, each of whom sets his own goals and seeks to realize them in his life, through private groups, and through various levels of government. Choices are hard, and costs heavy. They demand subordination of lesser goals to the greater. But the rewards are beyond calculation, for the future of our nation depends on the result.

At the same time, the United States cannot attain its goals alone, nor by offering the free world grudging alms or condescending leadership. We must lead, but in a spirit of genuine partnership. Together, the free peoples of the world can develop unmatched strength and vindicate the mighty vision of the Declaration.

2

PART I

GOALS AT HOME

1. THE INDIVIDUAL

The status of the individual must remain our primary concern. All our institutions—political, social, and economic—must further enhance the dignity of the citizen, promote the maximum development of his capabilities, stimulate their responsible exercise, and widen the range and effectiveness of opportunities for individual choice.

From this concern springs our purpose to achieve equal treatment of men and women, to enlarge their incentives and to expand their opportunities for self-development and self-expression. From it comes our insistence on widely distributed political and economic power, on the greatest range of free choice in our economy, and on the fair and democratic exercise of public and private power. It underlies the value we put on education. It guides the pursuit of science. It is the source of our interest in the health and welfare of every citizen.

The great ideas that have moved the world have sprung from unfettered human minds. The spirit of liberty, in which they thrive, makes one man hesitate to impose his will on another. It relies on the conviction that the truth will emerge from free inquiry and exchange of views.

The notion that ideas and individuals must be rejected merely because they are controversial denies the essence of our tradition. Schools and institutions of higher education, and the trustees, board members and legislators responsible for them, have a particular responsibility to ensure freedom of expression by students, faculty and administrators alike. We must bring up young men and women to believe in the individual and to act upon that belief. There are subtle and powerful pressures toward conformity in the economic, social, and political world. They must be resisted so that differences of taste and opinion will remain a constructive force in improving our society.

Unity of purpose must never be confused with unanimity of opinion. Vigorous controversy and the acceptance of dissent as a positive value will renew our strength and demonstrate to the world our calm confidence that truth and reason prevail in a free society.

2. EQUALITY

Vestiges of religious prejudice, handicaps to women, and, most important, discrimination on the basis of race must be recognized as morally wrong, economically wasteful, and in many respects dangerous. In this decade we must sharply lower these last stubborn barriers.

Progress toward realizing these ideals in practice has been extraordinary. We have ever more closely approached a classless society; there has been a revolution in the status of women; education is more nearly available to all; most citizens have opportunities which a century ago were dreamed of by only a handful.

Respect for the individual means respect for every individual. Every man and woman must have equal rights before the law, and an equal opportunity to vote and hold office, to be educated, to get a job and to be promoted when qualified, to buy a home, to participate fully in community affairs. These goals, which are at the core of our system, must be achieved by action at all levels.

Primary responsibility rests with individuals. Habits of prejudice and fear of social and economic pressure restrict employment opportunities and housing choices, cause exclusion from eating places, hotels, and recreation facilities, and inhibit the free action of public officers. No American should remain within the grip of these habits and fears.

The right to vote is basic. Private pressures and discriminatory administration of registration laws must not continue to obstruct it. Predominant state control of voting qualifications is traditional; but if necessary, the basic democratic right to vote must take precedence.

One role of government is to stimulate changes of attitude. Additional municipal, state, and federal legislation is essential.* The federal government should enforce the principle that federal funds shall not be disbursed to employers who discriminate on the basis of race. Similar policies should progressively be applied to federal grants for universities, hospitals, and airports, and to federal housing programs.**

By 1970 discrimination in higher education should be entirely overcome. Every state must make progress in good faith toward desegregation of publicly supported schools.***

3. THE DEMOCRATIC PROCESS

The degree of effective liberty available to its people should be the ultimate test for any nation. Democracy is the only means so far devised by which a nation can meet this test. To preserve and perfect the democratic process in the United States is therefore a primary goal in this as in every decade.

The democratic process functions only when the individual accepts his full responsibility as a citizen by forming considered opinions on public policy and by active participation in the choice of public representatives.

* See the Additional Statement by Mr. Meany, page 29.
** See the Additional Statement by Dr. Darden, page 24.
*** See the Additional Statements by Dr. Kerr, Dr. Killian and Mr. Meany, pages 26, 27, and 29.

Democracy gives reality to our striving for equality. It is the expression of individual self-respect; it clears the way for individual initiative, exercise of responsibility, and use of varied talents. It is basic to the peaceful adjustment of differences of opinion. It must not be curtailed out of impatience to find quick solutions.

The institutions of the federal government require improvement but not drastic change. As Mr. Rossiter's chapter points out, the conduct of the office of the President and the presence of high-quality people in key executive departments remain principal sources of effective policymaking and administrative performance.

Changing times require that the Congress reassess its procedures. Multiple hearings upon the same issue by several committees put an undue burden upon administrative officers and legislators. Congress could be more effective by focusing its attention on the determination of broad policies. Legislation has become unduly detailed. Congressional committees and their staffs too often encroach upon the administrative function. In the interests of efficiency and economy, Congress might well experiment with an occasional bill authorizing the President to eliminate or reduce specific items, subject to reversal by concurrent resolution.

Improvement of the democratic process requires a constantly better-informed public. Mass circulation periodicals have opportunities beyond their current performance. Television, although it has improved, can do better still in communicating serious ideas. In far too many communities, newspapers are inadequate in their coverage of significant public affairs. The problem of interesting and informing mass audiences, which most media must serve, is a constant challenge. The American people remain among the best informed in the world, but their sources of information must steadily be enriched to cope with ever more complex problems.

Private interest groups exemplify the rights of assembly and petition. Thus, the functioning of pressure groups of many kinds has become a part of our democratic process. Special interest groups must operate legitimately. The program of any particular group can be opposed most effectively by the formation of a counter group. There is need for more which represent broader interests such as consumers and taxpayers.

The vastly increased demands upon the federal government require at the higher levels more public servants equal in competence and imagination to those in private business and the professions. This involves a drastic increase in their compensation. The President should be given unequivocal authority and responsibility to develop a true senior civil service, along the lines suggested in Mr. Sayre's chapter. The executive branch must also place greater emphasis on the recruiting, training, and stimulation of career employees.

5

Employee organizations, dealing with the executive branch on wages and conditions of work, can play a constructive part.

National, state, and local governments collaborate and share power in many domestic concerns. To ensure dispersion of power within the system without obstructing solution of pressing national problems, we must pursue the following primary objectives: enlarge local discretion, as for example in the handling of matching federal grants; increase the financial resources of state and local governments;* represent urban populations more equitably in those state legislatures where they are now under-represented; further develop limited metropolitan authorities or governments.

Shared power (in Mr. Grodzins' phrase) is the key to the miracle of effective democratic government of a vast and diverse country. Our major cities and suburban areas need to find means to coordinate numerous local governments for the solution of common problems. State and local governments are increasing their activities more rapidly than the domestic sector of the federal government. Their load will continue to grow, and their capacity to meet it must be strengthened.

4. EDUCATION

The development of the individual and the nation demand that education at every level and in every discipline be strengthened and its effectiveness enhanced. New teaching techniques must continue to be developed. The increase in population and the growing complexity of the world add urgency.

Greater resources—private, corporate, municipal, state, and federal —must be mobilized. A higher proportion of the gross national product must be devoted to educational purposes. This is at once an investment in the individual, in the democratic process, in the growth of the economy, and in the stature of the United States.

Education is primarily a responsibility of the states. They have delegated responsibility for public elementary and secondary education to local authorities, and have chartered colleges and universities. This is the firmly established pattern; it can be made to function satisfactorily to meet the needs of our vast and diverse nation.

In a few states four-fifths of the youth complete four years of high school and one-half enroll in an institution of higher education. This is a majestic accomplishment. However, in many states less than half complete four years of high school and less than twenty per cent enter college. Clearly the goal is to bring every state nearer the present standard of the best. Within the next decade at least two-thirds of the youth in every state should complete twelve years of schooling and at least one-third enter college.

* See the Additional Statement by Mr. Meany, page 29.

There must be more and better teachers, enlarged facilities, and changes in curricula and methods. The enrollment in professional schools should be increased. Above all, schooling should fit the varying capacities of individuals; every student should be stimulated to work to his utmost; authentic concern for excellence is imperative.

Among the important things that should be done, along lines urged in Dr. Gardner's chapter, are the following:

• Small and inefficient school districts should be consolidated, reducing the total number from 40,000 to about 10,000. The local school district remains the key to good public education. Local boards should be greatly strengthened.

• Every state should have a high-level board of education.

• Teachers' salaries at all levels must be improved.

• Two-year colleges should be within commuting distance of most high school graduates.

• Graduate school capacity must be approximately doubled.

• Adult education should play a vital role, stressing a new emphasis on education throughout life.

Financial Support. Annual public and private expenditure for education by 1970 must be approximately $40 billion—double the 1960 figure. It will then be 5 per cent or more of the gross national product, as against less than 4 per cent today.

Most of these funds must continue to come from state and local governments, tuition payments and gifts. State and local appropriations have more than doubled since 1950. The federal role must now be expanded. Total government expenses at all levels must amount to $33 billion for education by 1970.

Federal aid to higher education must include increased scholarship and loan funds, support of research as an essential part of the educational process, and direct assistance for buildings and equipment.

The federal government should supplement state funds where per capita income is too low to maintain an adequate school program. It should also offer matching grants, for educational purposes to be determined by the states.* Since the Northwest Ordinance of 1787, the federal government has participated in the support of education without destroying local initiative and responsibility. In the future those values should still be safeguarded.

5. THE ARTS AND SCIENCES

Knowledge and innovation must be advanced on every front. In science we should allot a greater proportion of our total effort to basic

* See the Additional Statement by Mr. Meany, page 29.

7

research, first, to realize fully the rapidly unfolding opportunities to extend still further our understanding of the world, and second, to enrich applied science and technology so essential to the improvement of health, to economic growth, and to military power.

Today we must give high priority to those aspects of science and technology which will increase our military strength, but for the longer term we should recognize that our creative activities in science and all other fields will be more productive and meaningful if undertaken, not merely to be ahead of some other nation, but to be worthy of ourselves.

These objectives should govern our civilian space programs and policies. We should be highly selective in our space objectives and unexcelled in their pursuit. Prestige arises from sound accomplishment, not from the merely spectacular, and we must not be driven by nationalistic competition into programs so extravagant as to divert funds and talents from programs of equal or greater importance.

We should ensure that every young person with the desire and capacity to become a scientist has access to the best science education our leading scholars can devise. Given the availability of such education, science will find its fair share of the pool of talent. But this pool of talent must itself be enlarged to the maximum, by seeing to it that those who have the capacity for the rigorous academic discipline required for all the professions start their course of study early, are offered opportunities to develop their talents, and are urged to continue to do so.

We must use available manpower more efficiently. The practice of wasting highly trained people in jobs below their capacity, particularly in some defense-related industries, must be eliminated. On the other hand, we must recognize that many workers have potential for higher positions. We must intensify the practice of upgrading men and women who may not have had advanced training but who have demonstrated capacity.

As Dr. Weaver's chapter suggests, we should allot a larger proportion of federal research and development funds to basic research. The total program of basic research in industry and other institutions should be increased.

The federal government supports more than half of the research and development in the United States. It is of urgent importance that the administration of its scientific and technical programs be strengthened, but without resort to bureaucratic overcentralization and planning.

The humanities, the social sciences, and the natural sciences all are essential for a rounded cultural life. Literature and history are vital to understanding, to capacity to feel and communicate, to a sense of values. Economics, psychology, all forms of study of human relationships, have become more urgent as the conditions of living have become

8

more complex; our progress in dealing with national economic policy is an indication of what may be achieved by continuing to give these studies full weight. Our world-wide responsibilities require fresh emphasis on foreign languages and continued improvement in teaching them.

The arts are a vital part of human experience. In the eyes of posterity, the success of the United States as a civilized society will be largely judged by the creative activities of its citizens in art, architecture, literature, music, and the sciences. While an encouraging creative surge in the arts is already manifest, our society must, as Mr. Heckscher's chapter urges, stimulate and support richer cultural fulfillment. Our theater must be revitalized; it must have the kind of support in universities, colleges, and communities that will give it greater strength at the roots. Professional artists require rigorous discipline; provision should be made for the long years of training which are required. We should raise our critical standards and widen the area and depth of public appreciation. Thus far, television has failed to use its facilities adequately for educational and cultural purposes, and reform in its performance is urgent.

6. THE DEMOCRATIC ECONOMY

The economic system must be compatible with the political system. The centers of economic power should be as diffused and as balanced as possible. Too great concentrations of economic power in corporations, unions, or other organizations can lead to abuses and loss of the productive results of fair competition. Individuals should have maximum freedom in their choice of jobs, goods, and services.

Government participation in the economy should be limited to those instances where it is essential to the national interest and where private individuals or organizations cannot adequately meet the need. Government, of course, must maintain its regulatory control in areas such as anti-trust laws, collusion, and protection of investors and consumers. We must take special precautions to prevent government officials from being influenced unduly by the sectors of the economy they regulate.

Collective bargaining between representatives of workers and employers should continue as the nation's chief method for determining wages and working conditions.

Conferences among management, union leaders, and representatives of the public can contribute to mutual understanding of problems that affect the welfare of the economy as a whole.

Corporations and labor unions must limit the influence they exert on the private lives of their members. Unions must continue to develop adequate grievance procedures and greater opportunities for legitimate opposition. Professional organizations and trade associations should conduct their affairs on a democratic basis,

9

Pension rights should vest more rapidly and fully, to improve the mobility of employees.

Barriers to the employment of women and older workers must be removed. While women will maintain and enrich the home and the family, those whose children have left home for school, and those who are not married, are increasingly able to contribute their talents to jobs and voluntary organizations. They may well be the country's largest pool of inadequately used ability. Their enlarging opportunity will help significantly to meet the nation's needs.

7. ECONOMIC GROWTH*

The economy should grow at the maximum rate consistent with primary dependence upon free enterprise and the avoidance of marked inflation.** Increased investment in the public sector is compatible with this goal.

Such growth is essential to move toward our goal of full employment, to provide jobs for the approximately 13,500,000 net new additions to the work force during the next ten years; to improve the standard of living; and to assure United States competitive strength.

Public policies, particularly an overhaul of the tax system, including depreciation allowances, should seek to improve the climate for new investment and the balancing of investment with consumption. We should give attention to policies favoring completely new ventures which involve a high degree of risk and growth potential.

In practice, we must seek to keep unemployment consistently below 4 per cent of the labor force. Reduction in unemployment and operation of the economy closer to its capacity require steadily growing consumer demand, and proper management of interest rates, money supply, and government budget surpluses and deficits. If Congress were to raise or lower tax rates more readily, stabilization of the economy would be facilitated.

Increased reliance on research and improved technology will provide opportunity for American industry to expand its markets by producing new and authentically improved products rather than by too great a dependence on superficial changes in style. To these ends, universities, research institutes, governments, and industries should greatly increase basic research, the ultimate source of new ideas and new products.

Education at all levels should aim at a more capable and more flexible work force.

There is no consensus among the economists as to the growth rate those measures will produce. The chapter by Messrs. Stein and Denison presents carefully documented evidence indicating an annual increase in

* See the Additional Statement by Mr. Greenewalt, page 24.
** See the Additional Statements by Dr. Kerr and Dr. Killian, page 27.

the gross national product of 3.4 per cent without extraordinary stimulating measures. Other estimates made with equal care indicate higher growth rates up to 5 per cent annually. The higher the growth rate, the fewer additional extraordinary measures will be necessary. If the growth rate is lower, it will impel consideration of higher taxes, increased quantity of labor, and the greater individual effort and sacrifice exemplified by forced savings and reduced consumption.*

There is no merit in a statistical race with the Communist nations. The real test is capacity to achieve our own over-all goals. Our economic decisions must be governed by ability to meet our needs for defense, for education, for a healthy private economy with rising standards of living, and for foreign aid.

8. TECHNOLOGICAL CHANGE

Technological change should be promoted and encouraged as a powerful force for advancing our economy. It should be planned for and introduced with sensitive regard for any adverse impact upon individuals.

Education on a large scale is provided by many industrial firms for their personnel. Such activities combined with advance planning can minimize unemployment due to rapid technological change. Where re-employment within the industry is not possible, retraining must be carried out through vocational programs managed locally and financed through state and federal funds.

Private initiative can accelerate technological change in our non-military economy.

In our military economy, the federal government must strengthen the management of its programs in technology by improving its supervisory and contracting procedures. It must avoid undertaking impracticable and unnecessary projects and thereby wasting scientific and engineering manpower. Both government and industry need to encourage that combination of engineering and management talent which can master our increasingly complex technology.

We must continue to adapt the management and organization of the Department of Defense to changing military needs. We must encourage fundamental advances in military technology and their rapid introduction. Through bold and tough-minded management we should reduce lead-time in bringing new weapons to operational use. Civilian and military leaders, with the help and understanding of Congress, must make and make stick the difficult inter-service decisions required for the selection of major weapons systems from among available alternatives. The increasing complexity of these systems, the time required for their development, and their fabulous cost give these decisions overriding importance. Conservation of time is critical;

* See the Additional Statement by Mr. Meany, pages 28 and 29.

11

it may be more important than the conservation of funds. Saving time is likely to save money.

Throughout the economy, collective bargaining between management and labor will have a marked influence on the process of technological change. It should anticipate needed adjustments, through retraining and transfer policies, and, if layoffs become necessary, by such means as severance pay. Problems of technological change will require far-sighted planning by industry, labor, and government on a cooperative basis.

Public and private leadership are required where whole areas are economically distressed. As Mr. Watson's chapter suggests, measures to encourage industries to move to such communities and relocation programs for individuals are justified. Consideration should be given, where necessary, to state and federal government participation in loans and grants to aid community efforts and to underwrite support for programs of retraining.

9. AGRICULTURE

The relative financial return to agriculture in the economy has deteriorated. The ultimate goal must be a supply-demand equilibrium to permit the market, with a fair return to farmers, to determine the manpower and capital committed to this sector of the economy. To avoid shock to the economy, this goal should be approached by gradual stages.

A separate problem concerns the 50 per cent of farmers who operate at subsistence levels and produce only 10 per cent of farm output. For them new opportunities must be found through training and through location of new industries in farm areas. During this decade non-farm jobs must be found—where possible locally—for about 1.5 million farm operators who now earn less than $1,500 a year.

Mr. Soth's chapter makes clear that farm industry is a notable example of rapid technological change and difficult adjustment. Productivity in agriculture rose in the last decade about three times as fast as in the economy as a whole. Therefore, more resources—more people, and more investment—are employed than are required to meet our domestic and foreign needs.

Farmers are leaving the industry. There are a million fewer families operating farms than there were in 1950, a decline in the decade of about 20 per cent. This shift of occupation contributes to our economic growth, and ultimately to a healthy farm industry.

Major measures to reduce oversupply must include much increased retirement of farm land, with emphasis on whole farms. To increase demand we need energetic development of overseas markets. Agriculture could be competitive in world markets if there were reciprocal lowering of quotas and other trade barriers. In selected areas, our surpluses can meet human want without disrupting the markets of other nations. Improvement of nutritional levels for many Americans would not only increase the work efficiency of our population but also reduce farm surpluses.

Government programs of help for farmers, including price supports and other means to prevent collapse of incomes, will continue to be necessary for some time; they must be so managed that they cushion the shock of the transition, without unduly slowing the pace of necessary fundamental adjustments.

10. LIVING CONDITIONS

We must remedy slum conditions, reverse the process of decay in the larger cities, and relieve the necessity for low-income and minority groups to concentrate there.

We should also seek solutions for haphazard suburban growth, and provide an equitable sharing of the cost of public services between central cities and suburbs. In many parts of the country, the goal should be a regional pattern which provides for a number of urban centers, each with its own industries, its own educational, cultural and recreational institutions, and a balanced population of various income levels and backgrounds. The needs of a growing population for parks and recreation must be met.

To these ends, we need dedicated private leadership, together with public and private action to provide improved services and facilities for residents of slum areas, stepped-up urban renewal programs, and an increased rate of construction of lower-priced homes and apartment units. Effective regional planning is essential, and there should be fresh emphasis on considerations of beauty. We should seek elimination of racial discrimination in housing.

Experience in the past decade has taught us some of the steps which must be taken. Further urban renewal programs, costing as much as $4 billion per year, are needed to purchase city land, clear it of delapidated buildings, and make it available for residential and business use. Roads and rapid transit facilities should be planned and financed as a unit, and effective regional planning should deal with all transportation, industrial location, and government-assisted housing plans. Services to residents of slum areas, including particularly education, need the same emphasis as slum clearance.

Because experimentation is needed and solutions to these problems may well vary from place to place, federal housing policies should permit local authorities much more discretion. Where local laws prohibit discrimination, federal officials should withhold assistance from housing projects that violate the local fair housing policies. Consideration should be given to federal support, for a limited period, of an intensive moderate-cost housing program, as Mrs. Wurster's chapter recommends,

13

under which state and local governments could experiment with mortgage insurance, low-interest loans, non-profit corporations and other forms of industry-municipal cooperation.

Private and civic initiative are vital to such programs. The attainment of these goals will involve massive investment. In the long run this will pay handsome social and economic dividends.

11. HEALTH AND WELFARE

The demand for medical care has enormously increased. To meet it we must have more doctors, nurses, and other medical personnel. There should be more hospitals, clinics and nursing homes. Greater effectiveness in the use of such institutions will reduce over-all requirements. There is a heavy responsibility on the medical and public health professions to contribute better solutions.

Federal grants for the construction of hospitals should be continued and extended to other medical facilities. Increased private, state and federal support is necessary for training doctors.

Further efforts are needed to reduce the burden of the cost of medical care. Extension of medical insurance is necessary, through both public and private agencies.*

As our need for doctors rises, the number of applications to medical school is declining. To meet our medical needs, analyzed in Dr. Dixon's chapter, we must not only increase the number of places in medical school by about one-half in this decade; we must also make it much more practicable for young men and women of talent and modest means to enter the profession. Scholarships during medical school and internship training are necessary.

The study of environmental health measures should be increased. We need to mobilize our resources better to understand such problems as air and water pollution, radiation hazards, and food additives. This is necessary in order that the government may formulate wiser policies of regulation.

Some 17 million persons suffer from mental illness in this country; it costs state governments over $1 billion per year. A maximum research effort, a substantial increase in the number of mental health clinics, and further progress in improving state mental hospitals are all part of the necessary effort to cope with it.

An important welfare objective is to learn more about the causes and methods of prevention of juvenile delinquency and family breakdown. There is great need for sustained study in order better to understand this complex community problem. It requires cooperative attention and action by many professions, community services and organizations. It also requires special measures to find jobs for youth, while maintaining

* See the Additional Statement by Mr. Meany, page 30.

labor standards. **Additional trained social workers are urgently needed. Church and neighborhood action must continue to play a major part.** Continued attention should be paid to the social insurance system. The federal government, having relinquished to the states 90 per cent of the unemployment compensation tax, should encourage the states to meet a minimum standard of adequacy of benefit levels, duration, and fiscal solvency.* In addition, there should be established a federal reinsurance program for states with temporary acute employment problems. Public and private arrangements for maintaining income during sickness should be improved.

PART II

GOALS ABROAD

Introduction

The basic foreign policy of the United States should be the preservation of its own independence and free institutions. Our position before the world should be neither defensive nor belligerent. We should cooperate with nations whose ideals and interests are in harmony with ours. We should seek to mitigate tensions, and search for acceptable areas of accommodation with opponents. The safeguarded reduction of armaments is an essential goal.

The United States, though omnipresent, is not omnipotent. We and the nations which share our basic aims cannot hope always to prevent violence, the corruption of nationalist movements to Communist ends, or other adverse developments.

Whether nations will prefer freedom to totalitarianism is a vital issue. The free nations must exert themselves to the utmost to influence that choice, by assistance freely given to help develop political stability based on progress and justice, and to ease economic pressures. They must seek to prevent the denial of choice by Communist expansion.

Our goals abroad are inseparable from our goals at home. We must strive toward an open and peaceful world by making democracy ever more effective and individual life freer and more rewarding.

Information programs should be made more effective in counteracting distortion and presenting a balanced picture of American life and policy to people in foreign lands.

12. HELPING TO BUILD AN OPEN AND PEACEFUL WORLD

Foreign Trade Policy**

The healthiest world economy is attained when trade is at its freest. This should be our goal. The United States should join with other free

---

* See the Additional Statements by Dr. Kerr and Mr. Meany, pages 27 and 30.
** See the Additional Statement by Mr. Greenewalt, page 25.

world industrial nations in seeking a gradual reduction of tariffs and quota restrictions. **We should seek this goal while safeguarding the national economy against market disruption, against destructive competition as a result of grossly lower unit labor costs, and to preserve national defense. We must effectively counter totalitarian trade practices.** While many underdeveloped nations will insist, as the United States did for many years, upon tariffs and other forms of protection, we should continue to seek lowering of trade restrictions elsewhere in the world, especially barriers by larger regional trading groups. **Our export trade must be conducted with ingenuity and vigor.**

If the United States is to participate effectively in this process, some revision in our trade legislation will be required. Mr. McCloy's chapter makes clear that the so-called "peril point" and "escape clause" provisions may need some modification, since they put a floor on the reduction of tariffs, which has now been reached in many areas.*

Elimination or modification of these restrictions might lead to imports taking larger shares of particular domestic markets. Normally the reductions should be undertaken step by step. Where the impact of a tariff reduction is such that an industry or community cannot absorb it unaided, temporary government assistance toward retraining, relocation, and reinvestment is warranted.

Though the trend should be downward, there may be rare cases where increases will be necessary in the national interest.

Although exports have slightly exceeded imports in recent years, expenditures abroad for economic aid, military bases, private investment, and foreign travel have led to a deficit in international payments of about $3.5 billion in 1958 and 1959, and perhaps higher in 1960. **This unfavorable balance of payments is caused by many factors, some of which do not relate to foreign trade policy. At least three steps are essential to rectification: a much higher export surplus; larger participation of other developed nations in assistance to the underdeveloped; and more equitable sharing of defense costs among the Allies.**

The principal Western European nations are capable of larger capital export and aid to underdeveloped nations; this is notably true of the German Federal Republic. Similarly, it may be necessary for the United States to seek greater sharing of the cost of new weapons systems by the nations of Western Europe.

Aid to Less Developed Nations

Our principles and ideals impel us to aid the new nations. The preservation and strengthening of the free institutions of underdeveloped countries, and the defense of the free world, require a substantial increase

---

* See the Additional Statement by Dr. Darden, page 24.

in the amount of foreign aid, to be equitably shared by the major free nations.

International economic organizations, such as the World Bank, deserve our support. We must devise new forms of cooperation, in which developing countries have opportunities for participation.

The success of the underdeveloped nations must depend primarily on their own efforts. We should assist by providing education, training, economic and technical assistance, and by increasing the flow of public and private capital.

Through investment of about $20 billion a year, three-fourths of it from their own savings, the underdeveloped countries are increasing their production at an average rate of about 2 per cent. However, this economic growth is nearly balanced by population growth, so that the rise in living standards is barely perceptible.

Doubling their economic growth rate within five years is a reasonable objective. This could be accomplished if the developing nations increased their own yearly investment by about half, and if foreign investment rose from the present approximate $5 billion a year to about $9 billion in 1965—roughly 1 per cent of the Western industrial nations' combined gross national product. The United States share of such an effort would require by 1965 an outflow of $5 to $5.5 billion per year of public and private capital, as compared with $3.4 billion per year in the 1956-59 period.

Government funds for roads, port facilities, utilities, educational facilities and other institutions should account for a high proportion of these totals. The balance can and should be supplied by private investors. Broader guarantees and incentives will be needed to induce the required volume of private investment.

Better coordination of the assistance programs of the industrial nations will be necessary. The newly proposed Organization for Economic Cooperation and Development is a promising instrument for stimulating cooperation among the North Atlantic industrial nations, and with the nations to be assisted. The World Bank and International Development Association, with wide membership from both groups and high technical competence and experience, can and must continue to expand. Our special relationship to Latin America will call for an increasingly close cooperation on the basis of partnership.

We must encourage far larger numbers of qualified Americans to live and work abroad.

Half a million American civilians live abroad, as a result of private and government employment. Their number and their ability to represent the United States creditably must rise rapidly in the next decade if we are to attain an adequate level of exports and foreign investment and carry out programs for training and technical assistance. Universities, businesses, and the federal government should each in

17

appropriate fields greatly increase language and other specialized training for such work.

13. THE DEFENSE OF THE FREE WORLD

The Soviet Threat

Communist aggression and subversion, fully analyzed in Dr. Langer's chapter, threaten all that we seek to do both at home and abroad. Consequently, the maintenance of our independence and way of life, as well as our concern for the freedom of other nations, require the most effective counter-measures.

The power and opportunities of the Sino-Soviet nations are such that it will be a major task to prevent their expansion in the coming decade. Nevertheless, we must never lose sight of our ultimate goal: to extend the opportunities for free choice and self-determination throughout the world.

We must stand firm wherever, as in Berlin, our commitments and interests are squarely opposed to those of the Soviets. At whatever cost, we must maintain strategic and tactical forces of sufficient strength to deter the Communist powers from surprise attack and to cope with military aggression even on a limited scale. A secure deterrent is essential. We must meet Communist military threats used for political purposes. We must be ready to make the sacrifices necessary to meet the rising costs of such military capabilities.

We must also meet subversion by cooperation with other nations, by direct help on request, and through economic programs which, in addition to other purposes, reduce conditions favorable to subversion.

Nonetheless, we should try continually to find a basis for mutual tolerance and reduction of tensions. We should be prepared to negotiate on any reasonable basis. We should enlarge personal and cultural contacts.*

Communist China

Communist China's blatant hostility to the United States makes it especially urgent to strengthen our Pacific defenses and our ties with our Pacific allies.

Over the next decade, Communist China may be more aggressive than the U.S.S.R. Within a few years, Peiping may have the capacity to produce atomic weapons. Its strong conventional forces and rapid industrial progress already exert great impact in Asia.

Our policies in the Far East must include maximum cooperation with Japan in solving its difficult economic problems, continued support for the Republic of Korea and the Government of the Republic of China,

* See the Additional Statement by Mr. Meany, page 28.

18

programs of military and economic assistance to the free nations of South-East Asia, major assistance toward the economic development of India, and the maintenance of our own military forces.

Military Alliances

For the common defense, we must maintain and strengthen our military alliances. Our commitment to NATO in particular must remain firm. We should encourage the trend to greater military integration among the European members and the assumption by them of greater responsibilities. Our other military alliances and relationships in the Middle East and Asia must likewise be reaffirmed and strengthened. The Organization of American States must continue to have our unstinting support.

In support of these alliances, and in a few nations not covered by them, the United States must continue to furnish military assistance. To the extent that other nations gain strength, and local dangers diminish, it may become possible to reduce such aid. But major reductions are not in prospect. In some instances, our military aid is essential to progress toward political stability on an increasingly democratic basis.

Communist-dominated Areas

In nations subject to Communist domination or influence, our hope must be that the right of self-determination will ultimately be achieved. Trade, cultural exchanges, and occasionally technical or financial aid may be useful policies toward Communist-dominated peoples who are not hostile to us.

14. DISARMAMENT

Since a major nuclear war would be a world catastrophe, the limitation and control of nuclear armament is imperative. Disarmament should be our ultimate goal. It cannot be attained without eliminating the sources of distrust and fear among nations. Hence, our immediate task must be the step-by-step advance toward control of nuclear weapons and their means of delivery, with effective international inspection. A safeguarded agreement to suspend nuclear testing may well be the first step, and would tend to limit the number of nuclear powers.

In view of the complex interaction of arms control and national security, we must organize a major government effort for the study and analysis of political, military, and technical issues in order to provide a sounder basis for policy formulation and negotiation.

The essential condition of any stabilizing agreement must be that neither side be left in a position of significant advantage. Inspection measures providing adequate safeguards must be accepted by both sides, but we should recognize that any inspection system will have risks which must be balanced against the advantages of arms limitation agreement.

A real difficulty in progress toward arms limitation is to induce the Soviet Union to overcome its long habit of secrecy. The United States and its allies should emphasize their readiness to accept international inspection, although it will mean a degree of foreign presence and activity that will be novel and distasteful even in our open societies.

15. THE UNITED NATIONS

A key goal in the pursuit of a vigorous and effective United States foreign policy is the preservation and strengthening of the United Nations. Over the next decade, it will be under tremendous strain. However, it remains the chief instrument available for building a genuine community of nations.

This requires constant strengthening of world law, through the discovery and adoption of legal principles common to all or at least to many cultures, through improved methods for making existing international law accessible, and through the further development of the International Court of Justice.*

Through various specialized agencies the United Nations does significant work in many fields. It shows increasing effectiveness in technical assistance to new nations, and often assumes a major role in the control of violence and the settlement of disputes.

In a world in social, economic, and political ferment, international violence is a constant threat. Since nations have become so closely interlocked, there is danger that local violence will induce widespread conflict. Without abandoning, in justified cases, our right to unilateral action, the United States should join with other nations in seeking resolution of as many issues as possible through the United Nations, the Organization of American States, and other international agencies.

It must be recognized that the United Nations provides a forum for Soviet propaganda and tactics of dissension, and an opportunity for Soviet vetoes to block or delay free world advances. On occasion, the growing bloc of votes from the new and uncommitted nations may turn a decision in the United Nations against our interests. Nevertheless, we should give the world community, as represented by the United Nations, our steadfast support.

PART III

A FINANCIAL ACCOUNTING

Resources are a crucial test of a nation's ability to attain its goals. At the present time, federal, state, and local governments are spend-

* See the Additional Statement by Dr. Wriston, page 31.

ing about $135 billion each year, of which about $99 billion represents purchases of goods and services (as opposed to social security and similar transfer payments). These totals are 27 per cent and 19 per cent respectively of our total gross national product. We cannot now determine whether this proportion of our national product will be adequate for the role of governments in the Sixties.

The increase in defense expenditures is difficult to predict. National security expenditures, exclusive of veterans' benefits and interest costs due largely to prior wars, account for 36 per cent of the total amount spent at all levels of government. Foreign aid should be raised over the next five years, and there is little prospect for reduction in other national security expenditures.

Domestic expenditures are also hard to estimate. For education, we shall need a large additional sum. Expenditures at all levels of government for health, urban renewal, housing, transportation systems, and reservation of open space will certainly rise materially, and federal government support for basic research must be increased.

Economies can and must be made. Some savings in the federal agricultural program may be possible, and greater efficiency throughout government would reduce costs. But these savings cannot be counted on to offset rising expenses.

We therefore face the prospect, though by no means the certainty, that aggregate tax rates will continue at something like their present level through the decade, and may even have to be increased. We must face squarely the issue: if attaining the goals outlined in this Report should require a somewhat higher level of taxation, can we bear this level without consequences which themselves make the goals more difficult to reach?

Provided that economic growth proceeds at an annual rate of 3.4 per cent or higher, there is no doubt that we can do so. In aggregate terms, increasing public expenditures are very unlikely to reduce the level of average individual consumption in this country; the average citizen's standard of living would continue to rise, though perhaps at rates below those of the recent past. A moderate increase in tax rates need not, if its necessity were understood, materially impair the incentive or the morale of the American people, nor alter the primary reliance of the economy on private choice.

Tax systems which must allocate for governments about one-fifth of the national product must be both fair and designed to reduce to a minimum the impact of taxes upon growth.

A substantial reform of the tax systems is essential, whether public expenditures must be increased or can be reduced. It will facilitate the attainment of many national goals.

The federal tax system should be revised to eliminate unjustified exceptions to its general rules, to assure equitable treatment of all types

21

of incomes, to encourage the accumulation of risk capital so vital to economic growth, and to remedy the many contradictions and flaws which have grown up within the system.*

Many state governments must find new tax sources.** Local governments must be freed of unnecessary restrictions on taxing and borrowing powers, and the pronounced inequalities in the property tax bases of local jurisdictions should be corrected.

If these reforms are made and the minimum growth rate we postulate is achieved, it is this Commission's conclusion that the levels of public spending we would need to realize the recommendations of this Report are attainable. There must be no ideological preference for public spending as such. Costs must always be carefully weighed. But the needs outlined in this Report are themselves vitally related to ultimate freedom and individual development. We should not fail to meet them.

A CONCLUDING WORD

The very deepest goals for Americans relate to the spiritual health of our people. The right of every individual to seek God and the wellsprings of truth, each in his own way, is infinitely precious. We must continue to guarantee it, and we must exercise it, for ours is a spiritually-based society. Our material achievements in fact represent a triumph of the spirit of man in the mastery of his material environment.

The family is at the heart of society. The educational process begins and is served most deeply in the home.

From the first days of our history, every American has been responsible for his own life and livelihood, and for his family's, and has shared responsibility for his neighbor's. In our early years, the perils which threatened were close at hand, and the responsibility was inescapable. Now dangers, and opportunities as well, come from greater distance, and more subtly. But they are just as real. And it is as true as in the days of the frontier that the goals for Americans cannot be won without the efforts of all.

The major domestic goals of equality and education depend overwhelmingly on individual attitudes and actions.

It is the responsibility of men and women in every walk of life to maintain the highest standards of integrity.

American citizens will in this decade have countless opportunities to take the national interest into account in deciding their course of action. Negotiators for labor and management affect the growth of

---

* See the Additional Statements by Dr. Darden and Mr. Greenewalt, pages 24 and 25.

** See the Additional Statement by Mr. Meany, page 29.

the economy and its ability to compete with industry abroad when they reach a decision on compensation and working conditions, and thus influence the rate of technological change. Young men and women will help shape the course the United States will take by deciding in what occupation they will spend their lives. Americans who live or travel abroad can persuade countless people of the sincerity of American ideals and the values of democracy, or they can tarnish the nation's reputation. Voters will determine whether schools will be built, teachers' salaries raised, foreign assistance enlarged, defense needs fulfilled. Our goals will be attained and our way of life preserved if enough Americans take the national interest sufficiently into account in day-by-day decisions.

The American citizen in the years ahead ought to devote a larger portion of his time and energy directly to the solution of the nation's problems. There has been repeated occasion in this Report to emphasize the overriding importance of contributions by private groups and individuals. Many ways are open for citizens to participate in the attainment of national goals. To mention but a few: they may help to control delinquency by organizing a boys' club, serve on a school board, accept a tour of duty with government, participate actively in politics through parties or interest groups.

Above all, Americans must demonstrate in every aspect of their lives the fallacy of a purely selfish attitude—the materialistic ethic. Indifference to poverty and disease is inexcusable in a society dedicated to the dignity of the individual; so also is indifference to values other than material comfort and national power. Our faith is that man lives, not by bread alone, but by self-respect, by regard for other men, by convictions of right and wrong, by strong religious faith.

Man has never been an island unto himself. The shores of his concern have expanded from his neighborhood to his nation, and from his nation to his world. Free men have always known the necessity for responsibility. A basic goal for each American is to achieve a sense of responsibility as broad as his world-wide concerns and as compelling as the dangers and opportunities he confronts.

ADDITIONAL STATEMENTS BY INDIVIDUAL
MEMBERS OF THE COMMISSION

Statement by Dr. Darden

I am disturbed by the suggestion contained in the next to the last paragraph in *2. Equality.* The denial of funds to universities, hospitals, airports and federal housing programs where controversies over racial discrimination exist will result in many cases in the withholding of funds urgently needed by both races. It would be more effective to go on as rapidly as possible with the undertakings found desirable, relying upon education, persuasion and law to bring about a settlement of the controversies which arise. I wish to so record myself.

I have difficulty in reconciling the first three paragraphs of *12. Helping to Build an Open and Peaceful World.* With the first paragraph I am in accord. The observations in the next two paragraphs dealing with the "peril point" and "escape clause" provisions seem to suggest and approve tariff revisions so drastic as to violate our recommendation that the national economy be guarded against market disruption and against destructive competition as a result of grossly lower unit labor costs. Since adherence to this last principle is important, I desire to record my dissent from what I take to be a departure from it.

Mr. Greenewalt in his memorandum is dealing with tax revision and the possibilities for stimulating employment in this way. I wish to associate myself with his views on this subject. In addition to what he has to say I wish to record my view that the very high rates imposed are designed not to raise revenue but to confiscate incomes beyond a fixed figure and are a denial of opportunities for the individual upon which, and properly so, we place such emphasis.

Statement by Mr. Greenewalt

The goals here presented call for unprecedented increases in government expenditures over the next decade. Were these to be superimposed on our *present* economy the tax burden would be clearly unsupportable. Should the American people endorse these spending proposals, it becomes essential that the economy grow at a pace which will make the added funds available at tax rates no greater and, hopefully, even lower than those now being levied.

While the sections on economic growth, foreign trade, and tax policy contain much that is sound, they do not in my view adequately recognize this problem. A vigorous and expanding industrial economy is essential to our domestic well-being and to our position of world leadership. We dare not risk weakening it; we must do all we can to strengthen it.

The improvement of education and the allocation of increased resources to basic research are of course essential for the longer term, but even if implemented immediately could have little effect within a ten-year period. We must act promptly to improve the atmosphere for vigorous economic growth. Two things should be done. Depreciation policies, as indicated in the Report, should be modified to permit rapid amortization of new plant and equipment. This will encourage industry to undertake needed modernization and, more importantly, will facilitate entirely new and risky ventures with high growth potential.

The steep progression in our personal income tax rates should be abated. These high rates strike directly at incentives for personal accomplishment and cannot fail to weaken the drive at all management levels. If our business enterprises are to flourish, we dare not risk decreased initiative for those men and women responsible for the process.

High tax rates also tend to remove an important source for new venture capital—capital of the very kind likely to support bold new discoveries. There is insufficient recognition in the Report of the importance of *quality* in capital investment. The growth rate will be influenced much more favorably by a given number of dollars invested in plant for a completely new product than the same dollars invested in, let us say, a model change in a refrigerator or an automobile. New product ventures imply an inherently high degree of risk. Traditionally their conception and implementation has come from the initiative, creativity, and financial backing of individuals as well as from corporations. At present corporations have no difficulty in finding capital to meet new investment opportunities. This however cannot be said for today's Henry Fords or Thomas Edisons. The proportion of commercial successes from the invention of creative individuals is likely to be small. Financing must come from those who can afford to take the gamble and lose.

The section on foreign trade presents points of view that appear inconsistent and ambiguous. In certain portions of the section it is suggested that tariffs be reciprocally reduced so that imports and exports will be increased. Should such action produce unemployment in the United States, it is proposed that federal funds be made available for retraining and relocating the affected workers. I cannot agree with these proposals. To be sure trade between nations should be at its freest. We cannot, however, afford to accelerate the process if the result is to compound the very real problems of reducing present unemployment and absorbing more than 13 million new workers into a productive labor force. The problems of international trade are complicated by the gross disparity between American wage rates and those obtaining in all other industrial nations. Traditionally, improved technology in the United States, arising out of its great marketing area, has neutralized those differences. Today the creation of equally great trading areas abroad and technology fully equal to our own make such neutralization impossible.

Reduced tariff protection in the United States then becomes a clear invitation to greatly increased imports. To be sure industry should show initiative and vigor in increasing exports, and I have no doubt that progress can be made in this area. Reduction of tariffs abroad will increase these opportunities. I should point out, however, that differences in wage rates may be as effective in limiting our exports as they are in increasing our imports. For industrial England, Europe and Japan are not standing still—and the inevitable improvement in their industrial stature and in their ability to provide for the material needs of their citizens will make maintenance of exports at high levels progressively more difficult.

I should make it clear that I do not favor tariffs at rates so high that they bar imports in any industrial area. Competition from foreign products is as healthy for our economy as is competition among our own companies and industries. What is necessary, it seems to me, is the maintenance of tariffs which will no more than compensate for existing wage differentials. Were this to be done we would have the benefit of foreign competition on a fair, competitive basis. Imports would not be excluded but would have to compete on their merits with the products of American industry.

Finally, the section on taxation says nothing specifically about steeply progressive personal income tax rates. Here I make once more the suggestion that the slope of progression be substantially reduced. I find it a pity that a Report which speaks so eloquently of the rights of the individual should condone legislative strictures limiting him in some cases to less than nine per cent of the fruit of his labor.

Statement by Dr. Kerr

This Report represents the consensus of the Commission members. It is not precisely as any single member would have written it. But the Report accurately reflects general agreement on an impressive number of important issues, and I am glad to endorse it with the following reservations:

1. With reference to national goals in the area of equality of opportunity, I should prefer to state that discrimination in education (not only in higher education) should be entirely overcome by 1970. Similarly, our goal should be the complete elimination by 1970 of dis-

criminatory practices in employment, housing, and in the provision of other services and facilities. These goals are both essential and attainable. Granted that difficult problems sometimes exist, they can and must be solved during the present decade. The moral and constitutional rights of American citizens must take precedence over all other concerns.

2. In the economic sphere, I should prefer to state as our goal an economic growth rate of not less than 4 per cent, and, if reasonably possible, 5 per cent annually. Our many essential national objectives and tasks require such a growth rate and justify the measures which may be necessary to accomplish this rate of growth.

3. The experience of widely varying standards and requirements in state administration of unemployment compensation funds indicate that federal encouragement of specific standards almost certainly will not be enough. I believe the federal government will need to establish minimum standards for benefit levels and duration of benefits just as it has established minimum standards with respect to coverage and certain other features of our federal-state unemployment insurance program.

Statement by Dr. Killian

I wish to note my agreement with points 1 and 2 of Dr. Kerr's Statement above, dealing with desegregation of schools and with the growth rate of our economy.

Statement by Mr. Meany

The Commission has outlined goals for the United States in the fields of education, science and the arts, in city planning and urban renewal, in health, welfare and the improvement of living conditions that are of the first order. The role of the individual and the attainment of these objectives, through the full extension of the democratic process, is excellent.

In the area of world affairs, desirable goals are set forth on the basis of a full recognition of the threat of Communist aggression and subversion. These goals proclaim the need to preserve and extend the area of freedom and our duty to support the United Nations, pursue the objective of safeguarded disarmament, and to cooperate with friendly nations for both peaceful and defense purposes. Excellent positions are stated on the need for expanded foreign economic aid and improvements in international trade.

I am happy to associate myself with the above goals.

I find myself in disagreement, however, with the hasty optimism shown by the Commission in the international field in the references

27

to exchanges with countries under Communist dictatorship and control.

"To enlarge personal and cultural contacts" with peoples behind the Iron Curtain would be an undoubted good if there was thereby a really free exchange of ideas, opinions and information. It is possible that little harm results from exchanges of artists, scientists, actors and professional technicians. Damage is done, however, when government-ally-appointed heads of governmentally-controlled organizations from behind the Iron Curtain are welcomed as non-governmental delegates and are permitted to gain respectability and legitimacy in the eyes of the free world. This applies with particular emphasis in relation to trade unionism which is assigned such a key role in the subversive efforts of Soviet Communism and in its goal of penetration of workers' organizations throughout the free world.

I also stand in disagreement with some of the means proposed by the majority for the attainment of major domestic goals, or, in many cases, their failure to provide any adequate means for attainment.

Private initiative and incentive are important; state and local governments must expand their roles to meet new needs. But the superior resources of the federal government, collected through fair, equitable and progressive taxes and administered through a truly democratic structure, must be more greatly utilized. Failure to recognize this not only blinds one's self to reality, but would doom many of these worthwhile goals.

The Report grudgingly recognizes the role and responsibilities of the federal government and, when it does recognize it, sees it only as a last resort. Hoping that private initiative and/or state and local governments will do the job is just not enough.

The major question, with which the Commission wrestled but failed to conquer, is how to meet the costs of these programs without undue burden upon the nation's economy. The Report seems to say we can do it, maybe, but if not we are prepared to sacrifice.

I am in complete agreement with the need to sacrifice, if necessary through higher taxes and even a slower rate of progress in living standards.

But I am not convinced either is necessary for I firmly believe our economy can and will grow fast enough, given proper leadership, to permit the costs of these programs, many of which will also contribute to economic growth and expansion.

It is precisely here that the majority report fails. It speaks firmly and positively on goals; it speaks only timidly on methods for attaining them.

Let me cite the specific timidities to which I take exception:

1. The Report says, "There is no consensus among the economists as to the growth rate those measures (high levels of demand and adequate monetary and fiscal policy) will produce." The Commission tends to

28

accept as valid the projected 3.4 per cent growth rate that it had before it, though it concedes that other estimates of 5 per cent growth have been made by competent authorities. The majority admits that the 3.4 per cent growth may not provide the financial resources to insure achievement of its goals. It foresees the need for "extraordinary stimulating measures" to attain the higher growth rate and it proposes, as a last resort, "forced savings and reduced consumption." I am not prepared to accept this pessimistic approach. I am convinced, as are many sound economists, that the nation clearly can, should and must grow at an annual rate of 4.5 to 5 per cent, without resort to "extraordinary stimulating measures" such as forced savings and reduced consumption. America can meet its world responsibilities, insure its military security and increase the living standards of its people in the fully democratic and competitive society which is our heritage. I am not prepared to aim for less.

2. The Report sets excellent civil rights goals, but fails to support the action steps necessary in two major specifics.

a. In discussing private employment opportunities regardless of race or sex, the Report says, "Additional municipal, state, and federal legislation is necessary." It timidly stops short of supporting the only realistic legislative step: an enforceable federal fair employment practices law, supplemented by similar state and local laws.

b. It sets a 1970 goal for desegregation in higher education, but astoundingly sets no time goal at all for desegregation of publicly supported schools, urging only "progress in good faith." By 1970, all Negro children must have available to them the opportunity to attend all local schools, subject only to meeting uniformly administered academic standards.

3. The Report properly points out that "the financial resources of state and local governments must be increased," and that "many state governments must find new tax sources." It should go one step further and recommend that a federal income tax credit to the states be enacted by the United States Congress as a means of assuring a sound equitable way of raising additional revenue, rather than enacting regressive sales and excise taxes. A federal income tax credit is one sure way of reducing the reliance of state and local governments on the larger financial resources of the federal government.

4. Its education goals are excellent and the Report correctly observes that the percentage of the gross national product spent on education must increase in the coming decade. But it proposes only federal supplemental funds to states whose per capita income is inadequate and provides other states with federal funds only on a matching basis. What America needs is federal grants to all states with further supplemental funds to those states whose per capita income is too low.

5. In the field of medical care, the Report correctly assesses the need for reducing the cost burden through extension of public and private insurance. But, in the field of medical care for the aged, easily the most pressing problem in this area, the Report refuses to take the next, necessary step and say such insurance should be extended through the tried and proved Social Security system.

6. The Report recognizes the inadequacies of the present unemployment compensation setup but calls only for "encouraging" the states to meet a minimum standard of benefit levels, duration of benefits and financial solvency. We have just experienced eight years of "encouraging" the states to meet minimum standards with almost no record of success. The Report fails completely to recognize this fact and to call for what is necessary—requiring the states to meet such standards.

These specifics point up the fact that the Commission's Report marches right up to the issues, always faces them boldly, then often turns away, without making the necessary, if sometimes unpopular, proposals for attaining the very goals the Commission believes necessary.

It is not enough, in my opinion, to recognize the need unless we at the same time chart the path to attainment. The majority has correctly described the goals; they have failed, in certain instances, to point the way to achievement.

Statement by Mr. Pace

I have believed in the vital importance of the Commission on National Goals from its inception. This was not because I felt the Commission was capable of setting goals for Americans—only the people can do this—but rather to identify our major problems to our citizens who deeply want to contribute, but whose task has been made infinitely more difficult by the variety and complexity of the issues involved.

My conception of what this Commission has tried to do is to set out the things for which we should strive over the long term and to identify areas in which inaction might cost us dearly. It should be recognized that the Commission's task was to point out what this nation should do. It could not enter into the more difficult and detailed problems of priorities and the exact costing and paying for goals achievement.

A word about defense, with which I have had close association for over ten years. Clearly in so vast and complicated an area there are opportunities for improved administration and important savings, and these must be pursued vigorously. There are, however, three other areas that have commanded insufficient general attention and that are vital:

The first is the encouragement of revolutionary new ideas in weapons systems. Our greatest strength in our country is the free flow and interchange of new ideas. It is our best means of staying ahead of the Communists. Every effort should be made to encourage new approaches and to reward those who generate them. The lessons of the past are important, but clinging to the past is impossible.

The second is incisive selection at the earliest practical time of a new weapons system. In a period of enormous technological change, the variety of possible choices is so great that the selection process is most difficult. Responsibility for the selection must be clearly identified and centered in one place. Even recognizing that mistakes will inevitably be made, this still represents a lesser danger than that of pursuing too many programs inconclusively.

Finally, I want to emphasize the all-important problem of the time lag between the conception of a great idea and its production as a weapons system. Concentrating as we have on dollar savings, we lose sight of the fact that obsolescence through delay is the most costly single factor both in terms of dollars and the national security. The Department of Defense working intimately with the Congress in centering attention on improvement in this area can make a unique contribution.

A last comment: As an individual, I conceive of democracy as an expanding factor in the world—not expansion through force but through ideas. Democracy can never be allowed to become static or it withers. For it to continue to grow, our people must live it in its complete sense. In the long run the survival of our way of life depends more on the quality of family and religious life and on the full acceptance of the responsibility of citizenship in all its phases than on any other factors.

Statement by Dr. Wriston (with whom Messrs. Canham, Conant, Gruenther, Kerr, Killian, Meany, and Pace concur)

I believe that the discussion of world law (*15. The United Nations*) should include a specific recommendation for repeal of the Connally Amendment, which now limits the jurisdiction of the World Court.

Foreword
to the
Accompanying
Chapters

These chapters were written for the Commission as part of the basis for its consideration of the national goals. The authors were chosen from among people competent in the several fields, and were counselled by others whose familiarity with the subject matter was well established.

The Commission now makes these essays available to the public as interesting and relevant discussions of vital issues. The views stated are those of the authors, and are not necessarily shared by the Commission.

The Commission's own position is set forth solely in its own Report.

1

D ISCUSSION OF *the national goals of the American people must start from a reconsideration of the significance of the individual. In this introductory chapter, Dr. Henry M. Wriston reminds us of the convictions of the men who founded the nation, reviews our progress toward achieving their aims, and sets before us what yet remains to be done to attain them.*

Dr. Wriston is President Emeritus of Brown University, President of The American Assembly, and Chairman of this Commission.

THE INDIVIDUAL

HENRY M. WRISTON

I

FUNDAMENTALS

Why discuss national goals? A penetrating observation by Alfred North Whitehead suggests the answer: "The vigour of civilized societies is preserved by the wide-spread sense that high aims are worth-while. Vigorous societies harbour a certain extravagance of objectives, so that men wander beyond the safe provision of personal gratifications."*

That comment precisely describes the situation when the Declaration of Independence was proclaimed over 184 years ago. The economic position of the states would today be called underdeveloped; politically they were disunited, quarrelsome. The "extravagance" of the objectives of the new nation is thrown into bold perspective.

In drafting the Declaration of Independence, Thomas Jefferson did not impose his will upon the Congress. His colleagues deleted many of his cherished phrases and altered the substance of what he had written, to his acute distress. Yet one section was not weakened: ". . . All men are created equal, . . . are endowed by their Creator with certain unalienable rights; . . . among these are life, liberty and the pursuit of happiness; . . . to secure these rights, governments are instituted among men, deriving their just powers from the consent of the governed."

Those words expressed the deep conviction of the other members of Congress. John Adams, for example, differed from Jefferson on many fundamentals. But on this issue their views coincided. As Adams expressed it: "Let us see delineated before us the true map of man. Let us hear the dignity of his nature, and the noble rank he holds among the works of God." These ideas were "in the air"; it has been said that Jefferson "plagiarized the atmosphere." It was an unkind way of stressing a profound truth: he spoke for a deep consensus. Indeed the Declaration, he said, *was intended to be an expression of the American mind.*

A significant phrase preceded the quoted passage: "We hold these truths to be self-evident." This introduction to an astounding denial of what Europe regarded as beyond challenge accounts for the fact that no evidence was offered in support of the affirmations. As axioms they require no proof.

Familiarity with the words of the Declaration has bred inattention to their full meaning. In the most complete sense they were revolutionary.

* Whitehead, Alfred North, *Adventures of Ideas.* New York: MacMillan Co., 1956, p. 371.

35

Now that we have mighty power we tend to shy away from that word. But history cannot be denied; revolutionary they were. Kings had claimed their power by divine right, as vicegerents of God. Even where historic arrogance did not go so far, citizens were subjects, not rulers. The Declaration put the individual squarely at the center, as of supreme importance. It completely reversed the age-old order; it defined government as the servant of the individual, not his master.

Congress adopted the Declaration knowing that when they took up the pen they took their lives in their hands. They had moved "beyond the safe provision of personal gratifications." Signing, Benjamin Franklin exclaimed in deadly earnest: "We must all hang together, or assuredly we shall all hang separately."

Sometimes our War for Independence has been called a revolution of moderates, and properly in one sense, because the founders of the nation clung to so much that was good—the Common Law, for example. To the kings and ruling aristocracies of the day, whose right to exercise their "legitimate" power was denied, the Americans did not seem moderate, but ultra-radical. The founders of our nation deliberately set out to be innovators. They dramatized that faith and purpose in a Latin phrase engraved upon the reverse of the Great Seal of the United States: "Novus ordo seclorum"—a new order for the ages.

It has been well said that the American ideal blew mercantilist, monarchist Europe "off its moral base." The phrases of the Declaration and the motto upon the Great Seal were proclaimed in universal terms. The signers set a goal for "all men" and for the ages. If all men are created equal and the individual is the center of political, social, and economic gravity, there can be no elite class, no caste, no aristocracy, no master race, no chosen people, no favored nation.

The words were not said with tongue in cheek to produce a transient effect. They had none of the hollow ring of contrived and artificial expression. They were propaganda in the best sense—an eloquent and moving expression of profound belief.

Though the founders established principles, they set up a government too feeble to endure. As we watch the struggles of newly independent nations, we do well to remind ourselves of the collapse of our own first government. Remembrance will encourage patience and promote a measure of understanding.

When the Confederation failed, the founders met the crisis by drawing a new Constitution. It united a policy of strength to the philosophy of freedom: "In order to form a more perfect union, establish justice, insure domestic tranquility, provide for the common defense, promote the general welfare, and secure the blessings of liberty to ourselves and our posterity."

Nonetheless, memories of tyranny were not erased. The authors knew history. They saw the fallacy in the imperfect syllogism that assumes that "when we act publicly or privately, we are the same people" and that therefore the individual need have no fear of government. They were aware that strong governments are always tempted to overwhelm the individual. That danger, in the view of many, marked the new Constitution. Thomas Jefferson deplored "the want of a bill of rights to guard liberty against the legislative as well as the executive branches of the government." The Constitution could not be adopted until there was an implied promise to provide a bill of rights.

The first Ten Amendments set forth with great particularity a charter of freedom for the individual against the state. They stressed once more that the dignity of the individual is the end, government only the means. In the Olmstead Case, Justice Brandeis epitomized the ideal: "The makers of the Constitution . . . sought to protect Americans in their beliefs, their thoughts, their emotions and their sensations. They conferred, as against the Government, *the right to be let alone*—the most comprehensive of rights and the right most valued by civilized men."

The Bill of Rights is far from obsolete. Proof of its continuing vitality is to be found in the volume of litigation before the Supreme Court appealing to these amendments and to the restrictions upon government which they embody. There could be no more dramatic and decisive proof of the primacy of the individual in our whole scale of values.

The ideology of the Declaration and the Bill of Rights shaped our history. It set in train forces that moved, inexorably, toward democracy. It made this a land of opportunity for the oppressed of the world, and precipitated the greatest movement of peoples history had ever seen. Mere availability of land would not have produced that result. Other sparsely settled regions of the earth with greater unused natural resources saw no such tidal influx. The spirit of liberty acted as a powerful magnet; the commitment to freedom made us hospitable to others. The ideal of the equality of men set our course as a revolutionary force, a foe of colonialism, hostile to tyranny anywhere. For many years the United States was first to recognize revolutionary governments erected on the ruins of oppressive regimes.

The American ideal exerted a profound influence upon others precisely because it was so deeply rooted in our own national tradition. John Adams said it would lead to the "illumination of the ignorant and the emancipation of the slavish parts of mankind all over the earth." In that spirit Lincoln asserted that the Declaration meant "liberty not alone to the people of this country, but hope to all the world, for all future time." The same tradition assured Woodrow Wilson a tremendous welcome in Europe. When he spoke of a "world safe for democracy" it evoked a thunderous response in the hearts of men everywhere.

II

RECONSIDERATION

The Declaration and the Constitution date from the eighteenth century. What is their relevance for the current "new" world? We are assured that the world has changed more in the last two centuries than in all earlier recorded history. Indeed the pace of change is accelerating.

A philosopher, Whitehead, gave us one key to our history. A poet touches with sure insight the current significance of these ancient declarations. "The Black Cottage" is a poem by Robert Frost; in form, it is a conversation about an old house, long the home of the widow of a Union soldier. The Declaration of Independence entered the discussion:

> "That's a hard mystery of Jefferson's.
> What did he mean? Of course the easy way
> Is to decide it simply isn't true.
> It may not be. I heard a fellow say so.
> But never mind, the Welshman got it planted
> Where it will trouble us a thousand years.
> Each age will have to reconsider it."*

The seventh decade of the twentieth century is full of that reconsideration. Some voices will say, "It simply isn't true." Many more do not openly reject its truth, but by their acts deny that "all men are created equal."

The Communists regard the American dogma with mingled fear and scorn. Its root ideas are antithetical to their "dialectical materialism" which makes man not the reflection of his Maker but of his material interests. They realize that sooner or later one set of principles—theirs or ours—must become dominant.

For this reason they say, "We will bury you," partly as prophecy and partly as threat. Our best answer is complete fidelity to our ideal, confident that its truth will prevail—not soon, nor easily, but ultimately.

The new nations of Asia and Africa are also considering, as did our forefathers, the right of strangers to rule them. Leaders of these nations have almost all been imprisoned for their political beliefs; they feel a kinship with those American colonists who defied the mother country. They quote Jefferson both more frequently and more fervently than we do. Their understanding of him may be imperfect but still he is their inspiration. If their concepts of democracy are deficient, we should remind ourselves that our ideas took long to evolve, and are not yet flawless. If new nations fail to act upon the principle of the full equality of all men, we should recall how slowly and as yet imperfectly that ideal has developed in practice here.

* Frost, Robert, *Complete Poems.* New York: Henry Holt & Co., 1959, from "The Black Cottage," pp. 75-76.

Many new nations stress an almost forgotten passage of the Declaration: "Whenever any form of government becomes destructive of these ends, it is the right of the people to alter or to abolish it, and to institute new government, laying its foundation on such principles and organizing its powers in such form, as to them shall seem most likely to effect their safety and happiness." So deeply was this believed that Benjamin Franklin, as a member of the committee to design the Great Seal, wanted to inscribe upon it "Rebellion to tyrants is obedience to God."

Vast economic power and enormous physical power tend, by themselves, to evoke envy and fear. In the struggle to reach men's minds their negative effect makes the tasks of diplomacy difficult. Only moral authority can offset fear and suspicion. Historically nothing has contributed so decisively to the moral stature of the United States as its dramatic commitment to the right of the individual to life, liberty, and the pursuit of happiness.

The influence of the United States among the new nations will stem primarily from a conviction on their part that "these great truths" of the Declaration are still dominant in our political and social thought and action.

At best our influence will prove effective only slowly. Many of these nations have come to independence without the inheritance of legal systems, experience in local self-government, and many other advantages our forefathers had. Clumsy diplomacy, niggardly or awkward participation in economic development reduce the effectiveness of the United States abroad, of course. Nothing can so impair the influence of the United States with the uncommitted peoples as denials of equality before the law and equality of opportunity.

III

PROGRESS

It is the essence of statesmanship that its reach exceeds its grasp. Carl Schurz was an immigrant who came to this country after the failure of the European revolutions of 1848. He attained great influence here. Speaking in the "cradle of liberty," Fanueil Hall, in 1859, he said: "Ideals are like stars; you will not succeed in touching them with your hands. But like the seafaring man on the desert of waters, you choose them as your guides, and following them you will reach your destiny." The politician makes compromises essential to keep the daily business of government operative; the statesman sets a goal beyond the range of immediate fulfillment. The founders of the nation were both politicians and statesmen. They learned to make government work, and they set noble objectives which, as we reconsider them, are not yet fully attained.

Nevertheless, we have come a long way since 1776. The men and women who settled this continent came from rigid societies. A man was born into a class, from which escape was all but impossible, whatever his talents. Often he inherited his occupation; he had little or no choice regarding the kind of work he would do. Many migrated as indentured servants to escape what amounted to life-long bondage. Now rigid classes are gone; society is more fluid than ever before in history.

The individual can rise, by his own efforts, to positions of power and respect. Progress from log cabin to White House has historical verification. Six American presidents were born, literally, in log cabins, and under circumstances of extreme poverty and hardship. Six were sons of farmers and in their youth labored before sun-up and beyond sun-down. Four were sons of artisans, three of country parsons. Never in all history has there been such a succession of men rising from humble origins to responsible power. The individual can also sink; he can waste his substance, idle away his time, and go from mansion to gutter; no order of nobility or caste protects him.

The degree to which social fluidity has been attained makes irrelevant the whole Marxian dogma of the class struggle. A body blow has been dealt to the only economic and political doctrine which has arisen to challenge our ideals since the Declaration of Independence.

The Negro was neither indigenous nor an immigrant. He came involuntarily as a slave. When Jefferson wrote that all men are created equal, the phrase did not apply to chattels—human property, to be bought or sold, abused or well treated, at the will of an owner. Slavery was defended by ministers of the gospel as in accord with divine will. Even when Negroes were "free," they, and the Indians, were denied civil rights. It is not yet a hundred years since the full stature of the Negro's manhood was at last formally acknowledged.

Women constitute a majority of the population. The change in their status is dramatic. No woman signed the Declaration of Independence. No woman participated in making, or adopting, the Constitution. Such an act would have been literally incredible. No woman could vote, or hold office; all the professions and most occupations were barred to them. They were subjected to their husbands, their personal and property rights limited and curtailed in many ways. The change in their status is a true revolution.

Child labor was common and taken for granted; today there are only vestigial remains. Labor had no unions, no right to organize or bargain collectively. Now exploitation of workers has all but disappeared.

So far as this nation is concerned, the fear of famine has been banished; people are better fed, better housed, better clothed than ever before in history. The evils of poverty have been sensed; private philanthropy and public policies have softened its harsh impact. There has been a truly astounding advance in social ethics, in sensitiveness to poverty, disease, ignorance.

Progress in education has passed beyond the imagination of the founders. A larger percentage of the public now go to college than then attended common schools.

A generation ago we were told that the frontiers were closed. Since that time science and technology have opened new frontiers more challenging and offering greater rewards by far than those which our histories have glorified.

Life has been extended. Even within the bounds of this century expectation of survival has been increased by about twenty years. Moreover, great strides have been made in the pursuit of equality in this respect. In 1900 the expectation of life for a child of a laborer was thirty-four years—much less than for a child of the well-to-do. Today a workman's child has the same expectation of life as a child from any other social group. This is the fulfillment of the "unalienable" right to life. The productive period of life for the mass of men has been increased 50 to 75 per cent. In this dramatic achievement radicalism has been supreme. Surgeons perform operations which would have been entirely incredible when our nation was founded. Public health measures, sanitation, antibiotics, and hundreds of other developments have contributed to this astounding extension of life expectancy.

Developments in transportation and communication have broadened man's capacity for experience. When the sailing ship gave way to the steamboat and, again, when the airplane came, life literally took on a new dimension. Besides the armed forces, each year approximately four million Americans go abroad; and an enormous number live overseas. Telegraph, telephone, radio, television have put man in instant touch with all the earth and in less time than he used to get news from the next village—and with much greater precision and color. The slaves of the lamp and the motor have extended his powers.

Sometimes we hear complaints that with all our technological inventiveness we have not shown like resourcefulness in politics. That is a total misreading of history. Government of a nation of continental dimensions by the democratic process is a modern miracle. Not even Jefferson believed that an urban industrial society of such vast population and scope could be so ruled. Foreign commentators, such as Thomas Carlyle, predicted its failure. Yet with much less land, fewer natural resources, and smaller population we have outproduced larger nations; our people are more comfortable, and they are not ruled by any clique.

The fruit of all these massive achievements is that the individual is an individual in a sense new to the world. Freed of caste, clan, the taboos of superstition, the blindness of total ignorance, he is an integer

for the first time in history. A slave, an indentured servant, a man
tied to the land, a man whose trade was inherited, each was less
than free. He was governed by others; he was bound by tradition;
the range of choices open to him was narrow. Today the individual
not only has liberty to do his own thinking; if life is to be meaningful
it is he who must search out the values he will cherish.

This change has come so suddenly, the revolution in the status of
the ordinary citizen is so drastic that some cannot face themselves
and make rational choices. Efforts to come to terms with life as an
individual may occasionally be absurd, and we know that some people
fear liberty. But others, in their search for fulfillment, turn to art,
literature, science, healing, and thousands of creative acts. The
astounding fact is not the number of failures, but the measure of success.

Appreciation of past achievement is essential to a wise reconsideration
of our basic tenets. The old copybook maxim, "If at first you don't
succeed, try, try again," has its place. But in the grand sweep of
history success is built upon earlier success. If the heroes of our past
had launched a nation which failed, it would be hard to believe that
this generation could redeem so vast a calamity. But since there are
sound foundations both of philosophy and of action we can raise our
sights and set new goals. We can set out to appease our insatiable
desire for new and even greater triumphs. There is still wide scope
for advance, for, despite the victories of the past, there is much unfinished business. In some instances, wages are even yet pitifully low
and poverty is far from conquered.

IV

THE RACE PROBLEM

The "Negro problem" is the most conspicuous area for dramatic
new advance. Problems in race relations are not unique to the contacts of Negroes and whites. From time immemorial "stranger" was
equivalent to "enemy." Tensions have always been more difficult to
eliminate when physical differences accentuated the distinction. It is
one of the triumphs of civilization when that ancient prejudice is erased.
That it is possible to overcome prejudice is plain upon the record.
Different races live together in amity and effective cooperation in many
parts of the world. Hawaii offers a conspicuous American example;
peoples of many tinctures of skin, backgrounds of history, and varie-
ties of culture dwell together in peace.

The key is in the Declaration of Independence. If, in the poet
Frost's quotation, "it simply isn't true," no solution is possible. If,
on the other hand, we accept as fact that all men are created equal
and entitled, of right, to life, liberty, and the pursuit of happiness, race
relationships can become constructive.

THE INDIVIDUAL 43

The first unalienable right, without which the other two have no meaning, is the right to life. A truncated life will not suffice; men are entitled to life in all its fullness—length, breadth, depth. Yet for a Negro life expectancy, at birth, is about 7.5 years less than for a white man. At age twenty-five the life expectancy of a Negro is still about 5.8 years less than for whites. Clearly the difference does not arise wholly from higher infant mortality. This startling discrepancy between Negroes and whites is largely caused by inferior education, poorer living conditions, inadequate dental, medical and surgical attention. Those deficiencies are the direct consequence of curtailment of "unalienable" rights. Negroes who have had equal advantages in housing, education, and medical care have practically the same expectation of life as whites. That fact shows how needless is anything less. Cutting short millions of human lives negates in practice what we profess in the salute to the flag: "liberty and justice for all." Life is too sweet to be thus shortened by design, even the design of negligence.

A tremendous economic loss is involved. The working years of a colored person are roughly 12 to 15 per cent less than they should be. In terms of the production of goods and services, the growth of the economy, that is a waste we cannot afford. The loss runs far beyond what those raw figures indicate. Failure to give the Negro equal education condemns men to remain common laborers though they have a much higher potential. And common labor is a shrinking base. With a population of 180 million the United States needs fewer common laborers, not only in percentage of the labor force but in absolute numbers, than it did sixty years ago when the population was only 76 million.

The clear lesson is that if workers are not to be chronically unemployed and on the dole they must have better basic education and be more highly and more flexibly trained. The denial or curtailment of these essentials penalizes the Negro very heavily. It reduces the purchasing power available to the economy. It also lays a needless burden of higher taxes upon the rest of us. As the South accelerates its rapid industrialization, economic losses will become both more severe and more evident, for technological change requires constantly higher qualifications for the work force. It does no good to enact federal legislation declaring "full employment" a national policy, and then follow practices that ensure a labor force partly unemployable under modern conditions.

The agricultural revolution is no less dramatic than the industrial. There is no escape from the dead end of unemployment by using Negroes as "field hands." Mechanical cotton pickers and other farm machines symbolize drastic change. Here, as elsewhere, the common laborer is becoming a drug on the market. Better education and training are as essential for agricultural as for industrial work.

The Department of Labor lists over five thousand skilled and professional occupations. Most are effectively closed to Negroes. There is a glib explanation: "They do not meet the standards." So far as it goes that is unquestionably true. But the deeper truth, the overriding truth is that they have been deprived of proper preparation to meet them. Talent is distributed across the human race without respect to national boundaries, race, sex, or any other classification. No competent study ever found one race inferior in social, political, economic, or cultural potential.

Where barriers of prejudice have been lowered Negroes have made their way. Not until recently was big-league baseball opened to them; then they provided outstanding stars. Basketball and football show their quality. On our Olympic teams, they do far better than hold their own, and possess a number of world records. In boxing they have become dominant. Tennis, golf, bowling, swimming, and many other sports still offer barriers at the professional level which only an occasional Negro can surmount; he has to be sensationally good to be recognized.

In music, drama, and other arts, when given opportunity, Negroes compete on even terms. How much richer those contributions might have been if there had been equal opportunity, or may become if it is at last accorded, there is no means of estimation. Our whole cultural heritage can be vastly enriched by discarding legal—and even more, social—discrimination.

Northerners have no occasion to feel smug. Negroes continue to be excluded from the ranks of higher management by denial of a toehold on the executive ladder. If any large industrial, commercial, or financial enterprise is recruiting Negroes into executive-training programs it is a great rarity. When such artificial barriers fall, when Negroes are no longer handicapped in educational and social opportunity, in rights to own property, they will do well in many professions and in thousands of varied careers.

It is utter nonsense to insist that we are in a desperate competitive struggle with the Communist bloc and then handicap ourselves unnecessarily by depriving a significant percentage of our population of a fair opportunity to make their full potential contribution to the national effort. The economic loss runs to billions a year. From an economic standpoint alone, radical reform is necessary. The necessity is not proximate, but instant.

The loss in human satisfactions runs far deeper than the economic; it is beyond calculation. When people are denied fulfillment it is trespass upon the unalienable right to pursue happiness, to find, for oneself, the deeper satisfactions of self-realization.

Moreover, the political consequences are desperately bad. Needless barriers inevitably create and constantly multiply bitterness against a system which not only tolerates but ensures frustration. Whatever is done, at any level, public or private, to continue to foment resentment lays the axe at the root of the system of government to which we are committed.

Democracy, to be viable, requires a large measure of consensus. Deliberately to continue to impair that consensus among citizens is folly. The danger is increased manyfold when some have defied prejudice, broken through barriers, and secured higher education, gaining capacity for articulate leadership. They give voice to what have previously been mute discontents. They give direction to programs to attain the equality supposedly guaranteed by their citizenship. Troubles of an acute kind do not come from men without hope. The historical record shows that it is when people start to ascend in the scale of life that they become impatient to rise faster. We have reason to be thankful that, thus far, action is non-violent, that the new leaders counsel peaceful measures.

When it is urged that Negroes are not "socially acceptable" the statement misses the point. People are not born with social grace. It comes from education, training, environment—the whole atmosphere surrounding youth. The product is the result of the process. It is not reasonable to deny a proper environment and then complain of the consequences. We all know cultivated men and women of color who can hold their own in any society. There is not the slightest excuse any longer to limit freedom of movement, to exclude individual citizens from holding and occupying property where they please. The myth that a Negro neighbor always "impairs property values" has been shown to be just that—a myth. The best evidence is to the contrary, when social circumstances are adjusted. Hawaii and several places in the continental United States have demonstrated that men of all tints and shades can own property side by side and live together in harmony as neighbors if there is equality in education, in opportunity, in employment, and if there is the determination to see that all those things are present.

A current phrase, passed glibly from lip to lip, is the "revolution of rising expectations." The powerful tides that have swept over—and dissolved—empires are dominated by people of color. It may be said that many new nations are not "ready" for freedom. But the deficiency is not of their own making, and is swept aside. That accounts for the bitterness at imperialism. After colored Asia has been made independent, when Africa, "the Black Continent," is being released from colonialism, when tides of freedom are sweeping the world, they will surely wash our shores. Negroes know that men of color are the heads of almost half the nations in the United Nations. They know that many—perhaps most—of them have spent time in prison or in exile because they pressed for liberty.

Names now revered—such as Gandhi—set the modern fashion of civil disobedience that our forefathers earlier sanctified with the Boston Tea Party and defiance of the Stamp Tax. It makes no sense to attribute current unrest to "agitators." There is a contagion in the air—just as there was in the last quarter of the eighteenth century. It is futile to suppose that the infectious passion for equality could leave the American Negro unmoved.

All history and observable current dynamics show that a world in revolution—industrial, agricultural, scientific, political, and social— will not continue to tolerate denial of unalienable rights. It is all very well to counsel patience, but it was said long ago that "hope deferred maketh the heart sick." Patience with progress there can be, but none with efforts to block change. Stubborn refusal to move with the times and concede justice long denied will only multiply and magnify dangers, leave needless wounds it will take generations to heal. Those who suffered political disabilities and economic loss, those who were oppressed by carpet-baggers and wavers of the bloody shirt, those whose resentments have survived for more than three-quarters of a century, so that the political party guilty of those excesses is still taboo, ought not to neglect the lesson of their own suffering.

It comes with ill grace to complain that peaceful sit-ins and other non-violent acts violate piddling city ordinances and state laws cunningly devised to condemn a race to inferior status and deny it equality. Those who make the complaint do not come into court with clean hands. They have themselves helped nullify the Fourteenth Amendment of the Constitution. They have made decisions of the Supreme Court a mockery.

The "separate but equal" doctrine was uttered sixty-four years ago. Educational facilities have been separate; equal they have not been. No one is so bold as to pretend that the mandate of the Court has been observed. The Speaker of the House of Representatives of Georgia said in 1955, "Negro education in Georgia is a disgrace. What the Negro child gets in the sixth grade, the white child gets in the third." Such an admission makes massive resistance to the unanimous decision of the Supreme Court in 1954 intolerable. If Negroes had equal opportunity for education with the white children, the number of colored high school graduates would be much more than doubled each year.

But for defiance of our basic law and its acknowledged interpretation, in the North as well as in the South, by private individuals and by public bodies, many of the ills from which we suffer today would have been avoided, and others reduced to negligible proportions. Until the Declaration of Independence is taken to mean what it says, until the salute to the flag is not uttered with tongue in cheek, until the plain intent of the Constitution is not defied, talk of need for "law and order" is sheerest hypocrisy.

The price of massive resistance to law is not visited alone upon those who promote it. By reason of the high mobility of Americans, it has become a national problem. Denied education, equality, and the pursuit of happiness in their native states, Negroes have migrated to other parts of the country. They have brought with them the disabilities arising from earlier denial of their unalienable rights. They tend to be crowded together in cities; thus they form a clot in the blood stream of the body politic. When that occurs it makes absorption the more difficult; yet its continuation would be fatal.

The first and dominant goal with regard to the Negro problem is to treat men and women as individuals, and pay no attention to their pigmentation. The time has come—almost too late—for a determined and sustained effort to meet this issue at every level, federal, state, local, economic, social, personal. Like every other citizen the Negro must be not only allowed, but helped to fulfill his potential.

This goal is necessary not only in justice to the Negro but for the sake of the moral integrity of us all. One of our most perceptive scientists has written that "the strongest motivations for our striving are part of an essentially nonmaterialistic ethic . . . and what American society may need more than anything else today is a more explicit image to give us continuing belief and confidence." It is beyond question that feelings and acts of prejudice are corrosive of the moral integrity of our people. A national sense of guilt impairs both belief and confidence.

A new moral outlook is more important than new legislation. Nevertheless, use of intimidation and economic coercion to deny constitutional rights is intolerable. The power of the Attorney General of the United States to bring civil suit against anyone who attempts to deny the right to vote should be extended to protect all other constitutional rights as well.

We can take courage to make the massive effort required to purge ourselves by what has already been achieved in related matters. The Negro problem is not unique in our history. When Jews came in large numbers from Poland and Russia, they were subjected to bitter prejudice, evidenced in many ways. Now they hold high office in the land; in business of all sorts their contribution is enormous. The professions have given wide scope to their talents. There are still clubs and real estate developments—and some schools—that discriminate against them, but the number shrinks year by year.

The Irish immigrant was once ruthlessly exploited; prejudice against his religion was deep-seated and intense. Yet most of that has disappeared. In at least one state four-fifths of all office-holders are Catholics, and a good share Irish in origin.

It would be possible to follow the fortunes of one immigrant group after another; the record with minor variations would be the same. Orientals offered a more stubborn problem, but time and American citizenship have made striking advances there. Today the status of the migrant worker and his family constitute, in the words of a high official, a national disgrace. But public indifference is passing, and progress has been made.

The hopeful fact is that we now have citizens in full possession of their equal rights drawn from every corner of the globe, from many races and creeds. What has occurred in the United States, despite conspicuous imperfections, is a unique achievement in history; what remains to be done is less than what has already been accomplished.

In the case of the Negro the last two decades have shown gains. Desegregation has been achieved in the armed forces and the federal service. Headway has been made in transportation, in stores, restaurants, hotels, and schools. Enough has been done to show that desegregation is inescapable; it remains for all of us to make up our minds actively to cooperate with the inevitable.

V

THE INDIVIDUAL AND THE GROUP

The acid test of successful democratic government is the degree of effective liberty it makes available to the individual. That criterion establishes an order of values. Self-fulfillment is placed at the summit. All other goods are relegated to lower orders of priority; even personal security and comfort must have less consideration.

The principle is easy to state. Its application requires a continuous exercise of judgment and will. For there is a perpetual tension between the particular and the general, between individual whims and social necessities. Indeed, that is characteristic of life itself. Centuries ago Aristotle observed that man is a social animal. Each person has both particular and general interests, individual wants and social needs. When the general interest is overaccented, freedom declines and may disappear; first controls, then paternalism supervene. On the other hand, if individual interest utterly neglects social needs, anarchy is the end result. The consequence of either extreme is loss of liberty.

There has been a kind of uneven historical rhythm in the degree to which the state managed the lives of its subjects. Sometimes it left them alone to a great extent; at other times it intervened even in trivial matters.

For brief periods in history it has seemed that tensions between the state and the individual were slight. One can say relatively slight, but never absent; laissez faire was never a policy. It is a fantasy, and did not exist even as a tenable theory. The nearest that responsible men came to that concept was in the aphorism: that government is best which governs least. Even that statement was cast in relative, not absolute, terms. It was fully applicable only in brief moments when all good things—freedom, security, comfort—seemed to exist concurrently. Such eras in history have been rare and short-lived. Normally the tensions between liberty and other values we cherish are more acute. Often they rise to the point of conflict. In a society so completely, and complexly, organized as ours, in a world so interdependent and so disturbed, the choice between individual desires and social necessities becomes difficult.

It is made needlessly difficult when the basic value of freedom—human dignity—becomes confused with either comfort on the one hand or hardship on the other; neither measures human dignity. Economic determinism belongs to the Communists; let them have it. Dignity does not consist in being well-housed, well-clothed, and well-fed. Gandhi never lost dignity; in the deepest sense of the word he never lost security even when he lived in prison, was clothed with a loin cloth, and subsisted upon goat's milk. Other men, with "royal blood," have lived in luxury yet had no shred of self-respect and deserved no respect from others.

Dignity does not derive from a man's economic situation, nor from his vocation. It does not require a white-collar job or any other status symbol. It rests exclusively upon the lively faith that individuals are beings of infinite value. Abraham Lincoln had great insight in these matters. He had experienced abject poverty; he had worked as a common laborer; his education was the product of his own untutored determination. And he said: "It is difficult to make a man miserable while he feels he is worthy of himself and claims kindred to the great God who made him." In our reconsideration of the "great truths" of the Declaration of Independence, we need to be reminded of these things, lest our perspective become distorted.

Because of the increasing pressures of man against man in this shrunken and crowded world, there has been a growing number of compulsions upon the individual, designed to require him to do things for the general welfare, as well as his own benefit. The most inevitable is taxes—usually joined with death as the only absolutely unavoidable occurrence. The power to tax involves the power to destroy; in less extreme forms it is the power to redistribute wealth and reshape society, either to protect the individual or to impair his incentive and cripple his initiative.

One of the commonest compulsions is school attendance; its purpose is to develop the individual and protect society. Compulsory vaccination is a health measure—with like dual purpose. Social security is calculated to protect the individual in his old age, or his survivors if he dies; making him share the cost shields society from his possible dependence. Many other examples could be cited. Each is defensible when it does not inhibit essential free choices and when non-performance would involve danger, needless cost, or disadvantage to others. Those are the tests of the boundary between liberty and license; one man's freedom should involve no trespass upon others' rights to life, liberty, and the pursuit of happiness. They also mark the boundaries between freedom of the individual and paternalism on the part of the state.

At any given moment the decision regarding how far the state should intervene turns upon the current—and dominant—estimate of man's capacity to accept the bitter with the sweet. If the judgment accentuates his courage and strength, liberty will summon all his energies—physical, mental, moral—to wrestle with inescapable, and often intractable, problems. If opinion stresses his weakness, there will be a demand that government make choices for him, and care for him. That process, carried too far, puts comfort before freedom, government above the individual.

The dilemma is perpetual in history; it is new neither in form nor in substance. When the Declaration and the Constitution were being framed, Europe had rulers known as "enlightened" or "benevolent" despots. A good example was Prince Karl Frederick von Baden. He had many virtues; he developed agriculture and commerce; he sought to improve education; he reformed the administration of justice. Clearly he was enlightened. He was also benevolent; he held it to be the duty of his government "to teach his subjects even against their will how to order their domestic affairs," and "to make them, whether they liked it or not, into free, opulent and law-abiding citizens."

At that time the dominant economic theory was mercantilism. Characteristic of that system were economic planning and social engineering in extreme forms. The government was to tell citizens what to do: "It is in its hands to guide them away from error into the right path, and to teach them, even against their own wills, how they are to institute their households." The all-powerful, paternalistic state was familiar to the founders of this nation. With determined purpose they turned away from that ideal to establish a new order. Much later Dostoievski summed up the matter in a few words; he held even "tragic freedom" preferable to "compulsory happiness."

History is replete with manifestations of the acuity of that remark. When the issue is posed in sharp relief, the choice may be hard, but it is clear. From the standpoint of physical comfort and well-being many slaves were better off before they were freed and had to fend for themselves. Yet none is so ethically blind as to use this as a defense of slavery today. The black men of Africa cannot manage their economies, their public health measures—or many other things—so well as the Europeans did for them; but that they prefer tragic freedom to paternalism no one can doubt.

Usually the issue is less dramatically posed. We have been living in an era of moral fatigue. The characteristic historical tone of American life has been optimistic. But the disillusionment of two world wars that brought no peace, and of allies who turned (in both instances) into enemies; the reaction that always follows war's sacrifice; the shock of the great depression—all these combined to daunt our faith and supplant ebullience with pessimism.

In the mood stimulated by these shattering events, human misery came to seem more terrible than human freedom seemed beautiful. The individual was lowered in the scale of values, society exalted. For a brief time technocracy—the ultimate in materialistic determinism—had a great vogue, and was offered as a "modern" substitute for liberty under democracy. More generally men were referred to as "social units." A report to the President of the United States said that "the development of social technology" was "imperative." There were demands in influential places for "social engineering." Those are mechanistic concepts; they deal with individuals not as unique beings of diverse gifts and infinite worth, but as structural units to be built into a planned society.

Fortunately, we hear less of this subversive doctrine today, but other causes of tension have arisen to take its place. One is concern over competition with the manipulated economy of the Soviets, which has led to much talk of the "more efficient use" of "manpower" under the aegis of the government. Often this concept is pressed so far as to constitute an assault upon appreciation of the individual as free and self-directed. When the "manpower program" proceeds beyond information and counsel toward direction by authority the basic doctrine of our nation is countered.

During the persistence of the mood of doubt regarding our system—which often went so far as to assert that we had no ideology—the trespass upon individual rights could make subtle progress, and the inversion of values could proceed in small, but successive and cumulative steps. Security could be exalted above freedom, and intellect become suspect; checks upon thoughts and words, instead of deeds, were made to seem reasonable and necessary. Item by item government was called upon to make choices that had belonged to individuals. Reform was essential; in a few instances it went too far.

It must be emphasized that the rapidly growing federal government was by no means the only organization that tended toward submerging the individual. This is made abundantly clear by the fact that a large share of recent Supreme Court cases involving the Bill of Rights arose from actions of the states, cities, and lesser governmental units, such as school boards.

Moreover, the tendency to overwhelm the individual appears also in private organizations, which, like government, have grown greatly in size and influence. A business corporation may become so bureaucratized that only an "organization man" can survive. Corporate policy may oppose taking "controversial" positions on public questions or actively participating in a political party, particularly one not favored by the management. In dozens of intangible ways it may restrict freedom. All sorts of devices, even including "benefits," may reduce the mobility of the individual, and virtually tie him to his place of occupation. The tendency of every organization to eat up its members is perennial and must be fought every step of the way.

Unions were organized to protect the individual because he was in an adverse bargaining position facing the power of a corporation. In so doing they performed a vital service, of permanent value to our democratic society. But a union may go far beyond its essential service. By making membership compulsory, and collecting dues by check-off, sharp limitations are laid upon voluntarism. There have been instances where overstress upon uniform wages, seniority rights, work quotas, featherbedding "rules," and other devices accentuated losses in individuality arising from machine production instead of offsetting them. The union may curb merit increases and promotions; it may impair incentives. When the leader establishes an effective dictatorship, it is an assault upon freedom. Then the individual is a tool, not a master, as in the democratic process he has a right—and an obligation—to be.

A school can be an enemy of freedom if its discipline is too harsh, its curriculum too narrow, or dominated by some dogma. If it seeks to indoctrinate instead of stimulating originality of thought it is at war with its own reason for existence. A church that curbs political action, that interferes with matters beyond faith and morals, likewise becomes a barrier to liberty.

When any of these things happen, the state, itself curbed by the Bill of Rights, must curb the new threat. Paternalism upon the part of the state is vicious; it is no less intolerable on the part of a private organization. There is no doubt that in the 1960's the individual needs to be shielded from the tyranny of organizations. Any institution, political, social, or economic, that tends to stifle individual initiative or prevent individual innovation is a force for making the United States second-rate and regressive.

The Bill of Rights was not designed for corporations; free enterprise is only one fruit of liberty, not its root. Property and business exist for the benefit of individuals and have no inherent rights. Protecting individuals from the state did not destroy the state; it merely forced government to live with the democratic process. Protection from private threats to individuality will not destroy corporations or unions or schools, though they would have to conform to democratic requirements. Change is the order of life. As private institutions grow with change, they can meet changed circumstances.

VI
SELF-FULFILLMENT

The basic natural resource of the United States is its people. It follows inescapably that the first national goal to be pursued—at all levels, federal, state, local, and private—should be the development of each individual to his fullest potential. No limits are known to the degree to which, by the expenditure of adequate time, energy, skill, and money, the human mind can be developed at various levels of ability.

Democracy is the political aspect of the assertion of the supreme importance of the individual. It is predicated upon the measureless riches that arise from the variety of his inventiveness. The fertility of the individual mind is one of the mysteries of the universe. The source and manner of production of ideas no philosopher, no metaphysician, no scientist has ever been able to fathom. Somewhere, out of the void, that which did not exist before leaps into the mind of man. In freedom, each thinker and doer has the right to self-expression in vocation and avocation. Liberty puts the maximum reliance upon self-discipline.

This goal touches the foundations of democracy. From the first it was realized that popular government required an educated citizenry. The declaration in the Northwest Ordinance of 1787 is classic: "Religion, morality, and knowledge being necessary to good government and the happiness of mankind, schools and the means of education shall forever be encouraged." What was necessary then is doubly essential today.

The United States is the largest, most diverse, and most complex political structure ever to seek to manage its affairs by the democratic process. When achieved, that method of government is the most rewarding. But government at all levels has become so complex and problems so multifold that to attain success citizens must command greater intellectual resources than their forebears. Because the position the United States holds in the world is so influential, the success of the democratic process here is vital not to the United States alone, but to all the world.

The political necessity for the fullest, most competent, and most continuous education should be obvious. When any citizen, for whatever reason, is deprived of this development, it is a denial of one of his unalienable rights. It is a threat to the rights and well-being of the rest of us. It is a subtraction from the viability of our democracy. Every incompetent citizen is a menace to the freedom of all.

The economic argument is not primary, but it is exceedingly strong. Endless talk of the need for capital and machinery obscures the far more vital need for brains. To promote economic growth it is necessary to think not only in terms of what the federal government can do or what private capital can do, not merely in terms of law and regulation and investment. Far more vital is the development and exploitation of the innate capacities of people to the fullest degree. The most severe limitations upon the expansion of the economy are deficiencies and rigidities in the skills of the work force.

We have learned to glorify management; it receives special training at many levels, and large rewards. The research scientist, with his long years of preparation through arduous discipline, is at last recognized as essential to a growing economy. We are witnessing, dramatically, the shrinking need for the common laborer. Yet some of the crafts and professions—including teaching—pursue restrictive practices which deny many competent people access to their skills. Apprenticeships are limited to give a false "security" to current practitioners; in the guise of "standards" exclusion from professions is common. Restrictions where they persist should fall and an effort should be made to recruit more able people, rather than exclude them. The first way to expand prosperity and attain maximum economic growth is through a larger reservoir of people with higher competence.

The fullest development of every individual is hindered by underestimating the potential of a majority—women. They own much of the wealth of the nation; but in its management, in the direction of policies concerning it, not to say in the political operations which determine the atmosphere in which wealth is created, they are still discriminated against. At a time when women constitute nearly a third of the labor force, it makes no sense, from the standpoint of an expanding economy, to apply social sanctions which limit their earning power, and deprive the economy of their executive abilities, their capacity for scientific research, and even their higher technical skills. The union of family life and career is possible to a degree never before conceivable. Yet barriers of pride and prejudice are needless hurdles for women to surmount.

As political and economic reasons point to the need for greater personal development, so, also, does military security. It is irresponsible to talk as though arms, munitions, and money were primary. Estimates of defense requirements in terms of "hardware" offer a classic case of preparing for the wrong war. The first, and vital, necessity is more people of transcendent capacity and skill.

The importance of scientific and technical skills is appreciated. But they will not be enough. Indeed, by themselves, untempered by the humanities and social studies, they may heighten danger. We need people with such sophisticated knowledge and such calm judgment that no mass excitement could trigger an unnecessary war.

The twentieth century has seen Fascism and Nazism. Both were manifestations of mass hysteria; men were literally carried away from normal behavior. Victory in war over those institutions did not eliminate the danger of recurrence. Exaltation of one-man "leadership" leans in that direction. The urgent need is for widely distributed, not over-centralized, leadership and in many different fields. Many people must play important roles, lest the democratic process be ultimately prostituted to dictatorship.

Political strength, economic growth, security of the nation unite in demanding personal development. Social considerations make the same demand. An underdeveloped citizen—physically, mentally, morally— is not an energizer but a burden upon society. The vast growth of hospitals for the chronically ill and of prisons for the hardened criminal stresses that fact.

While schools are being improved, there must also be a massive assault upon whatever handicaps man physically—all the way from prevention of prenatal injuries to the postponement of senescence. In the closely intercommunicating world of today infections fly across land and sea; the protection of the individual is not only a local or even a national concern. It is an international obligation of urgent importance. Inescapable inferences for foreign policy flow from the concept of every individual developed to his highest potential. This puts in right perspective medical and surgical advances, availability of hospitals, the provision for adequate relaxation and recreation to repair the ravages of exertion and restore energy. Statistics on the loss of human resources by physical incapacities show that the scope of this concept is broad enough to challenge a myriad of talents.

The effectiveness of democracy—the most rewarding and most difficult form of government—rests not alone upon knowledge and judgment but upon character. Only the morally mature individual will be determined to do away with slums, end corruption, and help lift the load from the poverty-stricken at home and abroad. Only through moral sensitiveness can there be escape from the smugness that wealth and comfort breed. Moral sense resists avarice and self-seeking. It stimulates that concern for his fellow-men by which society escapes disintegration, while giving the individual maximum play for his talents, tastes, and interests.

With the combination of these elements, physical, intellectual, and moral, man rises to aesthetic appreciation—to culture. Without awareness of beauty life is barren even in the midst of luxury.

Once the individual as a physical, intellectual, moral integer is put at the center, the acceptance of tyranny, the tolerance of totalitarianism, and the readiness to exploit the ignorant and the poor have been made impossible. In a word, democracy becomes not only viable but absolutely indispensable.

All these considerations suggest the true character of education; it is the life-long process of growth, physical, mental, moral, aesthetic. It is not primarily training, though training is part of it. Central is the stimulation and the discipline of the individual. This does not require every individual to be a scholar. The wisdom of the world is not confined to the learned; often it is found in the perceptive experience of those whose schooling has not carried them into "higher education." Their shrewd insights on public as well as private matters are part of the historical record of progress.

There is no such thing as "mass education." Every use of the phrase is a denial of a vital reality; education is a wholly individual process. The life of the mind—despite all pressures to invade it—remains a private life. It occurs in each person uniquely. We do democracy no service in seeking to inhibit thought—free, wide-ranging, hazardous.

The American system is built upon the thesis that conformity is not the way to progress. Without independence of mind there is no freedom for the individual. Therefore education should never overaccent "adjustment." Whenever that emphasis is dominant, it is a deliberate effort to defeat the infinite variety that enriches society and the world.

The educative process should never be distorted by the nation's "need" for scientists, or engineers, or doctors, or any other specific profession or skill. Whenever counseling and curriculum stress vocation primarily they underestimate needs just as vital, though not statistically conspicuous. The nation needs philosophers, poets, artists, critics —and a thousand other sorts of people—in numbers which "manpower analyses" can never estimate.

Education and its objectives defined in these terms involve no less concern with classrooms, equipment, and teachers in adequate supply. But there must be vastly more concern to develop schools devoted to growth. It is not enough to pass child labor laws and compulsory attendance laws to keep young people off the labor market and immure them in buildings. The need is for challenge and stimulation.

If we make effective self-discipline in freedom the chief educational goal of the Sixties, we shall bring a fresh perspective to all our tasks. It would be a clean break with the materialistic determinism of the Soviets. It would establish the moral stance of the United States before the world. It would give us a vastly more efficient society.

No one can doubt that our nation started with extravagant objectives. Its success was so conspicuous that many people regarded progress as inevitable, some even called it "automatic." At that point what had been a manifestation of will and hard work and confidence became a complacent reliance upon factors other than effort and dedication.

Two world wars and the great depression rudely shattered such smugness. The pendulum of opinion swung too far in the opposite direction, and many doubted that there was any such reality as "progress." The ebullient optimism of the nineteenth century gave way to the pessimistic outlook of the mid-twentieth.

It is time to strike a new balance. The revolution in industry and agriculture wrought by science and technology opens enlarged vistas. The amazing economic recovery of Western Germany illustrates that dedication, skill, and hard work still make progress possible. The process is not even; we do not move forward on all fronts at once. Indeed, while advancing in one area, we may retrograde in another. Nor is the pace steady; progress comes in surges; in science it is sometimes called a "breakthrough" which must be followed by tedious and unglamorous consolidation of the new position.

For some years now, organization has seemed to mean more than individuals. The program of national defense has been so huge that stress has been on "team work." Even in science, group enterprises have seemed dominant ever since the Manhattan Project produced the atomic bomb. Industry has become huge, and corporate; unions have developed in size, structure, and resources. Politics has seemed to depend more upon organization than upon ideas.

The moment is ripe to remind ourselves once again that ideas come from individuals, that progress stems from ideas. In the same way morals are the exclusive possession of individuals; phrases like group morality cloud the reality rather than helping to clarify it. Ideals are the combination of individual imagination, intelligence, and moral clarity. Leadership, if the word has any meaning at all, is a characteristic which inheres in individuals who have energy, faith, and ability in unusual degree.

There are many legitimate goals for the United States. None of them—literally none—is attainable without the intelligence, courage, and industry of individuals. The central goal, therefore, should be a renewal of faith in the infinite value and the unlimited possibilities of individual development. Whatever constitutes a barrier to a man's unalienable rights should be swept away. Nothing whatever should curb his right to life—as long, as full, as rich as life can be. Liberty is his, because of his manhood; in liberty the infinite richness of his contribution to the life of others is facilitated. The pursuit of happiness is an endless quest; in it no one can "deliver the goods" to the individual, though the environment can be vastly improved. He must seek it for himself.

Walt Whitman was the poet of America. He summed up the goal in a characteristic poem.

> "I swear I begin to see the meaning of these things!
> It is not the earth, it is not America, who is so great,
> It is I who am great, or to be great—it is you up there, or anyone;
> It is to walk rapidly through civilizations, governments, theories,
> Through poems, pageants, shows, to form great individuals.

"Underneath all, individuals!
I swear nothing is good to me now that ignores individuals.
The American compact is altogether with individuals,
The only government is that which makes minute of individuals,
The whole theory of the universe is directed to one single in-
     dividual—namely to You."

2

THE DEMOCRATIC PROCESS

CLINTON ROSSITER

"WHATEVER WE *do, we must do as democrats—or perhaps not bother to do at all.*" *This is the theme of Clinton Rossiter's chapter on the nature of American democracy, the problems it now confronts, and the ways in which it should respond to them. Mr. Rossiter is John L. Senior Professor of American Institutions at Cornell University, and the author of many widely known books, including* Seedtime of the Republic, Conservatism in America, *and* Parties and Politics in America.

In preparing this chapter Professor Rossiter had the advice of the panel listed below. The author takes responsibility for the views expressed.

PANEL

S. M. LIPSET, Professor of Sociology, University of California; author of *Political Man.*

RICHARD A. MOORE, President of television station KTTV, Los Angeles.

WALLACE S. SAYRE, Eaton Professor of Public Administration, Columbia University, and author of the chapter on "The Public Service".

WILLIAM S. WHITE, newspaper columnist, Washington, D. C.; author of *The Taft Story* and *Citadel: The Story of the United States Senate.*

THE DEMOCRATIC PROCESS

CLINTON ROSSITER

The quickening debate over the public agenda of the next decade has given rise, happily and yet not surprisingly, to more unity than dissension among the American people. In this favored country we have almost always found more things on which to agree than to disagree, and the early 1960's appear to be a time of broad consensus on fundamentals.

The core of this consensus is a continuing commitment to democracy as the best of all possible ways of managing the affairs of men. The style of America has been democratic for more than a century, and it is hard for us to listen respectfully to those who argue that we must change that style radically in the next decade or begin the long decline to mediocrity and, beyond that, to extinction. Although we have never been more soberly aware of the faults of democracy, we have also never been more impressed by its strengths. All attempts to improve the quality of American life must, we think, be made in the manner and spirit of a free people.

I

WHAT IS DEMOCRACY?

One of the special strengths of democracy is that it encourages men to think for themselves, and experience proves that every thinking American can be counted on to have his own definition of this famous word. Yet amid the infinite diversity of our definitions there is a hard core of unity. When we say that America has been a democracy, and expect it to remain one, we mean it in each and all of several senses.

Our democracy has been, first of all, a process— a set of techniques for making decisions and managing affairs at every level of social organization. While our chief concern has been to practice democracy in the government of the nation, the process has also flourished, and given a special flavor to American life, in public communities and private associations throughout the land. Whether in operation in the Congress at Washington or in a school board in Palo Alto or in a service club in Keokuk, the democratic process has been a method of arriving openly, through discussion and compromise, at decisions in keeping with the reasonable wishes of the majority, and then pursuing these decisions with the fullest possible respect for the legitimate rights of the minority.

The essence of the democratic process has been respect for the rules; the guaranty of this respect in the public arena has been the spirit and practices of constitutionalism. Constitutionalism is the generic label for all those arrangements and techniques—separation of powers, checks and balances, due process, bills of rights, the rule of law—that force our governors to think, talk, bargain, and explain before they act, and that institutionalize the procedures through which public policy is made, administered, and enforced. Although the rule of the majority is, in Jefferson's words, the "vital principle" of the American republic, constitutionalism seeks to assure us that the majority will be clear-cut and cool-headed on all occasions, extraordinary on extraordinary occasions, and powerless on occasions when the consciences of men are at issue. Above all, it seeks to assure us that the consent of the governed will not be given lightly to decisions of great moment. This is why Americans have always believed stoutly that, while a government can be constitutional without being democratic, it cannot be democratic without being constitutional.

If democracy is procedures, it is also results; if it is a way of doing things, it is also things done. America has been a democracy not merely because our public and private governments have made many decisions openly, carefully, and in response to clearly-voiced popular demands, but because the decisions themselves were intrinsically hopeful and humane. While not every decision or activity of a government can be judged in these largely ethical terms, certainly in such fields as education and welfare the people of a democracy have a right to expect that policies will strengthen the fabric of civilized existence. A democracy, in this view, is a system of government that acts, whenever it does act, to foster justice, preserve liberty, erase inequality, promote morality, and expand opportunity; and such a democracy we have tried to be.

Finally, our democracy has been a spirit that has pervaded the thoughts and directed the actions of governors and governed alike. The essence of the democratic spirit is a belief in liberty and justice; the aspiration, a commitment to liberty and justice for all; and both essence and aspiration have pervaded the American temper. Enough Americans, it would seem, have had the instinctive preference for freedom and the reasoned respect for popular government that together make it possible for a nation to make the democratic gamble. The spirit of these men has been made real in a code of public and personal behavior that has governed our strivings for generations. It would be hard to overestimate the importance of this code to the proper working of the democratic process. Without the oil of the democratic spirit, in which humility and courage are mixed liberally with the belief in liberty and justice, the wheels of constitutional compromise would clog with the rust of fear and envy, or at best grind out results designed to serve only the vested interests of those men already in favor. And it is, after all, the presence of this spirit alone that gives a "democratic" quality to many acts of leadership in a system of government in which experts play an increasingly important part.

In all these ways—in process, in result (and thus in continuing purpose) and in spirit—America has long been a working democracy. More than a few men in power have corrupted the process and turned it to evil uses; more than a few laws and policies have served narrowly selfish ends; more than a few of us, thanks to our powers of self-delusion, have engaged comfortably in practices that flout accepted standards of humanity and fair dealing. Yet all this is simply to say that Madison was right when he reminded us of the universality of "the infirmities and depravities of the human character." None of it is to say that we could have wrought half so effectively or benevolently under the terms of any other system.

We have had, to be sure, many forces working in our favor. Democracy is a somewhat less weedlike plant than anarchy or autocracy; it will flourish only when conditions are favorable. We who live in modern America are blessed more than any other nation with the social and material conditions of freedom, for we have inherited a well-structured society, a productive economy, a bold and encompassing system of education, a civilized and equitable pattern of private property, and all the political and social tools of self-government. We are blessed more than most nations with the intellectual and spiritual conditions, for we have inherited a great tradition, a humane religion, a clear-cut morality, and a tested faith—faith, in particular, in the dignity of the person and in the fairness and competence of democracy. And surely we were favored in the days of our youth by the timetable of history, which gave us our major blessings in the right order: economic viability before political liberty, constitutionalism before democracy, a morality of self-control before a morality of self-expression.

Yet some of our blessings are the fruits as well as the fertilizer of democracy, and no one can say that we have failed to put both the process and the spirit to severe tests. We were the first to make the democratic gamble on a large scale; we made it with a thoroughly mixed bag of humanity, with men of every creed and national origin. It was not an easy experiment, despite all our good fortunes. At least once, in the decade before the Civil War, democracy failed us and we failed democracy. Yet in the grand perspective of history, which we should take more often than we do, it will surely be judged that over the years of their rise to greatness the American people were well served by American democracy.

II

TIME OF TRIAL

The question before us is how well it can be made to serve the American people in the years to come, particularly in the short span of years for which men in an age of disorder and innovation can reasonably plan. Although our answer to the question may be confident, it must not be offhanded, for plainly democracy is about to be put to a series of tests that will go beyond those of the past in profusion, severity, and perversity. The situation at home and abroad is hardly as favorable to the flourishing of democracy as it was, let us say, in 1900.

At home we are just learning to live with certain unforeseen consequences of our successful experiments in democracy and technology: urbanization and suburbanization, complexity and interdependence, the standardization of tastes and attitudes, the centralization of communications, the hypertrophy of organization, the institutionalization of self-indulgence. While it may comfort us to think that most of these consequences were inevitable as well as unforeseen, it cannot be denied that their cumulative tendency is to crowd the individual, place much of the responsibility for his well-being in the hands of men he cannot know or control, drown him with information he cannot digest or even understand, and thus push him, in his role as citizen, by way of impotence into apathy.

Abroad we are dealing with a world in which opportunity and danger, progress and decay, old order and new chaos are so explosively mixed that we must face this world, and thus face ourselves within, in a posture of defense far more elaborate than we have ever wanted to strike. More than that, it has not been easy for us to watch the rise of new societies whose methods are a vicious reproach to all that we cherish, and to recognize that these societies can do many of the things we have found worth doing—for example, produce steel or train doctors or eliminate illiteracy—and do them, apparently, with enviable success.

The result of all these developments is that American democracy is laboring under strains for which it was not entirely prepared. In the first place, it should be plain to see that, in operating the machinery, we no longer enjoy the margin for error of past years. The democratic process is grounded on common agreement to proceed slowly through techniques of compromise and to avoid steps that cannot be retraced. In order to work at its best it needs time and space—time in which to consider all points of view, to consult all interests, to build up a clear majority, and to reassure the reluctant minority; space in which to make mistakes and yet not do irreparable damage to the public weal or to private liberties. But time and space are both closing in on us. More and more decisions must be made quickly or go by default, be made correctly the first time on the assumption that there may be no second.

Another strain arises out of the sheer number of problems we face, a situation that has accelerated sharply the long-range trend in our public and private governments from smallness to bigness, frugality to costliness, and simplicity to complexity. The decisions to be made and executed each year are multiplying so rapidly that it is becoming harder to anticipate or coordinate them. We are certainly placing a load on the Constitution for which it was not designed by its framers; we are placing a load on many of its operators—for example, on our representatives in Congress—which compels them to be either dray horses or dilettantes.

And a third arises out of the nature of these problems. The tasks of government are qualitatively as well as quantitatively different from those of the past. The decisions to be made are more than numerous; they are also tougher. Those of the next decade may cut more deeply into the lives of the people than did all the decisions of the previous generation put together.

Numerous and tough though these decisions may be, they will have to be made. Once we could solve many of our problems by waiting for them to solve themselves, but those we face today seem to be of a different order. They will not disappear but only grow worse if approached in a spirit of careless or calculated negligence. Democracy, which has always counted heavily on the loose ways of spontaneity, must now make use of firm techniques of planning. It must think ahead as it has never had to think ahead before.

What we are up against, in short, is a shift from easiness to urgency in the circumstances under which American democracy must operate, and thus a shift from quiescence to activity in the style of American democracy itself. The quiet times are gone forever; forethought, decision, and energy are the order of the day.

And so the fateful question is put to us directly: Can democracy be active, at times even breathlessly active, and remain democracy? Can it be tough without being cruel, alert without being officious, effective without being overbearing, authoritative without being authoritarian?

Our answer, let it be repeated, should be a confident and yet measured "yes." It should be confident because we ought to have learned by now to respect the toughness and resilience of democracy. Experience, reason, instinct, and tradition cry out in unison against the judgment of despairing men that democracy is unequal to the tasks of a great nation in a revolutionary world, and against their advice that radically different techniques of decision-making and administering must be invented or imported wholesale. Democracy has proved its adaptability many times in our past; there is no convincing reason to believe that it cannot bear up under the strains of the future. Certainly no other form of government that has been developed or imagined can claim exemption from these strains. They are the growing burden of all governments everywhere in the world, and this burden will be borne most successfully by governments that make full allowance for the complexity and perversity of human events. The most thoroughly tested of such governments is constitutional democracy, which has unique resources for dealing with the problems common to all advanced societies.

At the same time, our answer should be measured because we ought also to have learned that democracy, perhaps more exigently than other systems, needs loving care if it is to perform at its best. We who are charged with such care—the active citizens of the United States— must do everything we can to strengthen the process, the conditions, and the spirit for the hard pull ahead. Of these three fundamental aspects of democracy, it is the process that most requires and best repays discussion. Let us therefore descend from the general to the specific and see what might be done to strengthen each of the major instruments and relationships of the American system of government. While no plausible case has yet been advanced (or is likely even to be listened to by the American people) for basic changes in this system, there are many small repairs and adjustments that could be made in an effort to tune it up for the heavy loads of the next decade.

III

THE BASIC INSTITUTIONS

To begin at the beginning, which is with the Presidency, our chief concern must be to keep this great office in effective command of the executive branch, especially of the agents of diplomacy and national security. All things considered, the health of the Presidency is good, and we can expect it to flourish indefinitely as a reassuring example of the capacity of democracy to adapt itself to the pressures of new conditions.

Yet there is always danger of the job getting out of hand. We have given the President so many tasks that he can do only a few of them thoroughly; we have made so many men responsible to him that he can control only a few of them directly. Our chief solution to this problem has been to create that amazing collection of agencies and officials known as the Executive Office, but this solution has in turn given rise to still another problem: the danger that the President may be made a prisoner in his own house.

The answer to this and to most other difficulties of the Presidency is clearly more personal than institutional. We should be extremely suspicious of such easy panaceas as the proposed creation of a supersecretary for national security to stand between the President and his principal heads of department. It is for the President himself, through the force of his will and candid assertion of his eminence, to keep his auxiliary machinery in good working order and thus to coordinate and dominate the protean activities for which he is constitutionally responsible to the people. This means, of course, the hardest kind of work. The President must insist that he be spared routine but not thought and decision; he must leave channels open to political and social pressures that express the realities of American life; he must remind his personal agents that they serve him and the nation poorly when they commit the prestige of his office to decisions he has not really made for himself. Only thus can the institutionalized Presidency display the steady show of leadership essential to alert and energetic government in a giant democracy.

The one sure sign of a healthy democracy is a vigilant, intelligent, self-disciplined legislature, and we may therefore take satisfaction in the determination of Congress to go on playing a vital role in the process of American democracy, no matter how accelerated the pace of that process may become. Capability must match and support determination, however, and there are plainly several steps that can be taken to make Congress a more effective body than it is today.

The road to improvement in this instance is partly institutional, partly personal. If Congress is to be an active partner in an active government—that is to say, a forceful instrument for legislating and appropriating—it must sooner or later move to reduce the power of its obstructionists to more seemly proportions. It must simplify its rules of procedure, confine the House Rules Committee to its proper sphere of action, place a reasonable check on the filibuster, and find some substitute for the traditional method of selecting committee chairmen. There are merits, to be sure, in the rule of seniority, which spares Congress an infinite amount of energy, intrigue, and rancor. Yet the rigid application of this rule has brought too many men to positions of power who are out of harmony, if not indeed out of touch, with the developing sentiments of their political parties and thus of the nation. The problem is a nasty one, yet surely the American political genius can find a workable solution to it.

If Congress is to be a responsible partner—that is to say, a prudent instrument for investigating and overseeing—it must be filled with men who are masters of their craft, respecters of the imperatives of organization, takers of the long view, loyal though not servile sons of their party. It must be filled, moreover, with men who have a knack for communicating essential information about the issues of the day to their constituents. All these considerations, to be sure, throw much of the burden of an improved Congress back upon the people. They might be helped to carry it a little more thoughtfully if they were asked by the Constitution to elect Representatives every four years instead of every two.

None of these changes would be expected to alter drastically the sensible relationship worked out by the Constitution and history between the President and Congress, nor, for that matter, would at least one useful addition to the President's arsenal of legislative and administrative leadership—the power to veto separate items in appropriations bills presented for his approval. In the interests of efficiency and economy, Congress might well experiment with an occasional bill authorizing the President to eliminate or reduce specific items subject to reversal by concurrent resolution. If we learn through these experiments that the power is one he ought to have and is unlikely to abuse, we could then catch up with forty states—and, for that matter, with the Confederacy—by writing it into the Constitution.

Despite the crossfire in which it finds itself today, the federal judiciary is probably the best prepared of all our institutions to meet the challenges of the next decade. We need more courts, and more judges on some of the courts we already have; we should demand of the President that his appointments be the most distinguished he can make. Further than that we should not go with attempts to influence the character of the judiciary and most particularly of the Supreme Court. If it is performing the tasks staked out for it in our system with any kind of courage and foresight, it is sure to be stirring the anger of more than one important group or section. That is the burden the Court must bear, and we should not permit angry men to make the burden intolerable. We must all learn to respect its independence even when we cannot agree with some of its judgments. We must understand why in making these judgments it cannot avoid making policy—as it has done throughout American history. Above all, we must remember that an upright and independent judiciary is a bulwark of constitutional democracy, and that the true test of such a judiciary is the manner in which it renders justice to men who are unpopular and helpless.

IV

THE CONDUCT OF GOVERNMENT

The processes of modern government are in large part administrative. Democracy must therefore be judged in terms of how efficiently it inspects meat and collects statistics and delivers the mail as well as how forcefully it makes foreign policy. If government is now the biggest business of all, we have a right to expect it to be run as well as the best—frugally, efficiently, responsibly, and ethically. While the President and Congress can do much with their techniques of control to raise the level of administrative performance, there is no substitute for a system of recruitment that brings men of talent and imagination into every rank of the public service and for a code of responsible behavior that gives them pride in their tasks.

One notable arm of the public service has always presented a special problem for democracy, and now, in a time of fierce and persistent stress, it must be managed carefully lest it weaken the process and deaden the spirit. This arm is, of course, the military, which has become so vast and costly an enterprise that its influence is felt powerfully in almost every corner of American life—and in almost every decision in foreign affairs. No easy solution exists for the problem of the military, not least because this influence, to the extent that it is unhealthy, is exerted unwittingly by men of good will rather than consciously by men of evil intent.

There are, however, several major points to have in mind as we go about the continuing task of keeping the military in its proper place. One is that the responsibility for civilian control be placed always in the hands of civilians who are in fact able to exercise control. This means, for one example, that the Secretary of Defense should be a man of quality who operates from a solid base of prestige and political power, and acts consciously as the strong arm of the President. Another point is that pluralism in the armed forces is not an entirely unhealthy phenomenon. A rigidly unified military arm might well present far more of a threat to the democratic process than does the present loose and yet honestly competitive pattern of command. And third, the real solution to this problem, as it is to most problems of civilized existence, is education. We must see to it assiduously that the wielders of our military might are infected early and often with respect for the democratic process and are trained to understand its methods.

The condition of our state and local governments, the distribution of responsibilities among the three major levels of government, and the coordination of activities in which all three levels have a hand are problems to which another chapter in this book is directed. It should be enough for present purposes to take note of the overriding need for more active and efficient governments at both the state and local levels. A strengthening of these governments would take us far toward solving the social problems that now beset us, and would do more to quiet fears of centralization than would any other program of action. The way to reverse the flow of power toward Washington, to the extent that it can or should be reversed, is not to weaken the national government but to bolster state and local governments. The states in particular have too important a part to play in the American system to be permitted the outworn luxuries of absurdly detailed constitutions, hog-tied governors, shamefully gerrymandered electoral districts, pressure-ridden legislatures, and chaotic administrations.

V

PARTIES AND INTEREST GROUPS

The democratic process is something more than a collection of offices and of men to fill them. It incorporates all those people outside government who have an active interest in the things it does and in the way it does them; and that, in a healthy democracy, is a large part of the adult citizenry. The process must therefore provide techniques that encourage citizens to gather and digest information, to form and exchange opinions, to debate issues, to communicate needs, and, in those areas where direct participation is possible and advisable, to hear the questions of their public servants and return their sovereign answers —and perhaps to put a few questions of their own. To accomplish these essential tasks of giant democracy we have created an amazing network of organizations. Three categories in particular are vital parts of the democratic process and deserve at least as much attention as we have given to the Presidency or Congress or the military: political parties, interest groups, and the media of communication.

The two-party system has served the needs of American democracy so long and, all things considered, so well that recommendations for its radical reform or total abandonment have a ring of unreality. Without the help of active political parties we could never hope to bring the eternal struggle for power into the open and under control; and we should be more understanding of the ways in which our two great parties have filled the largest gap in the Constitution by performing their vital functions as managers of elections, personnel agencies, sources of public policy, operators and yet also guardians of the machinery of decision and administration, schools of politics, and skilled buffers between individuals and society. Our parties are far from perfect in virtue, but that is only to say that they are managed by real men and women. They are far from high-minded in interest, but that is only to say that the interests they represent are substantial. And if they are not as clearly-divided, principled, disciplined, and responsible as some critics would like them to be, that is largely because they operate in a system in which power is divided vertically between nation and states and horizontally between executive and legislature, and because they seek to build majorities in a society of minorities. At the price of doctrine, and of at least some of their reputation, the parties have brought a vast measure of unity to a diverse nation. Few thinking Americans would want to argue that "the price of union" has been too high.

One could construct in fancy, to be sure, a party system better suited to direct the active government we can expect in the next decade, yet the one we have is the one we are going to have, especially because it is so remarkable a reflection of the realities of American life. When those realities demand action, action will follow. Critics who doubt the capacity of our major parties to make hard decisions would do well to recall two facts about the pattern of American politics. First, it is designed to check but not to frustrate indefinitely the will of the majority. When a majority shows itself clearly and persistently, it will push through the restraints of the party system just as surely as it pushes through those of the Constitution, which are also designed to delay but not to paralyze. And second, the rules of American democracy do not demand that every political decision be first of all a party decision. Partisanship must have a large place in the making of the great decisions before us, yet so, too, must bipartisanship and nonpartisanship. In the American system there are many ways to form and express majority sentiment, and even the best friends of parties would not presume to assert a monopoly of the democratic process.

This leads us naturally to consider the thousands of interest groups, known less fondly as pressure groups or lobbies, and more fondly as civic groups, that form one of the continuing wonders of American life. Whatever we call these groups, we are aware that they swing a sizable amount of persuasive power over the men who make and execute policy in all governments in all parts of the land, and that the democratic process would be very different without them. They do not have a high standing in the mythology of American democracy. Indeed, they are often represented as the worst enemies of democracy. Yet they are natural products of an open, plural, energetic society, serving effectively to institutionalize two of our most precious liberties: freedom of association and the right of petition. They, like the parties, can be no better, no more honest, no more broad-minded than the men who direct or support them. Laws that seek to regulate them can reach only a small way; most hopes for cleansing their methods and raising their sights begin and end with educating the active citizenry.

The one large objective that we might keep in view as we strive to make the interest groups a healthier feature of American democracy is to give a broader, more democratic character to the influence they exert. The serious doubts we have about these groups arise out of contemplation of their purposes as well as of their methods. Too many of them have too much energy to burn, money to spend, and thus influence to peddle in behalf of highly special and selfish interests. What the democratic process needs is the strengthening of existing organizations (and perhaps creation of new ones) that are broad rather than narrow in scope, general rather than particular in interest, public rather than private in operation. We need interest groups that speak out persuasively for majorities as well as for minorities—for consumers of natural gas as well as for producers, for parents of children as well as for teachers, for people who ride railroads as well as for those who run and man them. We need interest groups, too, that are not afraid of stimulating and ventilating intramural discussions, that make specific provision, to cite one intriguing possibility, for minority reports at annual conventions.

VI

COMMUNICATIONS: CIRCUS OR FORUM?

Democracy is at bottom an agreement to hold civilized discussion of issues that count, and those who cherish it must find and cultivate the techniques of reason. Giant democracy has found most of its own techniques in the wondrous media we have created—newspapers, journals, books, radio, television, polls, advertising, and the mails— to inform, educate, and entertain ourselves.

The trouble is, of course, that entertainment has almost swallowed up information and education in the operation of the mass media. Television, for example, is fast becoming the Circus Maximus rather than the Forum of American democracy, and we are missing out consistently on a rare opportunity to hold popular discussions of a range and influence unmatched in all history. While the Nixon-Kennedy confrontations were a welcome departure, they only scratched the surface of the democratic potentialities of this medium. A few brave spirits have done something to inform and educate the public on controversial issues, but for the most part television has not even come within hailing distance of the press as a device by which Americans can communicate sensibly with one another—not that the press is very far down the road to perfection.

Once again the fault lies with ourselves as well as with our trustees, who in this instance are the owners and managers of the mass media. Just as there is no panacea for the sensationalism of some of the press, for the vulgarity of much of radio, and for the presumptuousness of many of the polls, so there is none for the scarcity and sterility of public programming on television. This whole problem forms a jungle of doubt and unforeseen consequences in which we will have to feel our way along toward higher ground. It is possible, of course, that a stout-hearted Federal Communications Commission could compel the television stations of America to pay for the privileges they have been accorded in the coin of genuine public service, for example, by requiring them to set aside a sizable block of "prime" hours in each week for the use of civic groups anxious to communicate their ideas to the people and to men in power. There are also great opportunities for networks of non-profit public service stations.

Sooner or later we are going to have to face up to the harsh fact that the democratic dialogue is in real danger of being smothered.

Plainly we are in need of new rules and techniques for keeping this dialogue alive as an active ingredient of the democratic process. Plainly the mass media offer us a splendid opportunity, which we will lose at peril of losing democracy.

VII

PRIVATE GOVERNMENTS

This inquiry has concentrated of necessity on democracy in the public arena. We must not forget, however, that it is no less right and viable a force, whether as process or purpose or spirit, in the private activities of men. If democracy is a good way to conduct the affairs of nation and states, it should also be a good way to conduct the affairs of trade and professional associations, churches, unions, community projects, and perhaps even corporations and universities. Indeed, we could hardly expect the democratic process to function in the public arena if it were not also the standard pattern of action in the private. Where, for example, would most men be trained for the public offices of democracy if private organizations did not exist in profusion and perform many of their tasks as miniature democracies?

The affairs of these organizations are labeled "private," of course, only to distinguish them from those that are strictly governmental. Their decisions have far too profound an influence on the public at large to be thought of as something generically different from the decisions of a court or legislature. When a union decides to strike or a church to eliminate segregation or a corporation to close down the only plant in a New England town, it acts in the capacity of a private government, and we should expect it to act as deliberately and responsibly—that is to say, with as much concern for due process—as if it were in fact an arm of the state. We should also expect it, whenever the situation permits, to act openly. While the citizens of that New England town may have no right to override the decision of the directors of the departing corporation, they do have a right to present their views and to hear those of the directors.

We must not make a fetish of the democratic process and ask the impossible of these private governments. There are obvious difficulties in the way of running a corporation like a checked-and-balanced government; in the affairs of a large union the techniques of the town meeting may be as unworkable as they are in the affairs of a large city. For example, much of the clamor for "union democracy" overlooks the blunt fact that a massive infusion of populism into the operations of many of our big unions would either cripple them for the ongoing struggle with management or turn them into jungles of instability. Democracy is participation, but it is also responsibility;

it is the play of opinion but also the prudent management of affairs. In private and public governments alike it is an attempt to maintain a pragmatic balance between the urges of populism and the imperatives of organization, between the rights of the individual and the claims of the community, between the wishes of the led and duties of the leaders. The widely differing circumstances of the countless private governments in America must, of course, alter cases considerably, yet all such governments should be expected, within the limits of reason and strategy, to make provision in their operations for the techniques of constitutional democracy. Due process, publicity, open discussion, representation of the public interest, and accountability can be as good for General Motors—and for the United Automobile Workers—as they are for the country.

VIII

THE PURSUIT OF DEMOCRATIC GOALS

Democracy as results and goals rather than as procedures, as things done and still to be done rather than as methods of doing them, is the central concern of most chapters in this book. In them one reads of the goals of American democracy in the next decade; in them one discovers a many-sided program designed to preserve our liberties, expand our opportunities, and improve the quality of our lives. The pursuit of these goals will repay us twice-over for our efforts, for in winning them we will make even stronger the social, economic, cultural, and spiritual conditions under which the democratic process can operate.

The pursuit will prove futile unless it is made for and by all Americans. The goals of this book are goals for every citizen; the complicated process of deciding on priorities among these goals and then of working imaginatively toward them is one in which every citizen should be invited and indeed encouraged to join. Democracy, let us remember, has a fundamental commitment to equality, in the best and most realistic senses of that word: to equality before the law, equality of political voice, equality in constitutional rights, equality of opportunity, and equality of consideration. Somehow we must push farther and faster than we have in the past—through education, persuasion, example, and, where clearly necessary, force of law—to honor this commitment. Somehow we must eliminate the sordid or timid techniques of unequal treatment that still leave millions outside the circle of first-class citizenship in which most Americans are privileged to go about their affairs. While America is not a guaranty of success, it is a promise of opportunity; and we have no more pressing task in the decade before us than to see that the promise is made in good faith to all who live among us.

If this means that some men must renounce old privileges in order that other men may enjoy new liberties, then that is the way the knife of democratic aspiration will have to cut. It would be happier for all, to be sure, and far healthier for American democracy, if those who now deny other men their rights and opportunities as Americans could be persuaded to suppress their fears and to let democracy take its natural course. One way or another, however, the goals of the next decade, and of every decade after that, must be conceived and pursued as goals for all Americans.

IX

THE IMPERATIVE OF RESPONSIBILITY

In the end, of course, the fate of American democracy rests in the minds and hearts of men rather than in political machinery or social conditions. If enough minds in this country were to work rationally and enough hearts to beat kindly, the machinery of freedom could be far more rusty and conditions far less propitious than they are today —and still America would face the world as a proud, secure, confident democracy. Again and again we have had cause to note that the solution to most problems of American democracy is personal rather than institutional. Surely many of our techniques of decision and administration are about as soundly constructed as nature and art permit; they are simply waiting patiently for better men to operate them. To enlist, train, support, and instruct such men is a major task of American democracy in the years ahead. This task, in turn, calls for better men throughout the land.

Better men in government (or, more exactly, in the seats of power everywhere) means men who are upright, fair-minded, imaginative, and reliable, who practice the fine art of democratic leadership with skill and prudence, who summon up strengths rather than pander to weaknesses in the people with whom they must deal. Above all, it means men who are responsible, who act judiciously, openly, unselfishly, and correctly, who can bear the inspection of their constituencies with credit and await the judgments of posterity with confidence. There was a time—and not so long ago—when we could put up with large amounts of demagoguery, chicanery, and just plain bungling in our public and private governments. That time is long gone; the margin for political error, let it be repeated, has been reduced drastically by the revolution at home and abroad, most of all by the prodigious growth in the capacity of men to help and, by the same token, to harm one another. The great new dimension of industrial civilization is power for good and evil over the lives of men, and in this power we all share—the doctor with his antibiotics, the farmer with his pesticides, the pilot with his cargo of humanity, the manager with his plans to step up or step down production, the worker with his strategic place in the automated factory, the union official with his authority to call a strike, even the least of men who, dwelling in a great city, can flick a switch or mumble a few words into a telephone and bring discomfort if not indeed danger into the lives of thousands of persons on whose faces he has never looked.

This fact of power puts a new strain on all Americans, but especially on those who hold public responsibilities. We need only think, for the most persuasive example, of the challenge to the democratic process that arises out of the instantaneous and all-destroying nature of modern weapons. The men to whom we assign control of these weapons have none of the room in which to be silly or vainglorious or pig-headed that was furnished warriors of the past. Nor, for that matter, do the men to whom we assign control of our finances, public services, and schools, of our factories, fields, and facilities of transportation. They, too, hold far too much power over the lives of other men to be exempted from the growing demand for decision-makers and administrators who are first of all mature and prudent. What we might call the "imperative of responsibility" must pervade and stiffen the whole spirit of democracy.

So, too, must the "imperative of anticipation," for these same decision-makers and administrators must have a perception of the future, a grasp of the predictable and an instinct for the unpredictable, that managers of the democratic process have not found quite so necessary to cultivate in the past. The stumbling reaction of our government to the immense legal and administrative problems raised by the swift advance toward practical exploitation of outer space is example enough of the need for a new order of imagination all through the structure of democracy.

X

THE ROLE OF THE CITIZEN

Better men throughout the land means men who cherish liberty, who enjoy it themselves and respect it in others. Of such men, the democrats of the spirit, we can never have enough. Unless tens of millions of Americans are determined to be free themselves and to support other men in freedom, democracy is doomed to disorder and sorrow. The price of liberty, today as through all history, is self-reliance and self-discipline. Nothing has happened in this revolutionary age to relieve each of us of the prime responsibility for the state of his own freedom. Rather, the shift from independence toward power within the equation of personal liberty, and from untrammeled individualism toward a sense of community in the public philosophy, makes the practice of self-discipline more essential than ever before.

To say this is not in the least to deny the immense influence of social environment. But we cannot permit ourselves to become so bewitched by the new truth that liberty is socially influenced as to forget the old truth that it must also be personally cultivated. Liberty is offered by the good society, but it is achieved and practiced by the person. It is most securely achieved and practiced by men who submit themselves to the demanding self-disciplines of faith, knowledge, effort, virtue, and purpose. We have no more challenging task ahead of us than to strengthen old ways and create new ones in which men can be encouraged to choose liberty over sloth or surrender.

These considerations raise the familiar question of popular participation in public affairs. Whether for their own ends or for those of the community, whether at the polls or on public platforms or in private meetings, the citizens of a democracy are expected to take an active interest and role in the political process. Yet many citizens of American democracy do not participate persistently and enthusiastically, and many do not participate at all. The statistics of participation, whether measured in the total vote cast in presidential elections or in contributions to political parties or in attendance at annual meetings of school districts, are distressingly low. The statistics of voting are especially distressing because in a big democracy, which must count heavily on techniques of representation for expressing the wishes of the people, the choosing of leaders becomes the critical opportunity for participation. What are we to think of an enlightened community in which something up to 40 per cent of the eligible public will not vote in a presidential election and up to 60 per cent in a congressional election?

One thing we can think is that the community is not so enlightened after all, a thought that may encourage us to redouble our efforts at political education. Another is that millions of Americans find it difficult and often impossible to vote, a thought that may encourage us to move forcefully to clear away disabilities and discriminations. A third is that the remarkable "coolness" of American politics is, paradoxically, a sign of our confidence in the durability of democracy. And a fourth, perhaps the most important, is that the American future rests rather on the quality of our votes—and of our participation of every kind—than it does on the quantity. What America needs is not more voters, but more good voters, men and women who are informed, understanding, and reasonable. To produce such men and women in ever larger numbers should be a major goal of all labors to preserve American democracy.

XI

WE ACT FOR ALL MANKIND

Will the process and substance and spirit of democracy prove equal to the hard pull ahead? That is a large question to which history, not this or any other essay or prophecy, must make final answer. The most that we can do is to remember that democracy has always been a gamble, that few nations have ever been in a position to make the gamble, and that we, because we have been uniquely privileged to make it, have a responsibility for making it successfully that transcends our own fortunes. What Jefferson said of us in 1802 is every bit as true in 1960: We are "acting for all mankind" as well as for ourselves and our posterity. The failure of American democracy would bring democracy everywhere down into ruins. That is a thought to sober and inspire all Americans, and to stiffen them for the substantial sacrifices that lie ahead.

It may be, of course, that democracy as we have known it will have no place in the fantastic world—automatic, antiseptic, abundant, and presumably painless—that has been promised by the seers into the twenty-fifth century. So far as the eye of reality can stretch, however, it is the way of life best designed to serve the needs of the American people. As it serves our needs, so it expresses our traditions, without which we would be simply a mass of people occupying a large plot of land. Even if it could be proved that some other way of life might be more efficient in handling the problems common to all advanced societies, we would be foolish and dishonorable even to think of adopting it.

For what shall it profit a nation if it shall solve all its social problems and lose the character that made it a nation in the first place? Whatever we do, we must do as democrats—or perhaps not bother to do at all.

3

NATIONAL GOALS IN EDUCATION

JOHN W. GARDNER

3

FOR THIS *important chapter the Commission turned to one of the country's most respected educational leaders, Dr. John W. Gardner, President of Carnegie Corporation of New York and Carnegie Foundation for Advancement of Teaching. Dr. Gardner has outlined a concrete program for the decade. His specific recommendations deserve the careful attention of every parent, teacher, administrator, school board member, legislator, and voter.*

Dr. Gardner consulted with a group of forty leading educators, and was advised by the panel listed below. The panel desires to note that it is in general agreement with the views expressed in the chapter.

PANEL

ARTHUR S. ADAMS, President of the American Council on Education.

JOHN H. FISCHER, Dean of Teachers College, Columbia University and Vice Chairman, Educational Policies Commission of the National Education Association.

DEVEREUX C. JOSEPHS, Director, New York Life Insurance Company; formerly Chairman, President's Commission on Education beyond the High School.

NATIONAL GOALS IN EDUCATION

JOHN W. GARDNER

I

INTRODUCTION

Education is important in any modern society, whatever its political or economic forms. But a society such as ours, dedicated to the worth of the individual, committed to the nurture of free, rational and responsible men and women, has special reasons for valuing education. Our deepest convictions impel us to foster individual fulfillment. We wish each one to achieve the promise that is in him. We wish each one to be worthy of a free society, and capable of strengthening a free society.

Education is essential not only to individual fulfillment but to the vitality of our national life. The vigor of our free institutions depends upon educated men and women at every level of the society. And at this moment in history, free institutions are on trial.

Ultimately, education serves all of our purposes—liberty, justice and all our other aims—but the one it serves most directly is equality of opportunity. We promise such equality, and education is the instrument by which we hope to make good the promise. It is the high road of individual opportunity, the great avenue that all may travel. That is why we must renew our efforts to remove the barriers to education that still exist for disadvantaged individuals—barriers of poverty, or prejudice and of ignorance. The fulfillment of the individual must not be dependent on his color, religion, economic status or place of residence.

Our devotion to equality does not ignore the fact that individuals differ greatly in their talents and motivations. It simply asserts that each should be enabled to develop to the full, in his own style and to his own limit. Each is worthy of respect as a human being. This means that there must be diverse programs within the educational system to take care of the diversity of individuals; and that each of these programs should be accorded respect and stature.

This is a brief essay on a vast topic. It necessarily leaves out much that is important. We have dealt very sketchily with subjects that deserve more thorough treatment. And we have not touched at all, unfortunately, upon such important matters as the role of music and art in education, or the role of the school in development of children's character.

For the convenience of the reader, twenty-five of the more important recommendations are numbered and italicized.

II

THE TEACHER

Love of learning, curiosity, self-discipline, intellectual honesty, the capacity to think clearly—these and all of the other consequences of a good education cannot be insured by skillful administrative devices. The quality of the teacher is the key to good education.

During the 1960's the number of classroom teachers will have to expand by almost one-third to take care of population growth. (1) *To meet both growth and replacement needs, we must recruit at least 200,000 new teachers every year for the next ten years.* These are conservative figures. A number of educational leaders have urged a minimum of 50 professionals (teachers, counselors, administrators, etc.) to every 1,000 students. We are far from that today.

But an adequate *number* of teachers is only part of our problem. The other part is *quality.* We must raise standards of recruitment and training.

Both numbers and quality are particularly critical issues at the elementary level. Here, where individual attention is vital, there is today an especially grave likelihood of shortages. And the need for better trained elementary teachers is pressing. Every state should require the B.A. for new elementary teachers. (Four out of five states require it today.)

By 1970 every state should require one year beyond the B.A. for new high school teachers. (Only three states require it today.)

We should not deceive ourselves as to the recruitment problem. Low salaries and other conditions in the profession make it an unattractive career for too many people. We ought to have a large enough number interested in teaching careers so that we can pick and choose for the high qualities of mind and character we want in the profession. We are very far from that goal; indeed there is a serious shortage of teachers at this writing. If we are to bring enough good people into teaching, the community will have to accord the profession the respect it merits. (2) *Teachers' salaries must be raised until they are competitive with salaries in other fields for jobs involving comparable ability and length of training.*

Schools should continue to experiment with differentiation of professional roles. The use of teachers' aides to carry out routine tasks is one promising development. Another is the suggestion that the rank of Master Teacher be established for individuals at the highest levels of ability, training and experience, and that lower levels of functioning be defined for less qualified individuals. Such suggestions not only promise better utilization of the teaching talent available, but enable the best teachers to look forward to appropriate rewards of money and status.

Merit pay is another means of providing rewards commensurate with performance and should be universally adopted, with appropriate safeguards to insure fair treatment.

College faculties. Enrollments in higher education will double by 1970. To provide a staff commensurate with this growth and to replace all who resign and retire, we shall need some 468,000 recruits in the 1960's.

If we are to get anywhere near this number of qualified people, we must increase the output of our graduate schools. More important, we must create conditions which make the academic profession attractive to first-class people. A powerful factor is the public attitude toward intellectual endeavor, and toward higher education. If this attitude is one of respect, the profession will be attractive to young people. At a more practical level, the most important factor is compensation. As with school teachers, (3) *college faculty members should receive salaries that are competitive with salaries in other fields for jobs involving comparable ability and length of training.*

But the supporters of higher education cannot be expected to put up more money for faculty salaries if outmoded and extravagant practices mean that talent is misused. It is still common to use highly paid professors as drillmasters in subjects such as foreign languages. Administrators still indulge in false economies by refusing to give professors adequate secretarial and clerical help. And it is still the practice in all too many institutions to clutter the curriculum with courses of dubious value. College faculty, administration and trustees should discuss these matters—as well as questions of teaching load and student-teacher ratio —candidly and in good temper. The bill for higher education is going to be very, very large in the years ahead. It is reasonable to expect more discussion of how the money is spent.

III

THE STUDENT

Equality of opportunity. In dealing with students, the first goal is equality of opportunity. By 1970 we should have achieved a deeper understanding of this phrase than ever in the past. We should have become keenly aware of all of the forces that limit individual growth, and should have learned much about how to cope with these forces. We should insist that regardless of the individual's economic level, regardless of his color, whether he lives in a modern suburb or the backwoods or a city slum, he should receive the best we can give in the way of opportunity and encouragement to develop whatever abilities he possesses.

We are still losing large numbers of talented young people who terminate their education short of their full potentialities. Why do we lose them? Can we prevent the loss? We are just beginning to find answers to these crucial questions. During the 1960's intensive research should be applied to the problem of "talent salvage."

Our cities will still have slums in 1970, but the schools in them should no longer suffer the same blight which afflicts the neighborhoods (as is commonly the case now). In such neighborhoods the school must be *especially* good: the child outside of school may be subjected to conditions that do not stimulate (or actively hinder) his intellectual growth, and the school may be the only lifeline for development of his potentialities. Every city should develop special programs (such as the Higher Horizons Program in New York City) to put the best education at the disposal of underprivileged youngsters.

Similarly, in 1970 there will still be geographical areas in which economic backwardness, cultural impoverishment, or other conditions are unfavorable to individual development; but here again we should have learned how to maintain good schools in these areas to serve as lifelines for the youngster.

The battle to accomplish desegregation in the schools is a part of the broader effort to achieve equality of opportunity and respect for individual potentialities. The struggle to achieve desegregation will be a long and slow one. It will not be over by 1970. But it will be even longer if we let up in the relentless effort to accomplish this goal. Throughout the 1960's the struggle will have to continue on many fronts, and will have to be pursued in many ways. (4) *We should set as our minimum goal that by 1970 there should be no state in which desegregation is prevented by state action, no state that has not moved to comply with the Court decision on desegregation.*

The education of women. While the proportion of women in the labor force has been increasing rapidly—women are now about 36 per cent of the labor force—their rate of entry into the professions has declined. Although women win some 30 per cent of the B.A. degrees, they take only about 10 per cent of the Ph.D.'s. Such waste of talent is a relic of the past. We can afford it no longer.

From the earliest years, girls should be actively encouraged in the development of their intellectual capacities. Teachers, guidance people and parents should recognize that women are capable of advanced education in any field, including mathematics, science, engineering, medicine and law.

Women should be encouraged to enter every field requiring advanced training. A woman's family obligations may make it necessary to modify the pattern of graduate and professional training established by and for men. Her professional career may also involve departures from the masculine norm. Colleges and graduate schools should make it easy for women to continue their education part time (or to interrupt it) during the period of heaviest family obligations.

Each according to his potentialities. Having committed ourselves to equality of opportunity, we may properly turn to the second principle— that each child should be dealt with in terms of his own abilities. Every child should have the benefit of an educational program designed to suit his capacities and to develop him to the limit of his potentialities—whatever that limit may be. None should be required to fit a pace and pattern of education designed for children of other capacities.

In dealing with children of differing potentialities, we must remember that all are worthy of respect as human beings, all must know how to live and work together. They should never be handled in such a way that some youngsters appear to belong to an elite group while others are classified at a lower level. The comprehensive high school works to this end by keeping all students, whatever their ability, in the same educational community: students of every level of ability sit in the same homeroom, play on the same teams, act in the same plays, and have many other activities in common. (5) *It is essential that the tradition of the comprehensive high school be preserved and strengthened.*

To urge an adequate program for gifted youngsters is not to recommend favoritism. They do not need more attention than other children —in some situations they may even need less. They need a different *kind* of attention.

Attempts to identify children of unusual potentialities should begin when schooling begins. When a child's family and neighborhood background are culturally impoverished, the school may be the only channel through which his gifts can be nourished: the sooner they are discovered the better.

Children of high academic talent, most of whom will have to devote many more years to education than the average youngster, should be given the opportunity to move more rapidly. There should be various forms of grouping by ability from the earliest years of school; and every effort should be made in and out of school to provide enrichment for the gifted student.

In high school, every academically talented student should study four years of English, four years of mathematics, four years of one foreign language, at least three years of science, and three years of social studies. James Conant's Academic Inventory should be used to determine whether the ablest students are taking programs suited to their abilities.

The student not going beyond high school should also have academic subjects at the heart of his program. But he can profit greatly, too, by good vocational courses.

It is not wise to segregate vocational students into separate high schools, nor even into separate homerooms. Where such separation has acquired historic status, it will not be feasible to alter it, but the practice should be avoided where possible.

High school vocational programs should be thoroughly re-examined and revised. Like every other element of the curriculum they must change and improve. Today, all too many young people who will be exercising their skills in the 1970's are being prepared for the technology of the 1950's. Because most students will go through occupational lives characterized by constant learning of new skills, vocational programs should emphasize fundamental skills and fundamental ways of approaching problems.

It is especially important that thoughtful attention be given to the needs of the most limited group academically—the so-called "slow learners."

Guidance and testing. Guidance is an inescapable necessity of education today. By 1970 it should be provided by professionally trained people in all school systems. Every school should have a testing program beginning in grade one if not before.

Some experts have urged that there be one full-time counselor for every 250 to 300 pupils. That is a useful goal, but we must not be so eager to attain it that we accept unqualified people. The requirements are vague today and permit many unqualified people to become counselors. By 1970 no state should require less than the M.A., and certification requirements should insure that newly entering counselors are professionally competent.

IV

THE CURRICULUM

The curriculum is too large and too technical a subject to be dealt with adequately in this brief essay. The following comments touch only a few high points and are necessarily sketchy.

By 1970 the teaching of every subject from the elementary grades through high school should have received intensive reappraisal by teams composed of (a) the best minds in the subject-matter field, (b) curriculum specialists, and (c) the most experienced elementary or secondary school teachers of the subject. The best model for such reappraisal is the work that has been done in high school mathematics by several groups (e.g., University of Illinois, College Entrance Examination Board, National Science Foundation).

Reading and writing. Some subjects are more important than others. Reading is the most important of all. The first step to improve the teaching of reading is to improve the teachers. There are many superbly qualified elementary teachers, and it is no discredit to them to say that there are many others who are not qualified. It is a mistake to suppose that reading can be taught by an untrained person. Every elementary teacher who gives instruction in reading should have had courses in the specific methods of teaching reading.

In the primary grades individual attention is essential and it is hard to exaggerate the time that can profitably be devoted to reading. Remedial work should be prompt; in scheduling the child's program it is essential that adequate time be allowed for such work. From the earliest grades children should be grouped in such a way that rapid readers may move as swiftly as their capacities permit and the slow may receive thorough attention.

The teaching of writing, like the teaching of reading, can profit from more time and attention. The first requirement for a high school teacher of English should be competence in teaching composition. Written assignments are essential. In high school about half the total time spent on English should be on composition, averaging one theme a week. Teachers cannot meet this requirement if they are overloaded. English teachers should not handle more than 100 students each.

Mathematics. Mathematics is second only to reading as a priority subject in elementary school. And mathematics teaching, like the teaching of reading, will profit greatly by a general upgrading in the qualifications of elementary teachers.

As in reading, remedial work should be prompt and generous. The child who falls behind cannot understand the work that follows, and suffers a cumulative deficit. This often results in a fear of the subject that never leaves him. Ability grouping from an early age should enable the mathematically gifted student to move rapidly and the slower student to receive ample attention.

All teachers should be familiar with the great studies of the teaching of mathematics that have been conducted in recent years. Their cumulative influence should persuade teachers to communicate not only basic skills but comprehension of the underlying structure and concepts of mathematics.

In high school everyone should be required to take one year of mathematics; those who are going to a four-year college (or hoping to) should take four years. Exceptionally gifted youngsters should take calculus or analytical geometry in senior year of high school.

Science. The bottleneck in producing more and better scientists is the shortage of qualified teachers. Part of the answer lies in increased fellowship funds and expanded facilities for graduate work in science. There must be higher standards of preparation and certification for science teaching. Certification requirements should be revised to place greater emphasis on subject-matter competence.

All high school science courses should be revised in the light of current curriculum studies. New courses should reflect the best thinking of leading scientists and experienced teachers.

In high school a course in physical science or biology should be required. Every high school should offer elective full-year courses in biology, chemistry, and physics. High schools with a sufficiently large college-preparatory group may offer second-year courses in these fields. Students who hope to go on to a four-year college should study the sciences for at least three years.

Foreign languages. Teacher training institutions should certify the linguistic competence of graduates who are going on to teach foreign languages in the schools. Certification should be on the basis of examinations designed to measure listening comprehension, speaking, reading, writing, and understanding of the structure of the language and the culture of the people. School systems should hire only candidates who are so certified. It is a scandalous fact that today none of the 50 states requires that language teachers speak the language they teach, and many are incompetent to do so.

Foreign languages should begin no later than grade seven. In many schools they will begin in grade three. All teaching should be done by the modern methods which stress hearing and speaking throughout. Texts should be revised to fit these methods, and every high school should be equipped with a language laboratory. Every four-year college should require for entrance four years of high school study of a single foreign language.

By 1970 there should be no major world language that is not offered on a continuing basis by some university. There should be several places in the country where Chinese is taught in high school. Russian should be as widely taught as French—but we will not achieve that goal by 1970.

Social studies. In high school three to four years of social studies should be required.

As much as any subject in the curriculum, social studies needs a fundamental re-examination. In view of the rapid development of the social sciences in recent years, school courses in the subject should be thoroughly reappraised. Standards of teacher preparation and quality of texts should be raised.

V

INNOVATION IN EDUCATION

All the organizational arrangements, all the methods and procedures that characterize American education today were originally devised to help us accomplish our purposes. If they no longer help us, we must revise them. The arrangements and methods must serve us and not control us.

We would be in a better position to appraise the validity of present methods and the promise of new ones if we enjoyed a more vigorous tradition of research in education. The sooner we remedy this lack the better.

School organization. In seeking the most effective ways of accomplishing our educational purposes, we are going to have to take a flexible and experimental view of various established practices. A few examples will suffice.

The Self-Contained Classroom. The elementary school has been saddled with an inflexible tradition of the classroom in which one teacher stays with the same 25 to 30 children all day and teaches every subject. It is a tradition that cannot survive the requirements of modern education. But only careful experimentation will make it possible to modify the tradition without harm to the children.

Division into Grades. Some of the more advanced experiments in elementary education have partly or wholly abolished the division into grade-years. One school has done away with the first three grades, divides the children into nine ability groups, and allows them to proceed at the pace that suits their capacities. It is difficult to say where such experiments will lead, but they are well worth further study.

Utilization of Buildings. Most school and college buildings stand unused after 4:00 p.m. every weekday, all day Saturday, and throughout the summer. In the 1960's the nation will have to spend in the neighborhood of $25 billion on elementary and secondary school construction. Anything that can be done to diminish this through better utilization of present buildings will be money saved—money that could better be put into teachers' salaries.

Summer School. It is not just fuller utilization of plant that should lead us to re-examine the national summer shutdown in education. The summer session provides an important opportunity to supplement the school program—(a) for students who wish to take remedial work or repeat a subject; (b) for students who want advanced courses not offered in regular term; and (c) for driver education, typing and other courses students may not have time for in regular session. By 1970 all but the smallest unified school districts should operate tuition-free summer sessions (attendance voluntary). Every college and university should hold a summer session.

New teaching aids. The educational use of television holds great promise. But this marvelous tool of communication is powerless in itself to improve education. It may be employed to good effect or foolishly. One of the challenges facing education in the 1960's is to learn to use it well.

By 1970 every school in the nation should be equipped for instruction by television; and the advantages and limitations of educational television should be universally understood. Properly used, television could bring superb lectures and other presentations to school children throughout the nation. For example, demonstrations of scientific experiments of a quality that no single school in the nation can now afford, could be available to every school by 1970.

But the role of the teacher will remain secure. Television has notable limitations as a teaching device. There will always be some aspects of teaching that can be accomplished *only* in face-to-face interaction between teacher and pupil.

Exploring the classroom potentialities of the medium is not the only problem we face in educational television. There are questions of public policy to be settled. In the course of the 1960's, government and the educational world must undertake an unsparing reappraisal of the public service obligations of commercial broadcasters and of the availability of channels for educational purposes.

Another innovation that seems certain to have an impressive impact on the teaching process is what has misleadingly been called the "teaching machine"—and might better be called a self-teaching device. The best self-teaching devices and programs have proven remarkably effective, and students seem to enjoy working with them. Wisely used, they can remove a load from overburdened teachers, and give each student the luxury of a private tutor who proceeds at a pace determined by the student.

Where television holds the danger of standardizing instruction and of placing the student in a passive role, the self-teaching device can individualize instruction in ways that are not now possible—and the student is always an active participant.

As with television, the self-teaching device cannot replace the teacher. But by doing some things as well as—or better than—the teacher, it frees the latter to spend more time on those creative aspects of his job that no self-teaching device can duplicate.

During the 1960's the orderly development of these devices should not be marred by premature enthusiasm on the one hand nor misguided antagonism on the other. By 1970 a decade of experimental research on human learning, and application of the results to self-teaching devices and materials, should have made the best of these an adjunct to the teaching process that no school could afford to be without.

VI

HIGHER EDUCATION

The undergraduate years. The pressure on college admissions will continue, not only because of an increase in the college-age population, but because a higher percentage of that population will choose to go to college. Post-secondary institutions should be prepared to handle up to 50 per cent of the college-age population by 1970.

Even more than today, we shall be dealing with a wide range of abilities and motivations in the college population. Students will differ greatly in their educational needs, and will have to be served by diverse institutions and programs.

Some institutions (e.g., community colleges and two-year technical institutes) will specialize in those whose educational plans (or potentialities) are least ambitious. These institutions have a critically important job to do in American education. It is essential that they be given the resources and moral support necessary to do the job well.

At the other end of the spectrum, some institutions will limit their student bodies almost exclusively to those who intend to go on to graduate and professional work. Entrance requirements will approximate present standards for students requesting advanced placement, and almost all entering students will have taken advanced (college level) courses in senior year of high school. In short, students in these institutions will be a year ahead of the average college youngster today.

Many institutions, especially state universities, will accept students over a wide range of abilities but will enroll them in different programs. They will accept high school graduates with minimum qualifications, enrolling them in courses comparable to those offered by junior colleges. At the same time, some of these same institutions will operate honors programs comparable in difficulty to any in the country.

Though we accept the idea (long established in practice) that postsecondary institutions differ enormously in the level of education offered, we must insist that every college student be stimulated and challenged in terms of his own potentialities. A college education should be a reasonably arduous experience.

In the great variety of institutions and programs that make up American higher education there will continue to be both liberal arts and vocational programs. Each has its place. But *no* institution should be without a strong liberal arts component.

The junior college. We are moving toward more explicit recognition of the diversity in our higher educational institutions. An important ingredient in this diversity is the junior college or community college.

Such institutions perform highly useful functions. It is not vital that the functions be performed by institutions that carry the label *junior college* or *community college*. The functions can be (and often are) performed within a four-year institution. Some states prefer to do the job in institutions designated as branches of the state university or as extension centers.

Whatever the label, (6) *there should be roughly within commuting distance of every high school graduate* (*except in sparsely settled regions*) *an institution that performs the following functions:*

(a) *offers two-year terminal programs for students not going on to a four-year college career.*

(b) *offers transfer programs for students who do wish to complete a four-year program.*

(c) *serves as a technical institute for the community, serving local needs for vocational and sub-professional education.*

(d) *offers continuing education to adults.*

States should expect these institutions to take care of a substantial percentage of the future college population (perhaps 50 per cent of all who enter college for the first time).

The graduate school. The nation desperately needs men and women of high ability and advanced training. We cannot maintain our complex society nor sustain ourselves as a great nation without them. To educate such men and women is the task of our graduate and professional schools.

The graduate schools must expand their output to supply teachers for the vast growth of higher education, and to meet the increasing demands from government and industry for educated talent. (7) *We should be producing 20,000 Ph.D.'s annually by 1970 (compared with 9,360 in 1958-59) without a drop in quality.*

If the graduate schools are to achieve the necessary expansion, they need more good applicants. But they are not likely to get them until better arrangements are worked out for support of graduate students. Another requirement is that we strengthen and enlarge our present facilities for graduate education.

To achieve these goals, there must be increased support for graduate education, and particularly for fellowships, from every possible source. Graduate students preparing for college teaching should have the same benefits of loan cancellation under the National Defense Education Act as future high school teachers now enjoy.

Most experts agree that the program leading to the doctorate could be compressed. Total elapsed time should come as close as possible to the three or four years spent in actual study.

The professions. It is not possible within the space available to discuss every profession. We shall comment on the professions in general, and then take up three fields that have faced particularly vexing problems.

We are beginning to understand that true professional education takes place at the graduate level. A student headed for graduate professional education should spend his undergraduate years in a liberal arts program, majoring in one of the scientific or scholarly subjects underlying his future profession. Obviously this goal cannot be accomplished immediately in certain of the professions (e.g., engineering), but it should be recognized as a long-term objective.

Undergraduate schools that continue to emphasize vocational courses have a very important role to play as sub-professional technical schools for students not going on to full professional education. The effective use of manpower requires substantial numbers of technicians and sub-professional specialists who are as skilled at their levels as the highest professional at his level. Junior colleges and undergraduate vocational programs should meet this need.

The trend in all professional education is to emphasize the underlying scientific and scholarly fields, and to diminish emphasis on "how to do it" courses. In our rapidly changing technology, no student can learn specifically how to do his future job. The professional student should be educated chiefly in the fundamental fields of knowledge, in habits of mind, methods of analysis and modes of attack upon the problems of his profession. Above all he should learn to pursue on his own the lifelong process of re-education.

Teaching. One way to discover what are considered to be the important professions is to ask which professional schools receive highest priority in university planning. It would be a rare campus on which the school of education was ranked first. Yet in terms of our national future, teaching is the most important profession.

As in other fields, the term "professional" should not be applied to undergraduate work. The separate undergraduate teachers college should become a well-rounded liberal arts college—even though it retains a strong orientation toward preparation of teachers.

Every student headed for teaching should have an undergraduate liberal arts education, usually with a major in the subject he expects to teach. As a part of his liberal arts education he should give attention to those aspects of the behavioral sciences relevant to education. He should study the history and philosophy of education, and he should have both study and practice in the art of teaching.

In some—but by no means all—teacher education institutions, professional education courses have proliferated beyond good sense. Such institutions should prune and reorganize their offerings.

Every institution offering teacher education should make provisions for the liberal arts student who doesn't decide until senior year that he wants to teach. There should be a sequence of graduate courses and interne experiences available to prepare him for the profession.

There should be a thorough overhaul of certification requirements in most states.

Medicine. If we are to maintain the present ratio of physicians to population, and to supply personnel for medical research, industry and public health, our medical schools are going to have to turn out more doctors. The Bane Report estimated that we would have to graduate 11,000 annually by 1975 (as against 7,400 in 1959). In order to meet the need, the following steps are necessary:

(8) *Every medical school should re-examine its capacity to handle more students. Most medical school buildings are underutilized, and faculties have unnecessarily rigid notions concerning the limitations on student body.*

(9) *Federal funds should be made available on a matching basis for modernization and expansion of existing schools, and for the creation of at least 20 new two-year and four-year schools; states should not only match funds for the public universities, but give private universities some help in matching the federal funds.*

(10) *Present federal programs providing funds for research and patient-care facilities should be broadened to cover teaching facilities.*

(11) *Federal and state governments should substantially increase fellowship and loan programs for medical students. Resident physicians should be paid a reasonable salary by the hospital that employs them.*

Engineering. The long-term goal is to have students who are preparing for a professional career devote their undergraduate years to a liberal arts program with heavy emphasis on mathematics and the sciences. Undergraduate programs to prepare students for employment in various technologies should not be labelled "professional" and should not be regarded as suitable preparation for graduate work in engineering.

The future need for engineers will be great, and the colleges must expand their output. But numbers are less important than quality. We don't just need more engineers, we need more good engineers. The emphasis on mathematics and science as an ingredient of engineering education will have to be *very much* stronger.

The present 10,500 (full-time equivalent) engineering faculty should expand to at least 17,500 by 1970. Engineering education will need a faculty capable of teaching engineering at a higher level and with a deeper knowledge of mathematics and science. We should expect that 40 per cent of the engineering faculty will hold the Ph.D. (as against 27 per cent in 1959).

VII

EDUCATION OUTSIDE THE FORMAL SYSTEM

If we really believe in individual fulfillment, our concern for education will reach far beyond the formal system. We shall expect people to continue to learn and grow in and out of school, in every possible circumstance, and at every stage of their lives.

Education outside the formal system is already far more extensive than most people realize. Educational programs in industry and in the armed forces, for example, enroll tremendous numbers of students.

During the 1960's all organizations in our society—social clubs, women's groups, labor unions, industrial concerns, fraternal organizations—should seek to discover how they may help their members to continue personal growth. Each organization should find the specific ways in which it may be of help in (a) arranging for courses to be given by neighboring schools or universities; (b) assisting members to arrange group study programs; (c) building the philosophy of individual fulfillment into its organizational practices, so that every member has the opportunity to grow.

Many people who study outside the formal system do so for reasons having to do with their own fulfillment, and care little for academic credit. Others are concerned only with the immediate acquisition of skills, and credit is irrelevant here too. But many others do wish to obtain academic credit. We shall serve these people far more effectively when we have devised a flexible system of credit by examination. Such a system would assess and certify accomplishment on the basis of present performance. The route that the individual had traveled to achieve competence would not come into question. Such a system would permit many individuals to participate in higher education who now—by the nature of their jobs or other obligations—cannot do so. By 1970 many leading universities (and perhaps learned councils, state boards of education, etc.) should be offering credit by examination in standard academic subjects.

The 1960's should be a great decade for agencies with a special responsibility to facilitate learning outside the formal system, such as libraries, university extension divisions and adult education departments of public schools. The one hazard ahead is that heavy enrollments and straitened finances may lead universities and boards of education to cut the budget of what seems a peripheral activity. This must be avoided. It is no longer peripheral.

VIII

THE SPONSORSHIP OF EDUCATION

Local school districts. The local district remains the key to good public education. One of the gravest problems today is the existence of numerous school districts too small to operate efficiently. Small school systems are wasteful of personnel. They do not provide a sound basis for school finance. And small schools cannot provide an adequate educational program.

Experts have mentioned 2,000 as minimum enrollment for an efficient district. In 1957, more than 40,000 out of a total of 52,907 school systems had enrollments of less than 300!

Experience has demonstrated that voluntary provisions for school district reorganization do not work. (12) *States should pass laws making such reorganization mandatory under the direction of the State Department of Education. The approximately 40,000 school districts existing today should be reduced to about 10,000 by 1970.*

Given adequate size, the most important step the local district can take toward better education is to maintain a good school board. (13) *By 1970 informed Americans should have firmly in mind what a good board ought to be and do* (something most Americans today are far from understanding). They will ask these questions about their school board:

(a) Are the members devoted to education, well-educated themselves, outstanding in public spirit and integrity?

(b) Do they understand the nature of modern education, and carry on continuous evaluation of the district's educational program?

(c) Do they act in a disinterested manner, keep the board out of politics, and resist pressure groups which seek to shape American education to special ends?

(d) Do they distinguish between the policy-making function of a lay board and the professional responsibilities of the superintendent, principal and teachers?

(e) Do they work with citizens' groups who have the good of public education at heart, keeping these groups informed and giving them a sense of participation?

One of the most familiar problems the local district faces with respect to its school board is to devise a system for selection of board members that will insure the recruitment of able citizens and keep patronage at a minimum.   There are various ways of accomplishing such selection (depending on local circumstances).   The solution of this problem should be high on the list of goals for any community seriously interested in its schools.

State responsibilities. The states will play a greater role in public education than they have in the past.   To do so effectively, (14) *each state should have a state board of education, consisting of men of the highest integrity and reputation for public service.*   The board should be adequately staffed.   It should not be burdened with administrative tasks, but should be expected to conduct a continuous review of the adequacy of education in the state.

(15) *Each state should define minimum acceptable school services, should examine the capacity of each district to meet that minimum, and should devise an equalization program to bolster lagging districts.*   The program should be so designed as not to diminish local incentives to support the schools.

(16) *The state can help the districts help themselves—*(a) *by liberalizing (where necessary) state-imposed ceilings on local property taxing powers,* (b) *by liberalizing constitutional or statutory limitations on borrowing power of local districts, and* (c) *by reforming property assessment practices.*

As for the role of the state in higher education, there are heavy tasks ahead.   Enrollment in public institutions will rise from its present 59 per cent of the national total to 65 per cent by 1970.   Public institutions are going to face unprecedented problems of financing, construction and staffing.

Some states may awaken too late to the tremendous tasks ahead.

Not only must they act promptly, they must act wisely.   It won't be enough just to expand already gigantic state campuses.   Each state must design a state-wide system including universities, liberal arts colleges, technical institutes, and two-year colleges in whatever combination best suits its own needs. (17) *States that have not already done so should immediately undertake a study of their future needs in higher education.*

By 1970 higher education should be getting approximately 1.9 per cent of the gross national product (as compared with less than 1 per cent in 1957-58). It is reasonable to expect colleges and universities to make extraordinary efforts to increase their efficiency so that hard-won increases in support will not simply perpetuate extravagance and waste. Improvements in efficiency are possible, particularly in such matters as utilization of buildings.

Private sponsorship of education. At the pre-college level, non-tax-supported schools play a modest but significant role in our educational system (about 15 per cent of total enrollment). Since they share with the public schools most of the problems listed in this chapter, they have not been discussed separately.

At the college and university level, privately sponsored education is tremendously important (over 40 per cent of total enrollment). Whether it will continue as an important factor depends on whether it solves its financial problems.

Like every other source of funds for higher education, tuition will have to carry its share of the burden of increased costs. If it is to contribute the same proportionate share in financing higher education in 1970 that it does today, tuition in both public and private institutions will have to rise. As tuitions rise, it is essential that the scholarship aid available to able and needy students also rise. In the case of public institutions, it should be doubled or tripled. Even in private institutions, which now have far more adequate scholarship programs, these resources should be substantially increased.

In the case of private institutions, income from endowment and gifts should be more than doubled. Every college should have an organized program to enable its friends to participate in annual giving. Today about five million alumni are solicited annually by their institutions and give $25 million a year. In 1970 closer to twenty million alumni should be solicited and should give $700 million a year. Corporate gifts to higher education should double by 1970 (from the present approximately $150 million yearly).

The federal government. The federal government has been a factor in education for almost all of our national history. But its role is changing —and where the change is taking us no one can say. No one knows how best to design the role of the federal government in education. But one thing is certain: with education playing a vastly more crucial role in our national life, there is no likelihood that the federal government can escape greater involvement in it. Nor need we be alarmed at such involvement. Our tradition of local control in education is a healthy one, but we must not let it thwart us in accomplishing important national purposes.

The urgent requirements—and opportunities—of modern life make it necessary that we handle some problems at the state and national levels, whether the field be transportation, communication, commerce, law enforcement, or education. We are facing tasks of the gravest import for our future as a nation. Some of these tasks require long-term planning at the highest level. In such matters, we must act as a nation.

Most debate concerning the role of the federal government centers around the problem of financing, which is the most critical issue facing education today. Consider the scope of the problem. Total 1959-60 enrollment in the public schools was 35,917,000. This will rise to an estimated 44,428,000 by 1970. We must meet a present teacher shortage, recruit teachers for the rapid turnover characteristic of the teaching field, and build a larger corps of teachers for a growing system. We must raise salaries—in some areas drastically. We must meet a present classroom shortage, and expand facilities to handle future growth. And we must raise more money to meet inevitably higher costs ahead.

Primary responsibility for financing the schools must lie with states and local districts. But it is clear that federal support must be increased, and so designed as to offer minimum interference with state and local autonomy, and not to undermine local incentives to raise money for schools.

(18) *The most important task for the federal government is to supplement state funds in those states whose per capita income is too low to maintain adequate education.* (Legislation to this end was proposed by the late Senator Taft some years ago.)

(19) *The federal government should provide funds to the other states on a matching basis—to be used for construction or for other educational purposes as the state may choose.*

Education has become a centrally important activity in our national life. It must be represented at a high level in government. The present organizational structure is inadequate and should be altered. (20) *We must have either a separate Department of Education at Cabinet level or a National Education Foundation (patterned after the National Science Foundation).*

While this reform is being debated, there is a more modest action which may be initiated. (21) *Steps should be taken to create a Council of Educational Advisors, responsible to the White House but working closely with the Secretary of Health, Education and Welfare.* Such a Council would exercise no direct authority, but would be an effective voice both in government and in the educational community. If a separate Department of Education were established this Council could be disbanded, or placed under the Secretary of Education. If a National

Education Foundation were created, the Council could be absorbed into the board of the Foundation.

States that have resources to maintain an adequate educational system but do not employ them might be encouraged to do so by some form of tax credit involving federal sales or income tax credits to the states. This would put the federal taxing power at the service of the states with little danger of control. It is a possibility worthy of further study.

Higher education faces problems of comparable difficulty. Enrollments will double by 1970, and may rise well beyond that. Annual expenditures including capital outlays of the colleges and universities will rise to $11.1 billion (today: $4.3 billion) in dollars of 1960 purchasing power.

The financing of higher education will not undergo radical shifts in the 1960's. For public institutions, money will come chiefly from state and local government. For private institutions, the important sources will continue to be tuition, endowment income and gifts.

The federal government has had long and varied experience in contributing to the support of higher education. The familiar problem is to design a more active role for it which will not diminish the autonomy of the colleges and universities. There are several things the government can do which would meet this requirement.

(22) *Government grants and contract practices should let the universities charge the full cost of research—including indirect costs—and to amortize capital expenditures.*

(23) *The program of low-interest loans to colleges and universities for the construction of revenue-producing buildings should be continued and expanded. Matching grants should be offered for non-revenue-producing buildings of colleges and universities. (But grants should be made only when a college can demonstrate full utilization of present space.) Low-interest loans should be available for those institutions which will not accept federal grants for academic facilities.*

(24) *The government should expand its program of fellowships, particularly at the graduate level, with costs-of-education supplements to the colleges.*

(25) *The government should expand its program for student loans.*

IX

CONCLUSION

This essay has emphasized repeatedly the need for reappraisal of existing practices and for innovation. This need will not diminish in the years ahead. We must develop a philosophy and a technique of continuous reappraisal and innovation.

But new problems and new solutions are not the nub of our difficulty.

We still have plenty of old problems we haven't solved, not because we didn't know how but because we couldn't organize ourselves to apply what we knew. When he was offered the latest agricultural technique, the old farmer said, "What do I want with more knowledge? Right now I don't farm half as good as I know how." A good many of the recommendations presented here have been advocated repeatedly by public and private groups. The problem is to get action.

In some measure it is a problem of organizing ourselves to achieve our objectives. The somewhat blind evolutionary process of the educational past is no longer suited to the needs of our fast-changing society. That is why we must give special attention to such matters as the quality of school boards, the scope of state responsibilities and the adequacy of federal organization.

This report deals with concrete, practical measures. But all the arrangements will fail unless they are in the service of an authentic concern for excellence. We must raise standards in every phase of our national life. Education is no exception. We must do a better job. And the concern for educational quality must be widely shared. It has been fashionable to blame educators for every shortcoming of our schools, but educators cannot maintain standards of excellence in a community that cares more about a marching band and a winning basketball team than it does about teachers' salaries.

American education can be as good as the American people want it to be. And no better.

And in striving for excellence, we must never forget that American education has a clear mission to accomplish with every single child who walks into the school. Modern life has pressed some urgent and sharply defined tasks on education, tasks of producing certain specially needed kinds of educated talent. For the sake of our future we had better succeed in these tasks—but they cannot and should not crowd out the great basic goals of our educational system: to foster individual fulfillment and to nurture the free, rational and responsible men and women without whom our kind of society cannot endure. Our schools must prepare *all* young people, whatever their talents, for the serious business of being free men and women.

4

A GREAT AGE FOR SCIENCE

WARREN WEAVER

4

THE EXCITEMENT *of scientific discovery is captured in this chapter by Dr. Warren Weaver, Vice President of Alfred P. Sloan Foundation and of Sloan-Kettering Institute. A mathematician, a member of the National Science Board, for twenty-five years Vice President of The Rockefeller Foundation, and former President and Chairman of the Board of the American Association for the Advancement of Science, Dr. Weaver is eminently qualified to describe the strategy of scientific development, the contributions of science to modern life, and the goals we must pursue to make the future a period of rapid scientific advance.*

Dr. Weaver consulted with a large group of scientists, and in particular had the advice of the panel listed below. The panel wishes to record that it is in complete agreement with his conclusions.

PANEL

ROGER ADAMS, Emeritus Professor, Department of Chemistry and Chemical Engineering, University of Illinois.

GEORGE W. BEADLE, Chairman, Division of Biology, California Institute of Technology.

GEORGE R. HARRISON, Dean of Science, Massachusetts Institute of Technology.

CARYL P. HASKINS, President, Carnegie Institution of Washington.

A GREAT AGE FOR SCIENCE

WARREN WEAVER

"What science contributes to the national purpose is measured by what it adds to the sum of human knowledge; science serves the nation by serving humanity." *

I

SCIENCE

In the hundred-year period from 1840 to 1940 science made possible, directly and through technology, a total revolution not only in the circumstances of life, but also in our view of man's place in nature. In the twenty years since 1940 the change has been literally explosive. The mind of man has entered the nucleus of the atom and the nucleus of the cell, and man himself is now about to enter space.

The primary concern of science is the understanding of nature—of our physical environment and the world of living things, including of course man himself. This understanding of nature, as gained by science, has made possible a vast range and extent of practical applications, furnishing the basis for technology and contributing to problems of transport, communication, health, food, etc. Science and its applications comprise an essential part of the foundation for our economy, our defense, our material welfare and comfort, and our physical well-being. Science is now completely interlocked with social and political questions, so that wise national decisions cannot be made without sound scientific bases. "No modern statesman," says Abba Eban, for ten years Israel's Ambassador to the United States and her chief delegate to the United Nations, "can afford to be scientifically illiterate."

But all the practical, social, economic, and even political involvements of science must not be permitted to distract us from, or prevent our understanding of, the true nature and purpose of science.

It will thus be well if we turn our thought for a moment away from gadgets, rockets, antibiotics, plastics, and all the other useful material things made possible by science, and recognize that science is in fact a noble intellectual and artistic pursuit, one of man's major attempts to assess himself in relationship to the universe.

For example, we are just in the process of gaining a scientific picture of the total ascent of life. By far more vast and significant than the Darwinian view, this modern evolutionary doctrine begins with the ele-

* From the report of a committee of the American Association for the Advancement of Science, "Science and Human Welfare," published in *Science,* July 8, 1960, Vol. 132, p. 69. This excellent report contains much material that is relevant to the whole problem of our national goals for science.

mentary particles of the nuclear physicist and moves through the whole range of the atomic and molecular world up to the nucleic acids which, in their capacity to reproduce pattern and to pass on coded information, seem capable of forming the primitive basis for a living organism. From this point it is conceivable to move on to the gene, the chromosome, the cell, and ultimately human life. Whether or not man is the present climax of this ascent is itself now under question: for we have radar-listening devices, directed at inconceivably distant parts of the cosmos, seeking to determine whether there are other and possibly more advanced beings there, trying to communicate with earth-bound man.

When the sights are set as high as this, the view transcends all the compartments of science. This is not, in any exclusive sense, physics or biology or chemistry or astronomy. This is the whole of science, engaged with a problem of majestic dimensions.

The sweep and the depth of such a view of matter, man, and the universe fairly suggest what science really is—not a trivial business of tricky hardware, not the phony bubbling retorts of the advertisements, not strange men with white coats or beards, but the response, at once poetic and analytical, of man's creative mind to the challenge of the mystery of matter and life.

Science and the citizen. Here are the opening sentences of the March 5, 1960 issue of *The New Yorker:*

> "These are hard times for the layman. He is no longer thought competent to work out his own opinions on many matters, even many that touch him intimately. His very survival has become the property of committees and the subject of learned argument among specialists. He has little to say in the affair, poor fish, being largely ignorant of the information upon which plans for him are based."

There are three main reasons why it is imperative that the individual citizens of our democracy have an improved understanding of what science is, how it operates, and the circumstances that make it prosper.

First, science is now so heavily involved in many of the most difficult and important social and political problems (testing of nuclear weapons and control of space; dangerous adulteration of air, soil, plants, and food; radiation and genetics; population growth and resources, etc.) that these problems simply cannot be approached wisely or effectively without a reasonable understanding of the scientific aspects. And these problems, in a democracy, must be the concern of the citizens.

Second, the financial support of science has by now passed largely to governmental agencies—state and national—which are under the ultimate control of the whole body of citizens. These citizens cannot be expected to furnish a wise and adequate support for science unless they are given a chance to understand.

Third, a disastrous gap has opened up between the thinking of the relatively small body of scientists as contrasted with the beliefs, attitudes, and activities of the rest of our culture, notably the humanists, creative artists, and moralists. (Read C. P. Snow, *The Two Cultures and the Scientific Revolution.*) All citizens would be given a richer inner life if they could have a chance to appreciate the true nature of science and the scientific attitude.

For science is not technology, it is not gadgetry, it is not some mysterious cult, it is not a great mechanical monster. Science is an adventure of the human spirit. It is an essentially artistic enterprise, stimulated largely by curiosity, served largely by disciplined imagination, and based largely on faith in the reasonableness, order, and beauty of the universe of which man is a part.

This is not a view held only by aesthete-scientists. The television critic John Crosby, writing of some science shows in the *New York Herald Tribune* of March 30, 1960, declared: "There's something so ennobling, so uplifting, watching men wrestle with the mysteries of nature rather than punch each other in the nose."

Goals for science.* Science can be viewed as one of the major elements in our total way of life. As such, it is not possible to isolate it from the rest of life, nor is it very attractive or promising to seek to manipulate scientific activity in terms of a statement of formal plan or intent.

But science is also a tool—or set of tools—with which a culture accomplishes certain purposes. As such, one has a right to inquire as to the purposes, and as to the adequacy of the tools.

And although it is totally impossible to chart out the details of progress of science as one would plan the production schedule for a factory, and although there will remain, in a healthy scientific situation, important and delightful and exciting elements of variety and of unpredictability, it is nevertheless possible to inquire as to whether a segment of society (in this case, our own beloved country) is succeeding in producing an atmosphere within which science can prosper.

It is therefore relevant to review briefly the major factors which, in recent years, have been affecting the climate for effective and imaginative scientific progress. These factors, four of which seem dominant, have arisen—or at least have increased greatly in importance—since World War II.

First, there has been a great increase in types of scientific activity which demand elaborate and costly instrumentation and a numerous team of closely collaborating workers. The vast devices used to accelerate atom fragments to fantastically high speeds and energies, the great electronic computers, new types of huge radar and optical telescopes, oceanographic research vessels, aircraft and rocket-supported

---

* Near the close of this paper will be found a condensed summary statement of the science goals which follow from, and are supported by, the argument of the four main sections.

instrumentation for studying high altitude meteorology—these, with their dozens or hundreds of workers and their multimillion-dollar costs, are a far cry from the single scholar, working alone in his study or private laboratory.

Important and necessary as are the results of such team activities, there is a resulting danger of our losing sight of the transcendent importance of the imaginative *individual worker,* free to think about any scientific problem that arouses his curiosity and attracts his mind.

Second, science has recently become completely entangled in the development of weapons. Science has of course been an aid to military action since Archimedes or earlier, but the present involvement is quite new in its extent and character. Clearly science must do its utmost to defend democratic freedom; but the terms of this association with military affairs are in essence unhealthy for science. In particular, the whole concept of secrecy—of withholding facts, of limiting open discussion, of building guarded fences around scientific installations, and of locking doors in laboratories—this whole concept is wholly foreign to science.

In *The Affair* the great British novelist-physicist C. P. Snow has a passage in which the Cambridge University authorities are discussing the wisdom of undertaking thermonuclear research at the Cavendish Laboratory. It was mentioned that this would necessarily mean a special kind of security. "You won't like it," said one of the scientists to the Court of Seniors: "I don't like it. No one in his senses likes it. It's mostly bloody nonsense, anyway. But we've got to have it."

Third, there is a point closely associated with the preceding one, namely the fact that scientific development is now a main issue in the race for world prestige between our country and the U.S.S.R. The political aspects of this entanglement are as contrary to the true spirit of science as is the demand for military secrecy. These military and political involvements have brought large amounts of the taxpayers' money to the support of research—or more accurately, to the support of research and development, with the major sums going for development. But these involvements create real threats to the quality of the scientific output of the United States in the remaining years of the 20th century. Too often there has been forced haste to solve some practical problem, rather than the internally motivated drive that leads individual scientists to ponder patiently as one often must do in order to penetrate deeply into nature's secrets.

Fourth, there has been a considerable increase in the total volume of scientific activity, with a resulting high demand for able personnel with advanced training. It symbolizes this new situation that the Sunday *New York Times* carries numerous advertisements seeking—of all things—mathematicians!

It has been considerations such as these which have influenced the exposition of the succeeding four main sections of this statement, and which have led to the formulation of the goals listed in the concluding section.

It must be emphasized that the job here is to present the case from the point of view of science. Science is by no means all there is to life; our culture must recognize and respect other goals, very different in motivation and kind. The recommendations which conclude this statement are offered with the understanding that at a broader level of responsibility (perhaps by the Commission for which this statement is being prepared) due concern will be given to the priority of the goals here presented as compared with others, based on other than scientific considerations.

II

THE STRATEGY OF SCIENCE

Pure and applied science. The general public often confuses *science* with *technology*. The mild form of this confusion fails to distinguish between so-called "basic research" in so-called "pure science" with so-called "applied" or "pragmatic" research. A stronger form of this confusion even lumps together *basic research* and *development*. The latter term properly refers to the often extremely expensive task of making workable hardware (missiles, computers, high energy accelerators, rockets, space telescopes, etc.) *after* the basic ideas have been worked out.

The mild form of this confusion is very understandable, for the good reason that scientists themselves differ in their concepts of "pure" and "applied" research. Roughly speaking, pure research is motivated by curiosity and by a desire to obtain new knowledge and understanding, with little explicit concern as to when or how this new knowledge is to be used. In applied research one has a practical purpose or goal in mind and works backward from that, seeking methods—and often seeking items of new knowledge—which promise to serve the recognized purpose.

"Applied" researchers uncover lots of new knowledge; and "pure" researchers discover many useful and practical things. Thus the distinction between the two is often more a matter of temperament and motivation than it is of procedure or result.

Both types of research are of the highest importance and it is silly to view one as more dignified and worthy than the other.

Although the two types of research are interrelated and often heavily overlapping, it is nevertheless important to recognize the distinction. For "applied" research, having a practical goal in view, often has an advantage in obtaining support. To some it seems queer, unnecessary, and even foolish, to support a scientist who enjoys trying to understand nature.

And yet the whole history of science shows most impressively that the scientists who are motivated by curiosity, by a driving desire to *know,* are usually the ones who make the deepest, the most imaginative, and the most revolutionary discoveries—and those which, often as a result of the work of applied scientists, eventually turn out to be the most practical.

This point is so important that it will be well to illustrate it with a few examples. What are the scientific discoveries, the great concepts, which have deeply affected both men's minds and the circumstances of their lives? The list would be a long one; but let us choose, as rather varied examples, the universal law of gravitation of Newton (perhaps the grandest generalization man has ever made concerning the universe he lives in); the laws of electromagnetic induction of Faraday (which form the basis of the entire modern use of electrical power); the founding of genetics by Mendel (which gives us deep insight into the nature of heredity and which furnishes the practical rules for the breeding of improved crop plants and animals); the discovery of the laws of electromagnetic fields by Maxwell (upon which all modern radio and television is based, along with multitudinous other developments in modern electronics); and the total revolution of our concept of man in nature as brought about by Darwin's theory of organic evolution.

In all these cases the personal motivation was clear; it was the pure desire to know more, to experiment, to reason, to understand nature. The case of Faraday is a particularly moving one. The son of a journeyman blacksmith, at the age of 15 he read Watts's *Improvement of the Mind,* Mrs. Marcet's *Conversations on Chemistry* and the article on electricity in the *Encyclopaedia Britannica* and "found himself irresistibly drawn to a study of the facts of science." At the age of 21 and then a journeyman bookbinder, he broke away "from trade, which I thought vicious and selfish, to enter the service of science." This is the man whose discoveries made possible the generators and motors without which our modern living would collapse within an hour. This is the man who, when Gladstone asked him what possible use there might be for one of his discoveries, replied, "Why sir, you will soon be able to tax it."

Consider for a moment the three interrelated great movements in physics which occurred at the turn of the present century, and which are at present proceeding with great vigor.

The modern concept of the atom can reasonably be dated from J. J. Thompson's discovery of the electron in 1897. The first decisive step in quantum theory was the radiation law developed by Planck in 1899. The whole of modern relativity theory dates from Einstein's classical paper of 1905.

Thus within little more than a half-century our view of the physical world and the basis for our practical control of stupendous physical forces have been brought about by such leaders as Bohr, Dirac, Einstein, Gibbs, Heisenberg, Ernest Lawrence, Millikan, Pauli, Planck, Rutherford, Schrodinger and Thompson—all men who were clearly driven by the consuming passion to analyze more deeply, to learn new facts about nature, to advance basic knowledge. These men were truly great scientists. They have to a large extent created the practical facts of the modern world. But they were thinkers, not the authors of proposals for projects—they were not problem solvers, but free-ranging geniuses with poetic imagination and a driving force that came from within.

Research and development. It is specially important to distinguish between *research* (pure and/or applied) and *development*. The two are often combined in both organizational and budgetary statements, as the familiar initials "R & D" illustrate. By looking at the resources devoted to "R & D," one may get a dangerously incorrect impression of what is being allocated to "R."

The distinction in question has been defined by the National Science Foundation in saying that *research* is the "systematic and intensive study directed toward a fuller knowledge of the subject studied," whereas *development* is "use of that knowledge directed toward the production of useful materials, devices, systems, methods, or processes."

Research and industry. Years ago the academic scientists considered the industrial scientists to be rather dull persons, who chose to work for large salaries rather than for the love of discovery, and who were willing to be "directed" and "controlled". The industrial scientists, on their part, sometimes considered the academic scientists to be rather long-haired and dreamy idealists.

The remnants of this misunderstanding were largely eliminated in the industry-university partnerships of World War II.

A very few of the best of our industries have established a superb balance, within their own laboratories, between the necessary and proper mission of the company and the freedom of the individual researchers.

A great deal, however, remains to be accomplished. Certain industries pay eager lip-service to "basic research" but in sober fact do little or none. Anyone who doubts this need only check the facts concerning the volume of publication, from industrial scientists, in really scholarly research journals.

Although there has been a great improvement, industry as a whole does not furnish enough support to research and education in universities and colleges. Many industries do not contribute reasonably to the broad development of those fields of science on whose general vigor their own company health depends; and relatively few industries recog-

nize their broader responsibilities to the culture which makes it possible
for them to exist.

Crash programs. Ever since the dramatic success of the atomic bomb
project, our society has suffered from the illusion that any other large
problem ("the cancer problem" is a good example) could be promptly
solved by appropriating two billion dollars.

Crash programs cannot succeed unless there is available, ready to be
energized by the financial support, a suitable supply of properly trained
and adequately able personnel, and—this is critical—not unless the
underlying basic ideas and theories have already been established. What
is characteristically needed to make progress on these great scientific-
social problems is not to attack them with a feverish activity *from above,*
but to attack them *from underneath* with a long-range offensive of broad
basic research.

Closely related to the inefficiency and ineffectiveness of many types
of crash programs is the waste involved in trying to carry out development, at a wartime pace, of things that could be done better and more
cheaply if we would, with a little more national maturity, occasionally
ask ourselves "What's the rush?" We seem to get almost panicked into
spending huge sums on overlapping and unnecessarily competitive
developments, particularly in the defense and atomic energy areas.

Science and planning. There are some who believe that all the
science in our country should be master-minded by some one organization or group or person. Often the National Science Foundation is
nominated for this role, or the Science Adviser to the President, or a
proposed Secretary of Science.

At the other extreme are those who think they believe in a completely laissez-faire policy, this being qualified, in most instances, by the
condition that each advocate of this procedure be himself assured of
sufficient support so that *he* can do just what *he* pleases.

Most serious scientists agree that the former policy is bad. Most
realistic scientists agree that the latter policy is impractical and undesirable.

Some seek to solve the problem of planning by saying: "All one
need do is to let the scientists themselves make the decisions." But these
decisions are, of course, not made in some national town-meeting; and
therefore there has to be some procedure for selecting the "good" scientists who take the lead in making the decisions. And if one listens
to these good scientists one group at a time, then of course one discovers that the biochemists recommend more and better biochemistry,
the astronomers more and better astronomy, the solid state physicists
more and better solid state physics, etc.

Such advice is useful only if our society can afford to support the
optimum development of every branch of science—and this is clearly

not the case. Indeed if this were the case, the separate pieces of advice would be totally unnecessary.

Some middle ground must be found between over-planning and no planning. It *does* make sense for a group of varied experience to survey the entire scene to try to discern imbalances which are developing. For fads in science and the pressures of events, (Sputnik, for example, and other instances of what Dr. Kistiakowsky has so well called "technological spectaculars") do often tend to produce undesirable imbalances. Although the ability to predict phenomena is one of the prized characteristics of specific scientific theories, it is dramatically true that science as a whole is an almost completely unpredictable enterprise. Science is so completely, and so unpredictably, interconnected that it is necessary that the entire front advance as a whole; and it is both silly and self-defeating to attempt to force too deep advances on narrow segments.

This problem was not so severe when universities had the internal resources to support most of their scientifiic activity, and when there were numerous financial sources—personal, group, private foundation, estate, etc.,—of comparable magnitudes. For then the variety of sources created a situation within which the various factors of interest, promise, and significance could carry out a useful competition. As sources of support have become much more concentrated, particularly in a few federal agencies (National Science Foundation, National Institutes of Health, Atomic Energy Commission, Department of Defense) this problem of over-all national strategy is becoming more and more difficult.

No pat solution is available. Perhaps a few specific suggestions will be helpful.

First, we must preserve variety in the sources of support and of decision. Second, we must shift more of the massive federal support away from the short-term project basis, and towards stably-assured broad support of groups, university departments, and groups of departments. This inescapably forces decisions about major priorities, but leaves the details of decision with the scientists and scholars.

Third, the responsible boards of the relevant federal agencies must spend less time on details which they should leave to staff, and must give more attention to the matter of over-all priorities. And fourth, we must completely change our attitude towards the new role, principally in federal positions and in philanthropic foundations, of the scientist-administrator. To some extent, as in the past, *scientists* view these scientist-administrators as intellectually second-class citizens; and *society* does not provide these positions with adequate salaries and other working conditions, although industry has been much more realistic about its scientist-administrators. Not until government and the scientific community recognize the importance of this type of service can we hope to have, in the central positions of decision concerning science, an adequate supply of individuals who are able enough to meet the demands of their positions.

III

THE ROLE OF SCIENCE

Science and welfare. The beneficial relation of science to the control and elimination of disease; to the assurance of an adequate and proper food supply; to the prevention of accident; to the maintenance of sanitary conditions; and to all other aspects of the physical welfare of our society—all these are obvious and recognized.

The general health problems of our nation are at present undergoing certain major changes. The age structure of our population is shifting, and as a result there is new and growing importance to studies of the degenerative and other diseases manifested in later life. The prospect of ever-increasing developments in nuclear power and in other nuclear experimentation, moreover, makes it imperative that we increase our knowledge in the whole field of radiation biology, with special emphasis on the genetic effects of long-continued exposure to small amounts of high-energy radiation.

There has occurred a clear increase in our responsibilities, as a powerful and rich nation, for the welfare of less favored parts of the world. We must bring all aspects of science into a more effective relation with these global responsibilities.

In certain areas, notably in agriculture and in medicine, this aid can be given in a way which is unquestionably of great profit to the peoples involved. Aid to their internal transport systems, and to their resources for storing and utilizing water, is also, in certain cases, a fundamental sort of aid to their economy.

Some parts of the world are striving to become, on crash schedules, modern industrialized nations. This involves the sudden imposition of a technological and scientific superstructure on cultures which have had almost no experience with the analytical and quantitative modes of thought on which Western science is based. We must help these people not only to build factories and power plants; we must help them to reorient themselves in the thinking of the modern scientific world.

This more basic and more permanent sort of aid could, in many cases, well consist of assistance to their educational systems, with special emphasis on the introduction of modern scientific ideas.

Science and prosperity. An energetic development of science is absolutely essential to the continuing flow of new knowledge which leads to new inventions, new materials, new procedures, new industries, new opportunities for employment, and, in total, to a sound and vigorous economy.

A long report could easily be produced to illustrate the dependence of our national prosperity on the existence of a vigorous and imaginative scientific activity. But actually the relationship is so clear and obvious that little need be said.

Rather spectacular evidence may be found by observing that the rapidly developing portions of our economy—one could even say the fast-moving stocks on the Exchange—are those based upon relatively new scientific advances, such as in solid state physics (transistors, etc.), electronics, computers and automation, etc.

Science and national defense. The technological—indeed the truly scientific—character of the instrumentation and procedures of modern war are too obvious and too generally recognized to require exposition or emphasis.

One aspect is, however, often overlooked. Some have falsely assumed that the regulations of military security could really and permanently guard scientific secrets. It may be that such regulations can, with disastrous exception, control conversations between men and men. But science is a conversation between man and nature; and nature speaks freely and in all languages. Thus in science it is impossible to keep a secret for any significant period of time. The only thing that one can really "keep" is to keep doing one's best.

The lesson is clear. If for no other reasons, the requirements of defense make imperative a vigorous and large scientific effort; and the more fundamental and imaginative are the activities, the more likely is it that defense will be well served. The constant danger is that we have too much of yesterday's hardware, and too little of tomorrow's ideas.

Science and peace. It is deeply deplorable that science has become so entangled in competitive world politics—for science is one of the rare human activities that is independent of political boundaries. Science is not an activity of races, or creeds, or nations. Science is mankind's way of responding to the mystery and challenge of nature.

Given half a chance, men of all nations and all social and political beliefs find that they can collaborate scientifically with enthusiasm and with growing friendship and understanding. Especially is it true and obvious that in large areas of medical and agricultural research all men, wherever located on our planet, can work together.

But collaboration need not be limited to the more obvious fields. The extent and success of the world-wide collaboration during the recent International Geophysical Year—involving almost all aspects of our physical environment—demonstrated that it was one of the most heartening and promising social experiments ever conducted. We should energetically follow through with more collaboration in this same pattern.

These remarks do not in the least fail to recognize that there is a grim contest going on between our philosophy of the democratic life

based on the inherent worth and freedom of the individual, and the
Communist view. But it is both futile and wrong for us to use the reality of that contest as a goad to drive us into ill-considered, and at times
almost frenzied, activities, in order that we be "ahead of the Russians"
in science.

We will win or lose, in the contest between these two conflicting philosophies, depending on whether or not we do in fact possess, within
our system, the wit, the energy, the wisdom, and the dedication to demonstrate, *by our total way of life,* that individual freedom and true democracy offer men their highest hope.

As part of that demonstration we must make our scientific activity
as imaginative, energetic, and broad as possible. But we should do
this for positive reasons.

IV

SCIENCE AND EDUCATION

Human resources. The most important factor limiting the development of science in our country is the inadequacy of our supply of able
and well-trained scientists. We need more and better (especially better) persons in all categories. And the most serious need, as is doubt-
less the case in all fields, is at the top. We desperately need more outstanding individuals with real originality and imagination.

It is highly probable that we are not using at maximum effectiveness
the scientific manpower we already possess. Partly this is because there
may be wasteful stock-piling of scientists by certain industries and other
organizations which (often because they are operating under defense or
similar contracts) do not have to worry about either salaries or present
productiveness; and because these personnel, paid for out of contracts
or by tax-cheapened dollars, give management a comfortable assurance
against competition and against *possible* future needs.

The "normal" industries of our country, depending primarily on
the public rather than upon government contracts, operate in far too
competitive a market to be able to afford any significant amount of
human stock-piling. This problem thus is limited primarily to the
technical industries closely and largely related with defense.

The facts about the efficiency of our use of scientific personnel do
not seem to be very clear. Indeed, it is not certain that a serious amount
of stock-piling does actually occur; a few known instances tend to receive
exaggerated attention. But we should ascertain these facts, and then
act in accordance with them.

Another wasteful use of scientific manpower results from the fact
that we overload productive scientists with far too many committee,

study panel, and advisory commission duties, and with money raising and formal administrative activities.

The various groups utilized by the National Institutes of Health constitute at once a worrisome and a splendid example. There can be no doubt that these Institutes do a really marvelous job of focusing ability and experience on all the decisions for which they are responsible. But the April 1, 1960 booklet entitled "Members of Advisory Councils, Study Sections, and Committees of the National Institutes of Health" requires *127 pages merely to list,* in various arrangements, the scientists who furnish thought and time in connection with the allocation of the large funds provided by Congress to NIH. A current memorandum from NIH mentions that, in the two months of April and May of 1960, a total of 2,996 applications for grants were reviewed! The National Advisory Cancer Council which is, in effect, the board of trustees of the National Cancer Institute, meets three or four times a year, the meetings normally being of three days each. The special committees and boards of the Council have to have several additional meetings each year. The paper material sent to each member, which requires detailed study and preliminary mail vote on hundreds of individual decisions, forms a pile which is literally from fifteen to twenty inches high per meeting. To give conscientious attention to this material requires roughly a week of work preliminary to each meeting.

Are we developing decision procedures for the allocation of federal funds for research that are so complicated and time-consuming that we are lowering the effectiveness of our use of our best scientists?

The lost half. Granting, finally, that we could improve the effectiveness of the present supply of scientists, it remains true that we need more.

James B. Conant, as a result of his and other extensive studies, has estimated that we are giving higher education in our country to just about half of the young people who could profit by it. Among the "lost half" there must be thousands of potentially good scientists, probably a few hundred excellent ones, and possibly a few of genius stature. These, moreover, are persons who (even though they are at present given no chance to realize this fact) would really *want* to be scientists. Giving these lost persons a chance to be scientists need not involve competitive recruitment or unfairly glamorous salesmanship in order to lure them away from other intellectual careers.

There is a sense, quite other than that of Dr. Conant, in which one can speak of the lost half. For we have not made it part of our cultural tradition to arrange for the effective use, in scientific activities, of *women.* The biological facts must be conceded; but other nations are making it clear that it is possible to make adjustment to these biological facts, and give women full opportunity for creative careers in science. No one can visit Poland, for example, without being deeply impressed by the number of women in positions of scientific importance, and at the exceedingly pleasant fact of large numbers of husband-and-wife scientific teams.

As the pressure for able personnel increases, we simply must create new and appropriate opportunities for women. It is most heartening that Radcliffe College has just addressed itself to this problem in an energetic and imaginative way.

There seem to be two main things which we must do to improve our supply of boys and girls of scientific talent.

One of these is not too difficult but the other is admittedly very tough to accomplish. The relatively easy task is to assure that young people, particularly in the high schools, but also at even more elementary levels, are exposed to attractive, accurate, and competent (but not exaggerated) information concerning the careers, of all grades and sorts, which are available in science.

Science teaching. The very tough task is to improve the science teaching in the elementary schools and in the high schools. For a sympathetic, inspiring, informed, and competent teacher can have really decisive influence.

A variety of activity concerning the improvement of teaching material is now under way. Starting with the superb "Physical Science Study Committee Project" for reforming the teaching of physics in the high school, the movement is spreading horizontally to the other high school science subjects (mathematics, biology, chemistry), vertically down into the elementary school level, and to a minor extent vertically up into the college level.

There is also a fine activity, under the National Science Foundation, for improving the science education of the teachers of science subjects in the high school. Nearly 21,000 teachers of science are, during the summer of 1960, benefiting from this program.

These movements are excellent; but they are only a start. A basic need is for more and better persons to choose to become science teachers. This we can hardly achieve until our society assigns a higher place to teachers—higher in social standing and professional recognition, as well as higher in compensation. A position of honor and prestige for a whole profession cannot be created overnight nor by any one single act, however authoritative or dramatic. But ways to start, are, after all, obvious. First and foremost, we must pay teachers better. We must also give them better schools and physical equipment; we must give them more flexible opportunity to continue their own training and general intellectual development; and we must give special recognition and reward to special achievement.

In connection with the modern movements for curricular reform, a promising new partnership is developing between the "content" scholars and the pedagogical experts on "methodology." But scientists nevertheless continue to worry that too much emphasis may be placed on methods of teaching, and too little on the teacher's understanding of the science being taught. And scientists are troubled by the dilution of course content, as illustrated by the recent approval of the board of education of one of our great cities of a high school course on "Group Dating, Double Dating, Single Dating, and Steady Dating."

It seems clear that we have not sufficiently respected the minds of younger children. We should start some form of science education at the very earliest school age. Then our colleges and universities must raise the level of their freshman science courses as secondary education improves.

It is also essential that these high school and elementary school teachers be given vastly improved science courses as a part of their own preparatory training. And this brings us to the problems of science education at the college and university level.

Teaching and research. For centuries, intellectual and cultural leadership has resided in universities. The great traditional role of universities has involved the preservation of knowledge, the advance of knowledge, and—as the central educational function—the passing of knowledge and of the zest for new knowledge to the oncoming generation. A half century ago there were in the universities many, many instances of the great scholar-teacher. These individuals were dedicated to scholarship and research, but they also considered it a high privilege and a clear duty to teach younger students.

Nowadays scientists are being lured into jobs that admittedly give large research opportunity but which promise—as though that were a long-term advantage—only two or three or at most four hours of teaching, and sometimes teaching during only one term per year. At the same time there are many full-time research scientists around universities, their salaries paid from research contracts and grants, who are intellectual eunuchs, not at all involved in the propagation of their kind. Some distinguished scientists are glad to have post-doctorate students associated with them, but are unwilling to take on even doctoral candidates, to say nothing of lecturing to and discussing with undergraduates.

Thus the neglect and disparagement of the teacher, which has long existed at high school and earlier levels, has now seriously invaded the universities. *This trend must be reversed.*

We have been criticized and rightly so for using up *ideas* in application more rapidly than we have been producing basic knowledge. But this form of short-sightedness, bad as it is, is mild as compared with the short-sightedness of depressing, in our major educational centers, the educational function which must produce the *future supply of scholars.*

Topsy-turvy economic circumstances do not simplify this problem. The demand for certain types of scientists, particularly on the part of industries (and especially defense industries) is such that the recruiting officers tour the universities each spring, discussing the emerging Ph.D.'s with their major professors—and sometimes offering research jobs to these new Ph.D.'s at salaries which exceed the salary of the professor who has supervised the final theses.

The importance, the dignity, the professional recognition, the academic reward, and the personal satisfaction of *teaching*—all these our society must restore and emphasize. We must restore the older concept of a worthy and inter-reverberating comradeship between teaching and research. We must respect and reward the fine teachers who are intellectually alive and thus interested in the advance of knowledge, even though they are not themselves great productive researchers. A special opportunity exists in the large number and variety of smaller colleges.

In the past these smaller colleges—there are nearly 1800 of them, as against about 170 that have an enrollment of 5000 or more—have furnished a significant fraction of the students who go to the large centers for subsequent graduate work. The present importance, in science, of elaborate and expensive equipment has made it very difficult for these smaller institutions to compete for well-trained faculties. But our country—and science—and learning in general—will be vastly poorer if we cannot succeed in devising ways to preserve the integrity, the independence, the variety, and the excellence of these smaller colleges. And we must in particular devise ways to make them more active in science education.

The solid and wonderful word "research" gets applied, these days, to some pretty weird activities. Especially is this word misused in the advertising trade, in the attempt to invoke all the power and prestige of real science in connection with trivial tests of trivial products. "Research" with a "smellometer" indicates the supposed quantitative effectiveness of a deodorant!

At the other extreme, there exists a school of thought that takes altogether too precious an attitude towards research, belittling applied science as though it were stupid and inelegant. These are often the persons who do not respect teaching. These are the persons who still insist that "applied mathematics" is necessarily several cuts below "pure mathematics," and who would like to see every engineering graduate take a Ph.D. in physics. *We must avoid these silly extremes.*

The emphasis, in this portion of the chapter, on the importance of teaching runs the risk of misinterpretation. It may be wrongly inferred that *research,* deep and basic research, more and better research, is being given, here, a secondary role.

That is not at all the case. What is being argued is that teaching must not be given a secondary role: that *teaching and research should be equal partners*.

V

THE SUPPORT OF SCIENCE

The magnitude of support. How much should our nation be spending for scientific research? How much should this increase over the next five to ten years?

Largely because of the difficulty of defining the various categories of research, and partly because of great dissimilarity between the reporting agencies (colleges and universities, non-profit research institutes, commercial research organizations, industries, government laboratories and agencies, etc.), the numerical figures concerning our national support of research are not very satisfactory.

A brief summary of the figures, most of which have been taken from studies conducted by the National Science Foundation, will be found in a footnote. The details of the figures may be uncertain but the main conclusions are clear and apparent.*

For quite apart from the difficulties of detailed analysis, the figures unambiguously indicate a vigorous support of the more applied phases of research, and they indicate a tremendous increase in the support of development. But they also indicate that the more basic aspects of research, and especially the support of underlying research in universities and colleges, have not kept pace.

The sums required for developmental aspects (missiles, rockets, new types of aircraft, etc.) are simply astronomical. It is very hard for scientists to avoid the impression that the total annual national allot-

* Five years ago the total expenditure in our country for "R&D" (both basic and applied Research plus Development) was, from all sources public and private, about $5.6 billion. For the federal fiscal year 1959-60 the figure will be roughly $12.4 billion. This is a five-year increase of $6.8 billion, or a percentage increase, over that period, of 122%. This should be compared with increases over the same period in the Gross National Product (GNP) from about $397 billion to more than $500 billion, or slightly more than 26%.

Some 97% of R&D funds, and of the increase in these funds, goes into industry and into federal agencies. Roughly four-fifths of the national R&D money goes for development, leaving only one-fifth of the total for research, *both basic and applied*. For the year 1957, when the R&D total was somewhat over $10 billion, the National Science Foundation has estimated that the national *basic research* total was between $700 and $800 million—that is, between 7% and 8% of the total R&D. It cannot be too inaccurate to say that of the total R&D money, well under 10% and perhaps not over 5% of it is at present being devoted to the support of basic research.

Further light on the support of basic research is gained from looking at the situation in colleges and universities, the traditional centers of pure research and the training ground for our future supply of scientists. The figures indicate a five-year increase of university and college R&D money of $250 million, or 52%. This is less than half the rate of increase of R&D as a whole.

ment for pure research—which presumably now stands at something like $800 or possibly $900 million—could easily, profitably, and promptly be raised to $1500 million without increasing the national R&D figures. This could be done simply by enforcing a little common sense in the areas of wasteful development projects, some of which are a result of military interservice rivalry, and more of which are undertaken because of confusion as to our military objectives. We could also save huge funds by slowing down the hectic and costly pace of activity in certain areas—"space" is probably the major example—where we are motivated more by emotion than by reason, assigning extreme urgency to projects which are in sober fact not urgent. But whether or not financed by the suggested savings, the increase for basic research should be provided.

The increase from $800-900 million for basic research to about $1500 million should occur as promptly as personnel and physical facilities will permit—say in three years at the most. And in addition to this corrective increase in the fraction of our GNP which we devote to basic research, there should of course be a continuing increase to keep pace with our growing economy.

The distribution and character of support. The preceding section has urged greater emphasis on basic research, as contrasted with applied research and development. The present section is concerned primarily with the distribution of support not among the performers, but rather among the sources.

As federal support grows, there is a dangerous tendency to consider other sources as too small to be important. But it is of the utmost importance that we increase, rather than decrease, the absolute number, the variety, and the total potential of *all* sources. "Local" money continues to have a personal flavor, a stimulating concern, a willingness and possibility of being adventuresome and unorthodox, that can never be matched by dollars from Washington. Support of science by individuals, by clubs, by neighborhood organizations, by parent-teacher organizations, by near-by industries, by local foundations, by school boards, by labor groups—all this is doubly or triply effective. For it does significantly add to the support, it often adds in places and ways which would not otherwise be helped, and it builds science into the over-all pattern of information and concern of our society.

At an intermediate level it is equally important that larger units of our society—national foundations, industries, trade organizations, labor organizations, state governments, nation-wide health agencies—also continue to support, and increase their support, of science. Without this broad base of support, interest, and concern, we cannot have a sound and vigorous national development of science. As for the federal support of science, it has already become of prime importance; and it is clear and inevitable that its importance must increase. Only the federal government can command the resources for many essential activities.

In general, it would seem desirable that federal support move in two general directions. First, to the furnishing of broadly available facilities of the sort that cannot possibly be handled on a local scale. The National Science Foundation's creation of the National Radio Astronomy Observatory and of the National Optical Observatory are excellent examples, and there are various other opportunities, for example in the fields of large computers and high-energy accelerators. Broad programs which, often just because of geographical spread, are unsuitable for any support other than federal—the International Geophysical Year, oceanography, weather modifications, for example—also fall in this category.

Second, federal support should move to the furnishing of much more stable, long-term, less specified, large grants to universities, colleges, and research institutions, leaving to the local authorities much more responsibility for all details of decision.

If federal support—which has already moved cautiously in these two directions—would move substantially and courageously further, supplementing the continuingly useful project grants to individuals with large block funds granted to the universities under terms of maximum freedom, the control of science would be placed where it belongs. This procedure would incidentally free a large part of the time which scientists now devote to serving, at low over-all efficiency, as underpaid part-time administrators.

None of us wants the government to "control education"—or science either. But *broadening* and *liberalizing* the federal support of science in universities would enhance the independence of the universities and colleges.

The role of money, in aiding science, is to remove the limitations from creative scholarship. Whatever those limitations are, they must be removed. Sometimes the limitation is the lack of equipment or supplies; sometimes it is the lack of sufficient assistance. Sometimes it is the lack of books or journals, or of a good secretary, or the rent of a computer. Sometimes it is the need of travel to talk with other scientists and see what they are doing. Sometimes the need is that the government recognize that universities have to pay their bills—for janitor service, light, heat, upkeep of plant, grounds maintenance, etc.—with exactly the same kind of hard cash necessary for the salary of the Research Professor of Nuclear Physics. And sometimes the critical need is for *space*—for the remodeling of a laboratory, or for the extension of a laboratory, or for a new building.

We have a queer folklore about these matters. It is noble to pay for research assistants, and highly respectable to purchase scientific equipment. The employment of a secretary is a little dubious, and travel is almost suspicious. But money for a building! That is almost always what someone else is supposed to furnish. The government has recently made a limited number of grants for *half* of the part of a building, devoted exclusively to research, but the other half remains the responsibility of "someone else."

Granting all the force of the arguments for stimulating local support, it remains true that this policy is too inflexible, and that it should be broadened so that no critically important scientific development in our country be stymied for lack of suitable space.

Two aspects of the federal support of science raise serious questions from the point of view of the character and distribution of the support.

First, of the total federal research funds for the next fiscal year, it has been estimated that *two-thirds* will be devoted to the physical sciences, and only *one-third* to the biological and other life sciences. This preponderance of emphasis on the physical sciences is reflected in the 1200 fellowship appointments made by the National Science Foundation in the spring of 1960. Of these nearly 80 per cent were in the physical (including engineering) sciences.

Second, it seems undesirable that so large a fraction (about one-quarter, as estimated for the next fiscal year) of the total federal support of basic research is dispensed through the military establishments. As was observed in *Science* for July 8, 1960: "Because Defense has a fairly good idea of where it wants to spend its money, its mechanism for making grants is quite different from that of the National Science Foundation. The Foundation picks out what seem to be the most promising proposals submitted. Defense identifies certain areas it wants to support and then uses a sort of talent-scout system to seek out people in the universities and foundations who can do some work in the area." This procedure is legitimate and necessary from the point of view of defense; but it is not the way to achieve a broad and imaginative development of science.

VI

CONCLUSIONS AND STATEMENTS OF GOALS

The desirabilities of the goals presently to be stated are substantiated by the considerations contained in the main body of this statement. In many instances a given goal is connected with and justified by the argument of more than one of the sections. Thus it should be understood that the interrelated set of goals results from and depends upon the total preceding material.

Finally, a word should be said about the sense in which the word "goal" is used here.

Often one thinks of a goal as something which can be *attained*. But in the present context a goal is necessarily a *moving*, not a fixed target. The goals which one can usefully state for our national scientific development are *directions* in which we should move and keep moving, not fixed points which we can attain and then relax.

BROAD AND MAJOR GOALS

The following list starts out with the most important goal, and then continues with items of slowly decreasing priority.

Human Resources

This topic is put in the top position, for *people,* individual *human beings,* are of first importance. If we could interest the right *persons,* and give them the right education and opportunities to utilize their capacities fully, then all the other goals would take care of themselves.

(1) *Since science and all other fields that depend on educated manpower must compete within our national supply of talent, it is essential that every young person of intellectual promise be given an opportunity to develop to the full.*

(2) *We must ensure that students in high schools, and even in the elementary grades, be appropriately exposed to the interest, importance, beauty, and excitement of science.*

(3) *We must ensure that every young person who has the desire and capacity to become a scientist be exposed to the best science education our leading scholars can devise.*

(4) *We must recognize the importance of* teaching, *and reward the teacher at all levels of the educational system.*

Science and the Good Life

(5) *We should develop science in our country energetically and broadly, not merely to be ahead of someone else, but to be worthy of ourselves.*

(6) *We should vastly increase and improve all ways of giving every citizen a better understanding of science.*

(7) *We should make every effort to absorb science into the whole of life, bringing it to understanding collaboration with the humane arts.*

(8) *We should bring science—in its more applied aspects, in its basic aspects, and as a mode of thinking about the world—to the more effective service of the less favored countries and peoples.*

(9) *We should develop those scientific activities which contribute to international understanding and to peace.*

(10) *We should seek a balanced development of the totality of science, realizing that it is in fact an indivisible whole.*

MORE SPECIFIC GOALS

Support

(11) *We must substantially and promptly increase the national support for basic science from the $800-$900 million now devoted to this purpose to perhaps $1500 million per year.*

(12) *We should apply all our national ingenuity and devotion to increasing the number and variety of non-federal sources of support for science.*

(13) *We should very substantially increase the magnitude, flexibility, and stability of federal support of science in universities, including aid to good science teaching.*

(14) *We must provide federal support for science in the colleges and other smaller institutions, to re-establish the great role they used to play as major instruments in the recruiting and early training of scientists.*

Planning

(15) *We should avoid like the plague the enticing danger of too much, and too concentrated, planning of our national scientific development. The great majority of scientists agree that the supposed benefits of centralized planning are an illusion.*

(16) *But we must nevertheless devise some more effective mechanism for over-all comparative judgments about national priorities.*

(17) *We must acknowledge the new and growing importance of the (usually federal) science-administrator; and must give this function the organizational, intellectual, and financial recognition which will make it possible to attract and hold first-rate men in these critically important jobs.*

5

THE QUALITY OF AMERICAN CULTURE

AUGUST HECKSCHER

5

THE QUALITY *of American culture has important consequences for the character of American life. August Heckscher, Director of the Twentieth Century Fund, suggests in this chapter that our cultural values and attainments may not have kept up with our material progress. He recommends that steps be taken throughout the country to provide increased support and opportunity for the arts and the creative artist.*

Mr. Heckscher was formerly chief editorial writer for the New York Herald Tribune. *He is a member of the Art Commission of the City of New York, Chairman of the Board of the International Council of the Museum of Modern Art, and a widely read author.*

In preparing this chapter, Mr. Heckscher consulted with leaders in the principal artistic fields and was advised by the panel listed below. He takes responsibility for the views expressed.

PANEL

ALFRED KAZIN, free-lance writer and author of the well-known study of American literature, *On Native Grounds.*

LEO C. ROSTEN, Editorial Advisor to LOOK magazine; Visiting Professor of Political Science, University of California; author of *The Education of Hyman Kaplan.*

MRS. ALINE SAARINEN, free-lance writer and former art critic for *The New York Times.*

THE QUALITY OF AMERICAN CULTURE

AUGUST HECKSCHER

I

MATERIAL AND CULTURAL PROGRESS COMPARED

The United States has pioneered in the development of an industrial society, with wealth and leisure broadly distributed and a rising standard of living for all. It is committed to material progress; but it has intended that this be accompanied by spiritual and intellectual ferment and a deepening appreciation of the arts. As a people we face the question today whether our cultural standards can indeed be brought into balance with our material well-being.

Despite outstanding achievements by individual Americans, and signs of broad public interest in the arts, there is cause for serious uneasiness. An industrial civilization, brought to the highest point of development, has still to prove that it can nourish and sustain a rich cultural life. In the case of the United States, it is evident that cultural attainments have not kept pace with improvements in other fields. As the incomes of the people have risen, a proportionate share has not been devoted to intellectual and artistic pursuits. As leisure has increased, so has the amount of time given to unproductive and often aimless activities. Many of these leisure-time activities may properly be called recreational; too few can be judged to hold real meaning in the lives of individuals or of the community.

Amid concern for what the citizen does under conditions of modern industrialism, there is at a deeper level concern for what he is. The general advance in well-being seems to have brought with it a lessening of moral intensity and a readiness to indulge in secondhand experience. The ethic of the contemporary economic system emphasizes consumption, with "happiness" and "comfort" as the objectives to be sought. The end product seems to be a great mass prepared to listen long hours to the worst of TV or radio and to make our newsstands—with their diet of mediocrity—what they are.

The state of the arts in a society may be judged, among other things, by the beauty of its public monuments, the scale and fitness and the ease of human contacts provided by the squares and streets of its cities, the pleasantness of its country landscape. A people caring about dignity and excellence in its private lives may be expected to care also about the embodiment of these qualities in the public environment. The American scene today is not reassuring in this regard.

The earlier American achievements in community-building, such as the New England town, have been overrun and rendered obsolete by

127

the automobile. The newer cities have been allowed to take form without concern for the human values they should be expected to serve. The countryside, meanwhile, has been left as the prey of the bulldozer, the billboard and indiscriminate commercial exploitation. All this, it must be noted, has been occurring in a society which is lacking in no material boon and has perhaps a higher standard of well-being for the private citizen than any civilization in history.

II

THE NATURE OF GOALS

This chapter does not want to be a catalogue of the deficiencies—any more than a hymn to the virtues—of the American cultural scene. That there are lacks and deficiencies has been sufficiently indicated. The problem is what we can do about them—what reasonable objectives and goals we can set for the decade ahead. But a word, first, about the nature of the goals one can define realistically in this area of the national life.

The arts have sometimes been seen as an adornment, something added to society after science and economics have done their work. Such a view can scarcely be related to the concept of democracy, and it is definitely not the point of view of this chapter.

Democracy conceives of the whole pattern of existence as being unfolded from within. To the extent that the democratic process is not distorted by plebiscites or the manipulation of public opinion, it finds the people not merely consenting to legislative enactments but generating the forces and impulses from which legislation—and indeed every common purpose and aspiration—is born. The image of such a society is not laid up in heaven. It is being made and constantly remade by the myriad choices and decisions of the citizenry.

If this is true of the laws, it is certainly true of the arts in a democracy. The cultural life of a free people must be sought out. It cannot be decreed. It can be encouraged, guided, sustained. It cannot be imposed from above nor created by will or rational desire. For this reason goals in the cultural field must have a different scope from those that can be set elsewhere. In part the goals must consist of a sensitive appreciation of what is going on in the depth of society, a capacity for awareness, a gift for distinguishing between true and spurious forms of art. At their most ambitious these goals must consist of efforts to encourage and bring to fulfillment the best of what already exists in embryo.

To take this point of view is not to maintain that government at various levels has no role in the development of a democracy's cultural life. A people that truly values the arts will scarcely want to leave unused on their behalf the major instrument of common action. But the very nature of the arts, as here defined, sets bounds to what government can do. Its role must be limited and the expectations it creates must be modest.

III

TIME IN TODAY'S WORLD

The hopes for a rich cultural life have been based in large part upon the spread of leisure in the population. Leisure has traditionally been the seed-bed of the arts; an amplitude of time has in the past gone hand in hand with creativity. The shortened working hours and early retirement falling to the majority of today's men and women might have seemed, by analogy with earlier periods, to be an assurance that the quality of life would be improved. The analogy, however, does not seem to hold true. Today's leisure, possessed not by a class but spread through the population, is basically different from that which has existed in aristocratic societies.

What has happened is that time, as it has been passed from the few to the many, has been radically transformed. Its substance and its meaning in the lives of the people have been altered. Time could not have been created for the great majority without the occurrence of a number of interrelated developments; and these developments, in one way or another, have combined to make the leisure of the modern man very different from that of former civilizations.

The machine has been the great liberator, allowing today's worker to produce in a given period many times as much as his great-grandfather a hundred years ago. But the machine sets its own rhythm and exacts its price in terms of sensibilities blunted and energies drained. Urbanization has been the condition of industrial growth; and urbanization has cut off the worker from the natural harmonies and established traditions which gave to time a form and structure. Finally, the compulsion to consume the machine's output has rendered leisure steadily less contemplative and more keyed to material ends.

As a consequence of these interrelated developments, time in the modern world tends to be increasingly harried and gadget-ridden. Free time becomes the occasion, not so much for deeply felt human relationships and the experience of intellectual rewards, as for efforts to escape from boredom and for a seemingly endless pursuit of trivial distractions. Leisure, which should be the seed-bed of the arts, the source both of creation and enjoyment, too often becomes a round of activities undertaken as a result of disguised or overt pressure and for ends which appear to have less and less to do with the enrichment either of the individual or of society.

A positive concern with the constructive and life-giving aspects of free time is one of the first requisites if America's culture is to progress along with its material well-being. Time must come to be looked on, less as a boon in itself, than as a resource to be converted—an essence to be redeemed. We already can see the beginning of conscious efforts to educate men and women for leisure—though the "leisure skills" being experimentally taught are too apt to stress everything except the one which can carry a man unfailingly absorbed through life, the skill and the art of reading. We see, too, the beginning of a forward-looking approach to the preservation and use of out-of-door space.

Conservation in its earlier stages was a movement led by men who loved the natural world for its own sake; the new conservation must aim to organize and make available the gifts of nature to satisfy the needs of a growing population, remorseless in its leisure-time demands and often unwittingly bent on destroying the very boon it seeks. The need for recreation space over the next decades can be charted with reasonable accuracy. A society which puts a value on the quality of its national life will want to act resolutely in the light of such prediction.

A positive concern for the uses of time can easily be belittled on the ground that people want to be left alone in their leisure. The argument would be more appealing if the people's leisure were not already being conditioned and spoken for by powerful forces within our society. The rare individual may still set his own standards and keep time for himself. But too many citizens of the industrial society move in response to appeals and pressures of which they are scarcely conscious.

A man's leisure time is the way to his pocketbook, and even the way to his soul. The civic organizations, the professional groupings, the manufacturers of consumer goods, are all understandably intent upon claiming what was once thought to be the area of life most carefree and private. Almost no one is left alone any more; and there need be no apology for taking thought—and for taking steps wherever possible—to make possible a genuinely rewarding use of free time. If our society fails in this responsibility, it will discover that its much-vaunted gift of time has brought to the people neither true satisfaction nor even pleasure.

IV

THE MASS MARKET AND THE POPULAR ARTS

Life in America has become marked by a vast degree of organization. For purposes of industrialism and of democratic rule, the citizenry has been forged into homogeneous groups. Without the modern mass market, technology would not have been able to develop its potentialities. Without our two great political parties cutting across economic and geographic interests, democracy as we know it could never have been made to function. All this has had much to do with the nature of our life and the particular quality of our arts.

The organization of a market capable of absorbing the machine's inexhaustible output has abolished classes and greatly reduced the differences between individuals and groups. Women at different levels of income dress indistinguishably; the most luxurious housing units boast the same dishwashing machine available in almost any worker's home. All alike possess TV sets; all, or almost all, travel by the same means to the same places.

So, too, all are offered the same culture. The market which has been organized for consumer goods becomes a ready channel for purveying entertainment, literature or art. The public, not surprisingly, begins to think of art as something to be consumed not differently from other products. Buying books in the same store where it buys toothpaste, it can easily slip into considering the packaging no less important than the contents. It can look for the same qualities in culture as it finds in other merchandise: novelty, eye-appeal, enhancement of status and comfort.

Meanwhile those who create art in the industrial society seek—like the producers of goods or the managers of the political parties—the broadest possible audience. Television programs must, to be successful, cut across all social and economic lines. The museum director must attract a wide cross-section of the public. So American culture is increasingly directed to the mass market.

The result of this organization of society is a genuinely popular culture. It has its limitations, but it also has merits all too easy to overlook. In products adapted to machine production and keyed to the desires of the great mass, there can be as genuine a worth as in the folk art of an older, rural society. The variety and individuality of such products will derive not from the whims of the individual craftsman or local artist as in the past, but from cycles of popular fashion and taste. Modern industrial design thus has genuine roots; it can also have, as in machine-made glassware or simple tools, a purity and flawlessness of form which puts it close to fine art.

Where the commercial process introduces extravagance for the sake of novelty, something playful or humorously eccentric—even though flawed—may emerge. It takes only a slight shift of mood to discern in such excrescences as the tailfins of recent cars, or the streamlining applied to stationary objects, an exaggeration as harmless, and no less outrageously comic, than the flourishes which appear in the work of some old folk artist.

Valid forms attuned to the requirements of the mass media, like those springing from the industrial machine, may well be evolving under the very eye of those who discount mass culture as necessarily degraded and second-rate efforts. The movies, often in their less pretentious forms, can be examples of popular art at its best; a form of expression freshly created out of fresh needs, for an audience as broad as the community itself. Whether television has evolved, or is evolving, as a comparable art form is more difficult to say. But the opportunity exists for creative innovation, as it does in popular music and the musical theatre. The very rootlessness and restlessness of American life, its changefulness and diversity, may shape a culture admittedly different from anything known before, yet like folk art in being popular without being degraded.

Popular art is made to be easily enjoyed. Being shaped to the mass market, it does not require patrons or subsidies. Yet there are factors in the determination of taste not to be overlooked. Business in America has a major role to play in seeing that consumer products are well designed and that the appeal made through advertisements and other media is kept at a level which caters to something more than the lowest common denominator in the public. The level of general merchandise today is certainly higher in terms of taste and liveliness than twenty-five or fifty years ago. Advertising and commercial art have been improved by first-rate typography and photography, as well as by influences coming from other fields, such as painting and sculpture. In these ways business has to an encouraging degree done its share in maintaining the levels of popular art.

It is impossible, however, to separate form from content in advertising. Skillful or artistically refreshing techniques are debased if their objective is to carry a message appealing to the individual's fear of being different, to his hunger for superficial "status," or to the cruder impulses of sex. Too much of today's advertising does indeed have such objectives.

In the field of television we see the problem in its most acute and disturbing form. Here, more than anywhere, is cause for concern that the level of popular culture in America is being lowered. Third- and fourth-rate material seems increasingly to replace the better shows as the merchandiser reaches out for a wide market. The managers of the broadcasting companies seek the same large audience in order to sell their broadcasting time. Unlike the newspaper or magazine editor, they let the advertisers control the content of the program as well as the commercial.

The American system of broadcasting is deeply entrenched and is founded on the rock of freedom from government interference. It is not, however, beyond critical examination in the light of its performance. It is too easy to say that the people are getting what they want. The fact that large audiences can be attracted by fourth-rate material does not acquit the broadcasting companies, or the government which has an ultimate responsibility for use of this valuable and scarce resource, from asking whether the public interest is being adequately served.

Control by the government of the content of television shows is to be avoided at all costs. All the more necessary, then, are boldness and social imagination on the part of those who control the broadcasting companies. Beyond an appeal to enlightened leadership there is a range of suggestions for reforms which deserve serious consideration. It has been argued that the setting of standards, and the limitation of advertising time in any given hour, should be undertaken by the Federal Communications Commission. It has been argued that a public network be established and run as a public service. It has been suggested that a National Broadcasting Authority be created to produce public-service and noncommercial programs. In addition pay television, which has not been adequately tested, offers the possibility of direct payments by the listener.

What is required is some means of providing standards of excellence, a diversity of choice, and a way of not penalizing enlightened network officials by permitting others to fall below a certain level of operations. Social inventiveness has, as we have indicated, a large field to work in; its task is nothing less than to preserve popular culture, in a crucial sector, from becoming irredeemably trivial.

V

THE FINE ARTS AND THE CREATIVE FEW

Related to popular art but not synonymous with it is the realm of the fine arts—the creations of the few, directed to the comparatively small and specialized audience. It is this level of art which gives ultimate distinction to a civilization, being not only in itself the expression of human achievement at its highest but acting as a fertilizing and purifying influence throughout the domain of the popular arts.

The United States today has its own schools of painters, sculptors, composers and architects. It is producing significant results in the performing arts. No one in this generation is likely to ask, Who reads an American book? or, Who looks at an American painting? Critics in this country and abroad acknowledge a high degree of creative genius. Its museums and private collections show the foremost art of all centuries, and this is the object of wide public interest and appreciation. The great books are sold in inexpensive editions to very large numbers. In music, the classic compositions have an immense and continuous hearing; and the most famous works of the drama (particularly Shakespeare's) are kept alive for a broad audience.

Fine art is thus being created and enjoyed, both in the form of new works and of the classics. To keep the creative sources in our society open and productive must be a prime objective. In a world where ideology and the interests of the state seek in so many cases to control art and bend it to particular ends, the freedom of the American artist is noteworthy. At the same time we need to be constantly on guard against those who seek to judge or limit this freedom either because of ideological significance or the political affiliations of the artist.

In a more positive way, the artist must be encouraged and his work supported. It is being gradually recognized in this country that the teacher is entitled to a wage proportionate to the importance and dignity of the work he performs. The same fact must come to be recognized in regard to the artist. At bottom the problem is one of a changed attitude—a change which must begin with a different evaluation of the artist himself. Americans have been accused of being "anti-intellectual." In regard to art the charge could be even more grave: that they are not so much against it as indifferent to it. The artist has been allowed to make his way in a kind of freedom which has too often been bare and unprofitable because it was not part of an atmosphere of understanding. The place the artist has held in societies of the past, and holds in many countries of the present-day world, should by itself be enough to give Americans pause.

Disinterested and considerate help for the artist is particularly necessary because of the mass nature of our society. The innovator too far in advance of his times or too independent of current trends and fashions is likely to find the great audience unwilling to listen. The performer who does get the ear of this audience, moreover, is subject to subtle temptations and pressures to compromise the quality of his work. The existence of the popular arts in their present pervasive and insatiable forms provides, indeed, one of the obstacles to the highest development of the fine arts. The need is to make possible fruitful interaction between the artist and the mass audience, but at the same time to give the artist the means of keeping a life somewhat apart, under conditions allowing him to develop in his own way and at his own pace.

The relation between high art and popular art is subtle and complex. As we have said, the artist must be permitted by society a refuge and a sense of privacy; yet in the larger perspective it is his influence alone which saves the popular arts of industrialism and the mass media from becoming dehumanized and vulgar. How, precisely, is this influence to be exerted? If the artist's work is merely imitated and broadly reproduced, there occurs both a loss of quality in the original and a blunting in the perception of the great audience. The work of art is the expression of a unique vision, to be accepted as such, understood on its own terms and within its limited and necessarily rarefied sphere. Yet without that vision all areas of life and art decline.

VI

THE MAINTENANCE OF EXCELLENCE

It is not necessary here to try to trace out all the interactions between the high arts and the popular arts; the points at which they are linked or separated need not, for our purposes, be made precise. But it is necessary that our society be clear in regard to certain principles which can alone assure the maintenance of excellence and the concentration of an intense and undefiled artistic life.

These principles are not readily acceded to by the typical American. As a people we retain a lively, changeable culture, colorful and varied as befits a society constantly on the move and blessed with a bewildering variety of choice. We have fantastic devices for spreading this culture and a vast hunger to enjoy it. It is not easy, therefore, to maintain standards of excellence, to pursue without compromise the highest forms of art, to admit that not everything is simple or to be apprehended at a first glance. Yet it is essential that there be stated and kept in mind the hard, even bitter truths about the nature of art.

We list the following points, not as inclusive, but as some of the basic presuppositions which a people must come to accept and respect if its culture is not to fall into mediocrity.

1. Art is a matter for professionals. Its practice requires training, discipline and the most unflagging dedication. Nothing is more appealing in the United States today than the enthusiasm with which do-it-yourself culture is followed by the people. The activities of Sunday painters, amateur actors, weavers, wood-workers, musicians, etc.—all have their value. They are part of that constructive use of leisure of which we spoke earlier. But they do not attain, except in the most exceptional cases, the level of true art. The line between the professional and the amateur, between the artist and the audience, is one which any first-rate culture must maintain.

2. Art is not self-evident nor of necessity immediately enjoyable. It requires in the spectator an effort of the spirit and of the mind, sufficient to put himself in harmony with a vision other than his own. Americans have grown accustomed to say that they know what they like. We have had dinned into us that the customer is always right. These attitudes may be adequate for the consumer of mass-produced merchandise; they have very little to do with the person capable of appreciating art in any of its subtle forms.

3. Art is not a matter of numbers. The museums in our contemporary society may find it necessary for economic reasons to cater to a wide public. They may find it tempting and attractive to engage in various educational activities. Insofar as they do these things they may be community centers or educational institutions, both of which we

would be poorer without. But to the degree that they perform such services they are not concerned with art in the sense in which we have been speaking of it. Numbers and popularity are not related to this kind of art; indeed the preservation of excellence and the setting of ultimate standards may be incompatible with efforts to broaden public appreciation.

4. Art is not self-expression. Just as art cannot be understood without effort, so it cannot be created without travail. It lives by laws of its own, laws not always easy to communicate or to understand. But the true artist in any field is bound by these laws and is responsible for keeping them by a strict inner discipline. This is as true of the most abstract or experimental art as of objective and traditional art. Above all, art is its own end, and has nothing to do with therapy or emotional release.

Having stated these broad principles, it remains to add that the life of art requires a vigorous and independent critical spirit, embodied in a small group of men and women no less dedicated than the artists themselves. The critic, in a viable culture, is as sharply separated from the creator of art as the professional is from the amateur. For him to play his true role—understanding art not in terms of public preferences but in terms of its own nature and end—he must have objectivity and the chance to practice it consistently. A recognition by both the artists and the public of the critic's function is a sign of a viable culture. The United States has not been distinguished by the number of its critical journals of a high order nor in all cases by the capacity of its critics to withstand the commercial and popular pressures.

VII

FINE ARTS AND THE LIBERAL ARTS

In recent years there has been a striking emphasis upon the practice of art within American institutions of higher learning. The idea that there may be a close relation between the liberal arts and the visual and performing arts is comparatively new in America; it is certainly one that would have horrified the ancestral Puritans. Yet practical and theoretical affirmation of this interdependency has come from the citadel of old Puritan orthodoxy—Harvard University; and, not less surprisingly, from the high church of science and engineering, the Massachusetts Institute of Technology. Other colleges and universities, especially in the Middle West, have been pioneering in creative expression in a variety of forms. The contemporary student has sometimes seemed all too ready to flee the older disciplines of science and politics, taking refuge, medieval-wise, in the pursuit of an artistic ideal.

This shift has brought to the college campuses creative individuals—poets, painters, writers, musicians—who find a congenial home and a fortunate means of supplementing their incomes.

The marriage of the liberal arts with the fine arts has evoked questionings and problems. Insofar as the cultivation of the arts requires merely the transmission of an inheritance—the ability to recognize and appreciate a cultural tradition—there is no apparent difficulty in reconciling them. It is when creativity comes into play that the matter grows more complicated. The academician has cherished in regard to artists what has been called "the myth of the Inspired Idiot"—a conviction that original creation involves entirely haphazard and irrational processes. The academician, moreover, has taken it for granted that he is himself strictly a scholar and researcher; it disconcerts him to think that at some moment the professor of philosophy may actually turn out to be a philosopher—or the teacher of English literature, a poet. The bridge between what thus seem to be two races of man is built when it is recognized (as we have indicated above) that art is not mere self-expression but that it follows a law and discipline of its own. "The great artist is great both as an artist *and as an intellectual,*" says the Committee on the Visual Arts at Harvard University. "The university," it adds, "should welcome him."

There are dangers, nevertheless, in the alliance. The artist settled into the college is made comfortable; he is flattered by the adulation of immature minds; he may succumb to the contagion of research and teaching and forget his true vocation. The university, traditionally a refuge for excellence and a world apart, is itself being transformed by numbers and invaded by the standards of commercialism or suburbia. The real question, to quote the Harvard report once more, is whether, under such conditions, "the university can provide a home in which his [the artist's] genius can best flower."

That question will not be finally answered except by time and experience. Meanwhile there is much that is obviously attractive in the new arrangements. The liberal arts college or university is in a position to become over the next decades nothing less than the artistic focus of the community fortunate enough to shelter it. Already the American colleges provide some of the happiest examples of a rational and spacious environment, in contrast to the crowded and obsolete cities which too often surround them. These academic communities, with their museums and libraries, their theatres and auditoriums, are the essence in embryo of true cultural centers, not artificially imposed upon a society, but alive and growing from within.

These higher educational institutions provide a uniquely desirable audience, ready to accept the less well-known repertoire of music or the seldom-acted play. Conversely they provide performance for the community at large, and shed over the city outside the college walls the illumination of the distinguished artists and writers they harbor.

There is thus a whole new dimension in the relations between the college and the community. The traditional problems of "town and gown"—making excuses for bumptious undergraduates or justifying tax-exempt property—will be supplanted by considerations of a new depth and richness as the colleges and universities become recognized cultural centers.

It seems important over the next decade that the implications of this new function of the institutions of liberal arts be fully explored and developed. Uncritical or unsophisticated progress in this direction could raise new difficulties. As with every good thing, there are limits to what universities can and should do in fostering arts. Their function, apart from research, remains that of teaching and learning, not that of producing performing artists. The full, intimate experience of performance and creation are part of the learning process—perhaps a larger part than has heretofore been recognized; but a line still needs to be drawn, particularly at the undergraduate level, between the student and the would-be star. The distinction between professional and amateur, which has been drawn above, must not be further blurred by having our universities turn out young people who think themselves qualified as true artists, when at their best they have been made critics and seekers after truth.

Such hazards need to be stressed; but they do not obviate the task which has now fallen to our society, of bringing into a new harmony the hitherto divided liberal and fine arts traditions.

VIII

THE INSTITUTIONS OF ART

Art is the creation of individuals, but in many of its forms it involves individuals working together. By its life it gives life to institutions. The quality of art in a society will in large part depend upon the number, the vitality and the continuity of the institutions of art in its midst.

America has traditionally been rich in institutions. Its people have come together naturally to form committees; from committees have grown organizations. Many of these have been temporary or deciduous, disappearing and re-forming as purposes changed or interests shifted. In its cultural life there are examples not only of those vigorous shoots which embody a passing ideal or an aspiration, but of more lordly institutions, solidly rooted in the community, which make their own traditions and evoke established sources of support.

Insofar as art is embodied and carried forward within institutions, the money which goes to these should be on a scale commensurate with the significance of the work. Though support has come from many sources in the past, it has usually come haphazardly, even apologetically, as if society were ashamed of having to sustain these indigent institutions. But the institutions of art cannot by their very nature be expected to exist without aid; making funds available to permit their fullest flowering should be an act of highest satisfaction on the part of individuals and of the community as a whole.

Membership drives and admission fees may provide a significant proportion of running expenses; but there are dangers in being too dependent upon these. Museums, as well as other cultural institutions, must be constantly on guard against a deterioration of standards resulting from an appeal to what is immediately popular or even sensational. The pressure to derive fees from the public may have serious effects upon the basic purposes of the institutions. It is essential, therefore, that the community as a whole recognize on a stable and continuing basis its obligation to help meet annual expenses and in exceptional cases to build up endowment funds.

The sources of community support have been various. Individuals and foundations have found art an appealing form of benefaction. In twenty-one cities in the United States there have been established "United Art Funds," comparable to the Community Chests, which make their gifts to the cultural institutions of the community. Yet the support has been spotty, uncertain, and inadequate. The major source of subsidy still comes too often from the artist himself—from the musician, for example, whose salary is so far below a living wage that he is compelled to take two or even three jobs to supplement it.

Contributions by governments at the municipal, state and national levels are discussed elsewhere in this book. Private sources, however, have by no means exhausted their possibilities. The community drives now existing in a score of cities should become the rule rather than the exception. The corporation, which has come to the point where it feels fully justified in making contributions to education, must make the further step of contributing as generously—and on as rapidly growing a scale—to the institutions of art. The foundations, some notable exceptions notwithstanding, have neglected this field. A recent authoritative estimate put at only five per cent the amount of total foundation grants going to liberal arts—and much of this is for education, not the creative arts. The community foundations, which represent a growing force, should find the cultural institutions of the community a field as appropriate for their support as hospitals or scholarships.

All these agencies of support will find their way clear to supporting the arts without any radical departure from tradition, especially where art is embodied in vigorous institutional forms. What must be new is the scope and amount of support and the degree of commitment to the cultural life with which it is accorded.

While institutions make such support possible, the lack of institutions imposes a fatal handicap on the meeting of artistic needs. A few pioneering, imaginative programs may be successfully undertaken by foundations. The commissioning of works of art and the making of grants to individuals can within limits be carried out. But the steady flow of economic support depends upon channels already having been prepared and creative achievements having found embodiment in durable institutions.

The handicap caused by lack of institutions is especially serious in regard to the performing arts. With the exception of a few opera and ballet companies, there have been virtually no continuing groups. There is no national theatre, and there are only three or four cities with repertory companies. When the United States, following the example of virtually every other Western country, has wanted to send an acting group abroad, it has been compelled hastily to organize and train a band of actors, prepared to give a small selection of plays.

The lack of repertory companies has not only denied the theatre the kind of economic support which has gone to other artistic institutions; it has at the same time kept the theatre from reaching its fullest development as a medium of culture. Without stable theatrical institutions it is difficult to train actors in the discipline of their art or to give them the varied experience which evokes their full gifts. It has been impossible, also, to create theatre which draws upon the varied range of great plays by ancient and modern writers.

The theatre in the United States has persisted almost exclusively as a Broadway phenomenon, with each production a one-shot affair. Increasingly those plays tailored to a hit offer the only chance of securing the very large sums necessary for financial backing. There is a constant tendency toward fewer plays, and those adapted to special and limiting conditions. If the internal revenue laws were so altered as not to allow the entertainment of clients to be deducted as a business expense, Broadway as we know it, one competent observer has asserted, would almost certainly collapse overnight.

The "off-Broadway" theatre has provided in recent years a greater opportunity for experiment, but here, too, the general practice is to assemble a cast for each production; and often the ultimate aim is to reach Broadway. Summer stock, which seemed for a time one hopeful alternative to the Broadway practice, has given way to "package plays," put together and rehearsed in New York and then sent out upon the circuit. Where the work of a new playwright is produced in this way (and that is seldom enough) it is almost invariably with the idea of trying it out for a later Broadway production.

At the root of all this is the fact that theatre in the United States has been thought of not as an art form, but almost exclusively as commercial entertainment. Television confirms this tendency, as theatrical talent is increasingly drawn into the orbit of entertainment at the level of the mass audience. Yet the theatre remains important to all the arts and to the whole quality of American life. Perhaps no other medium can so effectively bring home to men and women the essential paradoxes of their existence, confronting them with the tragedy and the comedy everlastingly at the heart of things.

It seems highly important, therefore, that the creation of repertory theatres in the United States, situated in the larger cities, perhaps related to the universities, should be a recognized goal. This should be accompanied by a determination to see that funds from various public and private sources flow to the theatres as to other institutions of art. In addition there exists a large scope for imaginative experiment, on the part of foundations and other institutions, with the purpose of giving young actors, playwrights and scene designers opportunities for developing their gifts.

IX

GOVERNMENT AND THE ARTS

The role of government in the arts has been a matter of much controversy—and of considerable obfuscation, not least among those who themselves represent the cause of the arts. It seems necessary to speak plainly on this subject. For it would be an anomaly which could be explained only by the most unusual reasons if a people which really valued art were to take the position that government is excluded from action in this field.

Where government has entered directly into the field of art, the experience has too often been disheartening. Political influences have exerted themselves. The standards of the artist and the critic have been ignored, or where these have been permitted a measure of authority, the tendency has been for an artistic clique to entrench itself. The art which has been encouraged under official auspices has almost always favored the less adventurous and the more classically hidebound schools.

From this experience, leading figures in the art world have drawn the conclusion that anything is better than the intrusion of government. It may be questioned, however, whether such men are not thinking too narrowly as professionals, without adequate understanding of the governmental methods and institutions which in other fields, no less delicate than art, have permitted the political system to act with detachment and a regard for the highest and most sophisticated standards.

The judiciary itself is an invention of tremendous ingenuity, permitting laws to be administered independently of political pressure. The functions performed by the National Institutes of Health or the National

Science Foundation are, to take two modern examples, quite as complex as the encouragement of art; they are performed with a high level of competence and professional skill. Certainly in the United States of the next decades we should be capable of devoting as much ingenuity to the creation of adequate processes for the nurturing of art as we have for promoting health or science.

It may be argued that each public figure, if he does not think of himself as an expert on health or science, believes he knows what is good in art. We have urged in this chapter the necessity for widespread acceptance of the idea that art has its own standards, irrespective of one's personal preferences; that it is professional, disciplined, and is subject to the rational and informed judgments of the critics. As long as these principles are not accepted, it is perhaps impossible to hope that government can promote art without debasing it. But even that is not reason to despair. There already exist precedents of high officials upholding the verdicts of juries whose views on art differed admittedly from their own. There are notable examples of government cultural activity successfully protected from political pressure. The Freer Gallery and the National Gallery of Art remind us how private and public efforts can combine to produce results of highest excellence. The Library of Congress is a public institution which has made a notable contribution not only in its capacity as a great repository of books and information but through its Music Division by commissioning works by the foremost American composers.

It would surely be a counsel of despair to freeze our attitude toward government support of the arts on the basis of unhappy experiences in the past. What is needed is a cautious and tentative approach to new measures, undertaken with good will on the part of the politicians and of the representatives of art. The stakes are too important to let ignorance or prejudice on either side foreclose the issue.

What, then, should the government do in this field? It should consider, first of all, undertaking a number of relatively undramatic and indirect measures. The argument about the relation of government and the arts has been carried out within narrow limits, whereas there is in fact a wide area of choice. What is important is that leaders within our society—private citizens and public officials, scientists, curators, educators, artists—should agree that government must not thwart, and wherever possible must positively encourage, the development of the cultural life. Such agreement has been lacking, and as a result nobody has fully envisaged the scope and diversity of the action which might be taken.

Our tax laws could be combed over with the question in mind of where they could be adjusted to make sure that they do not penalize the pursuit of cultural attainments. Taxes which now burden the theatre and music should be removed. Tariff laws should be looked at from the point of view of art and cultural exchange. In virtually every department of the federal government there are activities touching the arts which should be coordinated and vitalized.

Nor should the role of the federal government alone be reviewed. At the municipal, county and state levels there are, as well, activities which could be fitted into an over-all policy toward the arts.

Various proposals for the establishment of a Federal Advisory Council on the Arts have been before the Congress. Something of this sort should certainly be passed, though it seems questionable whether such a council should be established, as is generally proposed, within the Department of Health, Education and Welfare. Provided its members were men and women really concerned with the issues involved—and not merely political appointments—the Council could perform a genuinely useful role in making studies of the whole field of arts in relation to government. There exist ample possibilities for creative innovations. It has been suggested, for example, that a subsidy for the transportation of art could help greatly in bringing it on a larger scale to the citizens. It has been suggested that a fee for the use of television channels might be charged and used for grants and subsidies to encourage those sources of art and talent from which television derives its sustenance. These measures, and many others, should be looked at with an open mind; they should be related to what is being done for art in other countries and to what is in accord with our traditional methods and habits.

In the main, government can be active insofar as the institutions of art already exist in the community. A local government could do actual harm by constructing a theatre where no repertory company exists or where a responsive audience is not in being. But where there are healthy institutions, government can lend its support as naturally to a museum as to a library, to a ballet corps as to a school. It can provide, or help provide, the permanent facilities within which art is performed. A city government without too much soul-searching will build a baseball stadium or a fair grounds. Is it unreasonable to ask, where there is a clear demand and sound institutions, that it provide a home for the opera or theatre company?

In the nature of things government cannot create art. That is no reason why it should not create a home for art—a feat which it is admirably qualified to perform. Nevertheless the congressional action on a National Cultural Center allowed no funds for the building. It is admirable that there should be plans to raise the money from individual, foundation and corporation sources; but the very fact that such activity is afoot should persuade the government of a positive duty in this field, apart from the provision of a site. It may be pointed out, incidentally, that the government, which feels restrained from building a cultural center in Washington, did not hesitate to build an extremely handsome one for the people of West Berlin. (In the latter case it kept its principles pure by action under the cover of a specially created "foundation.")

A significant though less dramatic example of the government's avoidance of what seems a plain responsibility is the fact that the United States pavilion at the international art exhibition, the Venice Biennale, is—alone among all such national pavilions—privately owned. It first belonged to an art gallery; it has since, at the government's urging, become the property of a museum. The building is inadequately maintained; more important, the private funds which are being devoted to this purpose could be used far better in promoting art through ways which the government cannot and should not undertake. The contrast between the attitude toward art of the United States and of European countries is strongly marked by the unfortunate condition of this Venice pavilion.

The support of going institutions of the arts and culture is something which government can and should do at every level. Municipal support is a well-established principle, with amounts ranging up to $5 million for one year in New York City, a little under $1 million in Philadelphia, down to $16,000 for the city of Washington. The programs supported are mainly museums and orchestras, although Houston provides a small sum for a repertory theatre. Support of the arts at the state level has been more spotty, with activity mainly confined to the appointment of commissions concerned with public buildings. But the concern of the states is increasing, and ought to increase markedly over the next decade. The entrance of the federal government into this sphere (going beyond its established concern for the District of Columbia), would present new problems as well as new opportunities. There is no reason why this should not be done, but the principle ought definitely to be established of having the federal government give grants to state institutions only on a matching basis.

Apart from activities in support of the institutions of art, government is itself the great exemplar in this as in other fields. It creates standards and sets style in the course of pursuing its basic objectives. This is true of government at all levels, but particularly so of the national government. Washington has been involved in one way or another with the arts since its founding. It has been the great builder, the great coiner, the great printer and collector of books, and inevitably the repository of great works of art. The question today is not whether the government shall do these things, but whether it shall do them well or ill.

Up to now it has too often done them—if not ill—at least in a spirit of mediocrity. American stamps and coins have been inferior in design. Official buildings, from the post offices in the smallest town to the great structures in Washington itself, have been undistinguished; and where fine buildings have survived from the past, they have often been damaged by tasteless additions or alterations. That the government can do much better than this is indicated by the embassies and consulates, works of foremost American architects, which have been constructed in different parts of the world since the war. It cannot be that the government, by this contrast between its brilliant achievements abroad and the mediocrities perpetrated at home, wants to indicate that its own citizens are somehow backward and not capable of appreciating the best in art. In the next decades, all that government sponsors and creates must indeed become the measure of the country's highest potentiality. Then it may be that our states and municipalities, catching the spirit of the federal government, will insist on something better in their public works than a meager spirit of utility.

Government's obligation is, in brief, to keep its own house with a sense of beauty and fitness. In doing this, as in supporting art in different ways and at different levels of the national life, government should be entirely clear about its own purposes. It should not seek to increase employment among impoverished artists. It should not conduct a welfare program for deprived citizens, nor try to win the cold war by showing that we have more and better art than rival regimes. It should seek to encourage art for its own sake as an expression of what is noblest in the people's lives; it should seek to create for the public the finest objects to which our culture can attain.

X

TOWARD A POSITIVE ATTITUDE

The most significant goal in the field of the arts is that their enhancement and development should be considered a goal—that the American people should recognize the objectives in this area of their common life to be on an equal plane with those to which in the past they have given their best efforts. It has been all too natural, during epochs when a continent was being subdued or amid the fresh responsibilities of world power, to think of the arts as something pleasant but peripheral. The time has now come when we must acknowledge them to be central and conceive their fullest development as essential to the nation's moral well-being.

This country is being watched by peoples—many of them as new to nationhood as they are old in cultural achievements—who ask whether under such a system as ours the highest values can be maintained. It is being watched—and judged. Among our own people, meanwhile, there is a deep and persistent questioning about the significance of our material advance. The ultimate dedication to our way of life will be won not on the basis of economic satisfactions alone, but on the basis of an inward quality and an ideal. Among much that on the surface appears to be complacency or materialism, the Americans—the younger generation especially—are looking for something at once more demanding and more genuinely satisfying than what passes for happiness by current standards. To minimize or frustrate this quest is to risk weakening the fabric of our whole society.

6

AN EFFECTIVE AND DEMOCRATIC
ORGANIZATION OF THE ECONOMY

CLARK KERR

6

THE CHALLENGE *to American economic organization, writes Dr. Clark Kerr, is to be both democratic and effective. We must preserve a great number of balanced power centers, protect the individual's choice among big organizations and his identity within them, and confine the government to defining rules by which we act rather than prescribing what we shall do. While doing all these things, we must also devise ways to make the economy effective in attaining our goals.*

A member of this Commission, Dr. Kerr is President of the University of California and an economist with a national reputation in labor matters. In preparing this chapter he was assisted by the panel listed below. He takes responsibility for the views expressed.

PANEL

JOHN T. DUNLOP, Professor of Economics, Harvard University.

ARTHUR J. GOLDBERG, Special Counsel, AFL-CIO.

MEYER KESTNBAUM, President, Hart Schaffner and Marx; Chairman, Commission on Intergovernmental Relations, 1954-55.

AN EFFECTIVE AND DEMOCRATIC
ORGANIZATION OF THE ECONOMY

CLARK KERR

A nation exists to serve the individual and common goals of its people. This is also true of the nation's economy. The American economy has served the people well over the nearly two centuries since the Declaration of Independence. The average American has enjoyed the highest standard of living in personal goods and services in the entire world; the non-agricultural labor force has generally worked the shortest hours among the industrialized nations; and the area of relatively free choice for workers and for consumers has seldom, if ever, been excelled.

Yet there are problems—even major problems—confronting the American economy in the 1960's. These problems arise both from internal changes in our society and from changes in the world beyond our borders. Other chapters in this series deal with the important questions of technological change and of the general health and growth rate of the economy. The focus of this chapter is the organization of the American economy and its relation to national goals.

A nation's economy may be organized in any of a wide variety of patterns, ranging from total state operation to total private operation, from heavily concentrated to widely diffused private ownership, even from domestic to foreign control in the case of colonies or underdeveloped countries with rich resources. The American economic system has evolved with a primary emphasis on the freedom of the individual to make economic choices. This was not happenstance, of course, but a reflection of the American people's belief, tacitly expressed in countless decisions on economic matters, that free choice in economic matters best serves our basic national purpose, which is, after all, the fulfillment of the individual. From the outset, we accepted as an imperative the proposition that a democratic political system can be successful only with a democratic form of economic organization. We gave relatively little attention to the effectiveness of the economic organization *per se,* implicitly assuming that economic effectiveness would result from the myriad of personal and group decisions and clashes within the economy. In some particular economic sectors—notably the development of our national railroad system after the Civil War—government policies were consciously directed toward increasing the effectiveness of the economy. For the most part, however, legislation and public influence were directed to keeping the economic system democratic and so, we believed, effective.

Our basic national purpose remains unchanged today, and so we retain as an imperative the necessity that our form of economic organization be democratic. But the rapidly changing conditions of modern life have caused us to examine closely both the effectiveness of our economy and our assumption that effectiveness will automatically result from the totality of individual and private group actions.

Industrialization has brought the individual rich benefits in health, material goods, and the leisure and means important to individual fulfillment. But it has also created large and powerful private organizations whose influence over the individual gives rise to new and often subtle questions of democratic procedure. And it has made individuals increasingly interdependent in many spheres. The economic success or failure of an individual or a private group today may depend upon or may affect many others. The complexities and costs of many desirable projects are completely beyond the scope of private individuals. Industrialization is resulting in new concepts of public responsibility and of public endeavors.

On the international scene, as well, we face as a nation problems of unheralded gravity and magnitude. Here, again, we are realizing that individual actions must increasingly be supplemented by public approaches. In today's world, our economic system must continue to serve the individual directly by providing opportunities for his material well-being and advancement. But this alone is not enough. Our economy must also serve the individual indirectly by enabling the nation to meet such challenges as the maintenance of an adequate, diversified, enormously expensive defense system; the acceptance of broad responsibility in the area of international cooperation, including especially assistance to underdeveloped countries; the maintenance and expansion of an educational system far greater in scope and quality than ever before envisioned, to meet the demands of the modern world; the provision of public services required by rapid and extensive urbanization and by rising standards regarding the minimum requirements of life in a civilized community—in short, the whole range of endeavors suggested throughout this volume as essential steps toward the continuing fulfillment of our basic national purpose. These public tasks call for immense resources and, obviously, for an economy of great competence and power.

Today's world and the vision of tomorrow's have brought us to the clearer realization that there are two great imperatives for the American economic organization. It must be democratic. It must also be more effective than ever before. We could afford a certain amount of economic waste and inefficiency in the past; we can ill afford it today. Precisely here lies the heart of the challenge to American economic organization in the decade just ahead. How can we as a nation direct our economic organization to the meeting of particular public tasks and standards of performance without at the same time endangering its basically open, democratic nature? The thorough exploration of this most urgent question is in itself a challenging goal for Americans in the 1960's.

This chapter cannot presume to provide any clear-cut answer to the question. But it can outline some of the aspects of each imperative— the democratic economy and the effective economy—which ought to be considered during the search for an answer.

I

THE DEMOCRATIC ECONOMY

Because he believed economic democracy to be an essential bulwark to political democracy, Thomas Jefferson favored a nation of small farmers and merchants with relatively equal economic influence. We have departed a long way from the Jeffersonian ideal, but the diffusion of economic decision-making to support the diffusion of political power remains a key point in our national policy. With industrialization there have grown up, since the time of Jefferson, large and powerful economic organizations—private and government corporations, trade unions, professional and trade associations. As they have grown, new issues have been raised over the distribution of power within and among these power centers. In a democratic industrial society, these are among the principles which can be applied to the reasonable distribution of power:

1. There should be as many power centers as possible, consistent with the effective functioning of the society. Local governments should be preserved as well as state and federal. There should be the maximum number of firms in an industry consistent with efficient operations and healthy economic conditions. The identity of individual national unions should be preserved along with that of the local unions within them.

2. These power centers should be roughly balanced in strength, when they face each other in conflict, so that no single one can dominate the other. This principle applies particularly to the equality of bargaining power in labor-management relations. Neither the company-dominated union nor the union-dominated industry is desirable if the contending positions are to be freely expressed.

3. Power centers should be separate one from another. Along with the doctrine of separation of church and state goes the essential separation of state and industry, and state and labor, and industry and labor; although these are not exactly parallel situations.

4. Individuals should be given as much choice as possible within and among these power centers. In particular, this means the widest opportunity to choose jobs and goods and services.

5. The participants in each power center should be able to exert at least an essential minimum of control over the leadership. Union members should have ultimate, though not day-to-day, control over their officials, and stockholders over the management of their companies. Employees and consumers need some protection against the power of the large corporation, as do individual members or single firms against the power of strong professional and trade associations.

6. Each power center should have an adequate judicial system to protect the rights of the participants—a grievance machinery in the corporation and the trade union alike.

7. Each power center should exercise only the minimum control over the lives of its participants consistent with its survival and effective operation.

8. Necessary governmental controls in the economy should be concentrated on procedures rather than on substantive issues. Instead of regulating prices, the government should seek to regulate mergers and the like; instead of regulating wages, the government should provide appropriate guidance to the process of collective bargaining.

These principles for the operation of a democratic industrial society have their counterparts in the governmental arrangements established by the Constitution and the Bill of Rights. These general rules, so well designed to handle the distribution of power in our political system, are increasingly applicable to problems of concentrated power in other areas than that of public government alone. The large corporations and the large trade unions may be viewed as private governments, with their own laws and their own means of enforcement. Traditionally as a nation we have been greatly concerned with the relation of the individual to the state; we have established our federal system of government, our checks and balances within each level of that system, popular control of government, and the rights of individual citizens. By and large, we have done very well in safeguarding the freedom of the individual and the group from the overwhelming dictation of the state. But we have paid less attention, until comparatively recently, to the growth of private governments, such as the corporation and the trade union, which now range alongside public government in the influence they have over the lives of individuals. Individual freedom is not affected solely by the relationship between the individual and the state, but also by the relationship between the member and his trade union or professional association, and between the employee, the consumer, or the stockholder and the corporation. Thus in the modern industrial society we face not alone the age-old question of making the political leaders responsive to the wishes of the people, but also of making the private economic organization responsive to the people it is intended to serve. The distribution of power in society has taken on new dimensions and new complexities.

Eight principles were set forth above which might be used to test the democratic character of an economy. They are not of equal importance but a fully democratic economy will reasonably meet the tests implicit in each of these principles. How does the American economy meet these tests in 1960? Before we attempt to answer this question, it should be clearly noted that the American economy is marked by great diversity, and that a thorough examination of the problem would require comparative analysis, industry by industry, of American performance and that of other highly industrialized countries. Also, brief answers, within the framework of a short over-all commentary on the organization of the American economy, cannot deal adequately with the vast complexities of problems in each of these areas. However, general and brief answers may serve to emphasize the areas of greater and lesser concern.

Area one: the multiplicity of power centers. It is common to comment on the growth of large corporations in the United States. And, certainly, our economy has moved a very long way from the concept of atomistic competition which, in fact, it never did approximate in most market situations. The more realistic standard is "workable competition." In terms of this standard the American economy appears to be doing quite well. There can be more competition among a relatively small number of firms than was once supposed, as the automobile industry has recently demonstrated. There is a surprising amount of actual and potential competition among different industries as science and technological research result in a stream of new and better products to replace old ones. Also, the new professional managers are alert to the dangers in the creation of a public image of a "monopoly."

However, "workable competition" is not guaranteed by the working of the economy alone, as is indicated, for example, by the practice of administered prices in some industries. Corporations are to a degree autonomous; markets do not set precise limits on their actions. They are to a large extent in control of their own corporate lives. It is one of the wonders of the economic world that corporations behave as well as they do, given, as they often are, such considerable latitude. Fortunately, this is an area where the American public has been alert to actual and potential problems of concentration of unchecked power for a number of decades. Public policy is formulated in fairly explicit and detailed manner through the anti-trust and related laws; and the continuation of this public policy is well accepted as essential to the preservation of a truly free enterprise system.

As to the unions, while there is now a single major federation of unions, it is a federation, and the life of the union movement takes place largely in the independent national unions. Within these national unions, the locus of power varies greatly and the historical tendency has been for it to concentrate more at national and less at local levels. The configuration of this power structure generally follows the structure of the industry; the national union is strong in nation-wide industries; the local union, in localized industries. This configuration is what realistically is to be expected. The most major recent change in the power structure of the union movement has been a tendency to strengthen the identity of local unions.

The current American scene is not marked either by "monopoly capitalism" or by a single all-powerful union movement; far from it. There are about as many centers of power in both the corporate and union areas of group action as can reasonably be expected in a highly developed industrial society.

Area two: the balance of strength. Power is seldom, if ever, fully balanced among institutions, and it is too much to expect that it should be. However, great imbalances of power as between conflicting institutions can lead to the domination of one by the other. In such an event, the system of checks and balances of a democratic system is disturbed. In the conflict between capital and labor in the United States, it is not possible to cast an over-all balance of strength. Collective bargaining is highly segmented; and it is not possible, nor is it useful, to say that the balance of power lies with one side in general or the other. Even in specific industries or areas, the balance of strength may vary with the immediate issue, such as wages, hours, pension plans, or automation. But one can accurately say that a rough over-all balance of strength prevails between management and labor in a great many segments of the American economy.

There are, however, two significant categories where this rough balance does not obtain. The first includes the many unorganized workers, despite a national policy of a quarter-century's standing which calls for "unions of their own choosing." In this area, federal policy offers a mechanism more nearly to balance the distribution of power. The second category includes many small employers, particularly in the service trades, who have no effective bargaining power against the union or unions with which they deal and who are sometimes even forced to belong to union-dominated employer associations. For this category, the best hope seems to lie with the creation of independent employers' associations. Governmental action cannot, of course, be called upon to redress all the imbalances which are bound to occur from time to time in a dynamic economy. It should be reserved for cases where the imbalance of power is serious and continuing. And we should recognize that general legislation applicable to all unions and managements cannot possibly assure that in particular situations one side or the other will not be dominant. Moreover, any quest for full "equality of bargaining" at all times could push the government further and further into details of bargaining and into specific legislation for particular sectors of the economy.

Area three: the separation of power centers. One of the classic potential threats to the workings of a pluralistic society is the collusion among power centers against the public interest. In the United States currently there are two areas of such collusion. The first is management-labor collusion to fix prices and restrain entrance to the trade. Outright collusion is largely unknown in large-scale manufacturing industry, but it is of significance in some of the small-scale trades. A more serious problem during inflationary periods is tacit collusion, with management granting wage increases on the assumption that the industry can always raise prices. Federal policy is against outright collusion, but the existence of violations is difficult to detect.

The other area is even more subtle. An increasing number of government officials and even agencies are being "captured" in whole or in part by private groups. Agencies which were established to regulate an industry sometimes gradually come to protect that industry instead. This "capture" occurs in quite legitimate ways. The agency comes to know the problems of the industry intimately and its officials to know the representatives of the industry; the "public" is not so constantly at hand. Aside from occasional legislative scrutiny of regulating agencies, what is needed is a strategy. Generally an interest group will prefer to have a single agency devoted to its problems; to meet no opposition in its dealings with that agency; to have the agency be as independent as possible from higher authorities. For an agency to be really "independent," it is better for it to have a wide constituency of problems; to be confronted by contending parties in seeking solutions to these problems; and to be subject to broad policy determination. Regulation which was meant to reform, otherwise often ends by preserving the status quo. A great deal of attention should be accorded methods of structuring governmental agencies so that in the conflict of viewpoints the public interest can best be served.

Area four: individual choice. Consumer choice in the United States is influenced in many ways, and it is limited by the range and quality of products sellers make available (the "choice" among television programs, for example, being fairly restricted at times). But individual choice of consumer goods and services is relatively free—with one very important exception. Members of minority groups are often denied free choice of housing, of recreational facilities and of other services. The same exception is found in the labor market, which otherwise works quite well. Most occupations are open to most people with suitable qualifications. But for members of minority groups many positions are closed to them, regardless of their qualifications—closed by the actions of employers, or unions, or both. In a nation devoted to "equality of opportunity," this is a grave defect in our economic processes. It should be a major goal of national policy to have a non-discriminatory product market and a non-discriminatory labor market for all our people.

Area five: ultimate control by constituents. Unions and corporations alike are, with very few exceptions, one-party governments. Their leaders are expected to behave responsibly in positions which daily require detailed knowledge and long experience as well as skilled judgment. It would be unreasonable and even unwise to expect members of these organizations to exercise democratic control over the day-to-day decisions of the leadership. But it is essential to provide some opportunity for an opposition to form and attain power in the face of continuing disagreement over basic policies. Stockholders' rights, while inherently limited by the distribution of ownership, are well established by law. And stockholders can readily transfer their shares. Union members can less easily change their jobs. Hence, democratic guarantees are particularly important for union members. Federal law now requires unions to conduct secret elections at stated intervals. Whether or not the bases for responsible actions by union leaders have in some circumstances been undermined remains to be demonstrated by experience. With reasonable membership opportunity to change its leaders, required union membership can give stability to collective bargaining relationships without unduly reducing the freedom of the worker.

Area six: judicial protection. One of the contributions of collective bargaining has been the introduction of independent judicial systems into much of American industry. Less attention has been given to the perfection of such machinery within the unions themselves, although certain unions have been most advanced in their provisions. The volume of grievances within industry and within unions is quite small, but the provision of adequate grievance machinery is nonetheless important.

Area seven: minimizing control over the individual. There is some natural tendency for power centers not only to grow in size but in the depth of their penetration into the lives of their participants. In the United States and Great Britain, alike, there has been concern over two major problems in this area. The first is the independence of the individual from forced political contributions or political participation by economic organizations, such as the corporation or the trade union. Public policy in both countries is wisely against such compulsion. The second is the freedom of the employee to change jobs without too great a penalty. In recent years there has been a growth of private pension plans which, when adequate vesting rights are not provided, tend to tie employees to their jobs. Fortunately, steps are being taken to improve vesting provisions; and further developments in this direction will help contribute to the freedom of the employee and to mobility in the labor market which is such an asset in a dynamic economy.

But there remains yet another area for concern, and that is the more subtle problem of organizational coercion of the individual in ways not subject to remedial regulation. The "organization man," the individual whose desire for security or fear of group disapproval leads him to surrender large measures of his personal independence to his organization, is a disturbing phenomenon of the times. Americans need to revitalize their convictions of the supremacy of the individual, so that economic or other organizations may remain the creation and servant and not the master of men.

Area eight: concentrating governmental controls on procedures. This has been the approach traditionally favored by the American people. Direct government control of substantive economic matters such as wages and prices has been accepted only during real national emergencies, as in the Great Depression or in wartime, and has been withdrawn as soon as the emergencies were over. The only direct controls generally acceptable have been those dealing with health and welfare issues such as hours and conditions of work for women and children, or in areas of accepted public interest such as banking and public utilities.

* * * * * * *

Americans throughout our history have been generally quite alert to the working of the economy as a democratic process. They have solved many problems along the way. There are still some to be solved. But the economic organization, by and large, has been compatible with and supportive of political democracy.

II

THE EFFECTIVE ECONOMY

Americans have over the decades accepted, some happily and some critically, the results of the free working of the economy; and these results have included a comparatively high average standard of living and an increasing measure of leisure. The "democratic" economy was also the "effective economy." Attention was directed to the improvement of the democratic processes, and public participation as represented by governmental action was largely limited to those regulatory measures believed essential to strengthen the democratic organization of the economy—measures dealing with the prevention of monopolies, the broad diffusion of economic wealth through the taxing structure, the protection of workers and investors and consumers against economic exploitation, etc. Many of these measures did contribute to the overall efficiency and growth of the economy, but that was not their primary purpose. In fact, it was more generally believed that government "tampering" with the delicate balances of the open economy would upset them and actually impair the economy's effectiveness.

Not until the harsh realities of the Great Depression did the American people generally begin to realize that the complexities and interdependence brought about by industrialization had made some profound changes in the economic scene. But the early 1930's made it all too clear that individual initiative alone, even though exercised with the greatest possible vigor and resourcefulness, might fail to suffice. A concept of public responsibility for the effectiveness of the economic organization was gradually taking shape. This concept received perhaps its most conscious and formal recognition in the Employment Act of 1946. The Act set forth "the continuing policy and responsibility of the Federal Government" as follows:

> "to coordinate and utilize all its plans, functions and resources for the purpose of creating and maintaining in a manner calculated to foster and promote free competitive enterprise and the general welfare, conditions under which there will be afforded useful employment opportunities, including self-employment, for those able, willing and seeking work, and to promote maximum employment, production and purchasing power."

The Act did not specify the level of employment to be maintained but it did recognize a federal responsibility to assure "useful employment opportunities."

Since the end of World War II other questions of public responsibility for the economy have been emerging. The inflation that accompanied the war and has continued in the years since the war has elevated the national concern for price and wage stability. The rapid development of the Russian economy and the economies of Western Europe, at rates substantially higher than our own, has called attention to national growth. Post-war strikes, and particularly the long steel strike of 1959, have renewed interest in the assurance of industrial peace. The "affluent society" of the "age of high mass-consumption" has raised questions about the direction of use of the new wealth; should there be more purpose to it than personal material gratification? These are among the new public tasks being considered for the economy: reasonable stability, faster growth, industrial peace, the "constructive" use of the new wealth. "Definite programs of action" are also being suggested, as in the last Rockefeller Brothers Fund report, for their own sake so that the "human impulse to idealism" may be satisfied and so that the people may "sense that large projects are under way and that they are part of some significant and enduring human enterprise."

The present economic process, developed over the decades after so much discussion, is geared to maximizing the freedom of individuals and private groups to make their own decisions. But these decisions have yielded depressions in earlier years and in recent years constant inflation, not stability; moderate rates of growth, not forced draft advances; strikes, not uniform industrial peace; additional durable consumers goods more readily than a new school, a new park, a new concert hall; an apparent sense of purposelessness, instead of visible public objectives. Consumer sovereignty and democratic unionism cannot guarantee stability or growth or industrial peace or public facilities. Neither the "invisible hand" of Adam Smith nor the "unalienable rights" of Jefferson, well as they may have served in the past, are alone sufficient for the new tasks.

How can we, then, give the necessary direction to our economic organization? Obviously, government participation has been and will be essential. But there are many ways and means of government participation, with varying effects upon an economy's effectiveness. The Soviet experience, for example, has shown that an economy directly controlled and operated by the state can be effective—at least in the short run and for the accomplishment of specific goals. But the stifling of individual initiative and creativity may prove in the long run to lead to dangerous loss of economic vitality. And, in any case, we cannot consider sacrificing all else for economic effectiveness. We still have to meet our other imperative, that of the democratic economy.

The problem becomes one of balance, as is always true of the operation of a pluralistic society such as our own. The public objectives which we may select for our economy must be weighed against their cost in the area of individual rights. Such objectives as price stability or economic growth are not desirable *per se;* they are desirable only as they ultimately lead toward the nation's basic goal of individual self-fulfillment. And government intervention is not evil *per se;* it is evil if it does not properly reflect the consensus of the people, or if the gains it might bring are clearly overbalanced by the resulting inroads in the individual's sphere.

The consumer price level in the United States has been rising over the past decade by about one and one-half per cent a year. Judging by the experience of many other free economies, this is quite moderate. How important is it to reduce this rate? The rate of growth of the gross national product in the United States has been about half that of Russia and Western Europe over the past few years; but the rate of the United States is measured from a substantially higher base and our nation has been in the lead technologically rather than catching up to the leader. How important is it that the rate of growth be raised? Or, again, strikes cost less in man-days lost than does the common cold; and how important is it that they be reduced at all or substantially? Furthermore, the worth of one public economic objective must also be weighed against the worth of another, for they may be mutually inconsistent. The policies and conditions which give rise to stability of the price level are not always the same as those which yield full employment or high rates of growth. These are complex questions, and the answers are often not at all clear. We need to devote continuing and intensive study to the economics of modern industrial society, which after all is a relatively recent phenomenon in the social science field and one which is changing almost daily. We need better methods of communicating the highly technical findings of the experts to the layman.

Having agreed upon valid public needs, we should next consider whether they can be adequately met through individual action alone. The role of government should be restricted to clear cases of national interest which cannot be served by private means, and the government should withdraw whenever its participation is no longer essential— when the particular public need no longer exists or when it can be adequately met by private economic activity.

When government action is required, we need to consider the most appropriate method of government participation. This, again, is a field which needs further study and experimentation. The government (federal, state and local) influences the economy in a very great number of ways: through action on defense needs, foreign aid, support to education and urban renewal and cultural and recreational facilities, through differential taxes and subsidies and manipulation of the interest rate. These influences are variously exerted by elected officials in the executive and legislative branches and by a host of different types of agencies, including service and regulatory agencies, policy-making bodies, and even public corporations which conduct enterprises. We need to make careful judgments about the best method of governmental action toward meeting a given objective—best from the points of view of both effectiveness and democracy.

One method which holds a degree of promise and which has not yet been as widely tested as it might is persuasive participation by the executive branch of government. The economic process developed over the decades has created a system which is reasonably responsive to the wishes of the people. If their wishes can be clarified and focused, they can be quite effective. Some of the devices might be the following:

1. The Council of Economic Advisors, established by the Employment Act of 1946, is already making continuing surveys of the general performance of the economy. These functions might be broadened to include the making of recommendations for actions necessary to the achievement of specific economic objectives.

2. The government, through its executive agencies, could exercise more initiative to assist industries through difficult economic adjustments. Some first steps in this direction have been taken to encourage and assist the progressive forces in the railroad industry to modernize policies and facilities; more could be done to ease the effects of automation through government cooperation with special re-training and placement and other programs to supplement the modernization efforts of various industries. The public benefits greatly from the economic returns of automation and has an obligation to ease the costs borne by individuals.

3. In some crucial and particularly sensitive or costly areas, the government's executive agencies will have to take the lead in

encouraging development. This is, of course, true of the activities of the Atomic Energy Commission and of many segments of the military services, as it has been historically of the Agricultural Experiment and Extension Services.

4. In the area of national emergency strikes, the government might enter earlier into potentially difficult situations and play a more aggressive role in making settlement proposals, but collective bargaining still works best when it is left to the parties. Compulsory arbitration leads automatically to wage fixing, as in Australia. And the Australian situation also indicates that it is very difficult, in a democracy, to make such arbitration really compulsory. There are several alternative courses to compulsory arbitration, including different degrees of mediation and of fact-finding and voluntary arbitration. Experience has shown that it is better to have several such courses of action available, to be chosen in accordance with the situation, rather than to rely on a single rigid course of action. The greater use of independent third parties to assist in collective bargaining, for example, has been helpful in several instances when major changes in rules and arrangements were involved.

5. The government can use the conference method more widely to spread information and to help form opinion as, for example, among industry and union leaders on the issue of price and wage stability. Such conferences can be, perhaps, more effective than in earlier times because of the greater consensus in our society and the more professional attitudes of leaders on both sides.

There are real limits to the effectiveness of such largely persuasive devices; but there are also real uses. They involve a more affirmative, constructive role for government, but they generally stop short of direct participation in the established decision-making processes of the economy. They would help identify national responsibilities and assist in the meeting of these responsibilities without heavily concentrating the power now widely diffused in our economy. They work toward a greater cooperativeness between public and private effort.

The American people want both participation and progress. It is easy, but fruitless, to praise the "free enterprise" system and then to demand of the system that it effectively meet selected public objectives. It is neither easy nor fruitless to explore the devices which can make the two consistent with each other. The exploration and development of means whereby the American economic system can best satisfy its two imperatives—democracy and full effectiveness under the new conditions—is an important and challenging goal for Americans in the 1960's.

7

FULL EMPLOYMENT, *economic growth and stable prices are goals of the nation and also means by which its other objectives are achieved. For help in formulating a program to attain them, the Commission turned to Herbert Stein, Director of Research, and Edward F. Denison, Staff Economist, of the Committee for Economic Development.*

The authors outline a program for reducing unemployment and bringing the economy closer to its potential capacity. They estimate the rate of growth which, in the absence of extraordinary measures, the economy might then be expected to maintain. They consider the adequacy of that growth rate to meet public needs. And they analyze the steps which can be taken to increase the growth rate further, together with the costs of taking those steps.

Not all economists will agree with the estimates Mr. Stein and Mr. Denison have made. But every reader of this thoughtful chapter will find new understanding of this complex subject.

The authors had the advice of the panel listed below. The views expressed are the responsibility of the authors, and do not necessarily reflect the position of the Committee for Economic Development.

A further description of the basis of the authors' estimates may be obtained on request, addressed to them at the Committee for Economic Development, 1000 Connecticut Avenue, N.W., Washington, D. C.

PANEL

NORRIS DARRELL, Partner, Sullivan and Cromwell, and member of the bar of the State of New York.

MILTON FRIEDMAN, Professor of Economics, University of Chicago.

NEIL H. JACOBY, Dean, Graduate School of Business Administration, University of California; member, President's Council of Economic Advisors, 1953-55.

ISADOR LUBIN, Arthur T. Vanderbilt Professor of Public Affairs, Rutgers University; United States Commissioner of Labor Statistics, 1933-46.

PAUL A. SAMUELSON, Professor of Economics, Massachusetts Institute of Technology.

CHARLES L. SCHULTZE, Associate Professor of Economics, Indiana University.

HIGH EMPLOYMENT AND GROWTH
IN THE AMERICAN ECONOMY

HERBERT STEIN AND EDWARD F. DENISON

The American economy works well. It produces the highest income per capita ever known, and a rate of growth that raises real income per capita by half from one generation to the next. This income, and its increase, are widely distributed. Economic advance has produced a revolutionary reduction in the hours and burdens of work. Americans have great freedom to use their resources and incomes as they choose. The system is highly responsive to the demands of the people, producing with exceptional efficiency, inventiveness and adaptability the particular goods and services for which a private or public demand is expressed. Unemployment remains a problem, but one so reduced in magnitude since the 1930's as to be qualitatively different.

America and the civilization to which it belongs stand at an historic turning point. They confront a critical danger and inspiring opportunities. The danger is indicated by the phrase "cold war." Among the opportunities are to help the billion people of the under-developed world realize their aspirations, to reduce nationalist and racialist limitations upon man's freedom and horizons, and to push back the frontiers of human knowledge in many directions. Neither avoidance of the danger nor realization of the opportunities *requires* that the American economy work better, although better economic performance would make both objectives easier to attain. Insofar as movement toward these more important goals depends upon the availability of economic resources, the American economy as it is and is likely to be can provide them. It would be tragic if the United States should fall prey to the danger or fail to grasp the opportunities because of preoccupation with the idea that it is not rich enough and needs to become richer faster.

Having said this, we can turn to the question of improving the performance of the American economy. Other chapters of this book deal with matters that would be part of a comprehensive review of the subject. We confine our discussion to three main aspects:

(1) The importance of reducing the average level of unemployment and raising production closer to its potential, the means for doing so, and the effect of doing so upon the growth of the economy.

(2) The relation between the production we can expect from the economy, if it operates near its capacity, and our "needs."

(3) Ways to increase the capacity of the economy, and the costs of such measures.

I

REDUCING UNEMPLOYMENT AND OPERATING CLOSE TO CAPACITY

In the period 1950 to 1960 unemployment averaged about 4.5 per cent of people wanting to work. That rate applied to present population and labor force would mean an average of about 3.2 million people unemployed. For most of the postwar unemployed, the period of unemployment was relatively short.

This is a good record as compared with American experience in the 1930's and with many of the longer-run expectations once commonly derived from it. Yet it should remain a primary United States objective to reduce unemployment further, for two main reasons: (1) its direct impact upon the unemployed, and (2) its effect upon total national production and the rate of growth of that production. Of these two reasons the authors regard the former as more important and by itself sufficient to justify national concern. Among the groups who for one reason or another do not share the benefits of the national prosperity, the unemployed are one of the largest. However, the reduction of unemployment is clearly also the least costly way of making a significant contribution to economic growth.

The importance of continuing attention to the unemployment problem is especially clear at this writing, in the autumn of 1960, when about 6 per cent of the labor force is unemployed. In fact, at no time in the recovery from the 1958 recession has the nation regained a satisfactorily high level of employment. The problem for the future is not only to improve on the postwar record, but also to make sure that we do not fall below it.

The United States has long since decided that high employment is an important national objective and that the government has a responsibility for its achievement. The real questions now are how this objective can be achieved at least cost, and what costs Americans are willing to pay for it. Reducing unemployment is an important objective, but it is not an absolute objective, that must be achieved regardless of cost—any more than other objectives are to be achieved regardless of cost.

The authors believe that means can be found to reduce the average rate of unemployment below that of the 1950's without costs so large as to outweigh the benefits. The cost that must be seriously considered is inflation.* So we are expressing the belief that unemployment

---

* We assume, and recommend, no attempt to restrict increases of prices or wage rates by government controls, formal or informal.

can be reduced without an increase of inflation that would overbalance its benefits.

1. The means to reduce unemployment. The essential requirement for the maintenance of high employment is a steady growth of total demand for goods and services at an adequate rate. The problem here is with the "steadiness". Total demand does tend, in the long run, to grow at an adequate rate and, if it does not, measures are known for stimulating its long-run growth. It is important to note that the problem is to increase demand when, and to the degree that, it would otherwise be inadequate. To add to demand "all the time" will yield little reduction of unemployment and much inflation. It will also leave unresolved, if it does not aggravate, the problem of increasing demand still more when it is needed. It is not only declines of total demand that should be prevented so far as possible. Failure of demand to increase at a rate proportional to the growth of the labor force and productivity must also be prevented if unemployment is to be kept low.

The United States now does much better with the problem of the steadiness of the growth of total demand than it did before World War II. There are two chief reasons. First, the supply of money grows much more steadily, because of changes in the financial system and in monetary policy. Second, the federal budget has become a much more powerful stabilizing force, generating large deficits in recessions and surpluses in booms. This is partly the result of the increase in the size of the federal budget, partly the result of changes in the character of the tax system and some expenditure programs, and partly the result of a policy that accepts these swings from deficit to surplus.

To go further or do better in these fields would require more precision in adapting the timing and scale of action to the fluctuating and unforeseeable economic situation. This becomes more and more difficult as we try to moderate fluctuations already of small scale and duration. The danger of doing too much or at the wrong time increases.

(a) *Budgetary Policy.* A major step that could be taken now would be to make tax rate changes available as an instrument of economic stabilization policy. Starting from present tax rates, there is room to stimulate private demand powerfully by cutting tax rates, or to restrict demand by raising them. At best there would be some lapse of time between recognition of the need for such action and enactment of the tax change, and possibly some further lag before the economic effects were felt. If there were prior agreement on policy, however, these lags could be shorter than would be probable with other methods of stimulating demand.

Two main obstacles, closely related, prevent the use of tax rate changes as a flexible instrument of stabilization policy. First, there is sharp disagreement in the country over the kind of tax cut that should be made if a tax cut should ever become appropriate. This creates a reluctance to initiate action to cut taxes, for fear that the cut would be —from the initiator's standpoint—the "wrong" kind. It also creates the danger that the time consumed in debate over the character of the tax cut would destroy its advantage as a flexible tool of policy. Second, it is apparently more difficult to raise taxes than to lower them. A tax cut adopted to combat recession may prove irreversible when economic conditions change, with probable inflationary consequences. Moreover, the possibility that an anti-recession tax cut will be permanent intensifies argument over the character of that cut.

There is no mechanical way around these obstacles. The only solution is improved understanding. We should learn that while the character of the tax system is important, there will be occasions when it is less important than getting taxes up, or down. We should also learn that if we are unwilling to contemplate tax changes except in time of open war, we are immobilizing one of our most powerful instruments for economic stability and for other national objectives as well.

Tax rates should not be lowered or raised in reaction to every small fluctuation in economic activity. But this instrument should be much more available than it now is for use in more serious situations.

On the expenditure side of the budget, stronger action to promote high employment will require more objective tests of the desirability of expenditures, better understanding of the counter-cyclical purposes, and better engineering and financial preparation.

(b) *Monetary Policy.* Whether we can expect from monetary policy a greater contribution to high employment and economic stability than it has made in recent years is uncertain. Hindsight reveals occasions when monetary policy should apparently have been looser or tighter than it was. But the problem of the policymaker is always to decide what action today will be appropriate at that future time when the action has its effects. In every appraisal of the future there is the possibility of error.

Two kinds of suggestions, pointing in different directions, for reducing the possibility of error in a stabilizing monetary policy are now current. One would prescribe a rule requiring that the supply of money grow at a steady rate, year in and year out. The other would ask the monetary authorities to base their actions more on their forecast of the future and less on present conditions. Each of these suggestions has some attraction, but it is not clear that either would yield better results than recent practice. Probably the most one can hope is that the increase of economic knowledge, through research and experience, will permit improvement of monetary policy.

Increase of knowledge would also help improve the use of government tax and expenditure policies to maintain high employment. Here, however, much more than in the case of monetary policy, there are political, psychological and procedural obstacles that prevent action as effective as existing knowledge would permit. At least in the short run, the authors would count mainly upon the reduction of these obstacles for improvement of overall stabilization policy.

2. The risk of inflation. In the past ten years, when unemployment averaged 4.6 per cent, the average annual increase in the consumer price index was 2.1 per cent. Even in the 1955-60 period when unemployment averaged 5.1 per cent, consumer prices rose 2.0 per cent per annum. Suppose that we could now reduce the average level of unemployment by a combination of general fiscal and monetary policies. Would this increase the likelihood of inflation? If so, how would this affect the wisdom of trying to reduce average unemployment?

These are questions on which books could be, and have been, written. Here we will only state certain observations and opinions:

(a) Other things being equal, the more demand is increased in order to reduce unemployment, the greater the danger of inflation becomes. There is a contrary view that by increasing employment, an increase of demand increases output per man hour, reduces costs, and holds prices down. The authors do not find theoretical or historical support for this view.

(b) The postwar period was special in too many respects to provide convincing evidence that persistent inflation will result if unemployment averages less than 4.5 or 5 per cent. During the earlier years of this period demand was clearly excessive. The wage and price trends and expectations of those years continued to exert an inflationary influence even after the excess demand had abated. Also, during most of the postwar period foreign competition as a factor tending to restrain U. S. price increases was much less influential than it will be in the future.

(c) The relation between unemployment and inflation depends not only upon the average level of unemployment but also upon its fluctuations. A steady rate of 4 per cent unemployment may be less conducive to inflation than an average rate of 4.5 per cent composed of intervals of 3 per cent and intervals of 6 per cent.

(d) How much inflation, if any, occurs at a particular level of unemployment is not unalterably determined by natural forces but can be affected by public policies. Agricultural and tariff policies, for example, have important effects.

The authors believe that it is possible to reduce unemployment below the recent average without more inflation than has occurred in the last three years and perhaps without any inflation. Even a little inflation, cumulated over an extended period, is inequitable in its effects. Some families are hurt by it while others benefit. We regard the benefit not as offsetting the hurt but rather as compounding the injustice. Against this injury to individuals resulting from inflation must be weighed the injury resulting from unemployment. There is no objective scale on which these injuries can be weighed. The community's conscience must decide. But we will express our own opinion that the small amount of inflation likely to be associated with a moderate reduction of unemployment would be less harmful than the unemployment.

Our assessment of the situation may be incorrect. There is a rather widely held view that the power of labor organizations and business is so great that prices will rise rapidly and at an accelerating pace if reasonably high employment is maintained. We do not share this view. But we cannot be sure that it is not true now or may not become true in the future. We do not recommend a policy of pushing for reduction of unemployment no matter what the inflationary consequences may turn out to be. We recommend that the United States try now to reduce unemployment, cautiously and flexibly, in readiness to take prompt countermeasures if serious inflation should threaten.

II

NATIONAL PRODUCTION AND NATIONAL NEEDS

From 1929 to 1957 the total production of goods and services in the United States increased at an average rate of 2.93 per cent per annum. We estimate that if unemployment is kept to about 4 per cent of the labor force, the annual rate of growth from 1957 to 1970 would be 3.27 per cent, and from 1957 to 1980 would be 3.24 per cent. The rates from mid-1960 would be higher—3.41 per cent and 3.31 per cent respectively —since the actual rate from 1957 to mid-1960 was below these estimated trends. The GNP reached an annual rate of $505 billion in the second quarter of 1960 and would have reached about $520 billion at high employment. At the estimated rate of growth it would be about $709 billion in 1970 and $972 billion in 1980.

This estimate of future growth assumes that no special measures are taken to accelerate growth other than the reduction of unemployment. It is based on an analysis of the probable contribution to growth that will be made by several factors—the number, hours of work, educational attainment and age-sex composition of the labor force, the stock of capital, the increase of knowledge, and others. It assumes, among other things, that the 1970 labor force will be about 19 per cent larger, and average annual full-time working hours about 5 per cent shorter, than in 1960; that the educational attainment of the labor force will increase sharply; that the capital stock will grow at about the rate indicated by past ratios of saving to national product under prosperous conditions.

Some of these assumptions may turn out to be incorrect. For example, the labor force projection postulates a continued rise in labor force participation of women that may not occur. However, these assumptions are not major sources of difference between our projections and those of other investigators. Certain other elements affecting growth, particularly the rate at which knowledge will advance and other changes affecting output per unit of input will take place, can be based only on past experience. Here, we have relied mainly upon estimates for the entire period since 1929, and for the decade of the Fifties.

Estimates of future growth under conditions of high employment have been made by other students. Some project growth rates similar to ours, others project higher rates. The difference generally lies in the weight given to the relations observed in the long period 1929-57 as compared with a shorter more recent period, especially 1947-1950 or the postwar period inclusive of those dates. This shorter period may be interpreted as evidence that a "New Era" began after the war, in which various factors, notably the advance of technology, will hereafter generate a more rapid rate of growth than previously experienced. Alternatively, since this short period was one of quite low unemployment, it may be interpreted as evidence that high employment by itself makes a very large contribution to the growth rate.

In the space available here we cannot discuss and defend the points of difference between our estimates and others. We would only say that we believe the longer period to be more reliable than a selected shorter period, in the absence of clearer evidence than now exists of a persistent change in some relationship. The immediate postwar period had many obviously special features that cannot be projected into the future. They have not, in fact, persisted during the past decade. High employment will influence the rate of growth through effects upon such factors as the input of labor, the rate of capital investment, and attitudes toward restrictive policies and practices that prevent the most efficient production. We have tried to appraise these effects. While we find them significant and worth seeking, we have not found them to be as influential as some other investigators have suggested.

Any estimates of the future may be wrong. We offer ours only as the most reasonable basis we know for considering any policy problems to which an estimate of future growth may be relevant.

It may be useful to indicate some of the possible patterns of spending that national products of the size projected would allow. Since most of the fears that have been expressed about the adequacy of growth concern alleged needs for more government spending, these patterns, shown in Table 1, focus on this component. We do not mean to suggest a preference among these or any other patterns.

Pattern I. If the proportional allocation of the projected national product among private consumption, private investment, and government purchases were to be unchanged from that of the second quarter of 1960, government purchases in 1970 would be up by almost $39 billion, rising from $98.6 billion to $138.4 billion. The same assumption for defense spending alone would mean an increase from $44.7 billion to $62.8 billion. This pattern implies a rise in per capita private consumption from $1831 to $2160.

Pattern II. With the same figure as Pattern I for private investment, an increase in per capita private consumption of 1.47 per cent a year, the average rate from 1929-57, would permit government purchases of $145.8 billion, up $47.2 billion. This pattern implies a rise in per capita private consumption from $1831 to $2126.

Pattern III. With the same figure as Pattern I for private investment, if private consumption per capita were held constant at its 1960 level of $1831, government purchases in 1970 could be $208.3 billion, up $110 billion from the second quarter of 1960. This exceeds any responsible projection of requirements that we have seen. For each billion dollars that government purchases are projected to fall short of this amount, private consumption per capita would be raised by $4.67. These calculations assume that the division of output between private consumption and public purchases does not affect the rate of growth of total output. The validity of this assumption would depend upon the character of the government expenditures, the character of the taxes to finance them, and perhaps on other factors.

Similar illustrative calculations for 1980 are also shown in Table 1.

The most obvious question to ask about the projected rate of growth is: Will it be enough? In one sense of course the answer is No. The growth of production is the source from which desires for goods and services are satisfied. These desires appear limitless. However fast production may grow, some desires will be left unsatisfied, and many will wish that growth were faster.

However, the rate of growth will not be increased by wishing. Steps will have to be taken to increase it. By and large these steps will involve some cost to someone—otherwise we could assume that they would already have been taken. (Remember that we are discussing the problem of raising the rate of growth above that which would otherwise result at high employment—whatever that rate may be.) The question then is not whether faster growth is desirable but whether it is sufficiently desirable to justify any particular step that might be taken to achieve it.

Table 1

Illustrative Distributions of the Projected National Product
(billions of 2nd quarter 1960 dollars)

	Total Gross National Product	Personal Consumption expenditures	Gross private domestic investment and net exports	Government purchases of goods and services
1960 2nd quarter (annual rate).....	$505	$329.0	$ 77.5	$ 98.6
1970:				
I.........................	709	461.9	108.7	138.4
II.........................	709	454.5	108.7	145.8
III.........................	709	392.0	108.7	208.3
1980:				
I.........................	972	633.1	149.1	189.8
II.........................	972	639.4	149.1	183.5
III.........................	972	476.7	149.1	346.2

Assumptions: I—Same percentage of GNP as in the 1960 2nd quarter.
II—Same investment as in I, per capita consumption increasing at 1929–57 rate of 1.47 per cent annually. Residual to government.
III—Same investment as in I, consumption per capita unchanged from 2nd quarter 1960 level. Residual to government.

This question may be concretely illustrated as follows. We estimate that if annual hours of work were to remain at their 1957 level, rather than to decline at the rate we project, our annual rate of growth from 1957 to 1970 would be 3.6 per cent instead of 3.3 per cent. Faster growth is a good thing and reduction of hours of work is a good thing. The question is whether increasing the rate of growth is more important than reducing hours of work. Similar questions can be asked about increasing immigration, or employment of women, or expenditures for education, or taxes for public investment, or tax changes to promote private investment, or expenditures for research.

When the question is put in this way it becomes obvious that the authors of this paper cannot responsibly pretend to answer it. We can try to illuminate the benefits of more rapid growth and indicate the costs of achieving it. But whether the benefits are worth the costs can be answered only by those affected or by those making the decisions. The costs and benefits are not reducible to any common terms that permit their objective measurement and comparison. In the end the decision will have to reflect subjective judgments, and insofar as they are collective decisions they will have to reflect some concensus of subjective judgments.

Whether a collective decision about the rate of growth should be made, through government, is in our opinion a real and serious question. The alternative view is that the desirable rate of growth and the correct means to achieve it are those that would emerge from private decisions. These would inevitably be affected by the action of government in discharging its important functions. But these functions do not include the explicit determination of the rate of growth. We believe that there is much to be said for this position, and we trust that it will receive due weight in public discussion of growth. We do not examine this position here only because it seems more fruitful to use our limited space to indicate what choices are available in the economic system if collective choices are to be made.

How much is growth worth?   If our economy grows at the rate we project, 3.3 per cent per annum, total output (Gross National Product) will be about $710 billion in 1970. If it grows at 4 per cent per annum, GNP in 1970 will be about $780 billion. The value of the higher rate of growth is $70 billion of output in 1970 and corresponding amounts in other years.

How much is this $70 billion worth? Obviously, the answer will depend upon what the $70 billion consists of and what wants it satisfies. If it includes critical defense expenditures, the caloric intake necessary for sustaining the population, the capital assistance that would set the underdeveloped world on the road to growth, then the $70 billion will be of the utmost importance. But anyone can think of possible uses of $70 billion that would be of little importance.

One can conceive of all possible uses of output being ranked in an endless descending series from the most important to the less important, to those of no importance at all, to those of negative value. Ideally, with $710 billion of GNP we would go down from the top of this list through the $710 billion most important uses. If we had another $70 billion of GNP we would take the next most important $70 billion of uses, all of which would be less valuable than any of the first $710 billion. The value of the additional $70 billion would be much less than 10 per cent of the value of the first $710 billion.

It may be that the actual American selection of uses of output does not conform to this pattern. Possibly we select more or less at random from the most important, less important, and unimportant uses. In this case the additional $70 billion of output might be as valuable, dollar for dollar, as the first $710 billion.

There might even be a systematic bias in the process, which causes the less important needs to be satisfied before the more important. If so, the needs satisfied by the additional $70 billion of output would be much more important, on the average, than those satisfied by the first $710 billion.

The importance of more rapid growth depends critically upon how well we allocate our output among our needs. This simply means that if we can count on devoting our expected output to satisfying our most urgent needs, additional output will be only as valuable as the satisfaction of our less urgent needs.

As the authors see it, the key current question about the allocation of output relates to the division between private and public uses. There may be limits upon the amount of public expenditure that keep critical public needs from being met, even though much less important private needs are met. Suppose, for example, that we cannot or will not spend more than 20 per cent of the gross national product for public purposes. If the gross national product in 1970 is $710 billion we can have only $142 billion of public expenditures, even though this may leave unmet many public needs more important than the needs satisfied by some of the $568 billion of private expenditures. The value of raising the GNP would then lie in the additional public expenditures it would permit.

It should be understood that in this paper we have made no evaluation of the need for additional public expenditure. Other chapters in this book consider that problem. Here we are concerned only to explore the implications for economic growth on the hypothesis that a very large increase of public expenditure is necessary.

There are two main possibilities to be considered. One is that we cannot raise tax rates above their present levels, at least without serious effects upon economic growth. The other is that we *will* not raise tax rates. In either case the yield of the existing tax rates sets a limit to public expenditure, and the only way to raise that expenditure would be to increase the yield of the existing tax rates by increasing the rate of economic growth.

Granted a willingness to raise tax rates, it must be recognized that certain patterns of tax increase might tend to retard the rate of growth. But substantial additions to revenue can be obtained without such an effect. This might involve some combination of (a) increases in the beginning rate of individual income tax (now 20 per cent), (b) a broadening of the income tax base by reduction of exemptions and exclusions and (c) increased taxation of consumption. Such taxation would be burdensome, but this burden is simply that which is implicit in any decision to sacrifice private consumption for public expenditures.

Whether higher public expenditures financed by higher taxes will retard the rate of economic growth depends not only on the character of the taxes but also on the character of the expenditures. If the expenditure increase is heavily weighted with public investment, research, education, and defense programs with a large research content, and if the taxation impinges almost entirely on private consumption, the net effect may be a higher rate of growth.

Even if taxes can be increased without adverse effects upon growth, the public and its government representatives may be unwilling to impose the additional taxes. In this case a higher rate of growth would be needed to permit more public expenditures by increasing the yield of the existing tax system.

The authors believe that there are unnecessary obstacles to an increase or decrease of federal taxes. Sharp disagreement over the proper distribution of tax burdens, exaggerated impressions of the consequences of the level and structure of taxes, the complexity of the tax system—all these make a tax increase or decrease excessively difficult. As a result, government expenditures tend to be adjusted to the yield of the existing tax system, even though the best level of expenditure might be higher or lower.

Too much should not be made of this point. At least in this century, no President has been unable to get an increase of taxes when he asked for it to finance expenditures that he described as essential to a vital national interest. Nevertheless, the tendency to regard the yield of the existing tax system as a limit to public expenditures is, we believe, a potentially dangerous obstacle to sound public policy. No law of history assures us that we can get safely through the twentieth century with the yield of the tax system we inherited from the Revenue Acts of 1950 and 1954. The American people should recognize this.

A more rapid rate of economic growth would reduce the importance of this obstacle. But we are doubtful of the possibility of circumventing this obstacle by raising the rate of growth. As we shall see in the next section of this paper, many of the steps that might be taken to increase the rate of growth would themselves require higher taxes. Is it likely that, being unable to raise taxes to pay for important public expenditures, we would be able to raise taxes to stimulate growth so that we could pay for these same expenditures? We think not, but we are not experts on what the American people can be persuaded to do. In any case we believe it would be a serious mistake to leave the American people with the impression that the rate of economic growth can be raised to whatever figure is necessary to make the yield of the existing tax system cover all desired public expenditures.

The argument to this point may be summarized as follows: If the national product is wisely used, the contribution of a higher rate of economic growth would be the satisfaction of less critical needs, not of the most critical needs. But the less critical needs are still worth satisfying, and should not be disregarded. They motivate a large part of the work done in this country.

If this country does not allocate its output to the most important uses, it cannot be sure that any specified rate of growth or level of output will satisfy its critical needs. In this case there are two possibilities. One is to increase the rate of growth, which would probably increase the likelihood that important needs would be met. The other is to become more intelligent in recognizing and responding to vital needs. The latter is essential whatever is done about the former. If we are not wise in the use of our resources, we cannot expect the abundance of our resources always to compensate.

The Competition of Soviet Growth. Up to this point we have been discussing the value of more rapid growth as a means of satisfying private or public needs for goods and services. In the present state of the world, rapid growth of the American economy may have an additional value.

Let us postulate this situation. The Soviet economy is now growing at a percentage rate higher than ours. If this should continue, the absolute annual growth of the Soviet economy will overtake our growth (it may already have done so). Although there are strong reasons to believe that the Soviet Union will be unable to maintain a growth rate faster than ours once it has achieved a comparable level of technical efficiency, let us nonetheless assume that it will do so. Suppose further that, despite this, the United States is able to maintain an adequate military establishment, provide for necessary public services and sustain a rate of growth of private income that is satisfactory to the American people individually. Would we then regard our rate of growth as adequate?

This is an extremely difficult question to answer. It requires us to project our imaginations into a totally new economic, political and psychological situation. We, our allies, neutral nations, and the Soviet bloc are all deeply affected by the vision of the United States as by far the world's richest and economically strongest country. It is hard to conceive a world in which this would not be true.

But it seems possible that a change to a situation in which the Soviet economy is generally recognized to be growing faster than ours, not only in percentages but also absolutely, not in spurts but steadily, and is approaching ours in total size, could have profound consequences. It could greatly strengthen the confidence of the Russians in their own system, increase the attraction of the Communist system for the independent, underdeveloped countries, worry our allies about their reliance upon us, and weaken our own morale.

These consequences might not follow. Certainly they are paradoxical on their face. They imply that in order to increase the attraction of our system to populations with average per capita incomes of $100 we, with per capita incomes of $2,000, must become still richer faster. They imply that even though we fully discharge our real obligations to our allies, they will lose confidence in us because we do not choose to raise our personal consumption more rapidly. They imply that the rest of the world will not evaluate us by the standards we choose for ourselves but will compel us to be measured by standards made in Moscow.

Moreover no one really knows what the standards are in the production race upon which world opinion is said to hinge. We do not know whether the Soviet GNP is now one-third of ours or two-thirds of ours, because the composition of their GNP is so different from ours. And it is not clear whether the race is in GNP at all, or in steel production, or in butter consumption per capita. Each side presumably wants to race on its own track and to persuade the world that it is the right track. The outcome may depend as much on the persuasion as on the running.

Nevertheless the possibility described cannot be ignored. Accelerating our pace in the production race is probably a positive factor for our national security. How important a factor it is, the authors cannot pretend to say. This is a question the American people will have to decide on the advice of people more expert than we in the politics and psychology of the cold war. If they should decide that it is important, this would, in our opinion, be the strongest reason for a collective decision to increase the rate of growth.

The costs of accelerating growth must still be considered. We do not do *everything* that might promote our national security. Especially, we want to promote our national security in the most efficient way. Somehow we must judge whether a cost of x spent in accelerating growth will yield more in national security than the same cost spent for weapons, or for foreign aid, or for space exploration, or for education, or for reducing racial discrimination, or for tempering nationalism, or for many other things that affect our military, political and psychological position in the cold war. Again this is a question that the authors cannot answer. But we will try in the remainder of this paper to throw some light on two elements of the problem—how much can we affect the future growth rate by alternative policies we might adopt, and what would they cost?

III

MEASURES TO ACCELERATE THE GROWTH OF CAPACITY

We have said that the nation should take steps now to bring the rate of actual production closer to potential production. It should strive in future to keep the economy operating close to capacity, consistent with reasonable price stability and freedom. The degree of success in this endeavor will influence the rate at which the productive potential itself increases.

The nation may also wish to increase the rate at which output grows by means other than fuller utilization of its productive capacity. Many ways of doing so have been suggested. To judge their desirability from the standpoint of economic growth, and determine the extent, if any, to which each should be pushed, even a rough quantitative idea of their potential benefits and costs is better than none at all. This chapter provides a simple framework for such an appraisal and applies it to various possible courses of action that might be considered to accelerate the growth of the national product. Most of these proposals should and undoubtedly will be judged mainly on the basis of considerations other than their effect on economic growth and their economic cost, but we cannot discuss such considerations here.

If the United States wishes to increase the total national product (other than by fuller utilization of resources) it must increase either the quantity or quality of productive resources, or output per unit of resources used. Our reference point in this analysis is neither the past nor the particular projection of future output presented above. What we are measuring in every case is the difference between the probable size of the national product if we adopt some course of action and its probable size if we do not.

Increasing Labor and Capital. We begin with proposals to increase the quantity or quality of labor and capital. The statistical analysis underlying our estimates included a third resource—land—which we exclude from the present discussion because in the underlying analysis land was defined as a resource that cannot change in quantity.

We need to know, first, by how much total production would increase if either capital or labor were increased by a given percentage. It is reasonable to assume as a first approximation that, other conditions being unchanged, if we could simultaneously increase the quantity, or average quality, of all productive resources by any given percentage we would increase the national product by the same percentage* But we need to know the result of increasing only labor, or only capital, without changing the quantity of the others, since we shall be considering measures that increase one or another resource above what it would otherwise be, and it is unlikely that all of them would be increased in the same proportion.

---

* It is sometimes assumed that increasing the quantity of *one* particular resource, usually capital, by a given percentage would increase national product by the same percentage. This is clearly incorrect, since it would imply that if labor and capital were each increased by one per cent, national product would increase by two per cent. It would imply that if we increased male labor, female labor, plant, and equipment each by one per cent national product would increase by four per cent.

We deduce an approximate answer to this question on the assumption, which we believe sufficiently valid, that the earnings of any factor of production, per unit, tend to equal the value of the amount by which output would be changed if one unit of the factor were added or subtracted. Assuming this, and knowing the earnings of each of the factors, we can calculate the contribution to production of a small increase in any one of the factors. With this method, and using 1954-58 data, we calculate that a one per cent increase in labor alone would increase output by 0.773 per cent, a one per cent increase in capital alone by 0.175 per cent, and a one per cent increase in land alone by .052 per cent.

These figures need to be raised somewhat to take account of the probability that the United States economy operates under conditions of "increasing returns to scale," whereby an increase in the total size of the economy generates efficiencies that increase the product of each unit of resources. We allow for this by raising the estimated per cent increase in national product for a one per cent increase in resources to .84 per cent for labor alone, .19 per cent for capital alone and .06 per cent for land alone.

These estimates do not mean that labor is in any sense more productive than capital, but only that a one per cent increase in labor involves a bigger quantity of resources than a one per cent increase in capital. In other words, 650,000 workers are much more resources than $10 billion of capital; they produce more and earn more.

We should also note that these estimates apply only to very small changes and are maximum estimates if bigger changes are considered. A big increase in any one factor, substantially increasing its amount relative to the others, will add less, per unit of the factor, to total production than if the relative proportions had been less changed.

With an estimated increase of 0.84 per cent in national product from a one per cent increase in the quantity or average quality of labor, to raise 1970 output by one per cent would require an increase of 1.2 per cent in labor input in that year. This would increase by one-tenth of one per cent the annual growth rate of the national product between 1960 and 1970. We use this calculation to estimate the contribution that various approaches to increasing labor input might make to raising the growth rate.

1. Immigration can, within wide limits, be altered simply by changing federal law. Recently, annual net immigration has averaged about 0.2 per cent of our population. As recently as 1911-15 it averaged 0.6 per cent. A return to the 1911-15 rate of absorption—which, of course, is not an upper limit—beginning in 1962 would mean a labor force larger in 1970 than it would otherwise be by perhaps 3 per cent and in 1980 by perhaps 7 per cent. Allowing for immigrants less thoroughly educated than the average American worker, and for their difficulties of language and unfamiliarity with the American scene, we might expect the national product in 1970 to be nearly 2 per cent larger than under present immigration policy. This would add about 0.2 percentage points to the growth rate of total product.

We believe such increased immigration would have a negligible effect on the per capita income of the *present* United States population, and in this sense would be approximately costless, although it might increase social problems.

2. Standard hours of work are of particular interest because, like immigration, they are generally established by conscious group decision—through negotiation between employers and employee groups and by federal and state legislation.

Economic welfare is greatest when individuals work to the point at which the additional disadvantage of extra work just equals the value of the additional production. There are two reasons to doubt that the existing process for determining hours of work necessarily leads to the greatest welfare. The first is that the relationship between standard hours and output is simply not known. We do know that the amount of work a man does in an hour is related to the number of hours he works. If the work week is sufficiently long, shortening it actually increases total output. For some range of hours below this, shortening hours will reduce total output but increase output per manhour. Finally, there comes a point beyond which a reduction in hours will actually reduce output per man-hour. But we do not know where these points are, either in general or in particular activities. The second reason is that hours-shortening often has been motivated not by the desire for less work and more leisure but by the desire to raise employment or keep it from dropping.*

A major investigation of the relationship between hours and output is needed to make rational decisions possible. It should cover an assortment of industries and occupations, and consider various patterns of weekly and annual hours. Unless we know the actual relationship between hours and output we cannot calculate what difference to the growth rate different levels of hours in the future would make. Our projection of the national product assumed that normal hours prevailing in 1970 would be 5.1 per cent shorter than in 1960, and that this would mean a national product 3 per cent smaller than if hours remained at the present level. Retaining present hours of work would

---

* We are not discussing here temporary hours reduction to spread work in periods of slack demand, but permanent changes in standard working hours. It is important to growth that permanent reduction of standard hours for the purpose of increasing the number of jobs be avoided, for this approach prevents increased efficiency from generating growth of output. A general environment in which job opportunities are plentiful is the best assurance against this.

raise the computed annual growth rate by three-tenths of a percentage point.

3. Increase in formal education has been a major factor in our past economic growth and will continue to be so. However, the returns from additional education are spread over a lifetime, and the immediate result of extending the number of years of school is to reduce the size of the labor force. Therefore, the effect that anything done now would have upon output in 1970 or even 1980 is limited. We have calculated, for instance, what would happen if, starting with those who would otherwise complete school in 1962, and continuing indefinitely, some action were taken that resulted in everyone remaining in school one year longer than he otherwise would. The calculation assumes (as would be in rough accord with our estimates), that the additional year would increase by 10 per cent the ability of these individuals to contribute to production. We estimate that the total input of labor, adjusted for quality, would be *reduced* 1.1 per cent in 1970, increased 1.4 per cent in 1980, and increased 7.4 per cent in 2010. Over the entire 50-year period from 1960 to 2010 we should have raised the average annual growth rate of national product by 0.12 percentage points.

Provision of an additional year's education would require the continuing use of 0.3 or 0.4 per cent of the national product, leaving that much less for other uses.

The authors believe that, in the field of education, the long view is the correct one. Our present growth rate is benefiting from the extension of education throughout the past 50 years. Improvements instituted now will affect our growth rate for the next half-century.

One additional point should be made. The number of days and years spent in school by the average student cannot increase indefinitely at the rate it has in the past. If formal education is to continue its past contribution to the economic growth rate, the rate of improvement in the quality of a day's education must be stepped up. Finally, it should be noted that on-the-job training and various other forms of adult education also improve the quality of the labor force, and more quickly.

4. Lost labor. Elimination of conditions that restrict labor input would allow a larger national product. Thus, we estimate that the potential national product is reduced about 4 per cent by labor lost as a result of illness and accidents, 3 per cent by labor lost as a result of seasonal fluctuations in nonfarm industries, 1 per cent by the presence of excess labor in agriculture, 0.7 per cent because individuals are imprisoned or engaged in crime, 0.6 per cent by long-term unemployment resulting from secular declines in localities and nonagricultural industries, and 0.3 per cent by work stoppages resulting from labor disputes. Some of this loss could be reduced by voluntary individual action—for example, driving more carefully, not over-eating, and obeying the law. A small part of the loss could be offset by steps, such as making more use of prison labor, that would involve little or no diversion of resources from other uses. But costs of this character *would* be required by the principal methods of reducing these losses, such as provision of better medical care, rehabilitation of criminals, greater efforts to reduce seasonal fluctuations, and steps to accelerate the movement of labor out of agriculture and depressed urban areas. Space limitations prohibit any discussion of whether a net benefit might be expected from such diversions of resources. We simply note that to add one-tenth of a percentage point to the growth rate over the next ten years would require that the proportion of total labor lost for all these causes be reduced by one-eighth.

5. *Potential labor.* If ways consistent with individual freedom and not involving compensating costs in reduced efficiency could be found to slacken the trend toward less labor force participation by older men, or to accelerate the trend toward greater labor force participation by women in the middle age groups, this would contribute to growth.* We do not know of methods that would make a substantial contribution to this objective.

Projections of the labor force indicate that the next fifteen years will see a sharp increase in the number of young people and women seeking part-time employment, many of them only a few hours a week. It is not obvious that even a generally prosperous economy will automatically provide enough part-time jobs to absorb these people. Unless means are found to create such jobs, there will be a slight loss of the labor input that would otherwise be possible.

Increasing the stock of capital. The growth rate could be increased by accelerating the rate of expansion of the capital stock.

The value of the United States net stock of private capital is around $1000 billion, or twice the national product. We estimate, from the division of the national income cited above, that an increase of $10 billion, or one per cent, in net private investment would increase total output by something like $950 million per year indefinitely. It follows that to raise the annual growth rate of the national product by one-tenth of one percentage point through private investment would require steps that would permanently raise the ratio of private investment to GNP by about 1.1 percentage points above what it would otherwise be. With net private investment running in the neighborhood of six per cent of the gross national product in prosperous years, this would be an increase of perhaps one-sixth in the average ratio of net private investment to GNP.

* Our projections assume continuation of recent trends in both these respects.

In addition to private capital, there is also a large stock of public capital—waterways, roads, etc.—which contributes to production. Its increase also contributes to growth, though we are unable to measure this contribution directly. Indeed, much of it is not reflected in changes in the real national product as this is actually measured. Nevertheless it is presumably the real output that concerns us, whether included in the measurements or not. We shall assume that the contribution of public capital to growth—per dollar—is the same as the contribution of private capital. It is generally not efficient to make public investments unless they would be as productive as private investment.

How can we increase the total of private and public investment? The problem can be divided into two parts: (1) increasing the supply of savings, and (2) assuring the existence of adequate incentives to get the savings invested. The two parts are closely interrelated. The savings will not be forthcoming if the investment incentives are not strong enough to use them, and an effort to increase investment must fail if savings are not available.

For present purposes we shall mean by *total* saving the sum of (1) private saving (individual and corporate), and (2) the excess of taxes over public non-investment expenditure, which we shall call public saving. This total will equal the sum of public and private investment.

The total of saving so defined can be increased by raising private saving, by increasing taxes, or by cutting public non-investment expenditures—assuming each to be done in a way that does not produce an offsetting effect on the others.

(a) Except for cyclical variations, private saving seems to have been quite stable in relation to gross national product for a long time, in spite of major changes in many apparently relevant conditions. Therefore, it is impossible to be confident that measures exist to change this ratio substantially. The greatest opportunities probably lie in shifting federal tax burdens from upper-income groups and corporations to lower-income individuals.

(b) Reducing public non-investment expenditures, without reducing taxes, would raise total saving and make funds available for public investment or, through the surplus, for private investment. We shall not try to canvass the opportunities for action on this front except to point out that the problem of increasing the rate of growth is raised in the context of the United States rate *vs.* that of the U.S.S.R. In this context it is hardly likely that cutting back the defense or foreign aid programs could yield a gain in growth that would offset the direct loss. Cutting back on education expenditures would surely impair growth. These are among the largest elements in public non-investment spending.

(c) Total saving can be increased by increasing taxes without increasing public non-investment expenditures. Even though the tax increase may reduce private saving, this reduction is unlikely to offset the increase in public saving.

We believe that, at any given level of national product, an increase in total saving, private and public, could be achieved through these measures, although we are less confident about the possibility of substantially increasing private saving alone. Whether, or up to what limit, it may be possible to increase productive investment, assuming the saving to be available, is a more difficult question and one on which economists are divided.

There are two extreme views of the limits to productive investment. One is that the limits to the amount of productive investment are, if not infinitely distant, at least very far off, and that an increase in the supply of saving will by itself produce an equal increase in investment. The other view is that, given their expectations with respect to an acceptable return, the amount of investment that potential investors are willing to undertake is at any time strictly limited, although it grows in the long run and fluctuates from time to time; that this limit is close to our normal supply of saving and often lies below it; and that therefore an increase in the supply of saving, whether alone or supplemented by other measures, will not evoke more investment.

To rehearse here the theoretical analysis and empirical evidence underlying these views would not only exceed the scope of this paper but would also be inconclusive. The authors offer the following as a reasonable hypothesis on which to base a try-and-see policy in our present state of uncertainty. We are not at the limits of productive investment. Actual investment may be restrained not only by the supply of saving but also by other factors, including those affecting the terms on which savers make funds available and the terms on which investors are willing to use funds. These factors can be influenced by certain policies which, given the availability of saving, will increase actual investment.

This hypothesis would call, if it is desired to stimulate the growth rate by the investment route, for actions to stimulate investment. It would also call for stimulation of saving, but only at times when this is appropriate. A tendency of investment to outrun saving, generating inflationary pressure, would call for measures to increase saving. A tendency to recession would indicate the need for further measures to stimulate investment, if these were available, and otherwise for stimulating consumption and, hence, curtailing saving.

Policies to stimulate investment might include the following:

(a) Providing greater assurance of the maintenance of high employment.

(b) Achieving any given degree of restraint on, or support of, aggregate demand that may be desired for the purpose of economic stabilization by maintaining an "easier" monetary policy, and tighter fiscal policy, than would otherwise be adopted.

(c) Stimulating research, which will generate new investment opportunities.

(d) Increasing the after-tax return on capital by shifting the tax burden so that it bears less heavily on capital. Particular attention should be called to the possibility of increasing depreciation allowances as a way of raising the profitability of investment.

(e) Providing a government subsidy for investment, or a guarantee of business loans.

(f) Pushing forward all public investment that will yield a return in the form of additional production, whether or not sold in the market, equal to the return on private investment, or, in case of serious unemployment, a lower but still positive return. (This does not mean that expenditures which fail to meet this test should not be made. Such expenditures would have to be justified, like many other policies, on grounds other than the promotion of economic growth.) This would require a more informed and sophisticated analysis of the costs and benefits of public investment than is now made, but this is desirable anyway.

Where to start with a policy of increasing both saving and investment depends upon the conditions existing when the start is made. As of this writing, in the autumn of 1960, the relevant conditions are these: We have not been at high employment for three years and show no signs of an imminent approach to high employment. Investment is running below the rate of saving that would come forth at high employment. With present tax and expenditure programs, high employment would give the federal budget a cash surplus in excess of $6 billion.

In these conditions it would be desirable, *if* a decision is made to promote growth by the savings-investment route, to start with the stimulation of investment. This would call for: (1) accelerating the rate of growth of the money supply; (2) reducing the taxes that bear most heavily on property incomes in order to increase private investment; (3) increasing public investments that will meet the test of productivity. The success of this policy would appear in the attainment of high employment. At that point, steps to increase saving would be in order, probably to be accomplished by increasing taxes on medium and lower incomes. Thus, we might proceed by alternate steps of investment stimulation and savings increase through the phases of the business cycle and reach higher levels of both saving and investment.

How far this process might go before a persistent unemployment problem signalled that a limit had been reached, we do not know. That is why a try-and-see policy is indicated.

The clearest cost of a policy to accelerate growth by increasing the rates of saving and investment would be the devotion to investment of resources that would otherwise be available for consumption.* Two other major consequences may be involved: a shift toward less equal income distribution, and a shift towards larger government expenditures. Whether these other consequences are costs or benefits, and how heavily they are to be weighed, are questions into which we cannot enter here.

Increasing output per unit of input. Thus far we have been discussing the contribution to growth of increases in the factors of production—labor and capital. There remains the possible contribution of steps that would increase the rate of growth of productive efficiency, measured by output per unit of input. These are all difficult to evaluate. Only the few that are more promising are discussed here.

1. *Eliminate obstacles to efficiency and mobility.* Over the years numerous laws and private restraints have developed that prevent the economy from achieving, or even moving toward, an optimum allocation of resources among the various lines of production. Legal provisions include obstacles to international trade erected by both our own and foreign governments, federal subsidies to various industries, resale price maintenance laws, farm price supports, selective excise taxes, and many others. In the private sphere, monopoly, restrictions on the entry of new workers into certain occupations, and discrimination in employment against minority races, are examples of barriers to the use of resources where they can contribute most to production.

In some industries the use of the most efficient techniques and tools is barred, usually either by workers or by workers and employers together. In agriculture, government regulations prohibit maximum production.

Even aside from the employment of excess labor in farming, which we have already considered in connection with labor losses, these various obstacles to the best allocation and most efficient use of resources probably cost us a few percent of our national product.

Elimination of these obstacles would permit us, as a nation, to obtain more real income without more work or any sacrifice of present consumption; in this sense additional output would be free. In principle, the public could even compensate individuals losing by their elimination,

---

* Since the nation would start from a position below high employment it might seem that the increase of investment could be achieved without a sacrifice of consumption. But if it is U.S. policy to get back to high employment anyway, the increase of investment should be regarded as an alternative to the increase of consumption that might be generated as a way of restoring high employment.

leaving everyone better off. Almost without exception, however, these laws and private restraints have resulted from deep-seated attitudes, or real or supposed needs, on the part of an influential segment of our population. Their abandonment will not come easily, nor without creating dissatisfaction. Even so, a determined and comprehensive assault upon them might well enable us to produce one or two percent more in 1970 or 1980 than if they remain unchanged. If they spread further, the opposite effect may be anticipated.

Increased mobility of labor (and capital) would help to bring the actual distribution of resources closer to the optimum, as conditioned by the circumstances just discussed, at all times. The major step of creating a comprehensive system of public employment exchanges has already been taken, and further improvements in furnishing job information to workers can hardly have a perceptible effect on the growth rate. (This statement refers to the allocation of employed resources not reduction of unemployment or underemployment.) Better counseling of students might be helpful. Private pension plans are commonly established in such a way that the employee loses his rights if he changes employers. For individuals with long service, and especially executives, this becomes a major barrier to job changing. Permitting workers to retain their accumulated pension rights would contribute to mobility, but would also add to costs and defeat one of the purposes—reduction in labor turnover—for which employers established pension plans. Quantitatively, an attack on mobility probably has little to offer to growth through improvement of the allocation of *employed* resources.

Very high marginal personal income tax rates probably tend to discourage risk-taking, prevent accumulation of investment funds in the hands of individuals most likely to undertake risky investments, and impair performance of the entrepreneurial function. The present authors cannot estimate the magnitude of these effects, but in view of the smallness of the revenue provided by the highest rates, consider that their reduction would be a sensible part of a determined program to accelerate growth.

2. *The advance and more rapid application of knowledge.* The advance of knowledge has clearly been the most important single source of past increases in output per unit of input. This is true even if, as is done in these computations, elements affecting the quality of labor, particularly education, are considered part of the contribution of labor rather than of knowledge.

This source differs from all others in one respect that is highly important in the present discussion: knowledge recognizes no national boundaries. With the very doubtful exception of "military secrets," any scientific discovery or theory or any knowledge of new products, materials, techniques, procedures and practices that arises anywhere in the world quickly spreads to all advanced countries. This fact has two important implications.

First, we can hardly hope to gain more than a very temporary advantage, in terms of relative growth rates, over Russia or any other advanced country by accelerating the growth of knowledge; what benefits one benefits all. Second, since we are only one of several nations that regularly produce it, only a fraction of the new knowledge that contributes to our growth is, even in principle, subject to our control.

Research is only one source even of new knowledge that originates in the United States, but it is probably the one most subject to alteration by deliberate decision.

There are familiar reasons for supposing that, in a competitive system, private enterprises will spend less for research than would be warranted by the total return to society from such expenditures. The main reason is that business firms get only a part of the gains from their inventions or other new developments. A second is that the results of research are highly uncertain, and firms may include a "premium for risk" in determining their research budgets.

The patent system was established to stimulate technological advance by allowing inventors or their employers to receive a larger share of the gains from inventions. However, it simultaneously discourages the general use of new knowledge during the period of patent protection, and it is a much-debated question whether the present degree of protection is too large or too small to maximize the advance of output per unit of input.

The income tax laws give favorable treatment to research expenditures by permitting them (except for investment in capital goods) to be charged off in their entirety as current expenses rather than requiring them to be "depreciated" over a period of time. Short of permitting more than the full cost of research expenditures to be charged, which amounts to granting a subsidy to owners of existing profitable firms (and in practice mostly to large firms since they do most of the research) there appears to be no way to provide a further stimulus to research through the tax laws.

The proportion of the economic gains from new knowledge that the individuals or firms responsible for it can secure varies greatly. It is far larger for the sorts of knowledge that may be loosely described as patentable than for advances either in basic science or in managerial technique. The scientists whose discoveries provided the basis for modern technology and the engineers who devised time and motion studies benefited, in a monetary way, only insofar as the resulting prestige enabled them to place a higher price on their personal services than could others who quickly adopted their ideas. Within the area of technology itself, the large firm can ordinarily gain more than the small from a new discovery. Insofar as we rely on monetary incentives, therefore, we are likely to devote too large a proportion of our research effort to applied technology and too little to basic research or research in management techniques; and within the first, too large a proportion to technical advance in industries characterized by large as against small firms. But we do not rely exclusively on the monetary incentive. The individual inventor is frequently motivated by curiosity, the hope of fame, or sheer love of tinkering. Rather large funds are provided from nonprofit sources for support of scientific research. The federal government supports much research in agriculture and medicine, and on a small scale many other research activities. This is in addition to its huge outlays in the defense and space categories, which exceed all other research and development expenditures combined and absorb an enormous proportion of our research talents, but contribute relatively little to economic growth unless quality improvement in military weapons and in space investigation is counted.

Expenditures for organized research have been rising sharply, and further very large increases clearly are in prospect—increases that may be large enough to absorb all the qualified personnel that will become available in the next decade. In addition to questions concerning the size and allocation of research expenditures, there are important issues requiring further study that relate to the best ways to organize and conduct research. Improvement of productivity in research activities themselves may well offer a significant opportunity to accelerate growth.

Growth could also be stimulated by bringing the average level of technique closer to the best that is known. To keep this gap as narrow as feasible, our society relies mainly on competition to force laggard firms out of business while encouraging expansion of the more efficient. Supplementary steps are possible. In addition to more and better formal education, these include improvement of means of disseminating information, through a wide range of media and institutions, and removal of obstacles to the adoption of new procedures. The latter may require better measures to prevent individual workers and groups of workers from suffering as a result of technological progress. The age of plant and equipment is an important determinant of the lag of the average behind the best known.

IV

SUMMARY

Various alternatives, in addition to maintenance of high employment, are available to the United States if it wishes to raise its growth rate above that which it will otherwise experience. The authors of this report make no recommendation with respect to any of these. Our purpose is to provide appraisals useful for the comparison of alternatives and formulation of policy.

The following summary is intended to facilitate such comparison. *On the basis of our estimates, the national product could be raised one per cent above what it would otherwise be in 1970, which would add .1 per cent to the annual growth rate over the next ten years, by any one of the following means:*

Double the rate of net immigration during the next decade; or

Curtail by about one-third the reduction that might otherwise be expected in standard annual working hours; or

Reduce by one-eighth the loss of labor resulting from illness, accidents, seasonal fluctuations, excess labor in agriculture, illegal activities, concentrated long-term unemployment, and labor disputes; or

Raise the proportion of gross national product devoted to net investment 1.1 percentage points above what it would otherwise be throughout the next ten years.

This result might also be achieved by an assault on obstacles to the most effective use of resources and on immobility; by an even greater increase in research outlays than is now in prospect; by more effective allocation and organization of the research effort; or by narrowing the gap between the average level of techniques and the best known. The yield from these has not been quantified, but we believe that the effort required to add one percent to the 1970 national product through any of these channels would be major, not trivial.

Increase in education is a major source of long-term growth, but it is already too late to raise 1970 output by lengthening the education of those now attending school.

We of course cannot estimate the effort that the American people might be willing to undertake to increase the rate of growth by these means. Without an extraordinary concerted effort, however, we doubt that the effect would be "big," if by "big" is meant the order of magnitude suggested by an increase from 3 per cent to 4 per cent, or from 4 per cent to 5 per cent. This is not a surprising conclusion. There is no reason to expect an increase in growth out of proportion to the increase in the forces that produce growth. An increase from 3 per cent to 4 per cent is an increase of one-third; an increase from 3 per cent to 5 per cent is an increase of two-thirds. The authors would not accept this criterion of bigness. We consider differences much smaller than this important and, if achieved by means that are worth their cost, well worth seeking.

*   *   *   *

Economic growth is a good thing, and it is tempting to elevate any good thing to the state of a goal of national policy. The main point of our paper is that the establishment of such a goal is wise only if the benefits of the "good thing" are worth its costs.   We have neither invented nor discovered the costs.   In fact, we suppose that consciousness of these costs has weighed in the decisions not to undertake the measures that might have given us more rapid growth in the past.

We should refer here to one kind of benefit and one kind of cost that we have not mentioned but that may be very important.   There may be value in having a "national goal" aside from the benefits of achieving any particular goal and almost without regard to what the goal is.   The goal may be inspiring, give "point" to life, and serve as a common bond holding the society together.   This may be a benefit even though at the present stage of history our psychological need would be better served by a goal less materialistic and less parochial than the growth of the American economy.

There is a limit to the number of goals that the American people or any people can pursue, the number of crusades they can engage in.   There is a limit to our supply of leadership for "pointing the way" and to the supply of attention and followership.   In this sense, any goal is proposed at the expense of others that are or might have been advanced, and the cost of elevating accelerated economic growth to the front rank of goals is that something else is deprived of that position.   The number of goals calling for our attention is large—to help set the underdeveloped world on the path of economic progress, to reduce the barriers of nationalism and racialism, to strengthen our national security, to improve the lives we lead with our immense flow of goods and services, to set a floor of economic security and welfare for all.   We need not feel guilty of negativism or passivity if we decide that accelerating growth is not one of our most critical needs.

In closing, the authors repeat what was said at the outset.   We do not, in this paper, attempt to decide what the public attitude toward the rate of growth should be.   This is a question that the people must decide, referring to the kinds of considerations discussed here but also in the end expressing their own values, their own views of what is worth what.

8

TECHNOLOGICAL CHANGE

THOMAS J. WATSON, JR.

8

THE RAPID *pace of technological change is one of the significant facts of the last half of the twentieth century. To analyze its effect on our national objectives, the Commission turned to Thomas J. Watson, Jr., President of International Business Machines Corporation, a businessman who sees technology at first hand. His chapter outlines a program for encouraging its development and cushioning its impact.*

Mr. Watson's panel is listed below. He takes responsibility for the views expressed.

PANEL

DAVID L. COLE, partner, Cole, Morrill & Berman and member of the bar of the State of New Jersey; Director, Federal Mediation and Conciliation Service, 1952-53.

CHARLES H. PERCY, President, Bell and Howell Company.

EMANUEL R. PIORE, Vice President for Research and Engineering, International Business Machines Corporation.

WALTER P. REUTHER, President, United Automobile, Aircraft, and Agricultural Implement Workers of America.

GEORGE P. SHULTZ, Professor of Economics, University of Chicago.

TECHNOLOGICAL CHANGE

THOMAS J. WATSON, JR.

I

INTRODUCTION

Technological change—a modern-sounding term—has been with us since the dawn of civilization. It is as old as a better stone-age axe and as new as a transistor radio—as commonplace as a can opener and as complex as a space vehicle. In its simplest sense, technological change may be thought of as the development of a better way of doing a known job or the discovery of how to do a previously impossible one. While not actually science, it draws heavily on science for its innovations.

The most discussed aspect of technological change, at least since the Second World War, is what we loosely call automation. This word generally describes the automatic linking of an industrial process to a device which checks the process and adjusts it to the desired standard. Automation in industry has greatly accelerated the whole process of technological change in our society. And many experts feel that the real impact of automated devices hasn't yet been fully felt, even in our technologically-advanced economy.

Technology has brought with it both great progress in better living and working conditions and a certain number of very real problems. We have only to look at recent history to see what amazing human progress has been made in a very short time. Just a century ago, steam and water power provided less than one-quarter of the energy needed for all production. Men and animals supplied the rest, with men giving by far the greater share. Today in the United States machines supply 98 per cent of all power for industrial work. Men have been freed, at least in our country, from much heavy physical labor. The average work week has been reduced from 60 hours in 1890 to 40 hours today and it will be reduced even further. More important, most workers today have safer, and generally more interesting, jobs than they had just a few years ago.

Technological change has not always brought a better life for all in the past. For this reason, it deserves more of our attention today than ever before. The population of the Western World remained approximately the same from 1200-1700 A.D. In the past 100 years, it has almost tripled. Out of this phenomenal growth has risen the huge working population of the United States and Western Europe.

And so while the automatic Jacquard loom of 150 years ago could move weavers from the hearth to the factory, the numbers involved were few and the movement slow. Now mechanisms available or predicted may, if not controlled, cause real displacement in the working population of this country. Some of these displacements have already taken place and we must do our best to protect all of our citizens today and in the future.

II

THE RECENT PAST

If there is any one factor most responsible for the phenomenal economic progress of the United States in the twentieth century, it is the enthusiasm with which we as a people have tried to create better ways and conditions of working and living. We have always wanted to do things more quickly, go places more quickly, and make more and better goods available more quickly. As a result, we have consistently removed more and more human energy from the production equation.

Today, the average worker in the United States works shorter hours, turns out more goods, receives higher wages, and has more energy harnessed and working for him than a worker anywhere else in the world. He is also backed up with huge capital expenditures—over $308 billion in the past decade alone. Equipment behind the average worker has increased by 139 per cent in the past fifty years and by 33 per cent in the last ten years alone.

This approach—supporting the U. S. factory worker with a maximum of power and tooling, management planning, and healthy environment— has been called the "American Use of Americans." It is a vital factor in allowing us to compete with foreign wage rates not even one-half— and in some cases not one-fourth—as high as our own. It has enabled us to increase output per man-hour over 35 per cent in the last ten years and at the same time employ more people than ever before in our history: 9 million more than were employed in 1950, 21 million more than were employed in 1940. It is enabling us this year to produce four times as many goods and services as we did fifty years ago—almost 40 per cent more than we did just ten years ago.

Even more exciting is the fact that technological development is continuing to help in the human upgrading process so precious to us in America. By taking over more of the mechanical production job, automation can, if properly applied and understood, give us the opportunity to put more production people into better jobs. Today, for example, over 20 per cent of the working force are classified as professional, technical, or managerial—whereas only 17.6 per cent were so classified ten years ago, and this upgrading process will continue. As the jobs requiring heavy physical labor or dangerous and boring work are taken over by machines, the challenge to America to put the displaced workers into interesting upgraded jobs is tremendous.

III

THE NEXT DECADE

The progress of the past has been amazing and fruitful. The next ten years may well bring about technological changes which will make that past progress seem small indeed. This will result from the rapidly closing gap between new knowledge and its direct application to our life. The principle of the vacuum tube was understood around the turn of the century, but it was not used in any major way until after the First World War. On the other hand, the transistor was discovered in 1948. Within five years, it was being widely used in many types of equipment. The solar battery was hardly born before it was flying in our satellites.

Future progress will come about as it has in the past—from internal economic stimuli and the pressing competitive need to make each industrial process as efficient as possible. Along with our own internal welfare, however, there is an equally crucial incentive: our long-term conflict with our Communist adversaries. They are convinced that their system will outpace our own. While we know that they are quite a distance from doing this, we would be foolish to be complacent.

The way we direct and expand our economy is very closely connected with our ability to triumph over Communism. We know our democracy has produced more for us than any other way of life man has tried, and we should not fear competition from any system that challenges it. As a people, we believe that a free environment enables men to think and create more effectively than a rigidly controlled environment. Now we must prove this belief by producing advances across the whole spectrum of human achievement at a substantially faster rate than the Soviet Union.

While the exact extent and direction of technological change during the next decade is impossible to predict, we do know that it will continue to be a major stimulus for growth through new investment, new products, and new industries.

Consider, for example, the electronics industry, certainly a product of rapidly advancing technological innovation. Sales in this industry have skyrocketed in ten years, from roughly $2.5 billion in 1950 to well over $10 billion today. Total employment has at least doubled— over 760,000 are now employed in electronics. In the next decade, we will see other new industries spring up and present ones expand, creating many thousands of new jobs and opportunities.

We will witness accurate world-wide weather prediction and television via satellites; the development of entirely new materials in response to rocketry's requirements for extreme heat resistance; and major breakthroughs in medical research and chemistry which, hopefully, will eliminate many of today's dread diseases.

We are living in an era of unlimited possibilities for a full, happy life for all people. Technological change is one of the means by which we can achieve this. But in the highly complex, competitive, and dangerous political society of the world, we must have a sure sense of direction. For this reason we need clear, realistic national goals in the area of technological change.

IV

GOALS

I would recommend these three basic national goals in the technological area as part of the platform on which we can continue to build a strong nation and a better world:

- *Technological change should be used to improve men's lives.* We have seen that it brings both progress and problems. Our goal must be to apply new technology so that it will improve the way men live and work. Necessary adjustment to an accelerating technology must be planned and carried out with human considerations paramount.

- *Technological change should be encouraged* to meet our own increasing industrial needs, to stimulate our social and economic progress, and to face successfully the long-term challenge of international Communism.

- *Technological knowledge should be shared* so that people throughout the world, particularly in the underdeveloped countries, may improve their lives and benefit from up-to-date technology.

1. Improving men's lives through technological change. We are in a time when changes of all kinds will continue to modify the way we live and work. This we must expect. New forms of energy, new kinds of machines, and new ways of organizing production are entering our economy and our way of life. Most of these changes are welcomed when they are understood, but there is no doubt that serious human problems are created by the speed with which our established economic and social patterns are being altered.

Already there have been shifts which can to a greater or lesser degree be attributed to technological change. There is, for example, a major, continuing change in our over-all employment pattern: far fewer people are producing a steadily increasing amount of goods. During the Fifties, total output of the manufacturing industry jumped 40 per cent, yet there was only a 9 per cent increase in total employees, and these were virtually all in administration, sales, engineering, and other non-production activities. Today almost half of the non-farm labor force is employed in managerial, professional, clerical or sales jobs.

Technological change in the form of new methods, machines, and chemicals has had its most violent impact on agriculture, an area sometimes obscured by today's emphasis on space exploration, nuclear energy and electronics. One hundred years ago, it took one farmer in the United States to feed five people. Today, one farmer feeds 32. Over 1,600,000 workers—or 20 per cent of the total—have left the farms since 1950, but farm output has increased.

Service industries, too, such as transportation, retailing, finance, utilities, and government service have undergone a major transformation. Until the late 1940's, there were always more people in production industries—manufacturing, agriculture, construction and mining—than in the service group. Now there are over 25 per cent more employees in the service than in the production industries, with an increase of over five million people in less than 10 years.

Perhaps the most promising fundamental change we can observe is the increase in skilled technical and professional workers, a change which should continue to grow in scope. The number of these highly trained people jumped 58 per cent just in the past decade. This is one of the most important human benefits attributable to recent technological change. These trends will in most cases encourage more education, more skills, and allow more time for self-development to people throughout the world.

(a) *Adjustment.* Fortunately, introducing technical innovation in industry has never been a sudden process and probably never will be. In a commercial organization, technological change generally cannot be brought about without vast expenditures of capital and major re-equipping of plants. Consequently, it comes about over a period of years rather than months or days. Certainly human adjustment to it should not be forced, rushed or humiliating, but must be carefully considered and carried out. This is a clear responsibility of both management and labor.

As an outstanding union leader has said, concerning the automation aspect of technological change: "Free labor and free management, in cooperation with free government [must] . . . plan as free people to meet the problems and to realize the promise of the greater abundance that these machines will make possible."

There are many signs that industry and labor are facing up to this problem of far-sighted adjustment to technological change. An outstanding experiment going on at the present time is the joint automation committee set up by a prominent meat processor and the unions. The committee is studying the effects of closing several out-dated plants, the possibility of workers retraining for new jobs and equipment, and job placement elsewhere when necessary. Whatever the outcome, this will serve as a useful laboratory model for further enlightened management-labor cooperation in planning for technological change.

(b) Displacement. Viewed in broad perspective, technological displacement is presently not a vast national problem. Our expanding economy has, decade after decade, absorbed into useful employment the overwhelming majority of the rapidly increasing work population, and this has facilitated human adjustment to technological change.

But we must not ignore the fact that technological displacement is a problem in some areas now—and the problem may increase in the future. It is likely to be most acute and worthy of special attention in depressed areas or in pockets of surplus labor. We must meet the problems of these areas, whether caused by technological change or by some other factor. As a human, practical matter, we must give sympathetic and prompt attention to the over-all problems of unemployment, for whatever reasons they occur.

The existing aids to depressed areas—governmental technical assistance, special consideration in awarding government contracts, and loans by the Small Business Administration—should be continued. But these programs must be vigorously supplemented by new approaches to ensure positive and prompt action.

When an area has been officially judged to be "distressed," the federal government should grant tax allowance for accelerated plant depreciation (similar to that granted defense contractors in wartime) to industries moving facilities into this area. State and federal governments should consider matching programs for local private funds when local citizens initiate campaigns to attract industry to distressed areas.

The minimum disturbance to the economic functioning of the country will come about by moving industry to the people who need jobs. But when this is not effective for a given area and there is a labor shortage elsewhere, an interstate plan of coordination and a "relocation" program for individuals should be worked out under the direction of the U. S. Departments of Labor and Commerce.

Depressed areas should be redeveloped in accordance with sound business and economic principles so that they will not become permanent responsibilities of the federal government. Federal guarantee of loans, and in some cases partial direct loans, seem to be the methods of assistance most in accordance with those principles. Private local groups would in such cases be directly involved and largely responsible for the business soundness of the development plans. Where necessary, federal loans would be made to individuals for relocation purposes, as well as to business and communities for development purposes. This approach has been applied successfully in Great Britain for many years.

A real and continuing effort should be made to improve both the benefits and duration of payments under federal-state unemployment insurance plans. Supplemental unemployment benefits might soften the effects of future lay-offs in certain industries. With an increasingly mobile work force, severance pay should be flexibly administered, with company and employee working together so that maximum benefit towards re-employment may be derived from the funds involved.

It has been suggested that a top-level commission of industry, labor and government be set up to study the effects of technological change upon our people and recommend appropriate action. If such a study cannot be effectively and promptly carried out by existing governmental departments, such a commission would be highly desirable. I would hope that the President would direct the appropriate departments to undertake this study at once. The private sectors of the economy—including both business and labor—should be called upon to take whatever voluntary action is needed. The President should then incorporate the appropriate recommendations of this study into his legislative program. To make such a program effective, business, labor and other interested segments of our economy must cooperate to the fullest possible extent. If such an effort does not produce concrete results, the new commission approach should be adopted.

American industry is accepting increasing responsibility for full employment in the United States. This trend must continue, for it is a national responsibility to ensure safe, interesting, and profitable jobs to all Americans who want to work.

2. Encouraging technological change. In a dictatorial economy, all aspects of production, education, finance, trade—and society itself, for that matter—can be manipulated to emphasize technological development or any other goal. But in our free society we have a more complex problem. How can we derive the maximum benefits of technological change and still make the appropriate social adjustments without endangering basic freedoms and human dignity? The answer is not a simple or quick one.

(a) Private industry. First and foremost, we must clearly recognize what has encouraged technological advances in our past and made us the most productive nation in history. The magic ingredient is our competitive enterprise environment, the most powerful force ever known for stimulating individual and cooperative efforts to make innovations for the benefit of mankind. It encourages and rewards those enterprises which make successful changes, and punishes or eliminates the inefficient who fall behind. Our patent laws, protecting for a specified time any individual achievements, are valuable elements of this environment. So are the anti-trust laws, which help maintain both the competitive stimulus to innovation and the competitive mechanism for sharing the fruits of technological change with the consumer. But we must not be satisfied with present strengths—we must build on them.

The federal government should encourage the updating of our capital equipment. Liberalized depreciation allowances should be given consideration as a means to this end when they would encourage new capital commitments and meet a need for increased funds for capital expenditure. Depreciation allowances should be kept under constant review to ensure that useful equipment life for tax purposes is realistic in terms of industrial practice.

We must continue to press for more liberal international trade policies both at home and abroad. These will broaden the application of technical innovations in the United States and in the developing nations. On the other hand, unimaginative and short-sighted tariff protection of marginal industries will neither strengthen our own economy nor win new markets or new converts to our way of life. While we must further our trend toward more liberal policies, the government must also give prompt consideration to helping our non-competitive industries re-orient their production capabilities into new areas.

(b) Government and defense spending. The federal government today plays by far the most significant role in the whole area of technological change. More than 60 per cent of all expenditures for research and development are now made through the Department of Defense, Atomic Energy Commission, National Aeronautics and Space Agency, and other federal agencies. These funds are certainly a most powerful and direct stimulus to technological change. As such, their administration is a key factor in shaping both our technological resources and our economy. The federal government's contract and administrative procedures, however, were originally designed primarily for procurement and purchase of weapons and equipment, such as airplanes and reactors. Consequently, they have done little to ensure that our technological capabilities and resources will be properly balanced and appropriate to our total national requirements.

The government should consider these suggestions to encourage technological change: First, within the government one group or agency should be made responsible for developing a national policy to support and encourage our technological effort. Increased support must be given to fundamental, basic research. While the National Science Foundation is now responsible for guiding and encouraging such basic research, perhaps its role should be expanded to include both basic and applied science, independent of any immediate departmental procurement needs. The government must understand the shape of the over-all national technology and determine what steps should be taken to strengthen or modify it, which areas should be accentuated, and what specific programs are needed.

Second, specific provisions for applied research and exploratory development should be included in certain government-supported projects. These are activities which translate new scientific knowledge into practical goods, procedures, and systems. There has been a lack of emphasis in the past, stemming directly from a "get-it-done" policy: "deliver *this* equipment with *these* capabilities on *this* date." Over-all technical progress inevitably suffers and often the final product is outdated before it appears.

Third, we need a careful study and a new approach to the administration of competitive bidding on government-industry contracts. While American industry has continually demonstrated the beneficial stimulus of competition in producing technological change, present government bidding procedures have often proved wasteful of technical manpower and specialized industry teams. Mere preparation of involved government bids has often occupied some of the nation's best technical minds in several companies for months on end. In defense areas, we must be as economical with our technological experts as with our technological dollars. We can certainly protect the American tradition of equal economic opportunity without being handcuffed to inappropriate and outdated contracting formulas.

Relationships between government and industry will never be simple, but they can and must be flexible. Responsibilities must be clearly spelled out on both the government and business sides. And finally, both groups must honestly look for ways to encourage our best technical minds to serve in government as well as in industry. Such encouragement must include both financial rewards and appropriate environment for creative work.

(c) Education. In the past, educators could plan reasonably well to prepare the student for a lifetime career as clerk, factory worker, mechanical engineer, or salesman. Most jobs and the qualifications were fairly constant. For example, the likelihood of radical change being required of a machinist or clerk was remote. New types of jobs were quite rare and generally involved very few people. Today this is no longer true. Educators at all levels now realize that education must enable graduates to undertake later career changes and be flexible enough to meet them successfully. Education and re-education must be a continuing process throughout the careers of most young people in school today. The range of problems facing them in the next ten years, in economics, space science, automation, life science, and almost every other field will demand far more open minds, and far better trained ones, than ever before in man's history.

We can no longer accept bleak projections such as the recent one which suggested that among young workers joining our labor force in the Sixties, 7½ million, or more than 30 per cent, will not have completed high school. Nor can we be complacent about the prospect that over 2½ million of them will not even have finished grade school—especially considering the fact that the rate of unemployment is much higher among those with less than a high school education.

The new education essential for tomorrow's citizen cannot be the prerogative of some all-powerful, intellectual group. It must be the common right and duty of every individual, within his capabilities. We cannot afford or permit educationally underdeveloped citizens in any part of our country.

We must devote a major part of our national effort to education, for it provides the surest basis for improving America in all ways. Specifically, we need additional schools, more and better teachers, higher salaries for them, and better instructional aids such as films and demonstration equipment. We also need continued and expanded education studies to provide more effective teaching methods. Where individual states cannot handle the financing adequately, there is certainly a federal responsibility to do so. Better education is by far the most fruitful and positive means of giving Americans the greatest chance to make a maximum contribution to the development of our country and the greatest chance for full employment throughout their lives.

Since jobs will change materially during the working lives of many in the future, a reassessment of our vocational education should be made by the states and the federal government. With the changing careers we contemplate, rigid vocational training seems to be of doubtful value.

College training of engineers must aim toward a far more broadly-oriented graduate. Engineering education must include more of both the basic sciences, such as physics and mathematics, and the humanities. Every major defense failure in technological development since the Second World War can be traced back to technical *and* management problems, not to technical problems alone. There have not been, nor are there today, enough top policy people in government or industry who on the one hand have been educated to understand the technological problems of our time, and on the other, possess the broad executive training, ability, and experience to plan and direct their solution.

3. Sharing technological change. The years since World War II have shown that it is impossible to win the world-wide political battle simply through alliances and financial or material aid. We must also win the battle for men's minds. But we must win it by offering these minds knowledge, skills, and opportunities to learn. One important facet of this process certainly lies in technological progress. If we help other nations to create stronger economies, happier and more prosperous citizens, the magic mottoes and platitudes of Communism will fall on deaf ears. If, on the other hand, we have as allies developing nations with a very small, rich ruling class and very large, very poor working class, our alliances will be frail indeed.

The quickest route toward building up these less prosperous countries is through broad and generous sharing of technological change. In the past, our own progress and strength have drawn heavily on the economic area: more goods and a better life for more people. Without a dedicated extension of this tradition to the fragile new countries of Africa and Asia, as well as to the underdeveloped nations in our own hemisphere, we cannot be successful members of today's world community.

There is still much want, suffering, and sickness throughout the world. A completely preventable, curable, and controllable disease such as malaria remains a grave threat to the lives of more than a billion people. There are still ninety countries or territories—with almost half of the world's humanity—which have bare survival incomes averaging about $100 a year per person. In struggling countries such as the Congo, with its population of 14,000,000, only a handful of people have university degrees. Unless we solve world problems such as these, the Communists will solve them for us.

In sharing technological progress, industry and private investors are in a unique position to further our political and economic goals. Foreign investment carries with it the capital, human resources, and know-how rapidly to increase the available technology in a less advanced country.

We cannot rely on private investment alone, however, to bring about orderly technological progress in underdeveloped countries. These nations need the basic structures upon which economic progress can be built—education, public works, communication networks, housing, and health services. Our government must accept an important role in providing increasing amounts of this kind of assistance.

Ten years ago, the United States took the lead in establishing a major program to "aid the efforts of the peoples of economically underdeveloped areas . . . by encouraging the exchange of technical knowledge and skills. . . ." Today we have over 5,000 technicians in almost sixty underdeveloped countries carrying out the exchange of technical information under the Mutual Security Program, operating in a variety of fields including agriculture, education, public administration, labor, communications and community development. The United States also strongly supports the technical assistance program of the United Nations and the Organization of American States.

But there is still much left to do. I have three specific recommendations:

First, more United States technicians should be sent abroad. I recognize that it is very difficult to get top technical people to accept relatively low government salaries and the rigors of living in less-developed areas, but this problem can be solved. For example, a number of university contracts have proved effective in maintaining a steady flow of technically trained people abroad. This approach certainly should be continued and expanded.

Second, the various programs for exchanging technical assistance must be more effectively coordinated. With aid coming from a variety of sources—government, the United Nations, and private organizations—there is a dangerous tendency for an unwarranted concentration in one area and a bypassing of other equally serious needs.

Finally, we must expand our exchange of technical information and more aggressively publicize our very real achievements in aid to these areas. The Soviets have recently leaped in with a substantial program of technical assistance, concentrating on those areas which bring them the greatest immediate public recognition. They support industrial projects, such as a steel mill or a cement plant or a factory. They conveniently overlook those less exciting but basic areas of health, education, communication, balance of payments support, and other public works which we stress. We must be sure our efforts are fairly presented, while still representing a balanced and useful development program.

V

SUMMARY

The three national goals recommended in the area of technological change—improving men's lives through it, encouraging it, and sharing it openly throughout the world—are deceptively easy to state. Achieving them even in part, however, will demand dedication, ingenuity, and sacrifice of special interest.

These goals cannot be pondered or debated or deliberated endlessly over the next decade. We can spend a lifetime pointing out the administrative complexities and problems involved. But while the problems are being debated, the opportunities may well be lost. Technological change continues to promise unparalleled leadership for the United States, the defensive strength needed to ensure a peaceful world, and untold abundance for all peoples, if we recognize and promote it as a basic national policy.

Finally, we must remember that technological change is man-made and must be man-controlled. Its total purpose: the benefit of mankind. We cannot afford to let the interest and excitement of the process distract us from its main purpose, the improvement of man.

9

FARM POLICY FOR THE SIXTIES

LAUREN K. SOTH

9

THIS CHAPTER *is a lucid statement of the farm problem and a proposal for meeting it. It is written by Lauren K. Soth, Editorial Page Editor of the* Des Moines Register and Tribune, *and author of the popular book,* Farm Trouble. *Mr. Soth was awarded a Pulitzer Prize for his editorials in 1955. He is Chairman of the Agriculture Committee of the National Planning Association.*

Mr. Soth was advised by the panel listed below. He takes responsibility for the views expressed.

PANEL

ERNEST T. BAUGHMAN, Vice President, Federal Reserve Bank of Chicago.

CHARLES E. BISHOP, Head of Department of Agricultural Economics, North Carolina State College.

ROBERT L. CLODIUS, Chairman, Department of Agricultural Economics, University of Wisconsin.

OSCAR HELINE, farmer, Marcus, Iowa; formerly, member of Farm Bureau State Board.

PAUL C. JOHNSON, Editor, *Prairie Farmer.*

FARM POLICY FOR THE SIXTIES

LAUREN K. SOTH

Agriculture is in trouble—the same nagging trouble of surpluses and low net income which has plagued farmers in three of the last four decades. In the Forties, the extraordinary demands of war, and then of postwar rehabilitation abroad, hid the underlying imbalance in commercial farming. But the Fifties saw a return to the surplus problem with a vengeance.

Farm families have not shared in the prosperity of the last decade. Their incomes have drifted lower in real purchasing power, while incomes of the non-farm population have climbed.

A large number of farm families, to be sure, are not greatly affected by commercial market conditions. They are *chronically* poor. The sweeping changes in farm population, in technology, in marketing of farm products, in government farm programs, have not shaken the hard core of poverty out of agriculture. This is still the nation's largest and most stubborn bloc of penury.

In setting goals for the future, America surely must place high priority on (1) achieving a better balanced and more stable commercial agriculture, and (2) liquidating its rural poverty.

I

THE PERFORMANCE OF AGRICULTURE

Yet by most standards of public measurement, agriculture in the early Sixties stands as a triumph of economic achievement. In considering national goals, one may ask, what performance does the nation expect from an industry—any industry?

Abundant production? Farmers in the United States have confounded the gloomy prophet Malthus, who said, "the power of population is indefinitely greater than the power in the earth to produce subsistence for man."

The U. S. public enjoys the lowest real food costs—in terms of human effort expended—of any people in the world, with one of the world's richest and most nutritious diets. Only about 21 percent of average consumer income is spent for food, as compared with 23 percent in the mid-Thirties. (If government expenditures for price supports are added to retail food costs, the current percentage rises to 22.) If Americans were eating the same foods as in the Thirties, food would absorb only 16 percent of the average family budget. There has been a massive shift from the cheaper, starchy foods such as bread and potatoes to the more luxurious, high-protein, high-vitamin foods: meat, milk, fruits, and vegetables. Moreover, the homemaker receives better quality and more packaging, processing and pre-cooking than before in the food she buys from the supermarket. So cost of the food alone has declined even more than these figures indicate.

Ability to serve the nation in an emergency? U. S. agriculture has vast reserves of stored grain, cotton and other products—available to meet a threat of war or other disaster, and for relief to other countries. It has even more impressive reserves in *capacity to produce.* Who can forget the magnificent response of agriculture to the demands of World War II? Today, farmers could do even better if called upon to expand their output—assuming the necessary increases in fertilizer, gasoline, machinery and other supplies were on hand. The Department of Agriculture estimates that if all farmers applied technical knowledge as fully as the top 25 percent, food and fiber production could be doubled! And output now is running six to eight per cent greater than can be consumed at present price levels.

Capacity to serve U. S. foreign policy by providing assistance to underdeveloped countries? Food and the ability to produce food are becoming major weapons in the cold war with Communism, as the opposing ideologies compete for influence in the hungry countries. In this war we are well armed. U. S. farmers are producing currently at a rate which accumulates large excess supplies of foodstuffs beyond domestic needs. These foodstuffs have become an important form of foreign economic assistance.

More significant for the long run, U. S. agriculture has the world's most highly developed system of farm research and education in the federal-state cooperative experiment stations and extension services. U. S. agriculture could deploy an army of engineers, agronomists, animal nutritionists and other technologists to serve the national purposes. About 1,250 agricultural technologists are already working overseas for the International Cooperation Administration. The industry also has a corps of more than a million able farm managers, who understand the newer technology and how to apply it under practical conditions. No other nation has the resources, not half the resources, for teaching others how to produce, store and distribute food.

Ability to increase productivity, thus freeing manpower for production of other goods and services? Agriculture has freed more than one-third of its labor force from farm work in the last 20 years. Output per man-hour in this industry has been going up in the last 25 years at the rate of about five per cent a year, as against less than three per cent in the non-farm sector of the economy. Since 1950, productivity in farming has been increasing at the rate of about nine per cent a year. Productivity gains in agriculture as a whole in recent years have been greater than in any other major industry. The value of output per man in farming still is below that of non-farm industry, because of excess labor in farming, but the difference is narrowing.

Today it takes less than seven million workers (ten per cent of the nation's work force) to produce an over-abundance of food. In Western Europe the percentage needed to produce an adequate supply is close to 25, and in the Soviet Union more than 40.

Stable production without sudden changes in employment or in purchases of materials and services from other industries? What industry can match agriculture in stability of output? There are ups and downs in production of some crops in localized areas because of weather. But U.S. agriculture as a whole produces at a remarkably stable rate year in and year out. And technology to some degree even is reducing the effect of weather as a cause of crop failure. The trend of total output is strongly upward (25 percent higher in 1959 than in 1950), and the trend of man-hours worked on farms is steadily downward (25 percent lower in 1959 than in 1950). But farming does not deliver sudden, disrupting shocks to the economy, as for example the metal-working industries often do.

Even when net farm income declines, as it has in the last decade, production is maintained, and there is no sharp reduction in purchases of fertilizer, gasoline, drugs, insecticides and other production supplies from non-farm industry. Purchases of consumer goods by farm families are reduced. But agriculture, being largely an industry of self-employed small businessmen, does not throw a hundred thousand men out of work and onto unemployment compensation (and relief rolls), as do major manufacturing industries. Farm people do not queue up in bread lines or social security offices. They tighten their belts and go on producing.

II

SOURCES AND SYMPTOMS OF THE FARM PROBLEM

Agriculture, in short, meets the highest standards of business performance in the public interest, when measured by these criteria.

What's wrong then? If agriculture is such a paragon in the U. S. economy, why is it in trouble? Why is there a farm problem? Why do we have government farm programs providing subsidies to farmers?

Inability to control output. The answer, simply, is that the modern economic system does not reward farm people according to the excellence of their performance in behalf of the public weal. In fact, it penalizes them for such performance.

Let it be said that farmers do not produce abundantly and with such impressive regularity because they are nobler than the rest of us. They can't do anything else but produce abundantly because of the structure of the industry: small, independent, competitive firms.

America has more than four million farm enterprises. Farm businesses are so numerous and so varied that they cannot act in unison to exercise appreciable discipline over production or marketing. An individual farmer can do only one thing to increase his income—produce as much (in the aggregate) as possible as cheaply as possible—although he can, of course, shift to different products as price incentives vary.

The great advances in agricultural technology of the last 30 years have not changed the structure of the industry. The technological revolution in manufacturing moved production from small home enterprises into large factories with hired labor and to aggregations of factories, with centralized decision-making. But the revolution in farming has been different. Although the average size of farm has increased greatly, the industry is still overwhelmingly made up of individual family farms, with the farmer and his family providing most of the management and labor.

When each farm operator strives to produce more, and does, the result is less income for the industry as a whole. This fact of farm economics seems most difficult for the public and even farmers themselves to understand. It conflicts with widely-held beliefs about the nature of the economic system and with the American set of values, and perhaps this is why our minds are so impervious to it. We believe the results *should* be good when every farmer tries to produce to the utmost, because the virtues of hard work and more output are intrinsic to our American ethic. And the results *are* good—for the rest of us—but not for the farming industry. Our folklore has not caught up with the facts of economics in the mid-twentieth century.

The demand for farm products in this rich, well-fed country is sharply inelastic. The public will not consume more than it is now consuming except at drastically lower prices. When the supply of food goes up five per cent, prices to farmers drop by as much as 15 to 20 per cent on the average. Returns to producers are less for a large output than for a small one. In 1959, U. S. consumers used 16 percent more food than in 1952, but they paid farmers less money for it. And farm production expenses were considerably higher in 1959 than in 1952.

But despite the clear evidence that more output means less income, farm production continues to march upward inexorably.

The recent decline in farm income. As production and productivity per man advance and farm income declines, more and more people leave the farm. There are about a million fewer farm-operator families now than there were ten years ago, and about five million fewer people on farms. Thus the national farm income is divided among fewer families. Yet for people still living on farms the income disparity as compared with non-farm people has widened.

In 1946, forty-one percent of all farm-operator families were in the lowest one-fifth of all families in the United States on the income scale. In 1953, the percentage had risen to 50 and in 1957 to 55.*

In 1946, 1947 and 1948, income per person living on farms averaged about 60 percent as much as income per person of the non-farm population. This was the highest ratio for any three-year period for which the Department of Agriculture has made estimates. (The farm income figures include income from non-farm sources, as well as non-money income in the form of food, fuel and house rent, for which a cash value is calculated. The non-farm income estimates include income received from agriculture, mainly rent, by people who are not engaged in farming.)

In 1957, 1958 and 1959, income per person on farms had dropped to about 45 percent of income per person of the non-farm population. In 1959 average income per person for the non-farm population was $2,216, and for the farm population $965.**

A more precise way to examine the trend in farm income is to eliminate from the statistics those farm families who produce little for market and whose incomes from farming remain low in good times and bad.

Farmers with annual sales of $2,500 or more who produce about 90 percent of farm products marketed had net incomes from farming averaging about $5,200 in 1949-51. In 1959 their net incomes had dropped to $4,200.

If income from non-farm sources is included, these commercial farm families averaged about $6,000 in 1949-51, compared with an average of $5,300 for all non-farm families. In 1959, average income of commercial farm families totaled $5,800, but the average non-farm family income had risen to about $7,600.***

The reduction in numbers of farms and of farm people has not been rapid enough to keep per capita or per farm family income from declining relative to non-farm income.

Underemployment and poverty. The widening disparity between farm and non-farm income during recent years is a result of soaring farm production against an inelastic demand. That is, it is a market problem, a commercial problem.

A large share of agriculture is but little affected by these changes in market conditions. Half the farms produce only 10 percent of the products for market. People living on these "non-commercial" farms did not profit from the boom times of the Forties, and they are not much worse off today. Despite heavy migration from such farms in recent years, the number of people remaining is excessive in relation

---

* U. S. House Committee on Agriculture, figures from census reports.
** U. S. Department of Agriculture, *The Farm Income Situation.*
*** Estimates by Walter W. Wilcox, senior economist, Legislative Reference Service, Library of Congress.

to the need for labor. Even at a much higher price level than the present one they could not earn enough from farming to make a decent living.

This lower half of agriculture is a serious blight on the U. S. economy. Some of the worst slum conditions in America today exist in rural areas of the Southern states and in spots all through the country. Many of these families are living at a level little better than that of people in Southern Italy, Greece or other Mediterranean countries—per capita incomes averaging $200 a year or less—this in a country where average income per person is above $2,000 per year!

This poverty sector of agriculture is a burden on the rest of the country, because it imposes welfare costs both in the home areas and in areas where migrants resettle. People from these areas are poorly fitted for city jobs, and they often add to the problems of delinquency and crime.

Because agriculture is an industry of free competition, it is easy to enter the industry—on a subsistence level—but it is often not easy to get out. Lack of opportunities in the rest of the economy tends to hold people in agriculture.

This is a costly waste of human resources which is too often over-looked or ignored. The four million persons listed as unemployed by the Bureau of Labor Statistics during 1960 do not represent the full degree of unemployment in the economy. Perhaps a million or more potential workers are living on subsistence-type farms where they produce little.

The extremely low incomes and excessive numbers of workers in agriculture are partly a result of restrictions in the non-farm labor markets. Agriculture is a free enterprise industry, a free competition industry. Many business organizations and labor unions are able to restrict entry and exercise control over prices and wages. These practices limit the opportunities for farm workers to move into non-farm jobs. So agriculture bears a disproportionate share of the burden of underemployment in the economy.

To some extent, subsidies to agriculture and the special adjustment programs for farmers are costs that society bears because it does not permit a free flow of labor out of agriculture into other kinds of employment.

There is no real solution to the problem of rural poverty without transferring many farm people to non-farm jobs. Some may be helped to become more productive in agriculture by education and financial aid so they can get control of larger amounts of land and capital. But in a general agricultural condition of surplus production, this can hardly be a satisfactory solution for many. To the extent that low producers in agriculture are made more productive, that merely intensifies the general problem of glut in commercial agriculture. Therefore, we must look for ways and means of helping large numbers of people on small, unproductive farms into non-farm occupations.

The solution to this problem of underemployment in agriculture obviously cannot be found within agriculture. It is a problem for the nation as a whole.

Better employment information and counseling, subsidies for movement of families to places where jobs are available, and the development of manufacturing industries in areas of surplus farm labor all would help. However, the fundamental need is for a higher rate of economic growth in the economy generally and a nearer-full-employment economy.

At best, the withdrawal of excess resources from agriculture is bound to be a long process. Agriculture has adjusted rapidly to the newer technology in the last 20 years—a reduction of its labor force in the magnitude of one-third since 1940! But assuming this rate of adjustment continues, agriculture is likely to be afflicted with surpluses and low prices at least during the next decade and probably longer.

The process of substituting capital for labor and reducing the numbers of farms has a long way to go. It is probable that production of farm products could continue to increase even if the amount of labor in agriculture were reduced by another 50 percent! *

The basic American farm policy. The tremendous rise in agricultural production and in the productivity of agriculture per unit of labor and per unit of total inputs did not come about solely by virtue of the competitive nature of the industry. Few Americans realize that the federal and state governments have been pumping new investment into agriculture for many years. This new investment has been in the form of improved technology and education, the most productive forms of investment.

From the very beginning, the United States adopted policies aimed toward a more productive agriculture. Not the least revolutionary of the ideas which guided the Founding Fathers was the idea that farming is an important industry and an honorable occupation and should be fostered. Jefferson's ideal of an independent yeomanry serving the nation as the foundation of democratic government was a powerful influence on our early development.

When America broke with the Old World, it broke with the idea that farming is a second-class occupation and that farmers are second-class people. Land was opened up for development by individual owner-operators. This policy was implemented by the Homestead Act of 1862 in the middle of the Civil War. In the same year came the Morrill Act which established the Land Grant college system of schools of agriculture. Later these state agricultural colleges became the key-

---

* "Our Embarrassing Agricultural Abundance" by Earl Heady, paper presented at Midwest Economic meetings, 1960.

stones of the federal-state agricultural experiment stations and extension educational services.

This network of agricultural research and education has had profound, and generally unappreciated, effects on U. S. economic development. It put tremendous sinews behind what became the nation's implicit farm policy of cheap and abundant food. The public promotion of technological improvement in agriculture was not intended as a cheap food policy. It was not intended as a subsidy to consumers. It was intended as a benefit to the rural economy, an encouragement to rural development, an expression of the Jeffersonian ideal and of the American vision of a farming industry of independent businessmen-laborers instead of the master-peasant system of Europe. All the legislation was written with the express objective of helping the farmer.

The Land Grant college system and other efforts to improve agricultural productivity *have* been of benefit to agriculture. When the demand for food was more elastic and when foreign markets were expanding under the Pax Britannica, plowing new knowledge into agriculture helped raise farmers' incomes.

But under today's conditions, with rich, diet-conscious consumers, this furious rate of technological advance in agriculture is placing a heavy burden on the farm population. It is yielding large returns to the public, however, in the form of cheap and abundant food.

This is a major factor in the present commercial farm problem. Critics of the price support and subsidy programs often say the farm problem was caused by government programs. That is partly true. The price supports of recent years have encouraged new investment in agriculture. Federal programs of land reclamation, soil conservation and technical assistance have stimulated output. And the long-run research and education programs have provided a continuing flow of new technical knowledge into practice on the farms.

The U. S. policy of agricultural development thus has expedited the continuous increases in output which are inherent in the competitive nature of the farming industry made up of small, independent units.

III

GOALS IN FARM POLICY

As we look at the next decade, what are the choices in agricultural policy? What goals should we seek?

We may assume that the American people want to maintain a strong, progressive agriculture producing abundantly. We may also assume that Americans, out of their basic beliefs in equality of opportunity and fairness, want farm people to be able to earn real incomes on a par with incomes in the rest of the economy—for equal ability and effort.

These are long-range goals—indeed, one might say these *always* have been goals in the American society.

At this stage of history, the chief problem, in moving toward these goals is to achieve a greater measure of equality of income opportunity for people now living on farms. This does not mean providing opportunity in farming for all who now live on farms—but opportunity in the economy *somewhere*.

It is evident that the reasons for the disparity of farm income in modern times are (1) overproduction of farm products in relation to the demand and (2) excess numbers of people in agriculture.

As short-range or intermediary goals for agriculture in the next decade, public policy should be directed toward:

1. *Liquidating the problem of farm poverty.*

"Liquidating" is a strong word, but it is not too strong a word to use as a goal for a nation as rich as ours. By the end of this decade the United States ought to have provided non-farm jobs for about 1½ million farm operators who now earn less than $1,500 a year in farming. There will be some migration from agriculture at the higher income levels. And some of the farmers on inadequate farms will be able to acquire larger operating units and to improve their incomes in farming. But as a general goal, 1½ million farm units eliminated seems a reasonable goal for the Sixties.

2. *Bringing farm production into reasonable balance with demand at prices approximating the 1959-60 ratio of prices of farm products to prices farmers pay.*

In 1959-60 prices of farm products averaged about 80 percent of "parity," as measured by the index computed by the U. S. Department of Agriculture. Farm output is running about seven per cent above the amount that would sell in a free market at current prices. The excess is being stored or disposed of in noncommercial channels by the government.

The goal sought—a seven per cent cut in total output—is a modest one, but it will be difficult to achieve. The price target also is modest. A somewhat higher level of prices of farm products in the market place would be desirable as a means of accomplishing goal No. 3. But considering the difficulties of supply management in agriculture, it seems wiser to shoot for a less ambitious goal at first.

3. *Raising real net incomes per person of commercial farm families on the order of ten per cent above the 1959-60 level.*

If efforts to accomplish No. 2 are successful, only modest government price and income supports would be needed to achieve No. 3—and perhaps could be nearly eliminated. The goal should be to keep farm income per capita rising at least as fast as the national income thereafter.

*   *   *

In line with these goals, all public policies designed to raise farm income in the Sixties should be consistent with (1) restraint of current agricultural output and (2) facilitating the transfer of labor from farming to other occupations.

Income-support programs which tend to increase farm production and to prevent the movement of people out of farming would hinder needed adjustments. Some income-support programs of recent years have stimulated output. However, there is no evidence that these programs have slowed the migration of people from agriculture. The disparity of farm income has been so large in most years that the incentives to abandon farming have remained strong.

Policies designed to bring about adjustment of human resources in agriculture, on the other hand, should not be such as to reduce current net income per farm family. If the present surpluses were to be disposed of by the government on domestic markets, and if all farm price and income-support programs were abandoned, this might speed up the movement of people out of farming. But the social cost would be unacceptable.

If the present level of farm income continues for another ten years, or drops lower, many of the best minds and most able managers will leave agriculture. The consequences might be ultimately to reverse the present farm problem of overabundance to one of scarcity and high-cost production.

Public policy should be designed, therefore, to keep agriculture an attractive enterprise, without perpetuating the maladjustment which now prevails. This is no easy task, and no simple, cure-all solutions are available. Wise public policy can alleviate the current income-disparity problem and make steady progress toward solving the long-range adjustment problem.

IV

FARM ADJUSTMENT POLICIES

Land retirement. One obvious policy which is consistent with the goals set forth here is a policy of land retirement. In a sense, this *has* been an American farm policy for 30 years.

Herbert Hoover proposed in 1931 that the federal government lease submarginal cropland and permit its use for pasture only, for 21 years, to bring farm production into better balance with demand. He said there was justice in the government compensating farmers for over-expansion of output created by government demand during World War I.

In most of the years since 1931, land has been held out of production of certain crops by the acreage allotment method. Since this land was used for other crops, however, the effect was not to reduce *total* farm output. It may even have increased output by encouraging better crop rotations.

The conservation reserve "soil bank" program of recent years keeps land entirely out of production for the term of the lease. This program in 1960 retired 28 million of the nation's 360 million crop acres.

To accomplish significant reduction in farm output by retiring land, a much larger acreage must be taken out of crops or converted to less intensive use such as pasture. Probably 60 million acres of cropland would have to be retired immediately to reduce total farm output by five per cent in the next few years.

We hear a great deal about the increasing use of farm land for roads, suburban developments, and other non-crop uses. Some writers even have expressed alarm about an imminent "shortage" of farm land. This is a false alarm. New technological discovery—the development of new types of capital inputs—has increased the substitutability of capital for land. The limitations of land on food output which Ricardo and Malthus wrote about simply do not apply in the U. S. economy of today. In the sense of such limitation, the nation has a larger supply of land today than it has ever had.

Retirement of farm land tends to facilitate the retirement of people from agriculture, especially if entire farms are retired. It is a valuable supplement to the social security program as a means of enabling elderly farmers to retire gracefully. It also helps make it easier for younger farmers to "get out from under" their farming enterprises and take jobs in the city. In a sense, it is, in the phrase of Prof. Theodore W. Schultz, a "homesteads in reverse" program.

In addition to a much larger land rental program, the federal government ought to purchase sizable areas now being farmed. Much of the land which should be retired from cultivation, in the Great Plains wheat states especially, would be better husbanded for future generations under government ownership. Some of it could profitably be used as parks and recreation areas, the demand for which is mounting rapidly.

The federal government once owned this land and turned it over to private owners for farming at a time when expanding agriculture made good sense for national economic development. It makes equally good sense now to take back some of this excess cropland to public domain, seed it to grass or trees, and remove it from crop production.

Public investment in agriculture. In the same line of reasoning, the public investment in reclamation, irrigation, drainage and other projects bringing new land into crop production should be stopped. In some river development projects, justifiable on grounds of power, navigation or flood control, irrigation of land may seem wise, because the marginal cost is low. Local interests demand it. But at a time when national policy requires a reduction in farm output and land retirement, it is hard to justify any public expenditure for farm land development. Every public policy which tends toward increasing land in crops should be examined with great care.

The same could be said for public investment of any sort which tends to add resources to agriculture.

Farm research and education. As has been pointed out, the public investment in agricultural research and education has been a major factor in the upsurge of farm output. It would be logical to reduce this investment under a policy of restraint on farm production.

Research, however, is not a readily adjustable resource of production. Even if research were stopped now, new technology would continue to flow out of past research for many years to come. By the time a cessation of research took effect, the needs of the country might have changed.

Besides, although public investment was the prime mover of the great advance in agricultural productivity, to a large extent the advance is now self-sustaining through private industry. The chemical, farm equipment, and other farm-supply industries are able to carry on their own research and education. Cutting the public investment in agricultural research and education by as much as one-half probably would not curtail the inputs of new technology into agriculture appreciably in the next 20 years.

The public budget for farm research and education is not one budget —it is partly federal, partly state, partly county, partly school district. Thus no central control over this investment is feasible.

So turning off this spigot of new technology would not be easy, nor, probably, very effective.

However, the public research and educational machinery might be switched over to work more intensively on the agricultural development problems of the poor countries of the world. The problem there is not over-production but under-production and poor diets. Many of the state and federal experiment stations could well devote part of their efforts to finding improved methods, better crops and livestock for countries such as India, Pakistan, Peru and Chile.

This does not contemplate demobilization of farm research and education facilities, but a shift of focus from an area where the need presently is minimal to an area where the need is great.

Technical assistance is considered a vital part of America's foreign economic development program, which in turn is an indispensable arm of the nation's foreign policy. In the agricultural research and education setup in this country, we have a ready-made instrument for pursuing this policy. The resources of scientific and educational skills and brainpower could be spared easily from work on U. S. farm development—not only because of the surplus situation but because private firms are able to do many of the jobs these public agencies are now doing. This conversion of a public agency partly to new duties would cost relatively little in public funds, but it would require the shift of some state-financed functions to the federal government.

The public facilities for research and education in agriculture also ought to be focused more sharply on the rural poverty problem here at home. The present Rural Development Program of the federal government has made a beginning, but much more must be done.

The main task is to facilitate movement of people out of farming to more productive jobs in factories, trade and services. Sometimes this means developing jobs in the areas of excess farm labor. For those who stay in farming, technical assistance, capital and more land are needed to make them productive farmers.

In this field, there is considerable knowledge of what to do and how to do it—the main things required are larger federal appropriations and a larger effort to get the job done. The Farmers Home Administration is the logical federal agency for this task. It has 25 years experience working with low-income farmers. FHA should be given a mission to help farm people into other occupations—by loans, grants, counseling, job training, etc. Its present assignment is wholly to provide credit and technical assistance to help poor farmers become more productive and to stay in farming.

There is no valid reason for not moving vigorously on this in the Sixties. Of course, the success of this program will depend importantly on how fast the economy grows and consequently on how many non-farm jobs are made available.

So much for the long-range policies which will smooth the adjustment of agriculture.*

Supporting farm income. A more rapid rate of economic growth, plus an expanded land retirement program, plus a vigorous educational, re-training and re-employment effort to transfer under-employed farm workers to more productive work would tend to ease the commerical farm problem. But it would be a mistake to conclude that such long-range adjustment endeavors would end the surplus crisis in commercial agriculture in the near future.

The United States government has been spending on the order of two to four billion dollars annually to support prices of farm products, and to store and dispose of surpluses. Even with this expenditure, farm income has declined. If this program had not been carried on, and all

---

* Mr. Baughman is of the opinion that greater emphasis than is indicated by Mr. Soth should be placed on market forces in bringing about the necessary resource adjustments in agriculture. He believes that the primary objective of government farm policy should be to facilitate these adjustments. The chronic poverty sector of agriculture should be treated as a welfare matter as poverty is in the rest of the economy. It cannot be corrected by income-support programs.

the stored grain had gone into consumption, net farm income would have been perhaps as much as one-third lower during the Fifties, according to research economists at Iowa State University.

If price supports and related programs were abandoned (except for 30 million acres in the soil bank), farm prices and net incomes would fall 30 to 40 percent in the next few years.* "The reduction in realized net income would be borne largely by the 2.1 million farms which market 90 percent of all farm products," according to the agricultural economists who made the estimate.

With 60 or 70 million acres of cropland in the soil bank and a larger flow of government rental payments to land owners and tenants, the decline in net income would be less severe. But it still would be a staggering blow to farmers who have undergone shrinking returns for a decade.

It would be a protracted blow, not just a quick recession which would "wash things out" and from which farmers would quickly recover. Agriculture would continue in a serious depression for many years. There is no reason to believe total production would fall off in the short run. There is every reason to believe it would continue to rise for some years in spite of a drastic price decline. Continued long enough (say 20 years), of course, such a policy would reduce output—and seriously damage the productive capacity of the farm industry.

So a policy of eliminating price and income supports must be rejected as both inequitable and inconsistent with a national goal of maintaining a productive agriculture. The 90 percent of the American people who are not farmers should remember that it is far better from the consumer's viewpoint to err on the side of abundance—even if it does require some subsidies to farmers.

What is the alternative, then, to present support programs which are piling up unmanageable surpluses?

The logical alternative is effective production control which would limit market supplies and raise prices in the market place. If such control could be established, farm income could be raised to a satisfactory level—but the productive capacity always would be available if needed. Agriculture would function as most other basic industries do in a modern economy. Federal subsidies could be eliminated.

Effective supply control would not necessarily reduce total food costs to the public. Consumers would pay less in taxes, but this would be offset, probably more than offset, by higher prices in the market.

Controlling supply, however, is extremely difficult in most branches of agriculture. Production restrictions are not equally acceptable among different commodity groups. Where some measure of supply management for a commodity can be established—as in many fluid milk mar-

---

* "Farm Price and Income Projections," a report from the Department of Agriculture, Senate Document No. 77. Income projections were made by a committee of Land Grant college economists.

kets, in tobacco, and in sugar—it ought to be employed. Experimentation is needed on both public and private devices which would introduce production and marketing disciplines for certain commodities.

The center of the farm surplus problem is grain. Almost every farmer produces or can produce wheat, corn, barley, rye, grain sorghum or oats. The problem cannot be successfully approached on an individual commodity basis, therefore. Prices are interrelated. Successful supply control for one grain could be undermined by lack of control of others.

The same is true of the different kinds of livestock. Quotas on hog production without control of beef cattle would be of limited effectiveness. And livestock output is closely related to grain production.

So the grain-livestock complex in U. S. agriculture, by far the largest sector of the industry, does not lend itself easily to centralized supply management.

Because of this, there has been much searching for other solutions. Greater use of grain for industrial raw materials has its "fans." But every responsible economic study of the prospects in the last 30 years, including one by the recent presidential commission, holds forth little promise. Even with grain prices cut to half of present levels, grain's most profitable use is mainly for human food, directly, or indirectly through livestock.

In the 1960's a renewed effort, in addition to voluntary land retirement, should be made to establish restraint of grain output.

Some further reduction in acreage of wheat and feed grains by the acreage allotment method should not be ruled out. This device is clumsy and inefficient. But at least it requires farmers to cooperate in an effort to hold production in line in return for their subsidies. It is ridiculous to continue the corn program as at present, with a guaranteed price to every producer and no compliance with acreage restrictions required. A minimum requirement for price protection should be participation in the soil conservation reserve program.

Grain is in surplus in most of the large grain exporting countries. So this is a problem that cannot be solved successfully by the United States acting alone. An international program, preferably through the United Nations, to make surplus grain available free or at low cost to underdeveloped countries must be developed. Commercial agriculture in the United States and Canada eventually will be compelled to adopt extremely strict production controls if it cannot find a better way of making its surpluses useful in the world. Our present Food for Peace program has been helpful, but it is too small and it incurs the opposition of other exporting countries.

A variety of programs. What is suggested here is not a new and miraculous "farm plan" but mainly a renewed effort to make present programs work better.

To the extent that the rise in output, especially of grain, can be checked; more grain used in foreign aid; new industrial uses developed which will return reasonable prices to farmers—to that extent government storage programs to maintain prices can be phased out. (An adequate grain reserve must be maintained against war and world relief needs, however.)

Meanwhile, direct subsidies on limited quantities of output—as in Canada—might be tried for some products, as an alternative to government loans and purchases. Such payments are most feasible for producers of perishable products, such as livestock, dairy products and eggs, which cannot be stored for long periods without waste.

The minimum objective of all these efforts should be a rise in net income per farm family in line with the rise in personal income for the nation as a whole. A secondary objective should be to achieve this with as small a public subsidy as possible—by supply management, primarily.

American agriculture is a diverse industry, or rather a collection of industries, and no one method of stabilizing income will work for all parts of it. A dogmatic approach to the farm problem, therefore, is doomed to failure—whether it is the "free market" theory or tight production control. When other programs which will maintain farm incomes at present levels are thoughtfully considered, even the sloppy surplus storage and disposal programs of today don't look so bad.

The nation is confronted with a serious overproduction problem in agriculture. The problem cannot be wished away or left to "nature." The public policies of the past largely created the conditions of over-rapid advance in farm production, and they cannot be easily or quickly reversed. But the nation can, by various stop-gap measures, prevent farm families from bearing the whole cost of the necessary adjustment.

10

FRAMEWORK FOR AN URBAN SOCIETY

CATHERINE BAUER WURSTER

N O DOMESTIC *issue is more puzzling or intricate than improving our rapidly growing cities and suburban areas. To prepare a framework within which the necessary decisions might better be made, the Commission selected Catherine Bauer Wurster, Lecturer in the Department of City and Regional Planning, University of California. She has for twenty-five years been closely associated with housing and related policies in this country and abroad. The wife of a leading architect, Mrs. Wurster is one of the country's best known and most influential critics of urban planning, housing and development.*

In the preparation of this chapter she consulted informally with a number of authorities on urban problems, and was advised by the panel listed below. She takes responsibility for the views expressed.

PANEL

ERNEST J. BOHN, Director, Cleveland Metropolitan Housing Authority.

MARION CLAWSON, Director, Land Use and Management Program, Resources for the Future, Washington, D. C.

LEO GREBLER, Director of Real Estate Research Program, School of Business, University of California.

DOUGLAS HASKELL, Editor of *Architectural Forum*.

JOHN T. HOWARD, member of the planning firm of Adams, Howard and Greeley, and Head of the Department of City and Regional Planning, Massachusetts Institute of Technology.

JOHN T. RYAN, President, Mine Safety Appliances Company, Pittsburgh; President, Allegheny Conference for Community Development.

ROBERT C. WEAVER, member of the Housing and Redevelopment Board, New York City.

BEN WEST, Mayor of Nashville.

FRAMEWORK FOR AN URBAN SOCIETY

CATHERINE BAUER WURSTER

The physical environment plays a dynamic role in human enterprise and welfare. As Winston Churchill once said, "We shape our buildings and then our buildings shape us." This chapter is about buildings, land, and the network of services and communications. It will focus primarily on metropolitan living patterns; but we must start with people, and some of the underlying issues.

I

CURRENT TRENDS AND SHIFTING PERSPECTIVES

People in 1970: the basic assumptions. The following projections might be altered by many different factors: war or peace; depression or more rapid economic growth; basic changes in social values, economic demands, technology, or public policies. But the trends are significant, however qualified, and they point up some of the issues that must be resolved in any effective approach to problems of the future physical environment.

The coming decade is likely to bring a population increase of at least 30 millions, one-sixth more than at present. Metropolitan areas will get the lion's share, around 25 millions, with an over-all growth of more than 22 per cent (although local rates will of course vary greatly). Two-thirds of our people will be metropolitan area residents by 1970, one-third in agglomerations of over a million, but most of them living outside the old central cities. Many cities will continue to lose population, and the rate of outlying growth may be around 40 per cent on the average, higher in the West and in larger communities. Outside metropolitan areas there will be a fairly substantial increase in non-farm residents, but the farm population will continue to decline.

The urban newcomers will include, as always, a large proportion of low-income, ill-educated families, seeking opportunity. Today they are mostly Negroes, but also Puerto Ricans, whites from backward rural regions, and others. By 1970 there will be a more even spread of racial and national minorities among cities throughout the nation. If present trends continue, however, the disadvantaged will increasingly dominate the old central areas while the newer suburban communities will be almost exclusively occupied by middle and upper-income white families.

By 1970 the present teen-age wave will have become a flood of young adults, which means a high marriage rate, a bumper crop of babies, and an increase of almost 50 per cent in job-seekers under the age of 25. The proportion of older people will also rise, and of workers over 45. As a result of the new age-grouping, the demand for employment, housing, residential services and educational facilities will grow faster than population.

About half of the manufacturing employment in the larger metropolitan areas is already outside the central cities, and this trend is likely to continue. In retail trade the central proportion is a little higher but suburban growth trends are strong. Business and government offices, wholesaling, and many specialized services, will probably tend to remain quite centralized although new patterns are visible in such places as Los Angeles, and the more mechanical office operations are sometimes being moved to fringe locations. Meanwhile, industry is still expanding outside metropolitan areas, but there is also the problem of depressed communities and regions, left behind in the shifting pattern of economic opportunity.

Automation and prosperity will tend to reduce the proportion of industrial jobs, increase employment in the urban professions and services, and shorten the hours of work. Incomes may well be considerably higher. Automobiles may increase by 40 per cent. Educational levels, and the demand for higher education, will continue to rise. These factors will bring many millions of low-income families up to a middle-class way of life, unless discrimination continues to impede normal progress by minority groups. But there will still be a substantial segment of the population below the poverty line and lacking adequate education, particularly in rural areas and among recent urban arrivals of all races. The chapter on farm policy underscores the need to provide new urban opportunities for a million and a half farm operators and their families, with present incomes of less than $1500 per year.

For most people, however, more leisure with higher incomes will greatly intensify the volume and variety of demand for recreational and cultural facilities of all kinds: in homes, in great and small urban centers, and in outdoor activities and travel. Whether added leisure is taken in the form of a shorter working day, a four-day week, or longer vacations, will affect the pattern of recreational demand and transportation requirements.

Technology has revolutionized our environment, usually in unforeseeable ways, and it is impossible to predict the ultimate effect of such possibilities as flying to work, closed-circuit TV, practical sea-water conversion, or the widespread use of new energy sources. But even if there should be no radical innovation by 1970, continuing technological progress in transportation and utilities, construction and consumer goods, is sure to have an important influence.

Most of these social and economic changes are essentially healthy and promising. They offer great possibilities for individual stimulus and fulfillment, for a richer family and community life. But realizing these opportunities depends, in very large part, on the quality and character of the physical environment. In this realm, growth and progress often seem to create more problems than they solve. Buildings and the vast service network represent large, immobile and long-term investments, subject to cumbersome private and public determinations. They do not respond easily to change. This is why it is important to try to visualize goals for future physical development.

The price of growth and progress. Natural resources and the rural environment have long received serious national attention in the United States, and the significant role of mass production methods in our economy is quite generally understood. Yet the metropolitan community, that far more complex institution which dominates our economic, social and political life today, is still a partially explored frontier. We have no clear image of its purpose and requirements, or how best to guide its destiny. But the cost and complexity push us gradually toward better understanding.

The social costs of the metropolitan environment are evident: the purgatory of the inmigrants, racial conflict, juvenile delinquency, the dreary lives of the aged, traffic congestion, the lengthening journey to work, the services that never catch up with need, slums and the chronic shortage of decent moderate-priced housing, smog, crowded schools, ugliness and noise in the center, monotony and inconvenience in the suburbs, the loss of natural amenity and the lack of recreational opportunity. Many of these problems also bring economic waste and inefficiency. But people and business keep coming, because this is the place to get ahead, with unique virtues and possibilities along with its evils. Somehow conditions must be improved, but the remedies are more expensive and more complicated than we once assumed.

The price of progress in a modern urban-based social economy is rising public "overhead," required for productive efficiency as well as for civic welfare. The necessary private investment in commercial, industrial and residential development depends on public expenditures for a basic framework of essential services and facilities, with attendant regulations. We are beginning to realize with understandable pain that these overhead costs and responsibilities are mounting even more rapidly than the rate of urban growth, because they are also enhanced by the greater size and complexity of metropolitan communities, by changing social and economic demands, and by the increasing burden of obsolescence as our central cities get older.

New civic responsibilities and the great opportunity. Big specialized operations are inevitable today, in government and urban development as well as in industry. The basic problem is how to adapt these powerful but often over-simplified tools to the infinite range of human needs, activities and possibilities.

The focus of this chapter might have been on the smaller-scale aspects of the problem: housing design, neighborhood planning, civic and commercial centers, industrial areas, parks, educational and cultural facilities, renewal programs and city planning, particularly in relation to rising qualitative demands of all kinds not yet fulfilled by the mass-produced environment. Or we might have looked through the other end of the telescope at the national environment, in terms of natural resources, over-all population distribution, and major regional trends. Or instead of any geographic view we could have emphasized the physical development process itself, which seems to be more than ever a "mixed enterprise," requiring coordinated private and public action whether for regions, cities, neighborhoods, or houses.

These are all important ways of looking at the environment, but the critical issue today is how to guide the future organization of the metropolitan community. A consistent framework for the social, economic and physical organization of metropolitan communities is needed, and this will be our primary focus. It is at this level that public policies and programs are most important. And it is here that government is weakest and most confused, lacking effective purpose or the means to carry it out.

At this new level of public responsibility we have a tremendous opportunity to shape the city of the future. But first we must decide what kind of urban and regional environment we want. And here there is a fundamental difficulty. Complicated large-scale operations, public and private, tend all too readily to exclude the individual from direct participation in the environment-shaping process, which he understands less and less in terms of cause and effect. Since he has more sense of personal power and choice in the consumer goods market, he tends to spend more money on household equipment than on housing itself, on automobiles than on public services, and is likely to vote down higher taxes even though a park, or less smog, might give him more personal pleasure than a second TV set.

For similar reasons, he may take an active part in the affairs of a small suburban enclave but scorn the big-city "machine," and feel no responsibility whatever for the metropolitan community. A distinguished mayor has described Mr. Average Citizen's day in sadly sardonic terms: his mounting irritation, from the moment he opens his front door, with smog, traffic, dirt, a degraded slum, the polluted river, and the need for civic improvements, ending up with fury at all those cheap politicians who want to raise taxes only to get more power for themselves.

The citizen is hardly more confused than the experts have been, however, as to the big alternatives and requirements. A generation ago most experts saw great crowded cities as a destructive anachronism, to be drastically altered by some form of decentralization. But suburban sprawl is clearly no solution, and the big centers have survived despite decay and mounting congestion. Now the new generation of experts and critics tends to glorify the economic and cultural virtues of the Great City, scorning decentralization in any form. But there is little sign of potential abatement in the outward push for space, and it seems likely that the extreme viewpoints represent half-world Utopias. There are forces that favor centering, while other forces favor dispersal, and they must somehow be resolved in a new kind of metropolitan community. We need a clearer image of the real alternatives for metropolitan life, along with the means required to achieve a given set of ends.

The opportunity is there, and also the duty, just because the environment *is* created by big decisions and big expenditures, which have to be made anyway whether or not they are related to a reasonably consistent set of goals. This paper is an effort to outline such a set of goals.

II

THE CONCRETE PROBLEMS

Renewal: the battle against slums, obsolescence and flight. In any list of goals, renewal of our older cities must be near the top. There is a great deal of seriously substandard housing in American communities, and spreading "gray areas" in various stages of actual or potential decay, plus commercial and industrial blight. It is quite evident that economic progress alone does not cure these evils, and that local governments cannot do the necessary job alone. Congress has therefore enacted successive measures granting substantial aid: for low-rent public housing since 1937; for broader slum clearance and private redevelopment programs since 1949; and for comprehensive renewal efforts, including rehabilitation and conservation of marginal property, since 1954. A social goal was clearly established more than a decade ago in the preamble to the 1949 Act: "A decent home in a suitable living environment for every American family." The economic goal is to revitalize the old centers, strengthening property values and the tax base. To achieve the latter ends, cities hope to gain more middle- and upper-income residents than they have at present, and they also seek new business and industry.

Can these goals be fulfilled by 1970? The answer is probably No, but with some additional tools and a greatly increased rate of public and private investment, tremendous progress could be made.

Over 400 communities have active renewal programs, with many important and even spectacular projects. Cities with broad-gauge achievements already visible include Philadelphia, Cleveland, Pittsburgh, Detroit, Chicago, Nashville, New Haven, Providence, Sacramento, and a number of others large and small. A new kind of public-private partnership is evolving, quite often resulting in distinguished planning and design. Efforts for code enforcement and neighborhood conservation are increasing. Businessmen are providing real civic leadership, along with many other interested groups.

But the over-all rate of progress can hardly equal the rate of obsolescence thus far, and has not even begun to affect the middle-class exodus. Since 1950 about 15,000 acres of slums and blight have been acquired for redevelopment and public housing, but several hundred thousand acres should be cleared. Perhaps a million and a half substandard homes have been demolished (only a fraction through renewal efforts), but up to 10 million more remain. Even at this slow rate of clearance, the relocation of displaced families has been the prime delaying factor. Moreover, despite uneven efforts to provide public housing or other assistance, most of the displaced people have probably crowded into other slums and blighted areas nearby, making them worse. It is all too evident that the supply of decent low-priced housing, old or new, is wholly inadequate to permit any large-scale clearance program.

Without some public housing, redevelopment would hardly have been possible at all. Outside New York City, however, this program has seldom been fully accepted as the general rehousing tool, even by slum-dwellers themselves. Rigid policies and large high-density projects have too often given it an institutional character, although a few determined cities, notably Cleveland and Philadelphia, have managed to humanize their programs somewhat. Rehabilitation efforts have been even less successful thus far. Plumbing and paint have improved many marginal dwellings, but usually have also taken them out of the low-income market. The basic problem in many localities is the chronic shortage at low price levels, which inhibits code enforcement, keeps substandard property over-valued, and prevents the normal market process of "filtering up" from operating effectively. As a New York report said, "the shortage of housing is currently the single most important reason for the spread of blight."

Meanwhile the new private projects on cleared sites are mainly luxury apartments for a very special and limited market. Exceptions are state- and city-aided projects in New York, including cooperatives, and civic efforts to provide non-profit middle-income housing in Cleveland and Pittsburgh. Lower land prices in redevelopment schemes would help, not only because low-density construction is much cheaper than elevator apartments, but also because most families would prefer garden apartments or "town houses" (i.e., the row house in modern dress). If the central cities are to attract many office workers with families, there must be substantial innovations in policy and practice.

The high density of much redevelopment may reflect unrealism about the future functions of the old metropolitan centers. They can certainly provide much of the specialized service and leadership required for the whole region and the main points of communication with the rest of the country. But this hardly means that either their working or residential population is likely to increase. In many cases there may well be a decline, which could profitably be used to reduce congestion. In the long run, only greater amenity will save the city.

The race question further complicates all these problems. In the big northern centers there is a strong push toward enforcement of non-discrimination in subsidized projects, public or private. At the luxury level this appears to cause little difficulty, since the minority demand is small. But in public housing it does not prevent a trend toward overwhelming Negro occupancy, which hardens the resistance to project location outside the ghettoes and frustrates the kind of gradual spreading out of minorities which appears to be feasible as well as desirable in a great many areas. Middle-income housing will confront the same problem, unless the suburbs begin to open up. In the South these issues have not yet become acute, and relatively more new suburban homes (as well as public housing) have been provided for Negroes, even if on a segregated basis.

In sum, despite renewal efforts the central city is more and more the abode of the poor, the rich, the childless and, to an ever increasing extent, all types of minority family. If this pattern continues, both the social and economic hopes for renewal are likely to be frustrated, with a resulting degree of political disorganization between central cities and suburbia far worse than exists today. At the same time middle-class families who might have liked to stay near their work will move farther away than ever. Outward commuting will also increase, by low-income and minority workers with suburban jobs who cannot find suburban homes, already a considerable number in many cities.

The resulting renewal goals are as follows (with housing tools considered later in more detail):

(1) A full range of housing opportunities outside the central cities for minority families, and for other low-income families who work there.

(2) An adequate supply of suitable housing for low- and middle-income families who need or want to live in central areas, at low as well as high densities. This will require lower-priced land in some redevelopment schemes.

(3) A much greater volume of investment, private and public, in renewal and redevelopment, in line with the Rockefeller Brothers Fund study which estimates a need for $4 to $7 billions of public expenditure per year for renewal and rehousing by 1967, as compared with $0.7 billions in 1957 and around $1 billion in 1960. These subsidies, largely federal as at present, would write down the cost of blighted property and subsidize rehousing where necessary. Such a volume of public expenditure would call forth more than $12 billions per year in taxable private invest-

ment, and although this would not do the whole job by 1970, it is probably all that could be effectively handled by that date, even with much better tools.

Suburbia: from scattered enclaves to urban maturity. The positive achievements of postwar suburban development must be recognized. The desire for space and family freedom, home-ownership and out-door life, is more than the old American dream, sometimes nostalgic or status-seeking. It is also the way a great many of us really like to live in the most concrete physical sense, including the fact that it suits modern principles of health and child-rearing. The intellectuals who attack suburban values in print, often with justice, can frequently be found at their typewriters in ex-urban retreats.

Since the war about 14 million one-family homes have been built, almost half with federal credit support, and many of them provide better physical living conditions than the owners ever enjoyed before. But they tend to be located in scattered subdivisions, as standardized socially as they are physically. These enclaves have neither the convenience and stimulating variety of an urban community nor the virtues of rural independence, and they have fostered a neurotic fear of minority or lower-class intrusion. There are some rising practical problems, however, which may help to create more varied and better integrated communities in the future.

One problem is "sprawl," the scattered pattern which makes utilities, roads and public services either inadequate or very expensive, and leads to chaotic local government. There is widespread feeling that more compact development would be desirable, with some smaller lots and higher density dwellings. This is reinforced by the need to preserve pleasant and useful open space instead of the random bits and pieces which the leap-frogging process leaves behind.

Another is transportation. Surveys suggest that many people are trying to bring their homes and jobs into a more convenient relationship. But the new middle- and upper-class homes are farther and farther out, with a large proportion of the professional and office jobs still in the centers. Meanwhile a great deal of industrial and service employment is springing up in the country. But unless they can find older marked-down homes or shacks, the lower-income suburban employees must commute from central districts. Only 30 to 40 per cent of the population can afford a recently-constructed private dwelling today, even on cheap land. And of course even well-to-do Negroes are usually barred from suburbs. The obvious answer is a better-balanced housing market at both ends.

Still another practical problem is the weak tax base of many newly incorporated suburban communities. This often merely results in "zoning out" houses which have low assessed values. But in recent years there has been a marked shift from the "exclusively residential" ideal to a desire for industrial development, to help pay for expensive schools and services. Often industries and shopping centers which locate where they pay only county taxes attract the same kind of resentment that central cities feel toward wealthy commuters. Stronger local government is gradually replacing the maze of "special districts," whether by annexation, big incorporations, or the granting of urban powers to counties.

Some suburbs are also overcoming their horror of mixing different kinds of dwellings and families. Apartments are included in a few tract developments, and zoning ordinances sometimes consider the needs of aged and single people. Even the mobile or trailer house (of which there are about a million and a half now in use as relatively permanent abodes) is increasingly accepted and planned for, along with the motel. In some areas, racial barriers are beginning to break down. Sophisticated builders realize that there will be no great flood, that discrimination will be outlawed sooner or later, and that restrictions only limit and complicate the market. Time alone will tend to modify the all-white, all-veteran, all-upper-middle-income tract.

In short, the suburb is getting to be more like a city, and a primary goal should be to reinforce this trend. We hardly need cities and centers today for the compulsory economic reasons which created them in the 19th century. Complete scatteration on acre plots would be quite feasible. But we need them more than ever for qualitative reasons: efficient government and good services; convenience for selective contacts and activities; stimulation and variety; and above all perhaps, for learning to live in an increasingly small and complex world full of different kinds of people.

The old centers cannot possibly provide these urban advantages for all the people in a big metropolitan area. They have not done so for a generation past, and a great many suburbanites never go "down town" at all today. Most of the urban elements are now scattered around in outlying areas: a variety of places to work and shop, libraries and colleges, banks, professional services, theaters, restaurants, hospitals, churches, embryo city halls and the rest. But they need to be pulled together into real cities.

Size, character, and degree of self-sufficiency would vary greatly, but the goal should be a relatively balanced community with a sound economic base, varied job opportunities, a wide range of housing types and prices, a strong and lively center, and plenty of space for outdoor recreation nearby. In some cases the city would need to be quite large, half a million or even more, with neighborhood sub-centers to meet daily household and children's needs. The predominant demand for one-family homes with yards must be served, but every effort should be made to encourage more compact development, and the modernized "row" or "town" house is a hopeful prospect. Some people will still commute to the old downtown district or other cities, and a great deal of interchange throughout the region will always be desirable. It would only be stimulated by better integration of the parts. Responsibility for the welfare and progress of the disadvantaged would have to be shared by all the cities, and this would help to save the old center.

Is this a brave goal? Perhaps, but there are signs of boredom in Suburbia along with the rising practical difficulties that lead toward urban solutions. A hopeful model is provided by Fremont, California, where the citizens of several small rural towns incorporated a huge area in order to plan it as a complete city of several hundred thousand, including its own wilderness amenities in the foothills.

In the small metropolitan areas, it may be primarily a matter of better integration with the existing center. And in many cases the present suburban towns can be strengthened. But where there is large-scale growth to come, entirely new cities and centers will be needed. Big developers are already moving in this direction more rapidly than the planning and policies required to guide them.

During the next decade, eight to ten million homes will be built on new land in metropolitan regions, with their complement of services and facilities. New jobs to support something like an equivalent number of people will also be created, primarily in outlying areas. Millions of acres of raw land will be developed, and the investment in housing and public services alone will probably be more than $200 billion. The economies inherent in a relatively compact and efficient urban pattern would pay for a great many amenities that are now lacking in suburbia. And metropolitan life could be greatly enriched.

Innovations in planning and policy will be necessary, however, including the following:

(1) Effective regional planning, and stronger land-use controls. Firm policies with respect to zoning and the provision of public services are essential, and open space reserves could be helpful. Public land acquisition for resale to private developers would be the most effective tool and, following renewal and reclamation precedents, this possibility is gaining support.

(2) Housing policy designed to make available a full range of dwelling types and prices, related to employment opportunities in the same city or general area, without racial restrictions.

(3) Incentives for effective planning, land-use control, and strong local government, in all federal and state programs of local financial assistance.

Housing: a wider range of choice for everyone. There will have to be about ten million additional homes in the United States by 1970, and there ought to be up to ten million more to replace seriously substandard dwellings and the large number normally lost for other reasons. Still another ten million or so will need some degree of improvement. Two million dwellings per year is about 40 per cent higher than the record output in 1950 and over 60 per cent more than the annual average for the decade. But this volume, plus rehabilitation and services, is well within the prospective capacity of the construction industry. Indeed, the pending flood of new job-seekers calls for a 20 per cent rise in total employment by 1970, and the Labor Department counts on an increase in construction opportunities "much faster" than 20 per cent, as a major source of additional jobs.

This rate of construction cannot be achieved if the market for new housing remains limited to the top 30 to 40 per cent of the population (less in high-density development), with a tiny volume of public housing (2½ per cent of new construction in 1959) at the bottom. Construction costs have risen faster than incomes.* High interest rates have further reduced the market. Under typical present conditions for a house with FHA-insured mortgage, a two per cent lower interest rate would mean about 25 per cent lower monthly payments, which would add about 15 per cent of all American families to the potential market, getting well down into the middle-income group.

Together, the new dwellings and the present supply of good or adequate homes must somehow meet the urgent needs of the poor, the aged and minorities—millions of whom will be forcibly displaced from their present quarters—as well as middle and upper-income white families. The homes must be varied enough to fit big and small households with differing incomes, tastes and living habits. A suitable choice of homes must be located within reasonable distance of local employment centers. And the housing supply in any locality should permit enough vacancies at all price levels to insure adequate choice and mobility, without exploitation.

This does not mean that a large proportion of the low-income households will necessarily need heavily-subsidized new housing. In central cities, and even to some extent outside, there is a big supply of moderate-quality older homes which could be made available, with modest grants and some rehabilitation where necessary, *if* there were enough vacancies to free up the market, encourage normal mobility, and permit the "filtering" process to operate effectively. This would require a great deal of middle-income construction, however, which is impossible with present costs and financial terms. Ample means must be available to provide new subsidized housing for displaced families (although not solely in large publicly-owned projects), wherever this seems to be the only immediate solution. Slum clearance operations which merely force the occupants into other slums are indefensible.

Cooperatives and other forms of non-speculative enterprise which

* Dr. Grebler states: There is real question whether the suggested increase in housing construction can be accomplished without a disproportionate rise in the cost of land and buildings.

have proven successful for both middle-income and subsidized housing in northern Europe should be further encouraged, and new sources of equity and mortgage funds should be sought out. Big redevelopment projects currently sponsored by the aluminum industry, in the hope of expanding outlets for its enormous productive capacity, exemplify an entirely new kind of housing enterprise which may have wide potential significance. The airplane industry is likewise scrutinizing the possibilties in the housing field.

The upward drive of 18 million Negroes and other minorities must sooner or later mean federal action against discrimination in federally-aided housing, as predicted and supported by the Commission on Race and Housing, an unofficial but nationally representative body. Laws against discrimination are already being enacted by city and state governments in the North. In the meantime there must be concerted public, private and individual efforts to give minority families more freedom of choice in housing and neighborhoods, particularly in outlying areas. This will not only ease the transition but also avert the ghetto trend in central cities and help solve the housing problems of everyone.

In the housing field the general goals are much clearer than the specific means. What we need primarily is responsible programming of local requirements, with a period of systematic but flexible experimentation. Working principles for the next decade are here proposed:

(1) Public agencies must set over-all goals, then provide assistance and incentives to private enterprise to carry out as much of the program as possible on their own initiative, with full encouragement for innovations. This is already beginning to happen in renewal programs.

(2) Future housing requirements, to insure a balanced inventory in both central and outlying areas and to meet the needs of displaced families, must be determined by local agencies on a metropolitan-wide and city-wide basis. This is an extension of the "workable program" principle, a condition of federal renewal aid since 1954. More refined techniques of housing market and needs analysis will be essential.

(3) Better coordination and greater flexibility are required in all federal and state programs related to housing, to meet the full range of local needs. Public policies have enhanced the disjointed, over-specialized, and generally inflexible character of the housing market, whether in standardized suburbia or in standardized public housing. Inducements rather than rigid controls are necessary, particularly to encourage responsible local programming of needs.

(4) To expand the effective market for new and improved housing, and the range of consumer housing choice, will be a major challenge to industry, finance, architects, researchers, and to housing,

renewal and planning agencies, with federal leadership and assistance required. Since there are no clear-cut answers as yet to many of the problems involved, programs must be designed to encourage local and private experiment instead of stifling it. Measures should include the following:

(a) A long-term nation-wide program of technological and design research, including systematic field experiment and public education, to lower construction costs, remove restrictive obstacles, and tackle rehabilitation. Substantial federal funds would be supplemented from other sources, and all kinds of industrial, academic and local agencies should be utilized, under broad federal leadership.

(b) An experimental program of federal financial assistance to localities, for new housing or rehabilitation which appears to be needed as part of a locally determined program. The program would be limited to five years, with maximum freedom to provide mortgage insurance, low-interest loans, annual or capital grants or other aid. These aids would be offered to both private builders and public agencies, but only on the firm condition of complete cost-accounting, for purposes of comparative analysis. Substantial funds should be made available, and a thorough report should be made to Congress and the public at the end of the period, to provide a basis for permanent legislation. This program would be used in part to encourage cooperative and other forms of non-speculative enterprise, to tap new sources of equity and mortgage funds, and also to facilitate technological and design experiments. All the regular federal programs for housing assistance should be continued, however, during the period of experiment.

(c) Legal and administrative action against racial discrimination, particularly in publicly-assisted housing. Pending federal action on a nation-wide basis, federal policies should fully support state and local laws, and should offer financial inducements for "open occupancy" housing, particularly in suburban areas.

Transportation: maximum mobility versus greater convenience. In recent years, the new freeways have made a spectacular change in our environment. They have opened up vast areas of cheap land for needed development and recreation, increased the job radius, and permitted many people to fulfill their desire for a private home.

But there is another side to the balance sheet. For many people, commuting costs and time have mounted, and consume a large share of their increased incomes and leisure. The total national expenditure on non-military transportation is now roughly $100 billion a year, or 20 per cent of the gross national product, with something like $25 billion devoted to passenger transport in urban and metropolitan areas. We spend almost as much to move around home as we do on housing itself. The public costs are enormous, in terms of local and state budgets and debt. And no leveling off is in sight. Traffic congestion often appears to be only temporarily relieved in outlying areas, and is creating an overwhelming crisis in central business districts.

One healthy reaction is the new appeal of the small automobile, but it may only stimulate more multiple-car families. Another is the rising effort to provide easy pedestrian circulation, separated from traffic, in residential, business and recreational areas. Of prime significance, however, is the brave stand against the automobile itself, by many experts and leading critics, in favor of a revival of mass transit.

If enough commuters would shift to it, the advantages are obvious. We must certainly save and improve what little is left of the regional rail networks which once served almost everyone everywhere. But any new rail rapid-transit system will be very expensive: half a billion dollars for the Washington, D. C. proposal, over $1 billion for the complete San Francisco Bay Area scheme. It will also be still another highly destructive element in the urban and natural landscape, unless it is put underground at further expense. And will most commuters really use it, if either their homes or jobs are far from stations? Furthermore, mass transit would probably have very little effect on the weekend traffic jam, which is likely to mount even more rapidly than commuting congestion.

The balance of costs and benefits will vary for different metropolitan regions. More self-sufficient sub-areas would reduce the need. But a network of large compact centers is exactly the pattern in which rail transit is useful and efficient, and a system can be designed to strengthen outlying centers as in the Bay Area plan. However, the decision to build a transit system will have to be weighed in each case against the critical need for other expensive public facilities.

In any event, there is little hope of avoiding major additional highway expenditures. Even with greatly improved rail transit, over two-thirds of the total public investment required to carry out Philadelphia's comprehensive plan will go for roads. With the possibility of 40 per cent more cars by 1970, it is expected that our present 10,000 miles of freeway will be increased to 50,000 miles in ten to twenty years. Half the current cost is in urban areas, and this ratio may increase.

Transportation costs are forcing a new look at the metropolitan development pattern, and some questioning of the whole approach to transport planning. A basic assumption, implicit or explicit, has been that maximum mobility throughout an ever-expanding area is a primary goal in itself, bringing added profit or pleasure for every dollar expended. But perhaps it would be more efficient, from many viewpoints, to try to minimize the need for ever-longer daily trips. This is what our goals for renewal and outlying development would do, by providing a wider choice of homes in somewhat closer relationship to a choice of jobs and other activities, within different sections of the metropolitan region. This means no revolution: in many areas a policy of minimizing transportation needs would help people and business to do what they are apparently trying to do anyway despite the obstacles. And those who must travel long distances daily, due to special living tastes or job requirements, would find commuting easier than it is today.

We need to know much more than we do about the desirable size and character of labor markets, and about important business linkages. For most economic purposes, however, it seems reasonably evident that a large metropolitan area can be broken down into smaller functional units.

Two principles for transportation policy are proposed:

(1) The first is a motto: remember that mobility is not usually an end in itself, but a means to other ends. Vacation travel may sometimes be a positive pleasure, but an extra ten miles on the journey to work is a costly nuisance.

(2) The second follows from the motto: transportation planning must be carefully coordinated with other kinds of planning, to shape a desirable development pattern. Such a pattern is likely to be one that maximizes convenience rather than mobility.

Vanishing open space and spreading pollution. The people in a big urban region need open space for many different purposes: to conserve water and other natural resources; as a reserve for future needs, often unpredictable; to maintain special types of agriculture which must be near cities; to prevent building in undesirable locations in order to avoid flood hazard or a wasteful extension of services; to provide a rural environment for people who want to live that way; for pleasant views from urban areas; for a sense of urban identity; for buffers against noise and other nuisance; but above all, for recreation, which can be combined with many of the other uses.

The demand for outdoor recreation is likely to increase ten-fold in 50 years, simply in terms of the expected growth in population, income, leisure and mobility. Already we are feeling the pinch. Much of the demand will be outside metropolitan areas, in mountains and countryside, historic places and quaint villages, at the seaside and lakeshore. All kinds of facilities (or lack of facilities) will be required, and if we take our increased leisure in longer vacations or a four-day week the rising demand for cabins, campsites and old farmhouses will become a flood. If our present preserves are not rapidly expanded, over-use will create many wilderness slums by 1970.

The federal wildland resources for vacation use are still quite large, if unevenly distributed. The crucial problem is in metropolitan areas and nearby, where it is a question of now or never. There should be at least 30 acres of reasonably convenient parks and wilderness per thousand people for active recreational use, with further acreage for other kinds of open space. But every additional thousand people will urbanize more than 100 acres of open land (even if our present wasteful practices are drastically curbed) and make the rest of it steadily more expensive. A million acres of wildland priced at half a billion today will soon cost several billions, if it is available at all. In the 22-county area around New York City, a detailed plan has been drawn up to increase the permanent open space by 150 per cent, or about 600,000 acres. But in this highly developed region the cost is $2 billion right now, and rapidly rising. In many areas urgent recreation plans are being prepared, of which California's state-wide program is another outstanding example.

Various measures to preserve natural amenities short of outright public purchase are increasingly promoted and employed: agricultural zoning, which is at least a delaying action; tax policies of various kinds; public purchase of easements or development rights. These are important tools which must be strengthened. A firm plan to attain our goal of more compact suburban development, with a refusal to provide scattered services, would also be helpful. But for permanent recreational use there is no real substitute for public ownership. This does not necessarily mean public management or heavy operating subsidies. With higher incomes, more facilities can be put on a use-charge basis. And for many kinds of activity, private operation is at least as good as public. Moreover, recreation equipment and travel are big-time business today, for which public park expenditures provide the necessary "seed-money."

For open space conservation during the next decade, the primary needs are two:

(1) The goal: acquisition of as much suitable wildland as possible in growing areas where the chance will soon be lost, related to present needs and plans for future development. There are now only about 6 million acres in state, county and municipal parks. In the year 2000 there will be a need for something like 50 million acres. A modest national goal to be reached by 1970 would be the public purchase of 5 million additional acres, as convenient to growing centers of population as feasible. Far-sighted prudence might well set a higher figure, and additional reserves of open land would greatly facilitate better urban development too, as earlier noted.

(2) The tool: such a program will require federal assistance, in the form of long-term, low-interest loans (or interest-free, following

agricultural precedents). Direct grants for planning would provide a relatively inexpensive stimulant, and should require that recreation programs be tied in with over-all physical planning at the state and metropolitan level.

Clean air is an even more basic natural amenity than open space. It too is disappearing in many urban areas. The belching smokestack is gradually being remedied, with rejuvenative effects on such cities as Pittsburgh and St. Louis. But new sources of smog are rapidly mounting: the trashburner, for instance, in our paper-addicted civilization, and automobile exhaust, the worst and most universal pollutant of them all.

The remedies for air pollution, such as the purifying gadget which California is preparing to require on every car, are costly. And knowledge is still inadequate. As the California Department of Health says, "Social aspects broader than air pollution control, even new patterns of use and development in metropolitan centers, are involved in the search for clean air."

Clean water for recreational purposes and general amenity, as well as for practical needs, is also a problem of resource conservation. The number of American cities with splendid waterfronts whose citizens drink diluted sewage and have no place to swim is a national disgrace.

Two immediate goals are indicated:

(1) Continued expansion of state and local programs for eliminating air and water pollution, carefully coordinated with over-all metropolitan plans.

(2) An expanded nation-wide research program on air pollution. An authoritative recent estimate calls for $32 million a year by 1968—40 per cent from federal funds, 28 per cent from industry, and 32 per cent from states and local governments.

The metropolitan impasse: is there a way out? For the past decade a rising tide of articles, speeches and reports has been calling for some form of metropolitan area unification. But are we getting any closer? Will the wave merely recede, as similar waves have done before? It may. In some areas it has already. But greater realism is evident, the essential needs are somewhat clarified, and a number of gradual steps have been taken which may hold promise. It is now clear that no single simple formula is applicable: metropolitan areas are big and small, old and new, with differing problems and possibilities. In most of the large complexes, at least, there will never be a single super-government taking over all the local functions.

But it is increasingly obvious that city and county planning are not enough, that "voluntary" regional planning is ineffective, and that the multiplication of single-purpose authorities for such functions as metropolitan transportation is creating a new kind of anarchy. What seems to be shaping up in many places is a loose but formal federation of local governments which will have a limited tax base sooner or later, engage in regional planning, wield considerable influence, and ultimately exercise some qualified authority over land-use.

If suburban governments continue to become better organized through large incorporations, city-counties or other means, the federation will thereby be greatly strengthened. A few relatively strong agencies can cooperate far more effectively than an elderly giant and a hundred wayward infants. Our basic goal, a multi-centered region with a network of strong balanced cities, would help to solve the perennial issue of metropolitan unification. These cities could also cope with the *local* responsibilities which are now being handed on to higher levels of government by default.

In the shifting metropolitan picture, state and federal governments can exercise a great deal of influence by making various aids contingent on effective regional planning and better integration. All current proposals for federal housing and renewal policy emphasize this point, and it is coming to be recognized in state highway, water and recreational programs. The move, here and there, toward state-wide physical plans may even stimulate local governments to do their own metropolitan planning, if only in fear of getting something worse from the State Capitol. We are painfully learning that metropolitan chaos is no victory for "self-determination": it merely results in the continuous transfer of local responsibility to the states and Washington.

The old dichotomy between "city" and "farm" is by no means dead in state government, however. Our political and administrative institutions were shaped in a period of rural domination, and are highly resistant to change. In most legislatures the rural representatives, sometimes aided by suburban counties, can still thwart the great cities. Many urban political leaders are therefore understandably sceptical about bringing the state into the metropolitan picture. But the political lineup is slowly changing, not only by reapportionment but also because farmers have more urban-type demands themselves, and because some of the country towns have become metropolitan centers with problems of their own.

In Congress there are similar difficulties, and in the Cabinet almost every major functional grouping is represented except the cities, with agriculture one of the most powerful and best supported. Pressure is rising for a full-scale department or some other means of focusing national attention and policy on the urban and metropolitan scene.

One proposal is a Department of Urban Affairs, and it can be argued that this is either too all-inclusive, or too narrow for the broad needs of metropolitan regions. Other suggested titles include Housing and Urban Development, and Urban and Regional Development. The first bill introduced for this purpose coined a new word, "Urbiculture."

tend to establish the framework, while private enterprise provides
of the superstructure. Had we focused on the house and the neigh
hood, instead of the big framework, there would have been m
greater emphasis on architecture, the building industry, consumer ch
and private decisions in general.

Third, over-all goals and guidance are needed for the metropol
community, since public decisions are so important in determining
development pattern which affects the whole economic and sc
structure.

Fourth, we must be prepared to devote a bigger share of our t
income to the physical improvements that growth and obsolesce
demand. The expanding metropolitan complex required by our so
economy is inherently an expensive institution, although its bene
should more than compensate for the cost. Economic growth will h
pay the bills, but the public share will probably have to be larger th
at present, if only to attract the huge volume of private investment t
will be necessary.*

Fifth, federal and state aids must be flexibly coordinated to se
locally determined ends, and to stimulate responsible local action.
another chapter in this book, our federal system is perceptively analyz
as a government of "shared functions," with numerous activities a
responsibilities involving all three levels of government. The auth
suggests that to improve this system its interrelated parts must be ma
to work together more effectively. Nowhere is this diagnosis mo
accurate than in the machinery to deal with problems of the physic
environment.

And finally, there must be better public understanding. The futu
environment offers many big choices for public decision that will affe
our whole way of life. But it is not the kind of choice available in
supermarket: selecting this or that item from among many independe
products, according to personal taste at the moment. Our environme
comes in enormous and expensive packages today, with the conten
predetermined and very difficult to exchange for something one migl
like better. The only way to affect it is by influencing the big decision
that produce the package. To do that it is necessary not only to kno
what we want but also to understand the possibilities and limitation
of the production process, and how the various elements in the packag
fit together.

Fortunately it is not the citizen-consumer's responsibility to acquir
and apply this knowledge entirely on his own. Politicians, expert

* Dr. Grebler states: While I agree that larger expenditures are necessary
the case for increasing the federal share is by no means clear in the light o
other demands on the Treasury and the potential financial resources of th
states and municipalities. Through increased real estate tax and other revenues
the cities benefit most directly from urban capital improvements.

Whatever the exact title or form, however, an agency is needed to help both cities and larger regions fit the pieces of specialized federal aid and policy together in order to create a more efficient and desirable framework for living and working. Programs related to urban and metropolitan housing, renewal, planning and community facilities should certainly be administered directly by such an agency. Probably other activities should be under its direction also. But there will also have to be a delicate mechanism for coordination with many activities in other departments, perhaps through a White House office, and even more delicate machinery to insure flexible service and stimulation, rather than rigid dictation, to local governments and private enterprise. Relation to state governments is another big question.

In some respects the Department of Agriculture provides a useful prototype. The agricultural extension program has a federal, state, university and local framework which combines research, experiment, financial aid, and education for citizens, consumers and producers, in many specialized fields, all for the improvement of farming and farm life.

The historic federal role in rural affairs reminds us, moreover, that the metropolitan problem is not only a question of governmental organization. It is also financial. The lag in needed physical improvements and services is due in large part to the lack of available funds. Recently, state and local tax rates have gone up three times as fast as federal rates, despite defense outlays. State and local debt has quadrupled in less than fifteen years. But the needs are mounting more rapidly than ever, and in many areas the limit of local public resources seems to be at hand, since the federal government has pre-empted the major sources of expansible revenue. Basic reforms in the tax structure may be called for, but the fact remains that metropolitan problems are created by exactly the same nation-wide forces that have produced our rising national income. They are the price of national growth and progress in the most direct and literal sense, quite as much so as the problem of rural relief and over-production. It is only reasonable that federal leadership, and a larger share of federal resources, are required for their solution.

The goals and means for metropolitan progress include all the proposals in earlier sections, but the key instruments may here be outlined:

(1) Stronger civic, business and political leadership at the metropolitan level, willing to accept the need for innovation.

(2) A federation of strong local governments, with a unified tax base adequate to the exercise of limited but positive powers including regional planning and land-use controls.

(3) Inducements for effective local integration, planning, programming and governmental structure, in all federal and state assist-

ance programs, including increased federal aid, and greater local freedom in its application, as a *quid pro quo*.

(4) A new federal department of Cabinet status, its exact functions to be determined.

The regional environment and the states. In some respects all our current emphasis on metropolitan communities as defined by the Census is too narrow, however important the focus for certain critical problems of growth and change. "Standard metropolitan areas" occupy less than a tenth of the national map and the boundaries are not as sharp as we sometimes assume them to be, even for local functions. Many areas overlap. Many communities outside the limits have more contact with the center than some of those within. New cities might sometimes be located beyond the present census boundaries. The metropolis uses, serves, and is influenced by a much larger region. And the rest of the country still has an important life of its own, with its own particular problems.

Urbanites need the hinterland, not only for food, raw materials and markets, but also for recreation, which is an increasingly important factor in the rural economic base. Along with natural amenities there is need to conserve such irreplaceable resources as the New England village, the Gold Rush town, and other pleasant communities with historic or merely rustic flavor. With longer weekends, vacations and years of retirement, a great many people can fulfill their desire for the small community life in such places.

Nor are the non-metropolitan cities dead. Most of them are still growing, with new industries and quite often with fresh leadership from individualists who have left the smog-bound commuting life.

The farm population is declining and more must leave. But electrification, telephones, automobiles and highways have modernized rural life, and the condition of farm housing, rural schools and other community facilities has in general been vastly improved during the past few decades, despite the gap between urban and rural incomes.

But there are many severely depressed or backward areas, rural and urban, which require special help to develop new resources in order to expand their economic and social opportunities. Both independent towns and rural counties have their own burden of physical obsolescence, renewal needs, and scatteration, which are combined in the shacktown, trailer and auto-court type of slum prevalent in semi-rural fringe areas. The basic issue here is the same as for the central city: if no adequate housing is available to the low-income migrant, where else is he to live? County regulations which prevent such slums merely create them elsewhere, or increase the crowding in central blighted areas.

In the big regional picture, the state plays a major role in shaping the development pattern, as the western water battles demonstrate. State activities such as highway and park systems, resource conservation and

industrial promotion, health and housing programs, tax pol numerous aids to local government, have a tremendous inflt our environment. In recent years there has been a revival of state in physical planning, not only through aid and encouragement agencies but also in terms of the need for over-all plans to co the state's own activities. Such plans could play an important relating metropolitan development to the bigger regional fram They could also provide a basis for guiding many federal decis in the resource field for instance—which are too often made narrow terms of highly specialized Washington agencies. As wi metropolitan community, if the state can decide what it really it will have more influence on federal policies.

Two needs should be emphasized:

(1) State-wide physical plans to relate various state and fe programs—particularly transportation, water and recreatic to some defensible hypothesis as to the desirable future distr tion of people and their activities.

(2) Greater attention to the special needs of small towns and r areas, in all federal housing and renewal programs, and by states.

III

IN CONCLUSION: ENDS AND MEANS

This paper discusses the physical environment primarily in ter of diverse problems associated with metropolitan organization in highly urbanized society. It proposes a framework which might to resolve the present conflict between forces that favor centraliza and those that promote dispersal, by guiding future development ward a regional network of strong cities, old and new, each offeri wide range of values and opportunities to a relatively balanced po tion. Others might propose an entirely different set of goals. whatever the framework desired, some fundamental conditions mu met if we hope to use our abundant resources to create a more factory environment.

First, we must recognize that the physical environment is indiv Houses, pipes, roads, schools, factories, offices, wilderness park dams are all part of the same organic system. Although many specialized activities are necessary, they must be related to goals and over-all patterns to be effective.

Second, a creative partnership between public agencies and enterprise is essential. The old battle between "private" and " fortunately disappearing at many points, has no meaning in to the physical environment, which is shaped by both. Public

critics, civic leaders, the press, all have important roles in translating the complexities of the physical environment into understandable terms and choices, a role which they have been fulfilling more and more in recent years. And "planning" in a democratic society is primarily a means of proposing and explaining possible future packages for public acceptance, rejection or modification.

This paper offers only one set of goals. But many other packages are possible, and they should all be publicized and debated if people are to act effectively in choosing their future environment.

11

F OR ITS *chapter on the health and welfare needs of Americans, the Commission sought the help of Dr. James P. Dixon, Jr. A doctor of medicine, the author was for four years manager of health and hospitals for the city of Denver, for two years Medical Director, United States Public Health Service, and for seven years Commissioner of Health of Philadelphia and Professor of Public Health and Preventive Medicine at the University of Pennsylvania. He was recently elected President of Antioch College, Yellow Springs, Ohio. He brings thoughtful perspective to this important subject.*

Dr. Dixon was advised by the panel listed below. He takes responsibility for the views expressed.

PANEL

DR. MICHAEL E. DE BAKEY, surgeon in private practice and Chairman, Department of Surgery, Baylor University, Houston.

G. MANTON EDDY, Senior Vice President and Director, Connecticut General Life Insurance Company.

FEDELE F. FAURI, Dean, School of Social Work, University of Michigan; formerly, Director, Michigan State Department of Social Welfare.

MARION B. FOLSOM, Director, Eastman Kodak Company; Secretary of Health, Education and Welfare, 1955-58.

ROBERT H. MACRAE, Executive Director, Welfare Council of Metropolitan Chicago.

DR. HAROLD M. MARVIN, physician in private practice in New Haven; former President, American Heart Association.

HERMAN M. SOMERS, Chairman and Professor, Department of Political Science, Haverford College, Haverford, Pennsylvania.

MRS. ALYCE M. WILSON, Executive Director, Woodson Center, Omaha.

MEETING HUMAN NEEDS

DR. JAMES P. DIXON, JR.

I

INTRODUCTION

We are a compassionate people. We have a strong desire to help persons in need. We believe that the individual is central to our society, that the principal asset of human society is human life itself, and that society must therefore help to protect the lives and interests of every individual.

We know too that the spread of juvenile delinquency, or an increase in the desertion of fathers, or widespread loss of income due to involuntary unemployment, creates a hazard for the whole community. Individuals cease to contribute to the community, and become dependent on it.

At the same time, deep conviction that the individual and his productivity are basic to our free society makes us reluctant to meet human needs in a fashion which might reduce individual initiative and self-reliance. In the planning, design, and execution of programs to improve the human condition, there is a constant dilemma: interference with individual freedom and self-reliance must be balanced against the need to maintain social justice and security for the group as a whole. Many decisions of the past and discussions of the present hinge on variations in perception of this moral judgment.

Most people handle most of their needs by themselves or with the help of family and friends. Society as a whole has two functions. It can develop ways by which people can meet their own needs more readily and fruitfully, and it can develop ways by which society as a whole can meet needs that would otherwise be unmet. There are individuals who will not meet their own needs, and others who cannot.

These two functions of society are performed through organized social institutions. A substantial number of these are privately run and supported. Private support is a distinctive characteristic of our general hospitals, as well as of many agencies which serve the needs of families and children. These institutions are of particular importance, for while they cannot extend their services to everyone, they have a major responsibility for setting standards of service. They provide a tremendous volume of services. They perform experimental and pilot functions. They are legitimate extensions of our economic system into the field of social service.

Another principal social institution involved in maintaining minimum standards of human health and decency is government. The role which government may play in devising and implementing new goals for human welfare depends conspicuously upon people's feelings about it, the responsibility we are prepared to vest in it, and our views concerning the effectiveness of voluntary efforts to meet human needs with or without government assistance.

Government's role should not be determined by the application of pious general principles. In modern society it is not possible to escape into the jungle and choose the threat of the lions as a substitute for the annoyances of bureaucracy. The tests should be these. In the particular case, will the use of government yield advantages unobtainable through voluntary efforts? Will it, in the specific instance, damage essential qualities of a health or welfare service so that standards of performance will be impaired? Will it interfere unduly with the personal and economic freedoms and responsibilities of either the provider or the recipient of the services?

In the first half of this century our capacity to attain new goals of decent living for everyone has dramatically increased. Greater knowledge, more wealth, and improved social organization now make it possible to consider a further improvement in meeting human needs, an improvement that could be substantial even when compared with the remarkable progress to date.

Three areas of human need call for specific attention in the decade ahead. These are improved health, the remaining unfinished business in our effort to lessen poverty through income security, and the reduction of juvenile delinquency, family breakdown and other instances of social disorganization. The reasons are manifest. Good health is necessary to the full functioning of the individual, poverty is destructive to the individual and to family organization, and social disorganization is destructive to our entire society.

Fully conscious of our moral, social, and economic objectives, and of the difficulties of establishing standards, let us examine present possibilities for improvement in meeting these human needs. We should seek ways which not only assure higher standards of decent living to more people, but also wherever possible contribute to the productivity and security of the nation as a whole.

II

HEALTH

Medical care for all. Health care is a continuous process. It starts with the prevention of illness wherever possible. It includes the adequate treatment of illness where it occurs. And it involves the rehabilitation of the disabled.

Prevention of illness is a particular responsibility of public health departments. New environmental hazards, such as exposure to X-rays, increased water pollution and increased use of agricultural pesticides raise additional problems for these departments in this decade.

Community health departments are becoming increasingly involved in the planning of medical services. No other existing agency has the capacity to identify a community's needs for medical care and to evaluate continuously the quality of its health practices and the adequacy of its health facilities and manpower.

The responsibility of a community health department to provide direct medical services to persons who would not otherwise be served should be equally clear. There is a myth which has it that only the very rich and the very poor receive high-quality medical care: the very rich because they can afford to purchase the best services available, the very poor because the community sees to it that the very best is provided for them. The fact, however, is that the seven million persons on public relief, and other low-income families, have more than their share of illness and receive by ordinary standards inadequate health care.

Recognition of a community health department's responsibility for the adequacy of medical care will not come easily. Opposition arises from a confusion between its role as the planning and regulatory authority on the one hand and as a provider of direct service on the other. As an agency of government, working in concert with other community agencies, it should be prepared to plan, coordinate, and regulate in a fashion which improves the medical care of the entire community. Its direct service programs should be designed to meet particular community needs. Thus some public health departments may well have responsibility for the provision of general hospital services to low-income families. Others may be responsible for seeing that medical care in acute emergency is available to all citizens, and yet others may be responsible for the setting of minimum standards in nursing homes. To the extent that local circumstances require direct medical care to be provided by a public agency, health departments are the agencies to do it.

Public health services have traditionally looked to the Surgeon General for guidance, and it is therefore particularly important that outspoken federal leadership be exercised toward enlarging health departments' responsibilities. And more than leadership is required. Increased financial support is needed from state and national governments to improve the planning, coordination, and execution of health services through health departments.

Just as the health department plays a principal role in the prevention of illness and the planning of health services, the hospital plays a central role in the treatment of illness. Increasingly, the physician relies on the hospital. Increasingly, the hospital becomes the center for emergency medical services. Increasingly, it is involved in the management of chronic illness. It has tremendous latent possibilities which have been barely exploited. The hospital can serve not just as a workshop for physicians, but in the larger role of community health center. It can improve its services for the treatment of acute mental illness. It can expand into nursing-home care. It can develop home-care services. For all these services, the need and the feasibility of using the hospital have been demonstrated.

Hospitals are under great public pressure to utilize their facilities more efficiently—to avoid the tendency toward unnecessary use of hospital beds needed for acute illness, and to design facilities and services to meet patients' needs more precisely.

The opportunity for full community use of hospital services is abridged by conflict between physicians and hospitals. This conflict is over the propriety of hospitals' entrance into the practice of medicine through becoming employers of physicians. This they already do in the provision of care to needy persons. The question is whether this pattern should be extended to those not in financial need.

To deny hospitals the right to play a larger role would sharply limit their capacity to improve the efficiency of community health services. Physicians and hospitals need to examine their respective roles. Increasing specialization requires increased organization of health services. In many instances the hospital is the proper community institution to organize these services most effectively. This means that it is frequently desirable for hospitals to employ physicians. Such employment need not interfere with the kinds of relationship between physician and patient necessary for good medical care. If hospitals cannot work out with the medical profession arrangements under which they can employ doctors, state legislatures should pass authorizing legislation. We cannot afford to under-utilize our hospital system.

Group practice clinics are an efficient form of medical care organization. They afford a quality of comprehensive and continuous care which is difficult for the physician in solo practice to achieve. They are economical to operate. As medical care becomes generally more available and more expensive, concern for its economic efficiency becomes vital. One of the barriers to the growth of group practice is the cost of facilities. Encouragement should be given by provision of long-term low interest loans from the federal government.

Voluntary health insurance has become an increasingly important factor in the extension of medical care. It deserves to be extended to its widest usefulness and should be enlarged to cover long-term illness and rehabilitation services. In addition we should continue to try to discover ways in which it may be effective in covering home-care and nursing-home services. Failure to cover these services tends to result in extensive use of hospital beds as substitutes for them, at much higher cost.

Rehabilitation. A second major health-service goal is that the physically disabled shall have opportunity for rehabilitation, even though correction of the disability may not return the person to economic productivity.

The Office of Vocational Rehabilitation in the federal Department of Health, Education, and Welfare is already deeply concerned with restoring the ability to hold a job. Sufficient funds should be provided to increase the annual rate of vocational rehabilitation from the present 81,000 persons to 200,000, the level of estimated need throughout the country.

But vocational rehabilitation is not enough. Rehabilitation services also vastly diminish the discomfort of the disabled, and their dependence on families or the community for care and total support. This has been well demonstrated by intensive services to persons with strokes.

Rehabilitative services are among the most costly now provided. It seems unlikely that voluntary insurance, contributed funds, or private resources can in an adequate number of cases finance rehabilitation which does not make the individual self-supporting. If the need is to be met on any wide scale, public funds are necessary.

In addition, we should encourage community hospitals to provide rehabilitative services, give particular attention to disabled children, and continue our emphasis on rehabilitation in the provisions of voluntary insurance contracts.

Medical care for the aged. There is widespread agreement that a third desirable health goal is to provide more adequate services to older people. The number of older persons is increasing. This is in part due to the victories of medicine and public health over the infectious diseases, especially of childhood. In part it is due to a rising standard of living. Older age involves a wearing out of the human body, and a consequent increase in demand for health services. There is disagreement as to how this demand should be met.

Older people, particularly after retirement, have limited income available to purchase health and hospital services. Frequently, when voluntary health insurance has endeavored to cover older persons, it has encountered difficulties by seeming to impose burdens on younger subscribers. Voluntary insurance has therefore not gone, and, indeed, it cannot go, as far in meeting the needs of older people as it has the needs of the younger, employed group.

Older people, like other citizens, tend to move about the country, and this mobility makes it difficult to work out plans for them on a state basis. Welfare assistance requires a test of financial need. The application of this means test to large numbers of people in our society is distasteful.

If we are to attain minimum standards of health service for older people throughout the nation, there must be national action. In the author's opinion, the logical choice is an extension of the present federal social security system. Such an extension would reflect the principle of contribution, during working years, of funds identified to provide as much health service as possible in old age. The Old Age, Survivors and Disability Insurance program is becoming a major factor in meeting minimum needs for older people, and it is logical to include the provision of health services in the same administrative machinery. Extension of the social security machinery is also advantageous because it is independent of the financial capacities of the individual states and avoids the application of a means test.

Relieving the voluntary insurance plans from a social obligation to cover health needs of older people should allow them to extend their coverage of the employed population even more rapidly.

The required action should be taken soon. Stop-gap measures providing federal assistance to states for medical care of needy older people only delay and confuse the attainment of the proper objective.

Mental illness. Mental illness is one of the most anguishing and exasperating health problems in our time. It has received great attention within the health professions, by community organizations, and by state and federal governments. It is an important cause of disability and an expensive part of our health service. Indeed, the cost to state governments alone is in excess of $1 billion. Some 17 million persons are estimated to be suffering from it in our country. The present state of our knowledge does not provide adequate means for its prevention and cure.

A fourth goal, therefore, is to accelerate research into causes and cures of mental illness. But as we gain and apply new knowledge, we should also push to improve the decency of the operation of our mental institutions and to encourage development of extra-institutional community health services.

In our country, support of research into mental illness and the principal support of its institutional services are acknowledged public responsibilities. To meet our obligation in the years ahead, more governmental attention should be given to this vast problem. As much federal money should be appropriated for research in this field as can be profitably spent.

Many of the services now provided for the mentally ill, particularly in institutions, are more for the custody of the ill person than for the treatment of his illness. These services are financed and operated by state governments. There is clear evidence that this custodial function would not require the isolation of many of the mentally ill in remote institutions, if there were proper community services permitting them to enjoy a family and home life.

State and federal governments should together undertake to fashion programs of coordinated community service that would permit a sensible relationship between the services of the community clinic, the community hospital, the home, and the specialized mental hospitals and clinics. State governments should at least elevate standards of service in their own mental institutions to the levels which they demand of homes and hospitals over which they have regulatory authority.

Voluntary health insurance has generally not provided extensive coverage for mental illness. There are encouraging experiments to enlarge such coverage. It is particularly important that voluntary insurance endeavor to cover forms of treatment which can be carried out over short periods of time in community or specialized hospitals.

An informed public. A fifth goal is to improve the general health knowledge of each person. This is necessary to enable us not only to distinguish between folklore and fact, but also to recognize the relationship of environment to health, and to understand that one's genetic inheritance, his family relationships, and even his job situation may influence both physical and mental health.

Moreover, as health-service machinery grows complicated, we need to improve individual capacity to select the service which is needed.

It has been said that in a state of total disaster each citizen would have to depend on his own medical resources for his survival. While we do not like to contemplate the necessity of facing such disaster, there is no substitute for knowledge. We should increase the emphasis in our educational system, particularly in the elementary and secondary school curricula, on the study of man as a biological organism and of the effect of physical and emotional environment on personal health. The health professions can best serve an informed citizenry.

III

THE REDUCTION OF POVERTY THROUGH
INCOME SECURITY AND WELFARE SERVICES

Low incomes mean that people are living at a level below an acceptable standard of decency. Such poverty is destructive.

In the United States, as in other western cultures, we have attacked poverty by significant use of devices to provide income security. While we have not devised a system of family allowances, such as is common in many countries, we have made extensive use of social insurance against the involuntary interruption of income. Social insurance in general involves contributions by the earner, so that when earnings are interrupted by death, injury, disability, unemployment, or old age, an amount related to earnings will be paid to him or his dependents. Social insurance is created by legislative action. Ours is not a tidy single system, but was established by such legislation as the federal Social Security Act of 1935, and workmen's compensation and federal-state unemployment insurance acts in all of the states. Social insurance is complemented extensively by private pension plans.

This system has evolved slowly, and it is quite natural that it should still contain some defects in its coverage. In addition to the need to extend social insurance to provide medical services to older persons, there are two other types of coverage which call for prompt strengthening. These are protection against income loss due to unemployment or disability.

Unemployment insurance is essentially a state responsibility operating under loose federal standards and assisted in times of emergency by federal loans. At present there are significant deficiencies in coverage of long-term involuntary unemployment. Indeed, only one state provides benefits for a period of 26 weeks, and at a level of 50 per cent of a worker's earnings in covered employment. Experience in the recession of 1958 indicated that the reserve funds in states with large unemployment were not adequate to service the existing benefit program.

To meet these inadequacies the states should continue to extend and enlarge the benefits. The federal government should furnish assistance in the form of loans or grants or reinsurance to provide against the drying up of state funds in a serious recession. This would require the federal government to be concerned about the fiscal solvency of state programs and might require federal legislation compelling states to improve the financing of their programs. In carrying out these recommendations it should be borne in mind that, as pointed out in the chapter by Mr. Watson, unemployment insurance is not a permanent cure. The cure for unemployment is more jobs.

Disability protection. In the field of insurance against wage and salary loss due to sickness or injury, there has been in recent years an extension of coverage following two major patterns. The first has been aid to the permanently and totally disabled, provided through extension of the federal Old Age and Survivors Insurance system. The second has been the extension of private protection by development of voluntary cash sick-leave plans and the purchase of individual and group disability insurance. The principal issue under discussion at the present time is whether protection against loss of pay due to sickness or other temporary disability should be made mandatory.

While it is clearly desirable that most American families have such disability protection, there is substantial disagreement as to how an enlargement in the coverage should be carried out. State-sponsored compulsory temporary disability programs are presently in effect in four states. These vary in form; some do and some do not make use of private insurance. It seems clear that there is also further opportunity for significant development of voluntary temporary disability insurance.

Under these circumstances it would seem wise not to prescribe a single course of action, but to work towards an extension of disability protection on all fronts, encouraging both public and private exploration and experimentation.

Even with the improvements we have suggested, however, social insurance will not cover all major family risks in the decade ahead. Public assistance and public and private welfare services will still be required, and careful attention to their development is necessary.

Some 350,000 persons in the United States are in desperate want, and do not fall within any of the categories benefited by the social insurance system or federal contributions. Their needs are met in some states by the provision of local funds, in others only by private charity. It has been suggested that federal matching funds should be made available to states for their assistance. There should be continued study of this issue and an effort toward its resolution.

IV

NEGLECT AND DELINQUENCY: ASSISTANCE TO CHILDREN AND UNDERSTANDING THE PROBLEM

The programs we have just described for income security and assistance to the needy have as their premise that the way to meet human needs arising from poverty is to supplement incomes. This is a valuable premise, when those who are in need will use the added income constructively, for it results in the least interference with the freedom and independence of the individual. But what should society do to meet the needs of children who do not have parents to care for them, or whose parents cannot be counted on to use financial help constructively, or who appear to fail to respond to their parents and society alike?

Services for neglected children. The question is acutely presented by the category of public assistance which is supported by federal aid to states and is known as Aid to Dependent Children. This program makes financial assistance available for the protection and care of 2,300,000 homeless, dependent, and neglected children, and children in danger of becoming delinquent. These children are found not only where a parent is dead or physically incapacitated, but also in families where there is desertion, divorce, or, indeed, where there was no marriage. For the most part, the assistance is paid to the parent with whom the children are living.

This program is now subject to widespread attack on the ground that it subsidizes immorality and desertion. It is no doubt true that the funds are spent in families where there is extensive family breakdown; that is precisely the reason the funds are needed. But there is little logic to the notion, which has its ardent supporters, that rates of illegitimacy will be reduced by withdrawal of assistance from families where the mother has borne two illegitimate children.

It is more likely that the relationships between the prevention and cure of family breakdown are akin to the relationships between preventive and curative medicine. Financial support or welfare services are forms of treatment directed to the needs of each child who is affected. They will not materially increase the extent of family breakdown, nor will they much reduce it. But our knowledge of how to prevent such breakdown is pitifully inadequate, and such services are the only way we know to offset the disadvantages a youngster may incur from his inability to choose his parents or from the social circumstances of his birth.

It is well to heed the advice contained in a recent report of the Department of Health, Education, and Welfare's Advisory Coucil on Child Welfare Services, and consider broadening the scope of assistance for children beyond the narrow limits in the present Act to include support for

> "those services that supplement or substitute for parental care and supervision for the purpose of protecting and promoting the welfare of children and youth, preventing neglect, abuse and exploitation, helping overcome problems that result in dependency, neglect, and delinquency, and when needed providing adequate care for children and youth away from their own homes, such care to be given in foster family homes, adoptive homes, child caring institutions, or other facilities."

This proposal goes beyond financial support to the parent of the disadvantaged child. It recognizes that it may be necessary to alter the environment of such a child, and develop new institutional settings for him. These should support and supplement his inadequate family situation and provide him the opportunity to develop his inherent abilities.

In the years immediately ahead, there will be not only a larger number of older people, but also more children. There is a clear likelihood that we shall in addition have an increasing percentage of working mothers. To the extent that reduced parental supervision is involved in the social breakdown of families, these demographic trends suggest that we may be headed for increased difficulties. Important as it is to extend a decent standard of living and health to older people, it is far more important to the nation that we maintain universal opportunity for a high quality of achievement by our youth.

Juvenile delinquency. Of all the symptoms of social disorganization, there is none more perplexing than juvenile delinquency. It has some of the characteristics of a contagious disease, for its presence constitutes a threat not only to the young person involved, but also to the life and property of citizens at large, who have not been directly involved in the development of the juvenile's delinquent behavior.

Like a contagious disease, juvenile delinquency spreads geograph-ically. Its heaviest incidence is in areas in American cities which have long had high rates. It is increasing in suburban areas adjacent to the city, and the rate of increase there is higher than in the central city. The present rate of increase in the number of cases coming before juvenile courts is about five times the increase in the number of young people aged ten to seventeen. If the present trend continues unabated, it has been estimated that by 1970 one boy in every five will be involved in at least one court delinquency during his adolescence.

The treatment and prevention of delinquency, if we may dignify our efforts by such terms, are far more complex than the treatment of spe-cific physical illness or the provision of income security at a time of unemployment. There are vastly varying perceptions of the role which heredity, home, physical environment, school, church, police, and other community institutions play in the cause and prevention of juvenile de-linquency; there is no certain causal relationship uniting it with poverty and broken homes. The only general agreement is that we are dealing here with a community problem which calls, if any progress is to be made at all toward understanding or correction, for cooperative study and ac-tion by many professions, community services, and organizations.

The two principal techniques presently in use to rehabilitate delin-quent youth are probation services and institutional care. There are not enough acceptably trained personnel to apply these traditional rehabili-tative methods. Only one out of ten juvenile probation officers has com-pleted social work training, and six out of ten have had no such training at all. Half of the cities in the United States above 10,000 population have no special juvenile police officer, and there are significant shortages of staff psychologists and social workers in state training schools.

This shortage of skilled workers is appalling evidence that we are far from using our best efforts in applying present techniques to the rehabili-tation of the delinquent individual. The deficiency will not be corrected simply by setting higher personnel standards, paying better salaries, and providing more adequate training opportunities, though all of these are needed. Much of this rehabilitation work is conducted within the ma-chinery of criminal justice, and much of the administration of criminal justice is based upon the concept that arrest and detention are useful deterrents to further crime. Firm and authoritative measures in han-dling the individual delinquent are important. But present evidence about human behavior supports the proposition that many delinquents are able with progressive assistance to make satisfactory adjustments in their social behavior, without resort to arrest and detention.

The school, as well as the police, is significantly involved in the iden-tification of the individual delinquent and the decision that he should appear in court. Heavy responsibility falls upon both these agencies. They must be equipped to distinguish between deviant adolescent behavior which can be controlled without resort to arrest and detention, and those forms of behavior which will become so severe as to damage both the community and the youth. Our schools, which are in the best position to anticipate delinquent behavior, are particularly laggard in preparing themselves to handle this problem. All too few have staffs of psychologists, psychiatrists, and case workers.

The search for understanding. We cannot ignore our responsibilities for the treatment of each case. But it is no more likely that we will substantially reduce juvenile delinquency in this fashion than it is that assistance to neglected children will affect the family breakdown that caused the neglect. We must set our future goals on some other basis. In establishing them we must recognize that we are dealing with the whole relationship of a youth to his family, school, and community. Like the very process of urbanization itself, such a complex of factors is not easily accessible to study or planning or action based upon planning. Despite these difficulties we should neither panic at the insistent increase of delinquency nor despair at the inadequacy of our present knowledge.

Here, as in the fields of mental health and family breakdown, we need to seek new knowledge aggressively. How important, for instance, is the absence of a father as a factor in the onset of delinquent behavior? Can we define more accurately the apparently contagious nature of the spread of this disorder? What is the cause of the changing patterns of delinquency—of, for instance, its rapid increase in suburban areas adjacent to the central city? Are there new combinations of authority and welfare services which might be useful? Should we rely more on private institutions such as church and settlement house? Should we require that financial assistance to a family which contains a juvenile delinquent be contingent upon the acceptance of professional services for that child? What is the effect of war on juvenile behavior? What is the effect of a predominance of women teachers on schoolboys?

We are a rational society and must believe that juvenile delinquency and other forms of social maladjustment have specific causes. We must also believe that patient research will lead us ever closer to a clearer understanding of those causes, and we must continue to hope that the clearer our knowledge becomes about cause, the more effective will be our techniques of treatment and our options for prevention. Whether we shall decide to exercise these options is a matter for decision in the future, for it is not necessarily true that society will apply knowledge in hand. In the end, we may discover that to reduce juvenile delinquency to the full extent our knowledge permits would require that we control human behavior more rigidly than we are willing to do.

We have no reason to be satisfied with the present state of our endeavors. Substantial new leadership for research, demonstration and training is needed. And substantial financial support will be necessary.

Because social disorganization is ubiquitous, it is proper that both leadership and support for these purposes should come from the federal government. It has demonstrated its capacity to operate national institutes effectively. We presently have institutes for specific diseases of man such as heart disease and cancer. What is needed now is an institute devoted to man in society.

Such an institute could promote and conduct research and training, drawing upon social, biological, geographic, juridical, and ethical sciences, to the end that we may develop a clearer view of both our expectations and capabilities for man in his present society, learning at the same time something more about the management of deviant behavior.

V

PEOPLE, FACILITIES, AND MONEY

People. We live in an age of specialization. The need for competent specialized personnel to serve in fields of human welfare is just as urgent as industry's corresponding need. There are indications that we are falling behind. At a time when the number of college graduates has been increasing, when new knowledge in the biological sciences has been multiplying exponentially, when the horizons for service to people in the field of health are enlarging, we find that the number of applicants to medical schools has declined from 24,000 in 1948 to 15,000 in 1958. While we are still able to fill all the places in entering classes, medical schools do not enjoy the degree of selectivity which they deserve. Of even greater importance is the fact, which Dr. Gardner emphasizes elsewhere in this book, that medical schools are not turning out enough physicians. The need for new graduates in 1975 is estimated to be 11,000, against 7,400 graduates in 1959.

The situation is similar in dentistry, and we have already noted the shortage of trained welfare workers.

Unless steps are taken, shortages of manpower will be the most crucial limiting factors in meeting the goals we have outlined. A variety of approaches is necessary. For personnel such as physicians, dentists, nurses and social workers, where training at the graduate level after college is necessary, we must find ways to introduce substantial scholarship support. In the natural sciences other than medicine, financial support of education toward the doctor's degree has generously increased in recent years. Medicine and the allied professions require very long periods of training, frequently seven, eight or nine years after the college degree. Traditionally we have regarded this as apprentice training and have not provided adequate stipends or scholarships. We need now a federally-supported program of scholarships for training at the graduate level, which would alleviate the economic hardships of the rigorous training programs for the health and welfare professions. Since this training is so much in the public interest, its support should not be hedged by commitments to future service, or its usefulness abridged by requiring repayment on completion of training.

It is unlikely that capital expenditures for new medical schools can be supported by the private sector of our economy. Wherever possible, states should continue to develop new schools as they have in the past decade. A program of matching federal support for medical school facilities would be desirable, not only to stimulate progress in states which have programs under way, but to make it possible for poorer states to develop adequate facilities.

In order to encourage young people to choose careers in the fields of social welfare, all employing agencies will need to increase salaries. The effect of the population explosion will be felt here as in education. One of the important responses of education has been to increase salaries at a rate much more rapid than the increase in cost of living. Social welfare agencies must follow suit.

Much more can be done toward active employment of older persons in health and welfare fields. In many of the community activities designed to bring usefulness and self-respect to our senior citizens, other senior citizens could well perform many of the required tasks.

In a free country there is freedom of career choice. Unless we make careers in the health and welfare services attractive professionally, rewarding economically, and respected as useful to the community, we cannot hope to apply present knowledge or develop new understanding.

Facilities. Specialized people alone are not enough. We require also specialized facilities. In addition to the needs for educational plant, we need facilities for extending the usefulness of community hospitals and group practice clinics, for serving the needs of the mentally ill within the community, for serving youth whose family setting is inadequate, and for conducting essential research.

Voluntary giving appears to be reaching the end of its capacity to provide capital financing in many metropolitan areas. Already hospitals in such areas that have not been helped by the Hill-Burton program of matching federal-state grants are laboring under the inefficiencies of obsolescence. Provision of mental health facilities is, on the whole, a problem for state governments. Perhaps the development of nursing-home and custodial facilities for older people should also be developed with state support, but it is probable that states cannot do the entire task alone. We should therefore explore the extension to other social institutions of federal participation of the sort which has proved so useful to hospitals in the Hill-Burton Act.

Money. Expenditures for health and welfare in the United States have been rising rapidly. In 1950 they accounted for 9 per cent of the gross national product; today the more than $55 billion spent annually for these purposes amounts to about 12 per cent of the GNP. Much of the increase was caused by larger private payments for health and health insurance; in the 1950's they rose from $9 billion to $19 billion. Even after allowing for changes in the price level and the population, this was an increase of over 40 per cent per capita. Most of the balance went to social security, which has been extended to cover new groups and which automatically grows as those who retire, after longer insured employment, receive larger benefits.

The continued pressure of substantial unmet needs suggests that the present trend of increasing expenditures for health and welfare should be maintained and could be profitably increased. The magnitude of the generally acknowledged health and welfare needs is so great that we might well not be able to satisfy them by 1970 even if we doubled the present rate of growth in these fields. It is unlikely that such an increase could occur, even if we wished it to; the decisions required in both the public and private sectors of our economy are far too complex to be made so quickly.

More reasonable objectives for the decade are that the over-all rate of growth be increased by about one-third. The social security program has nearly matured, and its costs (exclusive of extension to health care for the aged) should not increase as rapidly in this decade as in the past. More efficient use of hospitals and group practice organizations could slow down the increase in medical costs. But expenditures for medical care for the aged, rehabilitation services, expanded construction of capital facilities, and medical and social service education and resarch should rise far more than in the past.

The projected expenditures for health and welfare seem modest when compared with the human values involved, particularly when it is remembered that an earlier meeting of health needs, greater income security, and more rehabilitation of the disabled will increase our productive potential.

* * * * * * * * * *

There is an opportunity in the decade ahead to further improve the health, the economic security, and the quality of social organization of the American people. Present knowledge awaits application. Future knowledge awaits discovery. Progress depends upon the courage to make decisions about priorities, the wisdom to find ways in which careers in the service of man can be as attractive as careers in the pursuit of science, and the ability to continue to improve our capacity to use government as a device to produce realistic and expedient decisions, reconciling our aims for social justice and our concerns for the protection of individual independence.

Community and government are inventions of man and cannot, wittingly or unwittingly, escape involvement in responsibility for the improvement of the human condition.

12

T HE AUTHOR *of this chapter is Professor Morton Grodzins, a member of the political science faculty of the University of Chicago and director of its Federalism Workshop. His provocative thesis, which we believe represents a new interpretation of the American federal system, is that from the earliest days of the country all levels of government—national, state and local—have participated in all functions of government, from so-called "local" police activities to so-called "national" foreign policy. If he is right, his argument has profound significance for the way we should go about improving our federal system.*

Professor Grodzins takes responsibility for the views expressed in the chapter. He has been advised by the panel listed below. The members of the panel wish it to be noted that they are in general agreement with Mr. Grodzins' description of the way the federal system operates today, although several members of the panel have expressed differences of opinion which are noted in a footnote in the chapter.

PANEL

RICHARD CARPENTER, Executive Director and General Counsel, League of California Cities.

THOMAS H. ELIOT, Professor of Political Science and Department Chairman, Washington University, St. Louis; formerly, Member of Congress and General Counsel of the Social Security Board.

ARTHUR NAFTALIN, Commissioner of Administration, State of Minnesota; formerly, Secretary to the Mayor of Minneapolis.

JOHN A. PERKINS, President, University of Delaware; formerly, Budget Director, State of Michigan, and Under Secretary of Health, Education and Welfare.

EMMETTE S. REDFORD, Professor of Political Science, University of Texas; President, American Political Science Association.

WILLIAM J. RONAN, Secretary to the Governor, New York State; formerly, Dean, School of Public Administration, New York University, and First Deputy City Administrator, New York City.

THE FEDERAL SYSTEM*

MORTON GRODZINS

Federalism is a device for dividing decisions and functions of government. As the constitutional fathers well understood, the federal structure is a means, not an end. The pages that follow are therefore not concerned with an exposition of American federalism as a formal, legal set of relationships. The focus, rather, is on the purpose of federalism, that is to say, on the distribution of power between central and peripheral units of government.

I

THE SHARING OF FUNCTIONS

The American form of government is often, but erroneously, symbolized by a three-layer cake. A far more accurate image is the rainbow or marble cake, characterized by an inseparable mingling of differently colored ingredients, the colors appearing in vertical and diagonal strands and unexpected whirls. As colors are mixed in the marble cake, so functions are mixed in the American federal system. Consider the health officer, styled "sanitarian," of a rural county in a border state. He embodies the whole idea of the marble cake of government.

The sanitarium is appointed by the state under merit standards established by the federal government. His base salary comes jointly from state and federal funds, the county provides him with an office and office amenities and pays a portion of his expenses, and the largest city in the county also contributes to his salary and office by virtue of his appointment as a city plumbing inspector. It is impossible from moment to moment to tell under which governmental hat the sanitarian operates. His work of inspecting the purity of food is carried out under federal standards; but he is enforcing state laws when inspecting commodities that have not been in interstate commerce; and somewhat perversely he also acts under state authority when inspecting milk coming into the county from producing areas across the state border. He is a federal officer when impounding impure drugs shipped from a neighboring state; a federal-state officer when distributing typhoid immunization serum; a state officer when enforcing

*This paper is the product of research carried out in the Federalism Workshop of the University of Chicago. I am indebted to the workshop participants, particularly Daniel J. Elazar, Dennis Palumbo, and Kenneth E. Gray, for data they collected. I profited greatly in writing Part III of the paper from Mr. Elazar's prize-winning dissertation, "Intergovernmental Relations in Nineteenth Century American Federalism" (Chicago, 1959).

265

standards of industrial hygiene; a state-local officer when inspecting the city's water supply; and (to complete the circle) a local officer when insisting that the city butchers adopt more hygienic methods of handling their garbage. But he cannot and does not think of himself as acting in these separate capacities. All business in the county that concerns public health and sanitation he considers his business. Paid largely from federal funds, he does not find it strange to attend meetings of the city council to give expert advice on matters ranging from rotten apples to rabies control. He is even deputized as a member of both the city and county police forces.

The sanitarian is an extreme case, but he accurately represents an important aspect of the whole range of governmental activities in the United States. Functions are not neatly parceled out among the many governments. They are shared functions. It is difficult to find any governmental activity which does not involve all three of the so-called "levels" of the federal system. In the most local of local functions— law enforcement or education, for example—the federal and state governments play important roles. In what, *a priori,* may be considered the purest central government activities—the conduct of foreign affairs, for example—the state and local governments have considerable responsibilities, directly and indirectly.

The federal grant programs are only the most obvious example of shared functions. They also most clearly exhibit how sharing serves to disperse governmental powers. The grants utilize the greater wealth-gathering abilities of the central government and establish nation-wide standards, yet they are "in aid" of functions carried out under state law, with considerable state and local discretion. The national supervision of such programs is largely a process of mutual accommodation. Leading state and local officials, acting through their professional organizations, are in considerable part responsible for the very standards that national officers try to persuade all state and local officers to accept.

Even in the absence of joint financing, federal-state-local collaboration is the characteristic mode of action. Federal expertise is available to aid in the building of a local jail (which may later be used to house federal prisoners), to improve a local water purification system, to step up building inspections, to provide standards for state and local personnel in protecting housewives against dishonest butchers' scales, to prevent gas explosions, or to produce a land use plan. States and localities, on the other hand, take important formal responsibilities in the development of national programs for atomic energy, civil defense, the regulation of commerce, and the protection of purity in foods and drugs; local political weight is always a factor in the operation of even a post office or a military establishment. From abattoirs and accounting through zoning and zoo administration, any governmental activity is almost certain to involve the influence, if not the formal administration, of all three planes of the federal system.

II

ATTEMPTS TO UNWIND THE FEDERAL SYSTEM

Within the past dozen years there have been four major attempts to reform or reorganize the federal system: the first (1947-49) and second (1953-55) Hoover Commissions on Executive Organization; the Kestnbaum Commission on Intergovernmental Relations (1953-55); and the Joint Federal-State Action Committee (1957-59). All four of these groups have aimed to minimize federal activities. None of them has recognized the sharing of functions as the characteristic way American governments do things. Even when making recommendations for joint action, these official commissions take the view (as expressed in the Kestnbaum report) that "the main tradition of American federalism [is] the tradition of separateness." All four have, in varying degrees, worked to separate functions and tax sources.

The history of the Joint Federal-State Action Committee is especially instructive. The committee was established at the suggestion of President Eisenhower, who charged it, first of all, "to designate functions which the States are ready and willing to assume and finance that are now performed or financed wholly or in part by the Federal Government." He also gave the committee the task of recommending "Federal and State revenue adjustments required to enable the States to assume such functions."*

The committee subsequently established seemed most favorably situated to accomplish the task of functional separation. It was composed of distinguished and able men, including among its personnel three leading members of the President's cabinet, the director of the Bureau of the Budget, and ten state governors. It had the full support of the President at every point, and it worked hard and conscientiously. Excellent staff studies were supplied by the Bureau of the Budget, the White House, the Treasury Department, and, from the state side, the Council of State Governments. It had available to it a large mass of research data, including the sixteen recently completed

* The President's third suggestion was that the committee "identify functions and responsibilities likely to require state or federal attention in the future and . . . recommend the level of state effort, or federal effort, or both, that will be needed to assure effective action." The committee initially devoted little attention to this problem. Upon discovering the difficulty of making separatist recommendations, i.e., for turning over federal functions and taxes to the states, it developed a series of proposals looking to greater effectiveness in intergovernmental collaboration. The committee was succeeded by a legislatively-based, 26-member Advisory Commission on Intergovernmental Relations, established September 29, 1959.

volumes of the Kestnbaum Commission. There existed no disagreements on party lines within the committee and, of course, no constitutional impediments to its mission. The President, his cabinet members, and all the governors (with one possible exception) on the committee completely agreed on the desirability of decentralization-via-separation-of-functions-and-taxes. They were unanimous in wanting to justify the committee's name and to produce action, not just another report.

The committee worked for more than two years. It found exactly two programs to recommend for transfer from federal to state hands. One was the federal grant program for vocational education (including practical-nurse training and aid to fishery trades); the other was federal grants for municipal waste treatment plants. The programs together cost the federal government less than $80 million in 1957, slightly more than two per cent of the total federal grants for that year. To allow the states to pay for these programs, the committee recommended that they be allowed a credit against the federal tax on local telephone calls. Calculations showed that this offset device, plus an equalizing factor, would give every state at least 40 per cent more from the tax than it received from the federal government in vocational education and sewage disposal grants. Some states were "equalized" to receive twice as much.

The recommendations were modest enough, and the generous financing feature seemed calculated to gain state support. The President recommended to Congress that all points of the program be legislated. None of them was, none has been since, and none is likely to be.

III

A POINT OF HISTORY

The American federal system has never been a system of separated governmental activities. There has never been a time when it was possible to put neat labels on discrete "federal," "state," and "local" functions. Even before the Constitution, a statute of 1785, reinforced by the Northwest Ordinance of 1787, gave grants-in-land to the states for public schools. Thus the national government was a prime force in making possible what is now taken to be the most local function of all, primary and secondary education. More important, the nation, before it was fully organized, established by this action a first principle of American federalism: the national government would use its superior resources to initiate and support national programs, principally administered by the states and localities.

The essential unity of state and federal financial systems was again recognized in the earliest constitutional days with the assumption by the federal government of the Revolutionary War debts of the states.

Other points of federal-state collaboration during the Federalist period concerned the militia, law enforcement, court practices, the administration of elections, public health measures, pilot laws, and many other matters.

The nineteenth century is widely believed to have been the pre-eminent period of duality in the American system. Lord Bryce at the end of the century described (in *The American Commonwealth*) the federal and state governments as "distinct and separate in their action." The system, he said, was "like a great factory wherein two sets of machinery are at work, their revolving wheels apparently intermixed, their bands crossing one another, yet each set doing its own work without touching or hampering the other." Great works may contain gross errors. Bryce was wrong. The nineteenth century, like the early days of the republic, was a period principally characterized by intergovernmental collaboration.

Decisions of the Supreme Court are often cited as evidence of nineteenth century duality. In the early part of the century the Court, heavily weighted with Federalists, was intent upon enlarging the sphere of national authority; in the later years (and to the 1930's) its actions were in the direction of paring down national powers and indeed all governmental authority. Decisions referred to "areas of exclusive competence" exercised by the federal government and the states; to their powers being "separate and distinct;" and to neither being able "to intrude within the jurisdiction of the other."

Judicial rhetoric is not always consistent with judicial action, and the Court did not always adhere to separatist doctrine. Indeed, its rhetoric sometimes indicated a positive view of cooperation. In any case, the Court was rarely, if ever, directly confronted with the issue of cooperation *vs.* separation as such. Rather it was concerned with defining permissible areas of action for the central government and the states; or with saying with respect to a point at issue whether any government could take action. The Marshall Court contributed to intergovernmental cooperation by the very act of permitting federal operations where they had not existed before. Furthermore, even Marshall was willing to allow interstate commerce to be affected by the states in their use of the police power. Later courts also upheld state laws that had an impact on interstate commerce, just as they approved the expansion of the national commerce power, as in statutes providing for the control of telegraphic communication or prohibiting the interstate transportation of lotteries, impure foods and drugs, and prostitutes. Similar room for cooperation was found outside the commerce field, notably in the Court's refusal to interfere with federal grants in land or cash to the states. Although research to clinch the point has not been completed, it is probably true that the Supreme Court from

1800 to 1936 allowed far more federal-state collaboration than it blocked.

Political behavior and administrative action of the nineteenth century provide positive evidence that, throughout the entire era of so-called dual federalism, the many governments in the American federal system continued the close administrative and fiscal collaboration of the earlier period. Governmental activities were not extensive. But relative to what governments did, intergovernmental cooperation during the last century was comparable with that existing today.

Occasional presidential vetoes (from Madison to Buchanan) of cash and land grants are evidence of constitutional and ideological apprehensions about the extensive expansion of federal activities which produced widespread intergovernmental collaboration. In perspective, however, the vetoes are a more important evidence of the continuous search, not least by state officials, for ways and means to involve the central government in a wide variety of joint programs. The search was successful.

Grants-in-land and grants-in-services from the national government were of first importance in virtually all the principal functions undertaken by the states and their local subsidiaries. Land grants were made to the states for, among other purposes, elementary schools, colleges, and special educational institutions; roads, canals, rivers, harbors, and railroads; reclamation of desert and swamp lands; and veterans' welfare. In fact whatever was at the focus of state attention became the recipient of national grants. (Then, as today, national grants established state emphasis as well as followed it.) If Connecticut wished to establish a program for the care and education of the deaf and dumb, federal money in the form of a land grant was found to aid that program. If higher education relating to agriculture became a pressing need, Congress could dip into the public domain and make appropriate grants to states. If the need for swamp drainage and flood control appeared, the federal government could supply both grants-in-land and, from the Army's Corps of Engineers, the services of the only trained engineers then available.

Aid also went in the other direction. The federal government, theoretically in exclusive control of the Indian population, relied continuously (and not always wisely) on the experience and resources of state and local governments. State militias were an all-important ingredient in the nation's armed forces. State governments became unofficial but real partners in federal programs for homesteading, reclamation, tree culture, law enforcement, inland waterways, the nation's internal communications system (including highway and railroad routes), and veterans' aid of various sorts. Administrative contacts were voluminous, and the whole process of interaction was lubricated, then as today, by constituent-conscious members of Congress.

The essential continuity of the collaborative system is best demonstrated by the history of the grants. The land grant tended to become a cash grant based on the calculated disposable value of the land, and the cash grant tended to become an annual grant based upon the national government's superior tax powers. In 1887, only three years before the frontier was officially closed, thus signalizing the end of the disposable public domain, Congress enacted the first continuing cash grants.

A long, extensive, and continuous experience is therefore the foundation of the present system of shared functions characteristic of the American federal system, what we have called the marble cake of government. It is a misjudgment of our history and our present situation to believe that a neat separation of governmental functions could take place without drastic alterations in our society and system of government.

IV

DYNAMICS OF SHARING: THE POLITICS OF THE FEDERAL SYSTEM

Many causes contribute to dispersed power in the federal system. One is the simple historical fact that the states existed before the nation. A second is in the form of creed, the traditional opinion of Americans that expresses distrust of centralized power and places great value in the strength and vitality of local units of government. Another is pride in locality and state, nurtured by the nation's size and by variations of regional and state history. Still a fourth cause of decentralization is the sheer wealth of the nation. It allows all groups, including state and local governments, to partake of the central government's largesse, supplies room for experimentation and even waste, and makes unnecessary the tight organization of political power that must follow when the support of one program necessarily means the deprivation of another.

In one important respect, the Constitution no longer operates to impede centralized government. The Supreme Court since 1937 has given Congress a relatively free hand. The federal government can build substantive programs in many areas on the taxation and commerce powers. Limitations of such central programs based on the argument, "it's unconstitutional," are no longer possible as long as Congress (in the Court's view) acts reasonably in the interest of the whole nation. The Court is unlikely to reverse this permissive view in the foreseeable future.

Nevertheless, some constitutional restraints on centralization continue to operate. The strong constitutional position of the states—for example, the assignment of two senators to each state, the role given the states in administering even national elections, and the relatively few limitations on their law-making powers—establish the geographical units as natural centers of administrative and political strength. Many clauses of the Constitution are not subject to the same latitude of interpretation as the commerce and tax clauses. The simple, clearly stated, unambiguous phrases—for example, the President "shall hold his office during the term of four years"—are subject to change only through the formal amendment process. Similar provisions exist with respect to the terms of senators and congressmen and the amendment process. All of them have the effect of retarding or restraining centralizing action of the federal government. The fixed terms of the President and members of Congress, for example, greatly impede the development of nation-wide, disciplined political parties that almost certainly would have to precede continuous large-scale expansion of federal functions.

The constitutional restraints on the expansion of national authority are less important and less direct today than they were in 1879 or in 1936. But to say that they are less important is not to say that they are unimportant.

The nation's politics reflect these decentralizing causes and add some of their own. The political parties of the United States are unique. They seldom perform the function that parties traditionally perform in other countries, the function of gathering together diverse strands of power and welding them into one. Except during the period of nominating and electing a president and for the essential but non-substantive business of organizing the houses of Congress, the American parties rarely coalesce power at all. Characteristically they do the reverse, serving as a canopy under which special and local interests are represented with little regard for anything that can be called a party program. National leaders are elected on a party ticket, but in Congress they must seek cross-party support if their leadership is to be effective. It is a rare president during rare periods who can produce legislation without facing the defection of substantial numbers of his own party. (Wilson could do this in the first session of the sixty-third Congress; but Franklin D. Roosevelt could not, even during the famous hundred days of 1933.) Presidents whose parties form the majority of the congressional houses must still count heavily on support from the other party.

The parties provide the pivot on which the entire governmental system swings. Party operations, first of all, produce in legislation the basic division of functions between the federal government, on the one hand, and state and local governments, on the other. The Supreme Court's permissiveness with respect to the expansion of national powers has not in fact produced any considerable extension of exclusive federal functions. The body of federal law in all fields has remained, in the words of Henry M. Hart, Jr. and Herbert Wechsler, "interstitial in its nature," limited in objective and resting upon the principal body of legal relationships defined by state law. It is difficult to find any area of federal legislation that is not significantly affected by state law.

In areas of new or enlarged federal activity, legislation characteristically provides important roles for state and local governments. This is as true of Democratic as of Republican administrations and true even of functions for which arguments of efficiency would produce exclusive federal responsibility. Thus the unemployment compensation program of the New Deal and the airport program of President Truman's administration both provided important responsibilities for state governments. In both cases attempts to eliminate state participation were defeated by a cross-party coalition of pro-state votes and influence. A large fraction of the Senate is usually made up of ex-governors, and the membership of both houses is composed of men who know that their re-election depends less upon national leaders or national party organization than upon support from their home constituencies. State and local officials are key members of these constituencies, often central figures in selecting candidates and in turning out the vote. Under such circumstances, national legislation taking state and local views heavily into account is inevitable.

Second, the undisciplined parties affect the character of the federal system as a result of senatorial and congressional interference in federal administrative programs on behalf of local interests. Many aspects of the legislative involvement in administrative affairs are formalized. The Legislative Reorganization Act of 1946, to take only one example, provided that each of the standing committees "shall exercise continuous watchfulness" over administration of laws within its jurisdiction. But the formal system of controls, extensive as it is, does not compare in importance with the informal and extralegal network of relationships in producing continuous legislative involvement in administrative affairs.

Senators and congressmen spend a major fraction of their time representing problems of their constituents before administrative agencies. An even larger fraction of congressional staff time is devoted to the same task. The total magnitude of such "case work" operations is great. In one five-month period of 1943 the Office of Price Administration received a weekly average of 842 letters from members of Congress. If phone calls and personal contacts are added, each member of Congress on the average presented the OPA with a problem involving one of his constituents twice a day in each five-day work week. Data for less vulnerable agencies during less intensive periods are also impressive. In 1958, to take only one example, the Department of Agriculture estimated (and underestimated) that it received an average of 159 congressional letters per working day. Special congressional liaison staffs have been created to service this mass of business, though all higher officials meet it in one form or another. The Air Force in 1958 had, under the command of a major general, 137 people (55 officers and 82 civilians) working in its liaison office.

The widespread, consistent, and in many ways unpredictable character of legislative interference in administrative affairs has many consequences for the tone and character of American administrative behavior. From the perspective of this paper, the important consequence is the comprehensive, day-to-day, even hour-by-hour, impact of local views on national programs. No point of substance or procedure is immune from congressional scrutiny. A substantial portion of the entire weight of this impact is on behalf of the state and local governments. It is a weight that can alter procedures for screening immigration applications, divert the course of a national highway, change the tone of an international negotiation, and amend a social security law to accommodate local practices or fulfill local desires.

The party system compels administrators to take a political role. This is a third way in which the parties function to decentralize the American system. The administrator must play politics for the same reason that the politician is able to play in administration: the parties are without program and without discipline.

In response to the unprotected position in which the party situation places him, the administrator is forced to seek support where he can find it. One ever-present task is to nurse the Congress of the United States, that crucial constituency which ultimately controls his agency's budget and program. From the administrator's view, a sympathetic consideration of congressional requests (if not downright submission to them) is the surest way to build the political support without which the administrative job could not continue. Even the completely task-oriented administrator must be sensitive to the need for congressional support and to the relationship between case work requests, on one side, and budgetary and legislative support, on the other. "You do a good job handling the personal problems and requests of a Congressman," a White House officer said, "and you have an easier time convincing him to back your program." Thus there is an important link between the nursing of congressional requests, requests that largely concern local matters, and the most comprehensive national programs. The administrator must accommodate to the former as a price of gaining support for the latter.

One result of administrative politics is that the administrative agency may become the captive of the nation-wide interest group it serves or presumably regulates. In such cases no government may come out with effective authority: the winners are the interest groups themselves. But in a very large number of cases, states and localities also win influence. The politics of administration is a process of making peace with legislators who for the most part consider themselves the guardians of local interests. The political role of administrators therefore contributes to the power of states and localities in national programs.

Finally, the way the party system operates gives American politics their over-all distinctive tone. The lack of party discipline produces an openness in the system that allows individuals, groups, and institutions (including state and local governments) to attempt to influence national policy at every step of the legislative-administrative process. This is the "multiple-crack" attribute of the American government. "Crack" has two meanings. It means not only many fissures or access points; it also means, less statically, opportunities for wallops or smacks at government.

If the parties were more disciplined, the result would not be a cessation of the process by which individuals and groups impinge themselves upon the central government. But the present state of the parties clearly allows for a far greater operation of the multiple crack than would be possible under the conditions of centralized party control. American interest groups exploit literally uncountable access points in the legislative-administrative process. If legislative lobbying, from committee stages to the conference committee, does not produce results, a cabinet secretary is called. His immediate associates are petitioned. Bureau chiefs and their aides are hit. Field officers are put under pressure. Campaigns are instituted by which friends of the agency apply a secondary influence on behalf of the interested party. A conference with the President may be urged.

To these multiple points for bringing influence must be added the multiple voices of the influencers. Consider, for example, those in a small town who wish to have a federal action taken. The easy merging of public and private interest at the local level means that the influence attempt is made in the name of the whole community, thus removing it from political partisanship. The Rotary Club as well as the City Council, the Chamber of Commerce and the mayor, eminent citizens and political bosses—all are readily enlisted. If a conference in a senator's office will expedite matters, someone on the local scene can be found to make such a conference possible and effective. If technical information is needed, technicians will supply it. State or national professional organizations of local officials, individual congressmen and senators, and not infrequently whole state delegations will make the local cause their own. Federal field officers, who service localities, often assume local views. So may elected and appointed state officers. Friendships are exploited, and political mortgages called due. Under these circumstances, national policies are molded by local action.

In summary, then, the party system functions to devolve power. The American parties, unlike any other, are highly responsive when directives move from the bottom to the top, highly unresponsive from top to bottom. Congressmen and senators can rarely ignore concerted demands from their home constituencies; but no party leader can expect the same kind of response from those below, whether he be a President asking for congressional support or a congressman seeking aid from local or state leaders.

Any tightening of the party apparatus would have the effect of strengthening the central government. The four characteristics of the system, discussed above, would become less important. If control from the top were strictly applied, these hallmarks of American decentralization might entirely disappear. To be specific, if disciplined and program-oriented parties were achieved: (1) It would make far less likely legislation that takes heavily into account the desires and prejudices of the highly decentralized power groups and institutions of the country, including the state and local governments. (2) It would to a large extent prevent legislators, individually and collectively, from intruding themselves on behalf of non-national interests in national administrative programs. (3) It would put an end to the administrator's search for his own political support, a search that often results in fostering state, local, and other non-national powers. (4) It would dampen the process by which individuals and groups, including state and local political leaders, take advantage of multiple cracks to steer national legislation and administration in ways congenial to them and the institutions they represent.

Alterations of this sort could only accompany basic changes in the organization and style of politics which, in turn, presuppose fundamental changes at the parties' social base. The sharing of functions is, in fact, the sharing of power. To end this sharing process would mean the destruction of whatever measure of decentralization exists in the United States today.

V

GOALS FOR THE SYSTEM OF SHARING

The goal of understanding. Our structure of government is complex, and the politics operating that structure are mildly chaotic. Circumstances are ever-changing. Old institutions mask intricate procedures. The nation's history can be read with alternative glosses, and what is nearest at hand may be furthest from comprehension. Simply to understand the federal system is therefore a difficult task. Yet without understanding there is little possibility of producing desired changes in the system. Social structures and processes are relatively impervious to purposeful change. They also exhibit intricate interrelationships so that change induced at point "A" often produces unanticipated results at point "Z." Changes introduced into an imperfectly understood system are as likely to produce reverse consequences as the desired ones.

This is counsel of neither futility nor conservatism for those who seek to make our government a better servant of the people. It is only to say that the first goal for those setting goals with respect to the federal system is that of understanding it.

Two kinds of decentralization. The recent major efforts to reform the federal system have in large part been aimed at separating functions and tax sources, at dividing them between the federal government and the states. All of these attempts have failed. We can now add that their success would be undesirable.

It is easy to specify the conditions under which an ordered separation of functions could take place. What is principally needed is a majority political party, under firm leadership, in control of both Presidency and Congress, and, ideally but not necessarily, also in control of a number of states. The political discontinuities, or the absence of party links, (1) between the governors and their state legislatures, (2) between the President and the governors, and (3) between the President and Congress clearly account for both the picayune recommendations of the Federal-State Action Committee and for the failure of even those recommendations in Congress. If the President had been in control of Congress (that is, consistently able to direct a majority of House and Senate votes), this alone would have made possible some genuine separation and devolution of functions. The failure to decentralize by order is a measure of the decentralization of power in the political parties.

Stated positively, party centralization must precede governmental decentralization by order. But this is a slender reed on which to hang decentralization. It implies the power to centralize. A majority party powerful enough to bring about ordered decentralization is far more likely to choose in favor of ordered centralization. And a society that produced centralized national parties would, by that very fact, be a society prepared to accept centralized government.

Decentralization by order must be contrasted with the different kind of decentralization that exists today in the United States. It may be called the decentralization of mild chaos. It exists because of the existence of dispersed power centers. This form of decentralization is less visible and less neat. It rests on no discretion of central authorities. It produces at times specific acts that many citizens may consider undesirable or evil. But power sometimes wielded even for evil ends may be desirable power. To those who find value in the dispersion of power, decentralization by mild chaos is infinitely more desirable than decentralization by order. The preservation of mild chaos is an important goal for the American federal system.

Oiling the squeak points. In a governmental system of genuinely shared responsibilities, disagreements inevitably occur. Opinions clash over proximate ends, particular ways of doing things become the subject of public debate, innovations are contested. These are not basic defects in the system. Rather, they are the system's energy-reflecting life blood. There can be no permanent "solutions" short of changing the system itself by elevating one partner to absolute supremacy. What can be done is to attempt to produce conditions in which conflict will not fester but be turned to constructive solutions of particular problems.

A long list of specific points of difficulty in the federal system can be easily identified. No adequate congressional or administrative mechanism exists to review the patchwork of grants in terms of national needs. There is no procedure by which to judge, for example, whether the national government is justified in spending so much more for highways than for education. The working force in some states is inadequate for the effective performance of some nation-wide programs, while honest and not-so-honest graft frustrates efficiency in others. Some federal aid programs distort state budgets, and some are so closely supervised as to impede state action in meeting local needs. Grants are given for programs too narrowly defined, and over-all programs at the state level consequently suffer. Administrative, accounting and auditing difficulties are the consequence of the multiplicity of grant programs. City officials complain that the states are intrusive fifth wheels in housing, urban redevelopment, and airport building programs.

Some differences are so basic that only a demonstration of strength on one side or another can solve them. School desegregation illustrates such an issue. It also illustrates the correct solution (although not the most desirable method of reaching it): in policy conflicts of fundamental importance, touching the nature of democracy itself, the view of the whole nation must prevail. Such basic ends, however, are rarely at issue, and sides are rarely taken with such passion that loggerheads are reached. Modes of settlement can usually be found to lubricate the squeak points of the system.

A pressing and permanent state problem, general in its impact, is the difficulty of raising sufficient revenue without putting local industries at a competitive disadvantage or without an expansion of sales taxes that press hardest on the least wealthy. A possible way of meeting this problem is to establish a state-levied income tax that could be used as an offset for federal taxes. The maximum level of the tax which could be offset would be fixed by federal law. When levied by a state, the state collection would be deducted from federal taxes. But if a state did not levy the tax, the federal government would. An additional fraction of the total tax imposed by the states would be collected directly by the federal government and used as an equalization fund, that is, distributed among the less wealthy states. Such a tax would almost certainly be imposed by all states since not to levy it would give neither political advantage to its public leaders nor financial advantage to its citizens. The net effect would be an increase in the total personal and corporate income tax.

The offset has great promise for strengthening state governments. It would help produce a more economic distribution of industry. It would have obvious financial advantages for the vast majority of states. Since a large fraction of all state income is used to aid political subdivisions, the local governments would also profit, though not equally as long as cities are under-represented in state legislatures. On the other hand, such a scheme will appear disadvantageous to some low-tax states which profit from the in-migration of industry (though it would by no means end all state-by-state tax differentials). It will probably excite the opposition of those concerned over governmental centralization, and they will not be assuaged by methods that suggest themselves for making both state and central governments bear the psychological impact of the tax. Although the offset would probably produce an across-the-board tax increase, wealthier persons, who are affected more by an income tax than by other levies, can be expected to join forces with those whose fear is centralization. (This is a common alliance and, in the nature of things, the philosophical issue rather than financial advantage is kept foremost.)

Those opposing such a tax would gain additional ammunition from the certain knowledge that federal participation in the scheme would lead to some federal standards governing the use of the funds. Yet the political strength of the states would keep these from becoming onerous. Indeed, inauguration of the tax offset as a means of providing funds to the states might be an occasion for dropping some of the specifications for existing federal grants. One federal standard, however, might be possible because of the greater representation of urban areas in the constituency of Congress and the President than in the constituency of state legislatures: Congress might make a state's participation in the offset scheme dependent upon a periodic reapportionment of state legislatures.

The income tax offset is only one of many ideas that can be generated to meet serious problems of closely meshed governments. The fate of all such schemes ultimately rests, as it should, with the politics of a free people. But much can be done if the primary technical effort of those concerned with improving the federal system were directed not at separating its interrelated parts but at making them work together more effectively. Temporary commissions are relatively inefficient in this effort, though they may be useful for making general assessments and for generating new ideas. The professional organizations of government workers do part of the job of continuously scrutinizing programs and ways and means of improving them. A permanent staff, established in the President's office and working closely with state and local officials, could also perform a useful and perhaps important role.

The strength of the parts. Whatever governmental "strength" or "vitality" may be, it does not consist of independent decision-making in legislation and administration. Federal-state interpenetration here is extensive. Indeed, a judgment of the relative domestic strength of the two planes must take heavily into account the influence of one on the other's decisions. In such an analysis the strength of the states (and localities) does not weigh lightly. The nature of the nation's politics makes federal functions more vulnerable to state influence than state offices are to federal influence. Many states, as the Kestnbaum Commission noted, live with "self-imposed constitutional limitations" that make it difficult for them to "perform all of the services that their citizens require." If this has the result of adding to federal responsibilities, the states' importance in shaping and administering federal programs eliminates much of the sting.

The geography of state boundaries, as well as many aspects of state internal organization, are the products of history and cannot be justified on any grounds of rational efficiency. Who, today, would create major governmental subdivisions the size of Maryland, Delaware, New Jersey, or Rhode Island? Who would write into Oklahoma's fundamental law an absolute state debt limit of $500,000? Who would design (to cite only the most extreme cases) Georgia's and Florida's gross under-representation of urban areas in both houses of the legislature?

A complete catalogue of state political and administrative horrors would fill a sizeable volume. Yet exhortations to erase them have roughly the same effect as similar exhortations to erase sin. Some of the worst inanities—for example, the boundaries of the states, themselves—are fixed in the national constitution and defy alteration for all foreseeable time. Others, such as urban under-representation in state legislatures, serve the over-represented groups, including some urban ones, and the effective political organization of the deprived groups must precede reform.

Despite deficiencies of politics and organizations that are unchangeable or slowly changing, it is an error to to look at the states as static anachronisms. Some of them—New York, Minnesota, and California, to take three examples spanning the country—have administrative organizations that compare favorably in many ways with the national establishment. Many more in recent years have moved rapidly towards integrated administrative departments, state-wide budgeting, and central leadership. The others have models-in-existence to follow, and active professional organizations (led by the Council of State Governments) promoting their development. Slow as this change may be, the states move in the direction of greater internal effectiveness.

The pace toward more effective performance at the state level is likely to increase. Urban leaders, who generally feel themselves disadvantaged in state affairs, and suburban and rural spokesmen, who are most concerned about national centralization, have a common interest in this task. The urban dwellers want greater equality in state affairs, including a more equitable share of state financial aid; non-urban dwellers are concerned that city dissatisfactions should not be met by exclusive federal, or federal-local, programs. Antagonistic, rather than amiable, cooperation may be the consequence. But it is a cooperation that can be turned to politically effective measures for a desirable upgrading of state institutions.

If one looks closely, there is scant evidence for the fear of the federal octopus, the fear that expansion of central programs and influence threatens to reduce the states and localities to compliant administrative arms of the central government. In fact, state and local governments are touching a larger proportion of the people in more ways than ever before; and they are spending a higher fraction of the total national product than ever before. Federal programs have increased, rather than diminished, the importance of the governors; stimulated professionalism in state agencies; increased citizen interest and participation in government; and, generally, enlarged and made more effective the scope of state action.* It may no longer be true in any significant sense that the states and localities are "closer" than the federal government to the people. It is true that the smaller governments remain active and powerful members of the federal system.

Central leadership: The need for balance. The chaos of party processes makes difficult the task of presidential leadership. It deprives the President of ready-made congressional majorities. It may produce, as in the chairmen of legislative committees, power-holders relatively hidden from public scrutiny and relatively protected from presidential direction. It allows the growth of administrative agencies which sometimes escape control by central officials. These are prices paid for a wide dispersion of political power. The cost is tolerable because the total results of dispersed power are themselves desirable and because, where clear national supremacy is essential, in foreign policy and military affairs, it is easiest to secure.

Moreover, in the balance of strength between the central and peripheral governments, the central government has on its side the whole secular drift towards the concentration of power. It has on its side technical developments that make central decisions easy and sometimes mandatory. It has on its side potent purse powers, the result of superior tax-gathering resources. It has potentially on its side the national leadership capacities of the presidential office. The last factor is the controlling one, and national strength in the federal system has shifted with the leadership desires and capacities of the chief executive. As these have varied, so there has been an almost rhythmic pattern: periods of central strength put to use alternating with periods of central strength dormant.

Following a high point of federal influence during the early and middle years of the New Deal, the post-war years have been, in the weighing of central-peripheral strength, a period of light federal activity. Excepting the Supreme Court's action in favor of school desegregation, national influence by design or default has not been strong

* See the valuable report, *The Impact of Federal Grants-in-Aid on the Structure and Functions of State and Local Governments,* submitted to the Commission on Intergovernmental Relations by the Governmental Affairs Institute (Washington, 1955).

in domestic affairs. The danger now is that the central government is doing too little rather than too much. National deficiencies in education and health require the renewed attention of the national government. Steepening population and urbanization trend lines have produced metropolitan area problems that can be effectively attacked only with the aid of federal resources. New definitions of old programs in housing and urban redevelopment, and new programs to deal with air pollution, water supply, and mass transportation are necessary. The federal government's essential role in the federal system is that of organizing, and helping to finance, such nation-wide programs.

The American federal system exhibits many evidences of the dispersion of power not only because of formal federalism but more importantly because our politics reflect and reinforce the nation's diversities-within-unity. Those who value the virtues of decentralization, which writ large are virtues of freedom, need not scruple at recognizing the defects of those virtues. The defects are principally the danger that parochial and private interests may not coincide with, or give way to, the nation's interest. The necessary cure for these defects is effective national leadership.

The centrifugal force of domestic politics needs to be balanced by the centripetal force of strong presidential leadership. Simultaneous strength at center and periphery exhibits the American system at its best, if also at its noisiest. The interests of both find effective spokesmen. States and localities (and private interest groups) do not lose their influence opportunities, but national policy becomes more than the simple consequence of successful, momentary concentrations of non-national pressures: it is guided by national leaders.*

* Messrs. Perkins and Redford state:
    Professor Grodzins has made a significant contribution. The federal system has contributed to a "mild chaos" both administratively and financially. He accurately assesses the several quite futile attempts to disentangle the administrative and fiscal relationships of the states and the national government.
    At this juncture, however, it should be remembered that the present system of shared responsibility confuses rather than fixes responsibility. Ascertainable responsibility for policy, administrative performance, and financing is an essential feature of effective self-government. The possibility of achieving it needs to be explored.
    A reduction of the sharing of power would to some degree cause greater centralization of responsibility in the federal government. It would not necessarily result in loss of appropriate administrative decentralization and the loss of influence by the ordinary citizen over the activities of government. This is illustrated by what Mr. Grodzins himself says concerning the influence of the localized party structure on administration of centralized national functions.
    The chaos of party processes itself impairs leadership for national functions and national aims. Mr. Grodzins' conclusion that the costs of this chaos are tolerable may be drawn too easily. Whether the centrifugal pulls of party decentralization are so strong as to seriously threaten national leadership and responsibility in our government deserves careful assessment.
    Decentralization is an essential goal of American policy. So also are responsibility and leadership. Public concern needs to manifest itself about both of these goals.

13

THE PUBLIC SERVICE

WALLACE S. SAYRE

WALLACE S. SAYRE, *Eaton Professor of Public Administration at Columbia University, has dealt with personnel problems on all levels of government all of his professional life. He was director of personnel for the Office of Price Administration during World War II and has been consultant on personnel administration to the State Department, the Atomic Energy Commission, and other federal, state and local government agencies, as well as Commissioner of Civil Service for New York City. He was the Technical Director of the Sixth American Assembly and editor of its volume on* The Federal Government Service, *and is the author of numerous books and articles on personnel matters. This chapter outlines his program for improving the public service.*

The panel advising Mr. Sayre is listed below. He takes responsibility for the opinions expressed.

PANEL

DONALD C. CARPENTER, General Manager, Film Department, E. I. du Pont de Nemours & Company; formerly, Chairman of the Munitions Board and deputy to the Secretary of Defense for atomic energy matters.

GEORGE A. GRAHAM, Director of Governmental Studies, Brookings Institution; Staff Director, task force on personnel and civil service, Hoover Commission, 1953-54.

JOHN W. MACY, JR., Executive Vice President, Wesleyan University; formerly Executive Director, Civil Service Commission.

HARVEY C. MANSFIELD, Chairman, Department of Political Science, Ohio State University; formerly, Project Director, Connecticut Commission on State Government Organization.

THE PUBLIC SERVICE

WALLACE S. SAYRE

The events of this generation have given a new and special importance to the American public service. The emerging signs of the coming decade foreshadow its even greater importance. Three deep-running forces in our national life have converged to impose unprecedented and unremitting demands for high quality in ideas and in performance. The first and most urgent of these forces is the leadership role which the United States has acquired in a bipolarized world, a role in which political leaders and governmental staffs share fateful responsibilities for the safety of the nation and the world. The second great pressure upon the public service flows from the expanding functions of all levels of our government, embracing crucial assignments in the economic growth of the nation, the well-being and the expanding opportunities of its people. Accelerating and sharpening these demands upon the public service are the requirements for new policies and new modes of administration to govern satisfactorily the complex and interdependent metropolitan regions being created by the rapid urbanization of the United States.

The qualities of the public service required by these developments are almost self-evident. High competence in administration; integrity, stability and reliability in performance; and most significantly, the capacity for innovation and creativity are needed to envision and attain national goals.

In addition, these virtues must be achieved within the norms of a democratic society which demand that the public service be representative in its composition, responsive in its behavior, and responsible to popular institutions in its exercise of power. The governments of the United States face no easy task in combining all these necessary attributes of the American public service—competence, stability, innovation, creativity, representativeness, responsiveness, responsibility—into a coherent personnel policy, because some of the qualities desired may conflict with others equally desirable. Stability and innovation, competence and representativeness, for example, are often rivals rather than congenial partners.

Adding to these present and predictable difficulties is the discomforting fact that governments in the United States are not now, and are not likely to become, the most favored competitors in the talent market. In our society governments cannot claim by prerogative or tradition either "the first choice" or "a fair share" of the nation's skills and talents; each government—national, state, or local—must win its own share of talent in an increasingly mobile market against the attractions of other resourceful bidders. In this process, appropriate and necessary to a democratic society, the public service has been much more successful in recruiting talent than its extreme critics would have us believe, but present and future necessities demand a much more energetic effort.

The existing assets of the American public service in 1960 are impressive. In scope and diversity it matches, if it does not in fact exceed, any other comparable public service in the world. Almost 11 million people now work for the governments of the United States—about 15 per cent of the nation's total employment. Some 2½ million of these are in the military services, another 2½ million are civilian employees of the national government, and 6 million work for the state and local governments. The whole array of occupations and professions—almost every type of skill and talent to be found in the nation—is represented among them. Their duties range from simple routine to the highest levels of difficulty and importance. Many work in huge and complex organizations; but many, too, are in small and intimate units. Geographically and jurisdictionally they are widely dispersed; only a small proportion are in the national and state capitals. In all these respects, and in others, the public service of the United States is closely linked with, not set apart from, the patterns, customs and institutions of American society. Its representative quality is its most pronounced attribute.

I

THE FEDERAL SERVICE

The sharpest focus of past anxieties and future concern about the quality of the American public service is upon the civilian staff of the national government. This focus is appropriate because, although the federal service employs less than a third of all our civil servants, it has the most crucial assignments now and for the future, and it is most often the pace-setter for all others.

Goals and methods for the improvement of the federal service have been developed with care and stated with eloquence, in a series of studies and reports conducted and issued under high auspices during the past three decades. The program for progress gradually defined by these inquiries has been neither rejected nor wholly ignored. But so far it has been accepted as a statement of tendencies to be cautiously and sporadically encouraged, rather than warmly and firmly grasped as an opportunity for a bold transformation of federal personnel policy. The urgencies of the coming decade now give new relevance to the proposals of the 1934 Commission of Inquiry on Public Personnel, the 1937 President's Committee on Administrative Management, the 1949 and 1955 Hoover Commissions. The enduring recommendations of these studies and of other related inquiries may, in 1960, be summarized and restated as continuing goals for the federal service:

1. Give the President, as chief executive and chief administrator, unequivocal authority and responsibility for leadership of the federal personnel systems, and concurrently improve the machinery for Congressional participation in personnel policy.

2. Equip the Executive Branch, under the President's direction, to be a resourceful and energetic recruiter and developer of talent.

3. Base the recruitment and development of talent upon personnel systems which emphasize mobility, the opportunity for entry and reward of talent at all levels of skill and experience, and the interchange of careers between public and private employment and among all levels of government.

4. Seek systematically the qualities of innovation and creativity, as the scarcest elements in the personnel market.

5. Place the highest priority of the personnel systems upon the recruitment, development and effective assignment of the members of the higher civil service—the executives, the managers, the professional and scientific officers of the Executive Branch agencies.

6. Raise the prestige of the public service in American society.

The President in charge.   The most general and traditional characteristic of the existing federal personnel systems is their close supervision by Congress. The President, though he is the responsible head of the Executive Branch, and the members of the Cabinet, though each is responsible for the management of a major executive department, have secondary roles.

The President has the appearance of great formal powers over the personnel administration of the Executive Branch, but his actual exercise of personnel leadership is surrounded with difficulties and the administrative machinery through which he must work is awkward and inadequate. Some of the essential arrangements for effective leadership are missing. Critics of federal personnel systems sometimes say that Presidents and department heads give too little attention to their personnel responsibilities and fail to use energetically the leadership powers and opportunities they already possess. The history of Presidential efforts to become the center of initiative and leadership, however, is on the whole rather a record of Presidential frustration in the face of the inertia and rigidities of the established personnel systems. It is true that the extension of the merit system to include successively larger proportions of the civil service (after the passage of the Pendleton Act in 1883) has been largely the accomplishment of Presidential initiative. But Presidents have been much less successful in their attempts to introduce flexibility into the personnel systems.

Congressional interest in the personnel systems is of a different order from that of Presidents and heads of executive departments. Congressmen do not experience the direct pressures of executive leadership and responsibility; they do not see at first hand the costs of obsolete or inadequate personnel systems. Their interests tend to focus upon the rank-and-file of the civil service, not upon its higher ranks or the more specialized leadership groups. Congress as a whole, in fact, tends to accept the going systems, giving them little attention as such, although quite often criticizing the quality or the behavior of civil servants.

Congressional supervision over personnel policy and procedure is achieved mainly through the standing committees on the civil and military services. It is these committees, and occasionally the appropriations committees, rather than the whole Congress, which set the main tone of Congressional concern with the personnel system. Committee power is exercised in considerable part through detailed personnel statutes but more continuously through committee sessions in which face-to-face instructions and injunctions are issued to the numerous personnel managers of executive agencies. These committees are also the main point of convergence for the powerful interest groups concerned with the course and content of federal personnel policy—the civil service reform groups animated by anti-patronage objectives, the war veterans' associations seeking protections and preferences for their members, and the employee organizations driving for tenure guarantees, advancement by seniority, narrow pay differentials and other satisfying conditions of work for their membership. It is this meeting place of Congressional committees, personnel managers, and interest group leaders which is the center of gravity in personnel policy and personnel management in the national government. The consequence of this process has been the evolution of a series of personnel systems built upon accommodations to the objectives of these groups. Recognition of Presidential leadership and of the needs of department heads have not been prominent considerations.

The oldest formal personnel systems are in the military services. As systems they have many demonstrated virtues, but they do not, and seemingly cannot, escape the confines of parochialism and specialization. The general "civil service" system, launched by the Pendleton Act of 1883 and now embracing most federal civilian employees, has revealed similar if not greater tendencies toward a Congressional committee orientation and away from a Presidentially-directed personnel system. The more specialized personnel systems—those of the Foreign Service, the Tennessee Valley Authority, the Atomic Energy Commission, the Post Office, and others—exhibit comparable limitations. Indeed, the very multiplicity of these systems—at least a score in actual practice—is testimony to the absence of the integration which Presidential leadership would bring to the personnel policies of the Executive

Branch. No existing personnel system is as responsive to Presidential leadership as it is to the purposes worked out in the committee rooms on Capitol Hill.

Presidents are not likely to secure leadership over the federal personnel systems merely by requesting it. No doubt some power and opportunity in personnel has slowly accrued to Presidents in the last two decades. But future Presidents will need vigorous support and encouragement to seek and exercise active personnel leadership in order to become the center of energy in personnel policy. The leadership position, and the resources for its performance, which the Presidency has put to good use in national security policy, in budget policy, in national economic policy, and in general legislative leadership—through the establishment of the National Security Council, the Budget Bureau, and the Council of Economic Advisers—provide models for Presidential leadership in personnel policy.

Presidential leadership in personnel policy requires institutional resources for that purpose in the Executive Office of the President, a goal recent Presidents have sought but have not yet satisfactorily achieved. The President needs in his own office an agency for personnel leadership—especially for attention to the personnel policies and procedures affecting the higher ranks of the Executive Branch—which would possess status, responsibility and resources comparable to those of the Budget Bureau and the Council of Economic Advisers. This personnel agency should prepare annually, or even more frequently, a Presidential message to the Congress and to the public, reporting on the quality, the accomplishments, and the difficulties of the federal personnel systems and recommending measures for their improvement. Presidential leadership in personnel policy would be enhanced if changes were also made in Congressional machinery. A new Joint Committee on Personnel, or the creation of a new standing Committee on the Public Service (separating it from the details of Post Office affairs), or at least the creation of a new subcommittee on the higher public service, are among the alternatives deserving careful consideration.

The establishment of new levels of both Presidential and Congressional leadership is a necessary first goal for the federal public service.

The search for talent. For most Americans entering upon or changing their careers the government service is not the first choice, in preference to business or the independent professions. The prime task of government recruitment methods is to seek out and secure that portion of high talent which does regard government service as its first choice, and to persuade a larger portion to so regard it. For this task the established personnel systems are poorly equipped.

Most existing federal government recruitment procedures blandly assume a surplus of talented candidates so anxious to work for the government that they will painstakingly search out present opportunities and then patiently endure the slow and cumbersome selection processes which the personnel systems interpose between the candidates and government employment. There are some such candidates, but they have an unusual degree of dedication and determination, or else lack immediate alternative opportunities. In any event, they do not provide a surplus of talent available to the government on its own terms. Even the most optimistic appraisal testifies to the scarcity, not to a surplus, of the talents needed by the government, a supply which it must win in a severe competition. Only the transformation of the government's posture—from aloof participant to resourceful and vigorous claimant— will secure the talent required.

Comparable limitations attend the government's use and development of the talents its present staffs possess. High competence is often nurtured by the federal personnel systems, but it is most often specialized expertness within the narrow boundaries set by parochial assignments and by limited exposure to the larger world of the whole federal service or to the contrasting environments of private employment. The military services have given the longest systematic attention to the development of talent within their own ranks and have invested the largest resources of staff and funds for that purpose. In this, they have been aided considerably by the great size of their staffs, by the establishment of military institutes and colleges, and by planned rotation of assignments. More recently, such training and development efforts have been taken up sparingly and cautiously by the civilian personnel systems. Exhortations that more should be done are widespread and fashionable. The indisputable fact remains, however, that federal personnel systems lack comprehensive and coherent policies and procedures for the effective development of talent no less than for its recruitment.

The limitations on the federal government as a recruiter and developer of talent are largely the consequence of fragmented personnel systems, each heavily committed to its own specialized needs and values, deprived of the opportunities and resources which could be provided by the integrating leadership of a President conscious of the needs and assets of the federal service as a whole. Too few people now realize the room for talent in the federal service. There is also too little circulation of talented recruits, early or late in their federal careers, from one personnel system to another, from one agency to another, from one type of environment to another, from one type of responsibility to another. The result is too often a narrow career line, a competence in specialization but a parochialism in values which limits the potential capacity for high leadership positions.

The established personnel systems cannot now meet the necessities of recruiting and developing scarce talent because they are committed to serving other purposes. Congressional committee supervision, antipatronage goals, veterans' preference aims, tenure and seniority values—

each of these purposes has its own legitimacy. (For example, the anti-patronage reformers have a point which requires their constant vigilance in the public interest.) But none contributes directly to the recruitment and development of high talent for the public service. Only a Presidentially-led personnel system for the whole Executive Branch gives promise of assigning first priority to that end.

Mobility and choice. The doctrines of the federal personnel systems aim at the establishment of a "career service" for the federal government. In practice these aims have often been turned to the creation of a series of "closed" bureau career groups, to which new entrants are admitted only at the most junior level. These general tendencies have had the articulate and consistent support of the civil service reformers and the employee organizations, as well as the benevolent endorsement of Congressional committees and general public sentiment. In federal personnel policy the doctrines and, for the most part, the prevailing patterns of recruitment efforts, personnel development systems, compensation and retirement systems—all are based upon this doctrinal model. But the tendencies toward closed career services have not been unchallenged.

Much of the actual growth of the Executive Branch, especially in the twentieth century, has provided a contrasting model for staffing executive agencies. New governmental programs requiring innovations have most often been entrusted to newly-created agencies staffed by newly-recruited personnel. As the life-cycle of such a new agency advances, it tends to become the home of a closed career service of its own. But its formative and usually its most dynamic and creative years have represented the work of a staff as new to the public service as the program itself. The federal service is thus, and long has been, a blend of "career" staffs and staffs of "new blood."

The major difficulty in this state of affairs is the failure of existing personnel policies to accept the mixed system—that is, a blend of permanent staff and "new blood" at all levels of the federal service— as desirable in itself, rather than a series of regrettable concessions to necessity. Yet this model has a number of important characteristics which commend it to American society. It emphasizes mobility and freedom of choice for both public servant and private person. It promotes the interchange of talent between government and private employment. It increases the representative and responsive qualities of the public service. It provides to the government the innovative and risk-taking talents which its new programs especially require. It widens the career horizons of civil servants by opening up to them opportunities outside the public service, and reciprocally it adds the public service to the existing career opportunities of the outsiders. Importantly, too, it helps to keep the public service an integral and intimate part of American society.

The goal of an open and mobile public service is a natural and consistent objective in a personnel system under Presidential leadership, and in which the leaders of the Executive Branch are competing vigorously for available talent. With rare exceptions, the President, more than any other, feels the need for innovation, mobility, and speed in the executive agencies. Policies and programs, not the comfort of established institutions and staffs, are his prime concern. Department heads share importantly, though often in lesser degree, these Presidential urgencies.

Competence and innovation. Existing federal personnel systems tend to search for and give preference to technical competence acquired by specialized training or experience. Only the general tests for entrance at the most junior levels emphasize general intelligence. Neither of these procedures search for or directly reward candidates possessing superior capacities for innovation, for creativity, or for the critical analysis of ideas and institutions.

That this is also a defect common to most other personnel systems, private as well as public, does not relieve us of the necessity to devise methods for discovering and measuring innovative talents. The federal government's needs are the most urgent and its responsibilities for leadership are greater. The leaders of federal personnel systems—and especially those who directly assist the President in personnel methods—must themselves be innovators in their own field.

Because recruitment techniques are still quite primitive in their capacity to identify the qualities of innovation, the federal public service must depend greatly upon two supplementary sources. First, the leaders of the personnel systems need to see the opportunities, rather than the reluctantly embraced necessities, of recruiting new staffs for new programs. They must extend this practice rather than restrict it, perhaps often using it for the partial re-staffing of established agencies and programs in need of innovation. Second, the federal service must increase its capacity for the discovery, development and reward of innovative and creative talent within its own ranks. These are familiar practices. What is required is their more systematic, more purposeful, and more intensive use.

The leadership core. The highest priority in a new federal personnel policy must go to the recruitment, development and effective use of the leadership core of the federal service: the executives, the managers, the high professional and scientific officers of the federal executive agencies. This is not now the first concern of any existing personnel system.

The higher executives and professionals of the federal service stand, with the President and the Congress, at the center of the nation's policy process. Much of the process of decision-making is in their hands. The assembling of information, the discovery of alternatives, the analytical appraisal of these choices, the synthesis of risks and opportunities into innovative yet realistic recommendations, the process of bargaining and accommodations which transforms proposals into accepted policies, the execution of resulting plans and programs—in each of these stages effective participation by the higher executives and professionals is indispensable to the President and the Congress, being essential to the creation and execution of viable public policies. Without their contributions at a high level of quality our political system cannot meet the increasingly complex demands being made upon it.

Yet present employment rules and practices frequently interpose barriers between the government and the talent it needs. For example, "conflict of interest" statutes are so sweeping and ambiguous as to deprive the public service of many outstanding prospects. These statutes were framed, and tend to be administered, without sufficient concern for the government's recruitment necessities. The conflict-of-interest problem has been carefully studied for almost a decade, notably by the Hoover Commission in 1955 and by the Association of the Bar of New York City in 1960. As the Bar Association put it: "The national interest demands an integrated policy . . . that neither sacrifices integrity for opportunism nor drowns practical staffing needs in moralism."

Pay levels are another barrier. The strong tendency of the personnel systems is to impose a narrow spread between the lowest salaries and the highest, a policy directly traceable to the impact of close Congressional supervision over the personnel systems. The result is not only that the government is unable to compete effectively against the pay levels of private employers; it is also frequently compelled to ask severe financial sacrifices from the executives and professionals it must recruit or persuade to remain in the federal service. Still another handicap arises from the fact that the benefits of public and private pension plans are not transferable. And not least in the catalogue of barriers are the complicated and uncoordinated procedures of the personnel loyalty and security systems, which are almost as numerous as the separate personnel systems.

These barriers exist largely because the President has no effective help in looking at the leadership recruitment problem as a whole, no adequate institutional resources to balance the necessities of protection and economy against the equally urgent requirements for a high quality leadership corps.

In the search for this leadership talent, the heads of the executive departments should have a sufficiently loose rein to permit imaginative, even ingenious, experiments in attracting men of capacity. For example, each of a number of corporations was persuaded to promote within the firm one of its ablest executives on the eve of his tour of duty in the federal service and then to give him leave from the higher position, so that he would lose no career opportunities while absent from the firm and so that his status with his governmental and corporate colleagues would be clear. This is an example which should be multipled many times.

The plan which the federal government needs must be flexible—as to the numbers of executives and professionals required, the titles and rank of positions, the status of the members in the personnel system, the sources from which they are to be recruited, their orientation and qualities of mind. The President and his chief advisers can best decide, for his time and his administration, what is needed in the leadership group which is to energize and direct the Executive Branch during his Presidency. The leading Presidents are distinguished by the degree to which they have achieved this personnel goal for their administration.

Previous proposals for providing such a leadership group in the Executive Branch have emphasized the need for three elements of leadership: political executives, who would represent the President's policy positions; senior civil servants, who would provide expertise and continuity in administration; program executives, who would contribute expertise and energy to new programs. These are useful categories for describing the variety of talents required, and for emphasizing the several needs of the President in his broad leadership role. As categories for a formal personnel classification plan, however, they are too rigid and binding. Whether a particular executive is to be classified as a political, career, or program executive is a minor matter. The real concern is how he can be most useful to the President and his chief assistants at a given time. For this reason details as to number, outer boundaries, and internal divisions of the leadership group should remain flexible, capable of responding quickly and naturally to the needs for mobility and speed. In other words, the needed statute should treat the higher public service as a single entity, leaving to Presidential discretion the rules which would define its operation.

The plan for recruitment and development of the leadership group in the Executive Branch, then, should have as its core Presidential direction of a high-priority program characterized by flexibility and versatility in both concepts and performance, and comprehensive in its coverage (cutting across all the federal personnel systems, including the foreign service and other overseas systems.) Its essence would be its service to Presidential purposes. It would offer the rewards of public service to all members of the group, and life careers for some.

Recognition and prestige. American society is rarely deferential or uncritical toward any of the groups that exist within it. Yet there are solid grounds for believing that the public service tends to get more than its proper share of criticism and less than its proper share of recognition as a significant contributor to the well-being of the society. The American people have been slow to recognize the steady improvement which has been made in the quality of the public service, and this lag in turn slows down the rate of progress which might otherwise be achieved.

Improving the recognition and prestige of the public service is not a mere public relations task. It calls instead for more sustained and objective attention to the virtues as well as to the deficiencies of the public service by the President, the Congress, the leaders of the interest groups and of the communication media, and the leaders of the educational system. It calls, too, for greater restraint and objectivity by the leaders of the party out of power, who have long found the public service an inviting target while carrying out their obligation to criticize the administration in power.

The President, once he has assumed his rightful leadership role in the personnel affairs of the Executive Branch, would have the first obligation and greatest resources to secure more favorable recognition and prestige for the federal service. No other voice is so likely to be heeded.

II

STATE AND LOCAL PUBLIC SERVICES

The public service in the fifty states, the large cities, the numerous other local governments, and the emerging metropolitan regions shares many of the same urgencies as those of the federal service. There is a wide variation in the quality of these state and local public services— ranging from those which match the competence of the federal service to those which are clearly ineffective in the face of the new demands being placed upon them. In some of these latter jurisdictions, the prevalence of party patronage practices is a major barrier to the achievement of high quality in the public service.

In most basic respects the difficulties of these state and local personnel systems are comparable to those of the federal government systems. The chief executives are unable to exercise effective leadership in personnel policy and practice, the career services are overspecialized and inhospitable to new entrants at the middle and upper ranks, there is insufficient emphasis upon the talents of innovation and creativity, and there is a failure to gain recognition and high prestige for the public servants.

The severest problems here too center upon the recruitment and development of talent for the key executive, managerial, professional and technical posts. The handicaps of the state and local governments in the labor market exceed those of the federal government, and with rare exceptions they make a less energetic attack upon these problems. There is thus an even greater need for assigning high priority, in every state and local government, to a special personnel program which, under chief executive direction, would emphasize the recruitment and development of outstanding talent for leadership positions.

*   *   *   *   *   *   *

One of the most important national goals for the American democracy is the building of a talented, expert and innovative public service in the national, state and local governments. It is these public servants who must be relied upon to bring to the political process not only high technical expertise and a sense of continuity but also more than a minor share of the inventiveness, the long-range perspectives, and the conscious explication of those public interests which would not otherwise be emphasized in the public debate which precedes and follows the making of policy decisions. The responsibility for the continuous improvement of the public service rests most clearly and properly upon the elected chief executives, but it is also a task in which every leading institution in our government and society—legislatures, political parties, interest groups, communication media, and educational systems—has its own distinctive opportunity and high obligation to contribute.

14

THE UNITED STATES ROLE IN THE WORLD
WILLIAM L. LANGER

14

I N THIS *chapter Dr. William L. Langer describes United States foreign policy with clarity and precision. He sets forth both an underlying philosophy and specific positions he believes we should take on
difficult issues.*

*Dr. Langer, Coolidge Professor of History at Harvard University,
draws on a lifetime of study and experience, both in and out of government. He was Chief of Research and Analysis of the Office of
Strategic Services, 1942 to 1945, and Chairman of the Board of National Estimates, Central Intelligence Agency, 1950 and 1951. He is
the author of numerous books on diplomatic history and United States
policy.*

*In preparing this chapter Dr. Langer had the advice of the panel
listed below. He takes responsibility for the opinions expressed.*

PANEL

ROBERT BLUM, President, The Asia Foundation.

PHILIP C. JESSUP, Associate, The Rockefeller Foundation; United States
Representative to United Nations General Assembly, 1948-52, and
Ambassador at Large, 1949-53.

ROBERT A. LOVETT, Partner, Brown Brothers Harriman and Company;
formerly Secretary of Defense and Under Secretary of State.

CHARLES BURTON MARSHALL, Consultant, School of Advanced International Studies, Johns Hopkins University.

JAMES McCORMACK, JR., Major General United States Air Force (ret.);
Vice President, Massachusetts Institute of Technology; President,
Institute for Defense Analyses.

RAYMOND J. SONTAG, Ehrman Professor in European History, University of California.

THE UNITED STATES ROLE
IN THE WORLD

WILLIAM L. LANGER

I

GENERAL

The United States has, throughout its history, cherished ideals of independence, freedom and democracy. The energy and ingenuity of its people as well as the extent and resources of its territory have enabled it to attain a level of civil liberty, social equality and general prosperity never before achieved on such a scale by the human race. Its phenomenal progress has impressed and influenced the kindred nations of Europe and indeed the entire world. Even the countries most hostile to its political and social philosophy have set as their goal the standard of living enjoyed by the western nations and have bent their repressive, totalitarian systems to this purpose.

The revolutionary turmoil of the present-day world is in part due to the impact of American political ideals and in large measure reflects the growing awareness among emerging peoples of the gulf that separates them from the nations standing in the forefront of prosperity and growth. It is true that there has of late been a significant change in the relative strength of the most powerful nations, and that totalitarian doctrines have won many adherents. This means that in the years to come the United States must do more than hark back to a glorious tradition. It must strive increasingly to bring its own national life in line with its ideals and at the same time to provide strong leadership in a world threatened with the loss of what men of free spirit have always yearned for and held dear.

As yet the United States still holds a strong position. It is still looked to by many peoples for guidance and support; no amount of scoffing by Communist propagandists has destroyed the admiration and respect of the common man, even in the iron curtain countries, for the American achievement. The American people has, therefore, no reason to doubt its traditional ideals and objectives. On the contrary, it should actively vindicate them, while striving always to adjust and expand them to meet the requirements of a rapidly changing world.

The enduring objectives of the United States in world affairs are to safeguard its own way of life, and to promote the liberty, well-being and progress of all mankind. These objectives call for the defense of the independence of nations and for the reduction if not the prevention of friction and conflict between them. Their attainment is exceedingly difficult because of the forces operating in the world today. The old order has been shattered by two great world wars and for more than a generation the world has been in process of radical transformation. The most powerful nations are ideologically divided and bitterly hostile. At the same time fundamental changes are being wrought by technological achievements, one of the major effects of which has been to revolutionize warfare to the extent of threatening all mankind with destruction.

Only breadth of outlook, readiness to recognize the need for change, and ability to adjust to novel conditions will enable even the greatest nations to keep pace with developments and aid statesmen in charting their course through the incredible complexities of international living.

The present world situation is far from acceptable to the American people. The cold war itself, with its related ideological, military and economic antagonisms, was not chosen by the United States, but forced upon the world by Communist behavior. Change is now not only desirable but imperative if human society is not to embark upon self-annihilation.

No doubt many necessary changes will be brought about by force and violence, which in the past have played so large a role in the evolution of human affairs. It must be the aim of the United States, however, to reduce the employment of force, that is, to encourage the use of peaceful methods for settling disputes between the nations, if only to forestall further deterioration of the international situation and the correspondingly greater threat of general catastrophe.

The United States must, above all, have the will and power to resist even by force any attempt to bring about fundamental changes of the international order through the use or threat of military action. The great Communist nations, Soviet Russia and the Chinese People's Republic, have long since proclaimed the inevitability of ultimate Communist victory, and made no secret of their determination to further the "historical process" by every means at their disposal. They openly avow their intention to bury the democratic system and to organize the nations of the world in a new Communist order.

The United States, on the other hand, has no thought of imposing the democratic system upon other nations. It has long since abandoned the fond belief that it could, by its own influence and effort, make the world safe for democracy. For it now recognizes that many nations are for the present estopped by tradition, by poverty, by illiteracy and by other factors from rapidly transforming their present politico-social systems and abruptly adopting what for them must be an alien order. It recognizes further that even among advanced nations, political and social institutions are bound to be in continual flux, evolving steadily in response to changing conditions and requirements. In the free world of today there are almost as many variations in social and economic systems as there are countries. Such variations are not only acceptable, but unobjectionable, for in the last analysis no nation or people should be obliged to conform to patterns imposed by others.

Nonetheless, Americans are firmly convinced that both in principle and in practice democracy has proven itself. They also believe that over the long term free institutions can survive only in the setting of a community of free nations. It must therefore be a prime objective of American policy to encourage, support and defend those forces which, in the present-day world, are working in the direction of freedom, equality and representative government.

The United States should, at all times, exert its influence and power in behalf of a world order congenial to American ideals, interests and security, a world in which the peoples of all nations can find the opportunity for freedom and well-being. It can do this without egoism because of its deep conviction that such a world order will best fulfill the hopes of mankind and bring the greatest happiness and comfort to all peoples. Because this is so, the United States should be prepared to support other nations in defending themselves against Communist or other aggression, and in protecting themselves against economic pressure or political subversion designed to destroy their independence and force them into a totalitarian world order. It should likewise be willing to give unstinting assistance to the underdeveloped countries which are seeking an appropriate place in the modern world.

To the achievement of these ends, several broad policies are essential. In the interests of greater understanding and cooperation between nations, the United States should encourage freedom of communications and the development of cultural exchanges of all types. It should, furthermore, continue to promote the settlement of differences between nations by negotiation and diplomacy, avoiding as much as possible the propaganda exploitation of serious transactions and the spectacle of high-level gatherings which tend to arouse exaggerated hopes.

World law and the U.N. In an age marked too much by brutality and the use of naked power, the United States should bend every effort toward the re-establishment and expansion of international law. It is patently useless to strive for disarmament unless, concurrently, progress is made toward the development of procedures for the settlement of disputes by peaceful methods. This in turn requires constant strengthening of world law, through the discovery and adoption of legal principles common to all or at least to many cultures, through improved methods for making existing international law accessible, and above all through the further development of the International Court of Justice. The United States should, for example, abandon its present restrictions on the jurisdiction of the Court (the Connally Amendment) and show its good faith by its readiness to submit to the Court both cases in which it is the complainant and cases in which others complain against it. The development and further recognition of world law is a matter of urgent importance. Without it there is little likelihood of reducing tensions and avoiding conflict, and little if any chance of preventing the fantastic developments of the space age from plunging the world into chaos.

The United Nations organization obviously plays a key role in the furtherance of international cooperation and the safeguarding of peace. Despite imperfections in organization and shortcomings in its agencies and operations, the United Nations has, during the brief span of its existence, proved its potential not only as a forum for the airing of grievances, but also as a center for unobtrusive negotiation and as an executive agency for refugee administration, truce supervision and kindred assignments. Of recent years it has grown rapidly in membership, providing new nations with an easy introduction to active participation in international life. At the same time the secretary-general has taken an ever greater and more influential part as a negotiator and mediator, while great progress has been made also in the formation and utilization of international military forces to preserve order and forestall foreign intervention in disturbed areas.

The United Nations should never be regarded or used as a substitute for a responsible national policy. As a matter of fact, constitutional limitations prevent it from being an adequate instrument even for the treatment of certain international issues. Furthermore, its very evolution and growth create problems. The membership of the Council should be enlarged so as to be more representative. Meanwhile the admission of many new nations has so increased the membership that in the Assembly the great powers may soon find themselves outvoted by a majority of small powers, many of whom lack experience and understanding both in the responsibilities of freedom and in the realities of power. Great patience and diplomatic skill will in future be needed to prevent the Assembly and the whole United Nations organization from losing something in the way of effectiveness. The basic fact, however, is that conditions in the world today cry for the strengthening of international institutions and controls. The United Nations has demonstrated its advantages and its potentialities and it therefore behooves the United States to reinforce it and help it adapt to changing conditions and requirements.

II

THE COMMUNIST CHALLENGE

The salient features of the current international scene are (1) the acute ideological antagonism dividing the free world and the Communist bloc; (2) the phenomenal development of science and technology, making possible the invention and production of hitherto inconceivably lethal weapons and thereby tending to equate general or large-scale war with mutual annihilation; (3) the liquidation of European rule in Asia and Africa, and the precipitous emergence of new and for the most part politically inexperienced and economically underdeveloped nations.

The conflict of political and social philosophies and systems has of recent years spread over an ever-widening front. To political warfare of the propaganda and subversive types, the Communists have added economic and technical aid programs clearly designed to establish their influence and eventually their control over uncommitted regions of the globe. They have set themselves up not only as the champions of nationalism and the defenders of oppressed peoples against "colonialism," but have appealed to the peoples of the underdeveloped areas with slogans about the dictatorship of the proletariat and the organization of the "workers" state, despite the fact that such slogans have by now become outmoded and largely disregarded in the Soviet Union itself. Through their newly acquired ability to provide financial assistance and technical guidance, the Communists have greatly enhanced their power to enlist the allegiance of weaker states. The United States and the free world can meet this new challenge only by long-term planning and discriminating contributions to the programs of emerging nations.

Of equal if not greater importance is the striking growth and rapidly mounting strength of the Communist states, economically as well as politically and militarily. The Second World War brought in its train the subjection and economic integration of all eastern Europe with the Soviet Union. A few years later mainland China fell under Communist domination. Furthermore, within the last decade the industrialization of the Soviet Union has brought a tremendous upsurge of production, while in China the new Communist regime has laid at least the foundations for an economic transformation which could eventually make the People's Republic one of the major economic powers of the world.

Soviet intentions. It has been thought by some that these great changes might bring in their train corresponding changes in outlook and objective. The very rise in productivity and well-being, it is argued, may dampen revolutionary ardor and create among the Russians a more strictly national interest in safeguarding the gains they have made. Industrialization in Russia may well create attitudes and aspirations familiar from the history of the western countries. The Soviet Union, it is said, already reveals a social stratification and a marked trend toward state capitalism. Since Stalin's death the regime has clearly felt obliged to take into account popular dislike of collective farming and more particularly popular desire for a larger share in the fruits of industrial production. A new attitude, it is alleged, is reflected in the official doctrine of co-existence—live and let live, avoiding violence and war, recognizing the possibility of different social philosophies, and allowing history to move toward its destiny at its own pace.

There may be a measure of truth in this argumentation. Within recent years there has been a noticeable relaxation of internal pressures in the Soviet Union and a partial lifting of the iron curtain which isolated the population from the rest of the world. At the same time concessions have been made to the European satellite states in response to the reviving pressure for independence and liberty. The Kremlin has even gone so far as to proclaim that conditions in the world are now such that war between the conflicting social orders is no longer inevitable. Soviet leaders make great play with the doctrine of co-existence, and have called repeatedly upon the "imperialist" powers for high-level negotiations "at the summit."

The dispute which has arisen between Moscow and Peiping, in which the Chinese leaders take their stand by strict Communist doctrine and reject as treasonable any notion of peaceful co-existence between capitalism and Communism, would seem to suggest that the Soviet regime has indeed begun to move beyond traditional revolutionary theory. From the Soviet standpoint this debate must have ominous overtones, forecasting as it does eventual competition for leadership of the Communist world and more immediately obstructing any effort to improve the relations of the Kremlin with the western powers.

While recognizing the potential importance of these developments it would be a mistake, however, to overlook contrary aspects of the situation. There is, for example, abundant evidence that the rapidly growing economic and military power of the Soviet Union has given its leaders added confidence in their ability to equal and then surpass American production within the next twenty years and, in the meantime, to compete successfully with the western world in the field of foreign and technical aid. Their spectacular achievement has evidently strengthened their conviction that the triumph of Communism may be expected in the near future. Events of the recent past suggest that Communist leaders, far from modifying their basic revolutionary objectives, are pursuing them with ever greater confidence, vigor and boldness. They may change their tactics, but their goal remains the same. More and more it appears that to their minds co-existence means acceptance by their opponents of the forward march of Communism.

It is an integral part of Communist doctrine that military power, while indispensable, should be resorted to only when and if political and economic weapons have failed, or when and if military operations promise easy, quick success. The balance of nuclear power between the Soviet Union and the United States is such that, as Khrushchev has acknowledged, neither side could hope, even in a surprise attack, to destroy the other's retaliatory power. Thus the attacker would suffer terrific destruction. Soviet leaders may argue that in a general nuclear war they could wipe their opponents off the face of the earth and that, despite Russian losses, socialism would survive and prevail while capitalism would be destroyed. But there is nevertheless reason to suppose that large-scale war under present conditions is less than ever attractive to the Kremlin as an instrument of policy and that Soviet leaders will therefore lay increasing stress on the political and economic weapons through which in recent years they have extended their power and influence.

This does not mean that they will not, in the future as in the past, make the utmost use of military power as a threat. For this reason, they have made every sacrifice to attain military superiority. They have maintained huge conventional armies and have built a vast submarine fleet. They have made a massive, concerted effort to overtake the United States in nuclear armaments and to anticipate it in long-range rockets and in space exploration. So great is now the military power of the Soviet Union that the threat of nuclear attack, freely used as blackmail even before a substantial stock of missiles was available, is almost certain to become a prime instrument of Soviet policy.

In sum, whatever the changes in the Soviet Union, whatever the purpose of the so-called relaxation of tension and whatever the meaning of co-existence, the Soviet Union and the Communist bloc generally will, over the coming decade, redouble their efforts to extend Communist influence and control through economic aid, through political subversion, and through military threat. There is every reason to expect that in the immediate future the Western powers, including the United States, will be subjected to every kind of pressure, more particularly to severe nuclear blackmail.

Under these circumstances it is a matter of life and death for the United States and other nations of the free world to maintain their defenses at the highest state of efficiency. Barring an agreement on the limitation of armaments under adequate inspection and control, the United States cannot afford to relax its efforts to maintain and perfect both nuclear and conventional forces of sufficient strength to deter the Communist powers from a surprise attack or from military aggression, even with conventional weapons or on a limited scale.

For the next few years the United States may well be inferior to the Soviet Union in the number, if not in the quality, of its intercontinental missiles. During that period it will therefore be of the utmost importance to keep an adequate striking force of SAC bombers on constant airborne alert and to maintain or assist in maintaining bases in allied countries, properly equipped with aircraft and missiles. The Soviet government has been using nuclear blackmail freely to induce or to force NATO and other powers allied to the United States to deny bases to American bombers and missile crews. The rigor and persist-

ence of Soviet pressure serve to highlight the fact that, for the immediate future at least, the security of the United States and of the free
world from large-scale war will require multiplicity of dispersed installations, making it increasingly difficult if not impossible for the
Soviet Union, despite any superiority it may possess in the number
of missiles, to count on the elimination of NATO retaliatory power.

The dispersion of missile sites, the improvement in speed and accuracy of missile-firing, the hardening of both bomber and missile bases,
the development and expeditious multiplication of mobile launchers
for land- and sea-based missiles, such as the Minuteman and Polaris,
will all be of the utmost importance in buttressing the military posture
of the free world.   Numerous, dispersed, concealed or mobile missile
sites, making possible the extensive use of intermediate-range missiles
to offset inferiority in intercontinental missiles, would certainly lower
the odds in Kremlin calculations.

It must be a primary American aim to provide also against local
aggression, the more so as the United States is bound by treaty to
many powers in Asia as well as Europe to lend support in the event
of attack.   The over-all deterrent power of the United States is not
sufficient to ensure against Communist thrusts, especially in the Middle
East and Asia. Indeed, the so-called nuclear stalemate may serve as
an incentive to Communist operations of a limited type.   It therefore
behooves the United States to help strengthen the forces of allied and
friendly powers.

The extent and nature of this support should be re-examined peri-
odically with particular reference to any adverse effect it may have
internally or externally on the receiving country.   In general, however,
the existing program should be maintained and if necessary enlarged to
prevent the progressive subversion and ultimate takeover of such states
by Communist powers and the extension of their threat to areas thus
becoming adjacent.   Furthermore, American forces abroad should continue to be supplied with tactical nuclear weapons, if only to counter
the Communist threat of local nuclear war.   Since the use of tactical
nuclear weapons in a limited operation would involve a high probability
of general nuclear war, both sides would presumably be reluctant to
employ them. This means that in any local contest the decision would
hinge on strength in conventional weapons, especially of the modern
types. It would be difficult, therefore, to overstate the importance of
having available adequate conventional forces, to provide a deterrent
commensurate with the issues at stake.

Chinese power. It is difficult to evaluate the weight of Chinese Communist military power as a component of the larger Communist challenge. With a population of over 600 million, the People's Republic
has an unsurpassed manpower potential. Furthermore, the rate of
Chinese industrialization leaves no doubt that even now they are able

to provide modern armament for a huge conventional army. With this army they are already exerting great pressure on neighboring states. A crucial point will be reached when the Chinese Communist regime comes into possession of nuclear weapons, which may be at any time within the next five years.

The Soviet government has thus far given its Chinese ally assistance in the development of atomic energy, but is evidently reluctant to provide nuclear weapons or even to give much help in developing them. The Kremlin may well be apprehensive about its relationship with Peiping once the Chinese have the most modern instruments for blackmail and war. The bellicose attitude of the Chinese leaders and their avowed unwillingness to abandon the program of militant revolution bode no good for the world, especially for the United States. Even if there should be some break in the Sino-Soviet alliance, Chinese Communist power by itself will presently be a major threat to the security of the United States and other nations of the free world. Failing some progress toward a settlement of political issues or some success in the direction of arms limitation, there is no remedy for the United States and the nations associated with it but to keep all defenses strong and maintain the utmost degree of unity in preparing for the most ominous developments.

III

THE FREE EUROPEAN COMMUNITY

The threat of Communist subversion and domination hung heavily over Europe in the post-war period, when the eastern countries had already been reduced to the status of satellites and the central and western countries were exhausted, poverty-stricken and generally helpless. It was then that the United States government, recognizing that the strength of the free world depended to a large degree on the community of interest and action of the United States and the non-communist nations of Europe, launched a major campaign designed to restore the economic and thereby the military power of the menaced countries. Through the success of this program Western Europe has been re-established as one of the significant power centers of the world, a populous region distinguished by a high level of education and well-being, with a great productive potential.

The Satellites. It is a basic and continuing interest of the United States that the nations of Europe and indeed of the whole world should enjoy the right of national self-determination. Hence it must continue to support the claim of the Soviet satellite states to independence. The events of recent years have shown that at least some of these nations remain unreconciled to the Communist yoke and that the Soviet government cannot afford to ignore completely their aspirations toward freedom. There is, to be sure, no quick way by which the cause of nations forcibly subjected to Communist control can be vindicated. But these nations tend to look to the United States as champion of the elemental rights of peoples, which are the only sound basis for international order. The active and continued interest of the American people will help them remain true to their principles. The United States should, therefore, cultivate their friendship through cultural exchanges, furtherance of trade relations and, in certain cases, through the advancement of financial and technical aid.

NATO. The nations of western Europe and the Mediterranean were saved from economic collapse by the Marshall Plan. Following the Communist take-over in Czechoslovakia they became bound to each other and to the United States and Canada in the North Atlantic Treaty Organization (NATO), a military alliance designed for the defense of western Europe and North America against Communist attack. Under this organization the European powers provided bases on their territories for American troops and aircraft, thereby associating American forces directly in the common defense, with advanced stations from which strategic airforces could launch a multiple retaliatory attack.

The NATO countries have never reached the force-levels laid down in successive agreements, yet there can be little doubt that the alliance has proved itself one of the most successful peacetime coalitions in history. It created a strong community of feeling and interest between the European and American members, and, so long as the United States enjoyed superiority in nuclear weapons and the means of delivering them, it effectively discouraged even minor Soviet aggression in Europe.

The advent of the intercontinental missile has raised new and fundamental problems in the relationship of the North Atlantic nations. On the American side it has been argued that the new long-range missiles reduce the value of European bases for the defense of the United States; indeed, that it might be wise to withdraw American forces from Europe and "go it alone."

On the European side, some members of NATO have tortured themselves with the question of whether the United States would in the last resort risk its own devastation by intercontinental missiles in behalf of NATO or one of its European components. General de Gaulle, forcefully advancing this view, has argued that each nation must therefore assume responsibility for its own basic defense; each must have its own deterrent power, however modest.

This reasoning has led several European governments to consider the acquisition of nuclear weapons to build up a deterrent power in intermediate-range missiles. France has already devised and exploded an atomic weapon and evidently intends to persist in its program, despite the considerable cost in money and technical effort. Acquisition of nuclear weapons by many powers will greatly enhance the danger of nuclear war arising either from technical failures or from the ill-considered act of some panic-stricken government.

Actually, the revolutionary changes in the methods of delivering nuclear weapons have in no way diminished the interest of the United States in the continued freedom of the European nations. It is unthinkable that the American nations could long retain their freedom if the Communists should gain command of western Europe's resources and industrial plant, and were thus in a position to bring almost irresistible military and economic pressure to bear on the new world. The overseas bases of NATO will continue to be important to the United States, because they provide multiple missile-launching sites and make possible the wide dispersal of nuclear retaliatory power. Endless discussion and intensive study of the NATO problem on both sides of the Atlantic have failed to reveal any fundamental flaw in the concept of this coalition of free nations.

It should therefore remain the firm and publicly proclaimed policy of the United States to honor its present commitment to come to the aid of its NATO allies in the event of attack. Further, the United States should be prepared to consider sympathetically the needs created by rapidly changing conditions. The apprehensions of the European powers are understandable and should certainly be taken into account. To give nuclear weapons now to individual members of NATO would raise a number of difficult questions. It might be desirable for psychological reasons, however, to make such weapons available to the European NATO powers as a group, under collective NATO control. But in view of the difficulties inherent in collective control, it is doubtful that such weapons would be a significant addition to NATO deterrent power.

More far-reaching schemes, such as the transformation of NATO into a genuine military and political union, appear impracticable for the time being. At most one might envisage for the near term some kind of European Defense Union within the larger NATO framework. Such a union would involve a common foreign policy as well as close military and economic integration. It could no doubt deal effectively with the control of nuclear armaments specifically designed for the defense of Europe against either local or general attack. On the other hand, the known difficulties in the way of even the economic integration of Europe make the project seem over-ambitious. Furthermore, such a close coalition of the European members might tend to divide and undermine the existing alliance. Nonetheless, Americans should realize that the shift in the balance of nuclear power during the past decade has deeply affected the original concept of NATO and that, if the organization is to survive, it may be necessary to accept a greater measure of political and military as well as of economic integration in

Europe and possibly some further degree of cooperation within the entire Atlantic community.

The forces working toward economic integration have of late been running strong among the free nations of continental Europe, despite time-hallowed notions of national sovereignty and independence. It is in the interest of the United States and should therefore be one of its goals to encourage this movement. Integration would strengthen the general economic position of Europe, would make possible a more effective contribution to the common defense, and in the broadest sense would provide a real counterweight to Soviet power.

Unfortunately, basic differences of interest and outlook have resulted in the emergence of two rival groupings, the European Economic Community ("Common Market") and the European Free Trade Association ("Outer Seven"). This threatened division in trade policy obstructs the trend toward economic integration and endangers the healthy development of the free European community. The United States should, therefore, use its influence to reconcile these competing groups.

Germany. Of the unresolved issues of present-day Europe the problem of divided Germany is most prominent and most ominous. The phenomenal recovery of West Germany has demonstrated once again the unusual capabilities of the German people, while the growing German contribution to the NATO forces serves as a reminder of the Federal Republic's military potential. The Germans, relieved of their colonies by the victorious allies of 1919, are not obliged to dissipate their forces as the French have done. Thereby they become the more formidable as a European power.

It would appear incredible, to be sure, that the Germans could ever again invade the Soviet Union without the support of some major power. Nonetheless, the Russians and some of their satellites are probably concerned about the potentialities of a rearmed West Germany. Even if they do not believe that the United States would provoke the West Germans to attack, they cannot overlook the fact that the Federal Republic, as a member of NATO, is closely associated with Soviet Russia's most formidable opponent. They may fear that the free Germany, once it has rebuilt its military forces, might resort to military action to recover its lost territories, in the expectation that the United States would be impelled to lend support.

Since the control of East Germany has given the Russians a more advanced military base than they have ever before had in Europe, it is most unlikely that they will voluntarily relinquish their hold or agree to the reunification of Germany on other than Communist terms. The present German situation is also agreeable to Poland and Czechoslovakia, which hold territories formerly German and therefore share the Soviet distrust of a rearmed Federal Republic. Community of interest in the continued disruption of Germany has without doubt created a real bond between the Soviet Union and some of its satellites. Under these circumstances a solution of the German problem in terms acceptable to the free world is probably remote. Proposals designed to make reunification tolerable to the Russians, such as those for the withdrawal of Germany from NATO and its neutralization or demilitarization, are bound to be repudiated by the Germans themselves. Suggestions for disengagement, the creation of neutral zones, and kindred schemes may offer certain political attractions but involve such serious military disadvantages as to make them unacceptable not only to the Germans but to NATO generally. Any withdrawal of American forces from Germany, not to say from Europe, would tremendously weaken the NATO structure, while the Russians, having withdrawn behind their own frontiers, would still be relatively close at hand and certainly in a position to exert decisive pressure in German affairs.

It has been the policy of the United States for years to aid the recovery of Germany, to give the West Germans control of their own affairs, and to secure the Federal Republic in NATO. This policy has been one of both military defense and political design. Through the close association of West Germany with the rest of the free world it has been possible to encourage and support the forces of liberalism and democracy, as well as to draw upon German military capabilities for the defense of Germany itself and of all western Europe.

It should certainly be an American goal to maintain and develop this policy, more particularly to further in every way the reconciliation of France and Germany and the mutual understanding between Britain and Germany. As German military power and German influence in NATO councils continue to grow, there may be an increase of concern and even of distrust on the part of some NATO members. But this would serve only to underline the challenge confronting all NATO allies, namely to create a positive partnership with the free segment of the once powerful and still vigorous German nation.

The United States must strive to retain the confidence of the Germans, for the latter are only too well aware that the continued division of Germany is at least acceptable to some of their allies. The United States must therefore be ready to take the lead in exploring possibilities of German reunification. It must also contribute fully to the unflinching defense of the western position in Berlin. Existing arrangements with respect to that great city, while far from ideal, have proved workable over the years. If the Soviets continue to agitate the question of Berlin's status, it will be in the desire to force the surrender of several million Berliners to the satellite German Democratic Republic and so demonstrate that ultimate power resides in the Soviet Union.

The Soviets have thereby left the western world no choice but to stand by its established rights. The United States must continue to defend the Germans of West Berlin and to uphold free access to the city, even if Communist action creates the risk of war. A final solution of the Berlin problem must undoubtedly await a general German settlement, and is therefore hardly a question of the immediate future. This in turn means that the United States and its NATO partners will continue to be faced by a precarious and highly explosive situation. Since much more is involved than the fate of the city, the Berlin problem, like that of Germany in general, must be viewed as a crucial issue in the East-West conflict.

IV

THE FUTURE OF ASIA

Asia, as the largest and most populous continent, is bound to acquire ever increasing influence in world affairs. It is therefore a matter of prime importance to the United States and to the entire free world that the nations of Asia, many of them newly independent and still feeling their way, should develop in sympathy with the values for which we strive. Since there is no tradition of popular, representative government in Asia, there is constant danger that national leaders, under heavy economic and social pressures, may turn to totalitarian methods for solution of their problems. Asia today presents the spectacle of fully half the human race in violent flux, attempting desperately to cast off the fetters of the past, to overcome poverty and ignorance, and to find an acceptable place in the modern world. The magnitude of its problems and the power of the forces at work are such that only the wisest and most vigilant statesmanship can hope to deal with them.

Communist China constitutes the major threat to the free nations of Asia, as does Soviet Russia to free Europe. The Chinese People's Republic has a tremendous potential in natural resources, a huge and rapidly growing population, and a program of ruthless industrialization designed to make it one of the most formidable of world powers. Its leaders are moved by a deep resentment against western imperialism and by intense national pride, and they have succeeded in communicating something of their dynamism and patriotic fervor to the population at large. So confident and proud are they of their power that they have not hesitated to challenge their Soviet colleagues on matters of Communist doctrine and to admonish them to remain faithful to the program of undying conflict with the capitalist world.

A regime which in its very infancy dared defy the United Nations by intervening in Korea with huge forces may clearly be expected to press the Communist conquest of all Asia as quickly as its capabilities permit. The concentration of men and armaments against Taiwan is well-known and Chinese support of the Communist movement in Southeast Asia is no secret. The Peiping regime has conquered Tibet and asserted territorial claims against friendly India. Such states as Bhutan and Sikkim are directly exposed to Chinese Communist subversion and domination.

From the American standpoint, the most disturbing feature of the Chinese Communist regime is its uncompromising hostility to the United States and all that it stands for. It is the established policy of Peiping to stimulate its people to ever greater effort by systematic vilification of the United States, and it publicly proclaims its determination to destroy American influence in Asia at the earliest possible moment. Since the Peiping government is straining every nerve to equip itself with nuclear weapons, the United States and its Asian allies have every reason to expect Chinese Communist policy to become even more aggressive in the fairly near future. The United States must look constantly to its defenses, on the island chain extending from Japan to the Philippines, and in the area of the Southeast Asia Treaty Organization. Failure to do so will inevitably entail the successive subversion and subjection of the independent nations of Asia, not excluding either Japan or India.

The prospect of reconciliation and peaceful settlement with the Chinese Communists is extremely dim. The United States, nonetheless, should explore every possibility of furthering understanding and adjustment.

Taiwan and the Offshore Islands. The problems of Taiwan and the Quemoy and Matsu island groups are of key importance in the relationship between the United States and Communist China. Of these the problem of the offshore islands might be susceptible of settlement, for these islands have little value to the Nationalist Chinese regime on Taiwan except as they symbolize the hope of eventual return to the mainland. Militarily such a return is clearly impossible without large-scale American support, which in turn is beyond the intention or peacetime capability of the United States government. If the Taiwan government could be induced to withdraw from these exposed positions, nothing of much real value would be lost and at least one of the specific grievances of the Peiping regime would be eliminated.

The problem of the Nationalist Chinese regime on Taiwan itself is of quite a different character. It is patently impossible for the United States to withdraw support from an ally of long standing, and thus abandon Taiwan to Communist attack or subversion. At the most it can attempt to relieve tension in its relations with Peiping by reiterating its determination not to countenance an effort by the Nationalist Chinese to reconquer the mainland, and by proclaiming its readiness to explore with other interested countries any solution of the Taiwan problem that would be acceptable to the contending Chinese parties. Pending a settlement of this thorny issue, the United States should set as its aim the orderly growth of Taiwan as a state, recognizing that the cost of the necessary military and economic aid will be substantial.

There is little or no present likelihood that the Peiping regime would accept *de jure* recognition by the United States unless the latter were ready at the same time to repudiate or abandon the Nationalist Chinese government. Neither does Peiping show much interest in the development of contacts through the reopening of communications, cultural and other exchanges, or the promotion of at least a modest trade in non-strategic materials. Like the Soviet government in Stalin's time, it seems to think that popular ignorance of the United States and the free world facilitates the furtherance of its own program. Since this is so, there is little to be done on the American side, though it is definitely not in the interest of the United States to have great nations shut off from each other and deprived of the information and understanding on which alone a sound relationship can be based.

China in the U.N. The representation of the Chinese people in the United Nations has created one of the knottiest issues in present-day international relations. Thus far the Nationalist government, claiming to be the only legitimate Chinese government, has held a permanent seat on the Security Council and has enjoyed the support of a majority of United Nations members voting in the Assembly's credentials and political committees. But there has been a growing feeling in the United Nations that the Peiping regime, in effective control of the Chinese mainland with its more than 600 million inhabitants, should be admitted to the organization, despite the experiences of the Korean War and other considerations.

It is, in fact, unrealistic to argue, more than a decade after the establishment of Communist rule on the mainland, that Taipei rather than Peiping represents the Chinese people. It is equally unrealistic to exclude from world councils the most populous and one of the most formidable states of the present-day world. It is probable that within the United Nations pressure in favor of admitting Communist China will continue to rise and that before long the marked growth in the number of Asian and African members will bring about a majority vote to this effect. Thereafter the question of assigning China's permanent seat on the Security Council is bound to arise and the claims of the Peiping regime will almost certainly find considerable support.

In such a contingency the United States should exert itself to safeguard the claim of Taiwan to membership as a separate Chinese state, but it would be unwise to oppose a clearly expressed majority sentiment in favor of admitting Communist China. The mounting crisis in international relations makes it urgent that mainland China be brought into the world's councils, so that it may share in the decisions and responsibilities on which the fate of all humanity depends. Clearly no significant step can be taken toward arms limitation or control without the participation of the Peiping government.

Japan, like West Germany, has staged a remarkable recovery from the ravages of war and has during the past decade provided an example of reasonably stable government and rapid economic progress on a non-Communist basis. But Japan, despite its success in reducing the birth-rate and relieving the population pressure for the future, is still an overpopulated country and depends for its well-being on an active and extensive foreign trade. In the past, China was one of the largest and most profitable markets for the products of Japanese industry. It is therefore natural that there should be forces in present-day Japan working for an accommodation with Communist China that would reopen the continent to Japanese trade. While there is but little support for Communism in Japan, there has developed a strong pacifist and neutralist attitude, encouraged in the period of the occupation by American policy. As the one people which has actually suffered atomic attack and is at the same time particularly exposed to the fall-out resulting from Soviet nuclear tests, the Japanese are passionately opposed to the new weapons and to every aspect of nuclear war. The growth of neutralist sentiment has led to noisy agitation against the alliance with the United States and to opposition to the use of Japanese bases for nuclear purposes.

From the American standpoint Japan is as important for the defense of the free world in Asia as Germany in Europe. Japan is a key bulwark against Communist domination of all Asia. It is therefore a prime interest of the United States to contribute in every way possible to the maintenance of close military, economic and cultural ties. Fortunately a large majority of the population appreciates the need for the alliance with the United States if Japan is to hold its own against growing Communist power. But there is a genuine danger that extremists on the right as well as on the left may regain their influence through economic stringency or through inept American handling of their susceptibilities.

Since the prosperity of Japan hinges on its foreign trade, the United States should help to facilitate Japanese trade relations not only with the free nations of Asia, but also with European and American countries. It should devote continuing attention to the promotion of understanding between Japan and the United States and to the development of common interests. For example, the close association of Japan with programs for aid to the less developed countries of South and Southeast Asia would make for constant, intimate cooperation.

India, like most newly independent countries, has adopted a policy of non-commitment in international affairs, in the hope of being able to devote itself entirely to the modernization of its economy and its social system as well as to avoid the horrors of war. Though not definitely aligned with the nations of the free world, India has, however, chosen the democratic road. Its example is crucial to the further development of representative institutions in other Asian countries and it is therefore obviously in the interest of the United States to lend it sympathy and support.

The problem of economic development in India is of such magnitude that large-scale assistance on a long-term basis is indispensable. For the sake of the huge Indian population as well as for the safeguarding of free institutions in Asia, the United States should continue to give unstinting, long-term economic and technical aid. At the same time it should use its influence in behalf of compromise in the dispute between India and Pakistan over Kashmir, and should give India full diplomatic support in resisting the territorial claims of Communist China in the Himalayan area.

Southeast Asia. Several of the states of Southeast Asia are united in defensive alliance with the United States and other nations of the free world. These states, for the most part newly independent, lack stability and power and are directly exposed to Communist pressure and subversion. The United States has a genuine interest in aiding them through economic and technical support to strengthen their military defenses and develop representative institutions. Such a program, however, calls for much care and discrimination. Military support to one country may estrange another, and even economic aid must be of such a character and extent as not to upset conditions in the receiving state. The situation in Southeast Asia is at best precarious and the military resources of the Southeast Asia Treaty Organization are necessarily limited. The future of the area will therefore depend largely on the increase of stability through prosperity and confidence.

V

THE AWAKENING NATIONS

The spectacular and impetuous emergence of numerous new nations from the period of European rule and economic control in the Middle East, Asia and Africa has created or at least greatly accentuated the tension between the industrialized states of the northern hemisphere and the economically underdeveloped countries of the southern. Many of these new nations are moved by deep resentment towards their former European masters, are intensely jealous of their independence and at times unbearably arrogant, yet desperately anxious to overcome their ignorance and poverty, and wildly optimistic in their hopes for the future. Through their past contacts with Europeans and even more through modern communications media and propaganda, their leaders are more than ever aware of the prodigious disparity in the living standards of the advanced and of the newly awakened countries.

They are fanatically determined to improve their lot and to telescope long years of patient progress through some phenomenal transformation.

Aid to the underdeveloped. The problem of raising substantially the living standards of one-half of the world's population constitutes one of the major issues confronting the world today, even without reference to the Communist threat and the danger of nuclear conflict. There is little or no likelihood that the pressure of the emerging, restless peoples will diminish in the foreseeable future. The more prosperous countries of America and Europe must take large-scale action to reduce this pressure.

In the highly industrialized states, economic advance is so rapid that the standard of living may rise 100 per cent within a generation. The tendency therefore is for the gap in living standards between the industrialized and the underdeveloped regions to widen rather than narrow. Indeed, the initial result of improvement in public health facilities and in diet tends to be an increase in population which nullifies the rise in the standard of living. Even under the most favorable circumstances it will be a difficult, expensive, and long-term undertaking to improve the conditions of life in the underdeveloped countries to anything approaching those enjoyed by the industrial nations. Serious internal strains, instability and, possibly, resort to desperate measures must therefore be expected.

The United States, with the highest standard of living ever attained by mankind, cannot safely shirk a leading role in making available to the economically underdeveloped nations the benefits of the industrial and technological revolutions. In the interest of its own peace and progress it must assume a heavy burden, for it cannot hope to prosper in isolation. Its goal must be the creation of a world order compatible with American traditions as well as with American interests and security, one in which all nations will have a reasonable opportunity for economic progress and social well-being.

Recent events, notably in Africa and Latin America, have left no doubt of the determination of the Kremlin to compete in the economic development of the new nations and thereby to establish its political influence wherever possible. Unrest and instability provide an ideal setting for Communist operations, just as they militate against the orderly evolution of democratic institutions. It has been amply demonstrated in the course of the past generation that, discounting the cost in human suffering, to which industrially undeveloped peoples are inured, authoritarian regimes can be highly efficient in promoting economic development. Inevitably, then, the methods and achievements of the Communist world will be alluring to some leaders of emergent peoples who are in a desperate hurry to arrive at a distant goal. In other words, there is a real and immediate danger that some of the new and restless nations may jump from the frying pan of colonialism into the fire of

Communist domination. For practical political as well as for humanitarian reasons the United States and other nations of the free world must therefore make sustained efforts and substantial sacrifices in the competition to organize the new world order.

There is, of course, a limit to the amount of aid that underdeveloped countries can promptly absorb, lacking as they do seasoned leadership, trained personnel, honest administration, transportation and other facilities. There can be no doubt, however, that for a long time to come they could profitably utilize more aid than they have been receiving from the United States and European countries. Naturally conditions and prospects vary, and each country should be considered in terms of its resources, structure and aspirations. In the last analysis foreign aid, while indispensable, will prove ineffectual unless the population of the receiving country is itself willing to make a great effort and is prepared to abandon traditional institutions in favor of the organization, techniques and discipline essential to a modern state. At best foreign capital can provide technical knowledge, assist in the training of local talent, and furnish the financial aid necessary for the take-off to modernization.

It has been estimated that the industrial nations of the free world could more than double their present programs without expending more than one per cent of their own gross national products. It is clear, furthermore, that certain European countries could and should assume a much larger part of the burden than they have carried thus far. Present plans call for a concerted effort, through the International Development Association and especially the proposed Organization for Economic Cooperation and Development, to ensure the steady flow of investment without which long-term planning and sustained operations are almost impossible.

The United States should certainly use its influence and resources to launch a coordinated and continuing international attack on this crucial problem. But it should also, as a matter of urgency, review and improve its own aid programs. The selection and training of American personnel requires greater attention, and much could be done to reduce the number of agencies with responsibilities in this field, as well as to clarify their functions. Legislative authorizations and appropriations should be modified to permit longer terms of commitments and longer perspective in planning. The terms of aid should be simplified and alleviated, especially with reference to repayment. Surplus agricultural commodities should be made available on generous terms and all reasonable trade concessions extended to the underdeveloped countries.

In this field of activity much has been done over the past twenty years by private, voluntary agencies, through which the American people have expended some $2.5 billion for material aid and relief, technical cooperation, and educational projects. More than fifty private organizations are now working in conjunction with the International Cooperation Administration, which provides them with surplus food and the necessary transportation facilities. These agencies, representing both church groups and lay organizations, can add to aid operations a humane touch and, through their close contacts with foreign populations, can often work more effectively than the more impersonal agencies of government. Similarly, American businesses abroad often provide the most effective training in technical and managerial skills, and private consultants the best guidance in planning and promoting rational investment.

A crucial aspect of the problem is the educational one. Under the Military Assistance Program, tens of thousands of foreign officers and enlisted men were brought to the United States for specialized training. Through observation and contacts, as well as through the subject-matter of their education, many of these men obtained a better understanding of American conditions, procedures and objectives. The State Department Leaders' Program has served a similar purpose at high levels by bringing influential foreigners to this country for travel and consultation.

These efforts should now be expanded to provide training for foreign civilian personnel in technical, legal and administrative matters. Private foundations and universities have already embarked upon this task and there are presently almost 50,000 foreign students of all nationalities in American schools, most of them studying without American governmental support. A number of institutions of higher learning have received foundation grants to aid underdeveloped countries in organizing their planning and production. American citizens and institutions can exercise great influence through these efforts and it behooves the United States government to take the utmost advantage of the opportunities presented by private enterprise. Many young Americans with high ideals of service to their country and to humanity are prepared to serve abroad as teachers and advisers. What is now required is proper coordination and guidance of effort. It is certainly high time for the government to work out with universities, foundations and other professional and voluntary organizations a larger and more effective attack on this crucial problem.

Experience has shown the manifold difficulties in the way of assistance to the underdeveloped countries as they attempt to attain a sustained rate of growth and even a modest improvement in the conditions of life. Just because American levels are so high, the United States is bound to be envied, no matter how much help it may give. Just because these countries are inexperienced and poor, it will be difficult to apply democratic principles and establish standards of efficiency and honesty. Just because dictatorial regimes will at first be almost inevitable, there will be a strong tendency to look to the Communist states for help and guidance in a program of forced industrialization. And just because in these newly emerging nations human life has been held in low regard, there will be little inclination to weigh human misery in the mad race to attain overnight what it took far more developed countries a century to accomplish.

The United States and other free nations must therefore expect inefficiency, waste, frustration and ingratitude. But these must be accepted, for the task is not a purely humanitarian one. The objective of the United States is not to buy gratitude or friendship, but to help in reducing a vast area of international tension. The question is one of self-interest and self-preservation. In a world so closely knit, appalling disparities in wealth and well-being will undermine the entire community of nations, generating pressures and conflicts which even the most extensive and concerted aid programs may not be able wholly to circumvent.

The Middle East. The United States should support the nations of the Middle East in maintaining their newly won independence, in developing honest and efficient administrations, and in effecting with as little suffering as possible the transformation from the old social order to the new. Politically the regimes of these countries vary widely, from the relatively representative democracies of Turkey, Lebanon and Israel to the constitutional monarchies of Iran and Jordan, the popular dictatorships of the United Arab Republic and Iraq, and the absolute monarchies of Saudi Arabia, Yemen, Kuwait, and other Arab principalities. The United States can do little directly to influence the political evolution of these states beyond continuing to stress its faith in democratic institutions.

Several of the northern states of the area are bound to each other and to Britain in the Central Treaty Organization, with which the United States is loosely linked through participation in the work of certain committees. CENTO is designed to provide a measure of mutual support to Turkey, Iran and Pakistan in defense against Communist aggression and should therefore have a continuing claim on United States military as well as economic aid.

The Turkish Republic in particular plays a crucial role in the defense of the free world not only because of its strategic location and its long tradition of resistance to Russian expansion, but because of its active membership in NATO. Although in Turkey modernization has been under way for more than a century, the country still faces grave economic and social problems which are reflected in the instability from which the government at times suffers. It is obviously a major interest of the United States and of NATO to support the Turkish Republic economically and militarily, and to encourage in every way the progressive development of its democratic institutions.

Iran and Pakistan have also aligned themselves with the nations of the free world. These countries, like others of the area, are undergoing rapid and painful changes inescapable in the process of transformation from feudalism to modern democracy. They should continue to receive American military and economic aid to the extent of their ability to utilize it advantageously.

The Arab states have been free of Turkish rule for little more than a generation and have but recently attained their full independence. In international affairs they have almost all adopted a neutralist policy, due partly to their hostility to their former masters, and partly to their resentment toward the United States because of its part in the establishment and maintenance of Israel.

Much of the Arab world is in a state of chronic unrest, the reflection primarily of the economic and social tension resulting from the rapid transition from the old tribal system to the modern industrial order. This unrest finds expression in the bitter rivalry of popular leaders and even more in uncompromising hostility to the Israeli state. In these circumstances the United Arab Republic has accepted large-scale military and economic aid from the Soviet Union and other Communist countries, though apparently without irrevocable commitment to the Communist bloc. Unless it does so the United States should maintain friendly relations with the Arab Republic as with the other Arab states, using its influence and power to help them stand on their own feet, overcome their mutual differences, and achieve the social reforms which are essential to any basic improvement in their standard of living. It is clearly in the interest of the United States not only to keep these nations from falling victim to Communism, but to see them grow in prosperity and stability, to develop trade relations with each other, to establish active cultural as well as business communications, and to cooperate in resisting territorial aggression of any kind.

The existence of Israel will indubitably contribute to the prolongation of instability in the Middle East as it already does to the continuation of hostility between the Arab states and the western powers. Since the United States has firmly committed itself to support Israel's integrity, it should aim to bring about a reasonable and mutually acceptable settlement of the Arab-Israeli issue. The United States should reiterate its determination not to permit the conquest and extinction of Israel and should induce other powers to join in a guarantee of the present territory of the Israeli state. It should continue to take an equally strong stand against further expansion of Israel, and so help to give the Arab states an assurance of the territorial *status quo* without which any compromise settlement is unthinkable. Official recognition of the *status quo* by the Arab states is probably politically impractical for the present. But it would no doubt be furthered by a settlement of the status of the Arab refugees, almost one million in number, whose position is every year becoming more deplorable. The United States cannot of itself solve this problem, but should certainly use its best influence to bring about a compromise, recognizing that this might involve the return of at least a limited number of Arab refugees to Palestine.

Africa. The continent of Africa is bound to be a center of turbulence in world affairs for years to come. European control of vast areas is being relinquished quite suddenly and new, independent states are emerging more or less pell mell. The difficulties inherent in any such precipitate transformation are enhanced in the case of Africa by the fact that the population, poor and illiterate, is still living for the most part on a tribal basis. Trained and experienced leadership is almost entirely lacking and many of the new states, as successors to arbitrarily defined European colonies, lack the traditions and characteristics of real nationality. The leaders almost without exception have exaggerated hopes and expectations of progress and prosperity.

These new states cannot defend themselves unaided against a major power. Economically, too, they will long remain dependent on the financial and technical support of more advanced nations. To date such assistance has come to the new states primarily from their former masters, the British and the French, who have been providing about a billion dollars annually in public and private investment. Both Britain and France are prepared to continue their programs of support, though perhaps at a reduced rate. The question is whether the newly independent states will accept such aid. If not, it may prove more practicable to provide the large-scale economic and technical assistance required through the agency of the United Nations.

It has been the policy of the United States to recognize the preponderant role of the former colonial powers who, because of the magnitude of the task, should be encouraged to continue and even increase their contribution. But the time has clearly come for the United States to assume a larger responsibility, either directly or through the United Nations. For it should be the goal of the United States not only to forestall military aggression against the African states but also to support them in resisting undue pressure of a political or economic kind. The Communist states have already established footholds and are exerting their influence wherever possible. The United States should formulate without delay a comprehensive, long-term policy, to assist the African states in organizing effective systems of government and administration, and to give the technical and financial aid required to enable them to establish reasonably sound economies and to make some progress in education and social well-being.

In the uncertainty that is bound to persist for some time, the United States should try to foresee and mitigate territorial and other disputes between the new states, and if possible negotiate international agreements regulating the supply of armaments to avert huge and dangerous military outlays. It should encourage the formation of regional groupings which would help to eliminate or reduce territorial disputes and at the same time provide for sounder economies through the creation of larger communications systems and broader markets.

In those parts of Africa where there has been large-scale settlement by Europeans, there is an ever-present danger of violent race conflict. The whites are everywhere in a minority, being only about one-fifth of the total population even in the Union of South Africa. It would appear hopeless in present world conditions for such minorities to continue their discrimination against the majority and persist in their attempt to keep it permanently in subjection. Racial war is certain to ensue and would surely have serious repercussions throughout the world.

The United States must therefore use what influence it has to encourage and support such readjustments as may seem essential. With understanding and a readiness to accommodate, the whites of Africa could, with their greater education, experience and resources, still play a prominent and effective role. Difficult though the transition might be for them, they will be well advised to accept the racial equality towards which the pressure of events is leading the states of the new Africa.

VI

LATIN AMERICA

The Monroe Doctrine has, for well over a century, notified to the world the particular interest of the United States in maintaining the independence of the countries of Central and South America. The historical and geographic circumstances giving rise to this special concern have created a special relationship among the republics of the New World. This special relationship has, in turn, found expression in institutions such as the Organization of American States, which provide for prompt consultation and cooperation. Now that both Soviet Russia and Communist China are making determined efforts to undermine the position of the United States and establish their own influence in Latin America, it must be the continuing objective of United States policy to uphold the partnership principle and to work constantly towards even closer and more intimate relations between the nations of the western hemisphere. This involves not only common planning and action for mutual defense, but also consultation and collaboration in world affairs. It implies also an unremitting effort to improve mutual understanding and trust through cultural exchanges of all kinds.

Despite the imprint of European culture upon the countries of Central and South America, the large populations of Indian descent still live to a great extent in poverty and ignorance. Social imbalance has made for political instability and instability has tended to engender revolution, involving not infrequently the establishment of dictatorship. The United States and its Latin American neighbors are committed to a policy of non-interference in each other's internal affairs. Without infringing this principle the United States should encourage in all possible ways the growth and acceptance of democratic ideas and practices, while avoiding aid and comfort to dictators or dictatorial cliques.

One obvious method to further the cause of democracy is to give unstinting support to the economic and social development of these countries. Even at substantial sacrifices the United States should assist in the diversification of their production and the establishment of a large if not a general market. United States businesses have already made huge investments in Latin America. The further expansion of such investment could be promoted by some form of government insurance against loss, in return for which private enterprise could be coordinated with a major government program of technical and other economic assistance.

The task to be accomplished in Latin America is enormous, and even heroic efforts may fail to meet the full requirements. For the foreseeable future there will continue to be a vast disparity between the living standards of the United States and its neighbors to the south and this will inevitably provoke discontent, criticism and resentment, which in turn will create an atmosphere conducive to the spread of Communism. Nonetheless, the United States must persist, for there is little use in embarking upon grandiose projects for the new Asian and African nations if the American people and government prove themselves unable to deal successfully with the needs of their immediate neighbors and traditional associates. The goal is clear and the time has certainly come for common study and planning preliminary to a great and concerted effort towards greater prosperity for all the American peoples.

VII

LIMITATION AND CONTROL OF ARMAMENTS

The tension in international relations generated by the conflict between democracy and Communism has of late been greatly enhanced by the phenomenal development of science and technology, and by their increasingly direct impact on armaments. Revolutionary discoveries have been made in military technology every few years, the changes coming with such rapidity that the human mind, trapped by its own achievements, can no longer grasp all their implications.

The United States and Soviet Russia are annually investing tens of billions of dollars in fabulously expensive engines of destruction, many of which are apt to be already obsolescent when they come off the assembly line. In return they have exposed each other to an ever greater danger of a surprise attack of inconceivable destructiveness. The point has already been reached at which each of the two super-powers possesses weapons and the means to deliver them sufficient to the destruction of its opponent several times over, yet without much likelihood of ever being able to attain a decisive superiority. All humanity now lives in constant danger of war by intercontinental missiles, while the advent of the space age adds to existing terrors the prospect of nuclear satellites. The accomplishments of science, on which the enormous productivity of the modern world depends, have had also the contrary effect of bringing humanity to the brink of self-annihilation.

Armaments were in the past regarded as reliable symptoms of international tensions. The new thermonuclear weapons, however, have themselves become a prime source of tension. It must therefore be a primary goal of the United States to arrive at a systematic reduction of armaments under adequate inspection and control, and more especially to establish international regulation of the most lethal instruments of destruction.

Limitation and control of nuclear weapons are all the more urgent because without them other nations, possibly in considerable numbers, will presently equip themselves with such armaments. The expense involved, as well as the further problem of acquiring the means of delivery, may deter most smaller powers. But these factors would have less weight with others, notably West Germany, Japan, and the Chinese People's Republic. Communist China in particular may confidently be expected to join the so-called nuclear club within the next three to five years and to use its nuclear power as a political if not as a military weapon.

An increase in the number of nuclear powers may not enhance materially the potential self-destructiveness of mankind, but it will certainly render the conditions of human living even more precarious. The number of issues from which nuclear war may result will be multiplied and the employment of nuclear blackmail for political purposes must be expected to become far more widespread. Furthermore, the number of persons in a position to unleash nuclear war will be vastly increased. Not only technical failures but the hasty act of some unbalanced or panic-stricken individual might draw the great nuclear powers into what had begun as a relatively minor conflict, and so plunge a large part of mankind into the holocaust.

Since nations arm against each other out of distrust and fear, as well as for deliberate conquest, it is unthinkable that anything approaching complete disarmament can be achieved in the foreseeable future. To be sure, the Soviets have proposed the speedy abolition of all armaments, but this proposal is so patently illogical and impracticable as to stamp it a cynical propaganda fraud.

It does not necessarily follow, however, that the Soviet government is uninterested in the limitation and control especially of nuclear weapons, or opposed to the adoption of a program to this end, modest though it be. Despite Khrushchev's boasts, there is no reason to suppose that the Kremlin is less keenly alert than other governments to the dangers of nuclear war, or less fully aware of the implications of space war. Even though superiority in long-range missiles may provide it with a powerful instrument of blackmail, it may have real misgivings about the acquisition of nuclear armaments by its bellicose Chinese ally. Soviet leaders express deep concern about the possible nuclear arming of West Germany.

Every effort must be made to advance, even though but slightly, toward arms limitation and control. The difficulties and complexities, technical as well as political, are enormous; progress is bound to be slow and painful. But partial, even informal agreements may be feasible and might well open the way to more substantial achievements. The problem of inspection and control will continue to be a stumbling block, but should not be carried to such extremes as to make agreement impossible. No inspection system can provide ironclad assurance of security; a degree of risk will always be involved, whatever the safeguards.

A beginning might well be made with an agreement to suspend nuclear testing. Prolonged negotiations on this subject have resulted in informal agreement on many items, even on the delicate questions of inspection and control on Soviet territory. Though no firm or official agreement has been concluded, the ban on testing has been observed for some years by the United States and Britain, and presumably by Soviet Russia. Communist leaders, while making the utmost propaganda capital out of the armaments issue, may be groping for a solution of this overriding problem and may even be ready to accept some measure of international regulation and control, if only to ensure the security of their own impressive gains.

An international agreement between the present nuclear powers to desist from further testing of nuclear weapons would have the effect of freezing further development and slowing the "technological runaway." It would probably serve also to limit the increase in the number of nuclear powers by further arousing world opinion against the testing that would be necessary. It might also pave the way for agreement on the terms of an effective nuclear stalemate.

The United States and Soviet Russia are at present locked in such a stalemate, since neither can hope in a first strike to destroy the other's retaliatory power. A freezing of this situation, if possible at a reduced level and certainly under a system of rational arms control, would help alleviate tension and gain time for further negotiation by providing a more stable military environment. The end to be sought, without which there can be no security for anyone, must be effective international control especially of nuclear weapons in all their aspects: research, testing, production and stockpiling. Toward this end the United States is bound to strive with all its might.

In the past, discussion of the arms problem has suffered not only from the deep distrust between the nuclear powers, but to some extent from lack of unity of purpose and plan on the American side. Key agencies of the government, to say nothing of Congress, have contended against each other and thus hindered or delayed the formulation of sound and consistent policy. Furthermore, there have been neither funds nor staff nor proper direction for a continuing study of the political, military and technical problems involved, including the implications of specific plans and proposals. If American policy is to inspire confidence, if our negotiators are to be effective, if in short any real progress is to be made in the crucial matter of arms control, much better provision must be made, perhaps through a special agency, for research, planning and the coordination of policy. This matter will brook no delay.

VIII

NATIONAL GOALS AND NATIONAL PURPOSE

National goals are not the same as national policies or even immediate objectives. They contain a large measure of idealism, for they represent what a nation considers ultimately desirable not only in its own interest but in that of the whole international community. As such, they are for the most part not immediately attainable. Indeed, they may remain forever in the realm of aspiration. Nevertheless, they give meaning to national and international life and set for a people an end toward which it may strive and toward which specific plans and policies may be directed.

The definition and establishment of national goals must remain an idle exercise unless a people is deeply convinced of their validity and willing to make a concerted and sustained effort toward their progressive achievement.

The American people has, over the past half century, made notable progress in understanding its position in a rapidly changing world and in accepting the responsibilities incumbent upon it as a world power. It has certainly come to realize that, however great its desire to devote itself to its own concerns, the world will not leave it to its own devices but will force upon it ever greater attention to the demands of the times. The United States has already fought in two world wars in behalf of its principles as well as its interests. Of recent years it has made great sacrifices in defense of freedom and democracy throughout the world.

But the process of learning is never-ending. It requires time and effort, and also leadership and instruction. The American public is still prone to evaluate the results of diplomacy in simple terms of success or failure, if not in terms of personal achievement or ineptitude. There is far too great a tendency to criticize and condemn American foreign policy and more particularly to attack the State Department which conducts it. Such criticism is justified and helpful only if it is grounded on full understanding not only of the issues but of the difficulties in the way of their solution. The American people must realize that success in foreign policy depends not only on a few government officials but also on considerations of power and interest, on the aspirations and policies of many other states. Diplomacy implies constant adjustment and compromise. One cannot expect, in dealing with international problems of great complexity and importance, to come out with clean-cut, consistent victories. Some major issues may never be definitively solved. In ever changing terms they may create difficulties and dangers for any foreseeable future. In short, there are marked limitations to diplomacy, which preclude anything beyond alleviation of tension and progressive adjustment to changing conditions. Knowledge, skill, flexibility and patience are all called for, not only on the part of official negotiators, but on the part of the people on whose understanding and support they must rely.

In the continuing education of the public the government itself has an important role to play. It should make every effort to counteract the tendency to shroud difficulties in the cloak of secrecy and should, on the contrary, devote much more attention to the provision of prompt and reliable information through mass media, as also to the more effective coordination of policy and public relations among agencies. Nothing can be more harmful to the sound conduct of foreign policy than the confusion created in the minds of the people and their representatives in Congress by the conflicting statements on crucial matters emanating from different officials or agency sources.

Goals in world affairs necessarily lose their validity unless they are related to domestic programs. The United States cannot play the role of a great power unless it maintains its own strength, spiritually as well as militarily, politically and economically, unless in its own affairs it tries to live up to its principles. On the government level a continuing effort must be made to keep the organization of the Department of State, the Department of Defense, the International Cooperation Administration and kindred agencies abreast of the new demands, and to ensure sound formulation of policies. The need for able and well-trained personnel is great and it is therefore urgently necessary that methods of recruiting, clearing and training personnel be improved.

The success of the United States in world affairs is bound to hinge in the future more and more on the efficient mobilization of human resources and on the full utilization of all potentialities. The government should take greater account of the capabilities of private institutions in the foreign field and reduce the many obstacles that at times still obstruct their efficient operation. Thought should be given also to the constant improvement of the Information Service, which plays so important a role in conveying an image of the United States to foreign peoples, and to further development of cultural exchanges which contribute to better international understanding.

In conclusion, national goals, if they are to have meaning, must be consonant with domestic goals and with the nation's capabilities and attitudes. One and all, these matters are not the concern exclusively of government officials, teachers and news commentators. They are the concern of every American citizen, without whose understanding and support no government can, under the democratic system, hope to succeed.

15

JOHN J. McCLOY, *now Chairman of the Board, The Chase Manhattan Bank, was President of the World Bank, 1947 to 1949, and United States Military Governor and later High Commissioner for Germany, 1949 to 1952. His broad experience qualifies him to prepare the Commission's chapter on trade and tariff policy, assistance to underdeveloped nations, the balance of payments problem, and other complex issues of foreign economic policy.*

Mr. McCloy was advised in the preparation of this chapter by an informal group of consultants and by the panel listed below. He takes responsibility for the views expressed.

PANEL

ROBERT R. BOWIE, Director, Center for International Affairs, Harvard University; Director of Policy Planning and Assistant Secretary of State, 1953-57.

EMILIO G. COLLADO, Director, Standard Oil Company (New Jersey); United States Executive Director, International Bank for Reconstruction and Development, 1946-47.

LINCOLN GORDON, William Ziegler Professor of International Economic Relations, Harvard University; Director, Program Division, Economic Cooperation Administration, 1949-50; Minister of Economic Affairs, United States Embassy, London, 1952-55.

ALFRED C. NEAL, President, Committee for Economic Development.

ANDREW N. OVERBY, Vice President and Director, First Boston Corporation; Assistant Secretary of the Treasury, 1952-57.

FOREIGN ECONOMIC POLICY
AND OBJECTIVES

JOHN J. McCLOY

Foreign economic policy of the United States in the decade of the Sixties promises to be of decisive importance. Involved are relations with other nations on a wide range of vital matters—foreign trade, our aid to less-developed lands, foreign investment, and a host of other interconnections that serve to tie nations together. How we handle these relations and our attitude toward them form an integral part of our general foreign policy. At the same time the policies pursued are bound to exercise a broad impact on the domestic scene. The nation's security, the material well-being of its people, and even the shape of the world in the future—all are at stake in the process.

Today the United States plays a major role in the free world economy. Our nation turns out 40 per cent of all industrial production; we are the world's largest exporter, as well as one of its major importers. From our fields and factories flows an indispensable stream of goods— goods which in the early postwar years helped put Europe back on its feet and more recently have been of critical assistance to many less-developed lands.

Yet our economic relations with other peoples are in no sense a one-sided affair; nor is our position one of dominance. We depend on other lands for many critical materials and amenities of life. Large as are our imports, those of Western Europe taken as a whole are considerably greater. We serve as only one element in the determination of world prices, and shifts in the buying of other nations can materially affect the fortunes of our own producers. Even more important, our fate as a nation in this nuclear age is closely linked with that of other nations. The ties that bind us to other peoples cannot merely be political and military in character; they must have a solid foundation of common interests and objectives that are economic as well.

The truth is that we now live in a world which has grown increasingly interdependent. The speed of communications has foreshortened the world and reduced nations to the size of the City States of earlier times. Man lives in ever closer proximity to his fellow man, nations nearer and nearer to one another. At the same time we are witnessing a continuing revolution in the techniques of production and warfare: a revolution which has bound the free world closely together in terms of markets, the flow of materials and defense, while increasing the possibilities of aid and technical assistance to less-developed areas.

331

Paralleling these changes we are confronted with a massive political movement which aims to reverse the nineteenth and twentieth century trend of the world toward democracy and liberalism. Great military strength, a re-invigorated production system, an absolutist regime based on suppressive policy methods and propaganda—all combine to create the challenge of a new imperialism quite comparable to those of the most extensive empires of the past.

I

THE AIM OF FOREIGN ECONOMIC POLICY

Within this context the basic aim of United States policy can be simply stated. It is no less than the purpose which guided the country and inspired Americans from the beginning: to help build a world at peace, in which all men have an opportunity to lead lives of purpose, freedom and fulfillment. By and large, Americans have remained consistently faithful to this ideal over the years. But the obstacles to its achievement have been shifting and formidable—and perhaps never more formidable than they are today. In recent years four broad developments in particular have confronted the nation with new challenges and have helped to shape the character of our policy. Very briefly these are:

- **Revolutionary change in the less-developed lands.** Peoples of the less-developed lands, observing the experience of the industrial countries and the Soviet Union, are no longer content with their lot. They aspire to a new and better life, and seek to organize their societies in a way that can assure this objective, even though revolutionary change may be involved. Moreover, as a part of this same process, thirty-eight new nations, chiefly in Asia and Africa, have come to life under conditions which often have destroyed old ties and relationships.
- **The growing economic strength of the Communist bloc.** The Communist lands, particularly the Soviet Union and China, continue to grow in strength and in their potential for external economic expansion and aggression. Today these lands comprise a fourth of the world's population and account for perhaps a fifth of world production. Their policy is aggressive and their avowed intention is to spread the Communist philosophy and way of life to all other peoples. The United States and the West must prepare for increasing competition from the Communist bloc, particularly in their relations with the developing countries.
- **The economic resurgence of Western Europe and Japan.** Countering in part the increase in Communist strength has been an economic resurgence in both Western Europe and Japan. These

areas are now growing in economic terms more rapidly than the United States. They have an ability to shoulder burdens of defense and economic aid which a decade ago was lacking. At the same time, they have modernized industrial plants and are employing mass-production techniques which formerly were the hallmark of United States industry. All this acts to enhance the strength of the free world as a whole. But it also presents problems of heavy competition and adjustment for United States industry, both at home and in world markets.

- **The trend toward regional economic groups.** A related aspect of the growing strength in Western Europe has been the formation of the European Common Market and the European Free Trade Association—each a prospective trading unit, designed to eliminate internal trade barriers between members, while maintaining tariffs and other barriers against outsiders. Moreover, this tendency to develop regional groupings for economic purposes is spreading elsewhere—to Central America, South America and perhaps next to the Middle East and Africa. Paralleling these developments, too, is a growth in the number and use of international institutions for specific economic purposes.

These then, in capsule form, are some of the important forces and trends which have a bearing on the position of the United States in world economic affairs in the decade of the Sixties. The criticism is sometimes expressed that too much emphasis and attention is directed toward the Communist challenges and not enough toward our own independent objectives. It is said that many of our problems would exist quite apart from the Communist threat. To a certain extent this, of course, is true. Nevertheless, at the center of a great number of our problems and policies, and overriding many other considerations, does lie one single inescapable element: the ominous conflict with the Communist bloc over the form and shape the world is to take in the future. Although this conflict will continue to have significant military aspects, the weapons with which it will be fought are more likely to be economic and political. The Communists have made no secret of their aim to convert the less-developed lands to their way of life. It requires little imagination to foresee the consequences for the free industrial nations if in the end the Communists were successful in their objective—if South Asia, the Middle East and much of Africa, let alone South America, were closed off to the West. Freedom as we know it would be difficult to maintain in such a restricted and menacing world.

What is required over the longer-run—and more than a decade is involved, perhaps as much as a half century—is to build a world that can accommodate not only our own aspirations but those of the peoples of less-developed countries as well: a world in which the free institutions that are vital to our way of life are not only preserved but extended. Such a task will require all the energy, resources and imagination we can muster. It cannot be undertaken by the United States alone—the whole of the free world will be required to cooperate in it. Nor is the problem solely one of economic aid. Involved is the whole network of economic relations between nations: foreign trade, private foreign investment, the development of regional groups and international agencies. All of these are interrelated, and policies fashioned for each must be consistent with the others to form a unified whole. It would make little sense, for example, to assist less-developed countries with aid, while denying them outlets for essential exports.

At the same time, if we are to be successful in the great tasks that confront us, domestic policies must be correlated with the foreign. If we are to continue to have any freedom of choice in our foreign economic policy (as well as our foreign policy as a whole) we must act to preserve our very great but still finite economic power.

Rising costs at home in the face of improvements elsewhere, the dampening effect of our present tax system, the waste involved in some of our national programs—all these become factors in our foreign economic policy. As a leader of the free world it is essential that we have a secure and solid base from which to discharge the tremendous responsibilities which Providence and, to a very large degree, the Communists have placed upon us. In the world of the Sixties we cannot afford to fritter away strength in wasteful featherbedding on the part of either industry or labor. Government budgets must be held under stern discipline; inflation must be avoided; and payments between nations maintained on a sound basis.

The role of economic growth. A central objective of policy throughout the free world should be sound economic growth, without inflation. It can be said of economic growth that it is not an end in itself, but merely a means to other ends—to a stronger, more alert and public-spirited society. Free peoples and their economies thrive in an atmosphere of growth; they encounter difficulty and hardship in an environment of stagnation. A growing United States economy means an expanded market on favorable terms for the products of other nations. At the same time it enhances the ability of the United States to render assistance, economic and political, wherever needed.

Economic growth is even more essential for the less-developed lands. For many of them it is a matter of life and death, with large numbers of people still living on the edge of subsistence. For all it is an important concomitant to political stability, and failure to achieve growth increases the risk of the adoption of institutions and techniques which are alien to freedom.

One of the most significant and challenging developments of the twentieth century lies in the fact that man now holds in his hands the technical basis for eliminating hunger, epidemic disease and privation on a wide scale. In large sections of the Western world this goal has already been achieved. The possibility exists for realizing it eventually on a world-wide scale, although many difficult political, economic, social, and cultural barriers would have to be overcome before it is achieved. Nevertheless, men are stirred by great objectives, and there is every reason why men with vision should now look forward to a day when the presently less-privileged lands can enjoy many of the advantages now achieved in more fortunate countries. It is not out of keeping, therefore, to set as some of the most important of our goals the following, even though their actual realization in some instances may seem remote:

(1) Elimination of hunger in countries of the free world willing to cooperate in programs directed to that end. Minimum diets would be assured as a result of local economic development, including expansion of agriculture in areas most suited to it.

(2) Virtual elimination of epidemic diseases and the achievement of minimum standards of medical care by all free world peoples.

(3) Expansion of elementary education to the vast majority of individuals, with the opportunity for secondary and higher education open to as high a proportion of talented people as possible.

(4) Achievement of a rate of economic growth in cooperating countries which would assure substantial improvement in living conditions over a period of years.

Progress toward these objectives would, of course, carry with it profound political implications as well. As suggested above, programs necessary to this end would require far-reaching cooperation and the adoption of a consistent framework of policies. Subsequent sections of this report discuss United States policy in the light of the foregoing needs, as well as in terms of other objectives. Included are sections concerned specifically with the following:

(a) United States policy on world trade.

(b) Our policy toward regional economic groups.

(c) Aid to the less-developed nations.

(d) Policy with regard to the Sino-Soviet bloc.

Concluding sections give consideration to the impact of these various policies on the United States balance of payments and suggest new forms and approaches which will be needed for free world cooperation if our goals are to be achieved.

II

OUR POLICY ON WORLD TRADE

The most pervasive of our foreign economic policies is that relating to trade with other nations. Such trade is important to our own material well-being; it is vital to our arrangements for defense; and it is essential to progress in the less-developed lands. Most of our allies could not live without exchanging goods with other nations, and any viable system must include trade with the United States. Likewise, the less-developed lands require machinery and supplies from the industrial nations and it is essential that they earn a good portion of these through exports, particularly to the industrial nations.

For more than a quarter century now the United States has maintained an enlightened and consistent trade policy. Broadly speaking, it has been our objective to reduce and remove barriers that block the flow of trade between nations. We have sought also to promote *multilateral* trade—that is, unrestricted trade between all countries, with no attempt to balance exports and imports between specific countries. Our Reciprocal Trade Agreements Act, our promotion of the International Monetary Fund, and our adherence to the General Agreement on Tariffs and Trade (GATT) have all acted to support these broad policies.

Trade policy in the Sixties.   The Sixties promise to be a period of critical decision for the United States and the free world generally on trade policy. At the moment existing policies are under increasing criticism and there are some in our country who would now move toward greater protectionism. They point in particular to the growing competition of imports in many fields, as well as to a troublesome imbalance in our international payments.

The fact is that protectionism is no way to set about correcting an adverse balance of payments—and doubly so in the circumstances of the Sixties, since it would carry the United States in precisely the opposite direction from that required to meet the overriding need that confronts us in our relation with other peoples. On the contrary, if the free world is to tackle its problems successfully in the coming decade it must move to re-energize the policy of relaxing controls and encouraging expansion of trade between nations.

At the same time it must be recognized that the United States cannot act unilaterally in pursuing such a goal; nor can it be precipitate or quixotic in its approach to the problem. Other nations, particularly industrial nations, must also be persuaded to remove trade barriers, and as a means to this end it will be necessary for the United States to retain leverage to exercise pressure in bargaining. Today tariffs are higher in countries like Britain and France than in the United States. Moreover, the European Common Market, with its eventual aim of a common external tariff for all members, will act to raise tariffs at the outset in countries with low barriers like Germany, Belgium, and The Netherlands. (Tariffs in France and Italy, however, will be reduced somewhat in the process of averaging.) Indeed, if any of the newly formed regional groups are not to restrict trade over a broader area, and affect world commerce adversely, they must be induced to reduce external tariffs and quotas.

Thus, it should be the objective of the United States over the next decade to bring about in the Common Market and other industrial areas a movement toward a lower tariff level, say a reduction of 50 per cent in the average of tariffs on industrial products. This tariff goal in the industrial countries should be reached only by steps taken over a period of time, in order to ease the problem of adjustment. At the same time the industrial countries should be required to honor their undertakings under the General Agreement on Tariffs and Trade to eliminate quotas and other quantitative restrictions on trade—again over a period long enough to work out needed adjustments. This would require the eventual removal by the United States of such quotas as it imposes in return for reciprocal action on the part of other nations. Other arrangements for stabilizing prices of certain industrial raw materials might be developed (page 348). As a matter of general policy, however, it is difficult to see how quotas which protect high-cost or inefficient production, and at the same time support artificially high prices, can be defended in the public interest as a permanent policy. If for reasons of defense or other national interests it is desirable to continue high-cost production, the payment of outright subsidies normally would appear preferable.

In this regard it also would appear to be in the best interests of all nations, including the United States, to move toward freer trade in farm products. Again this would be possible only if action were taken by other countries as well as the United States. For with few exceptions agriculture today is the most heavily protected of all industries. It might be added that in a world with fewer restrictions, the United States would undoubtedly be fully capable of competing on a price basis with other areas. In fact, farm exports might expand considerably, to the mutual advantage of farmers in the United States and consumers in other industrial nations. That should be our long-term objective.

A revision of trade legislation. If the United States is to participate effectively in the process of further reducing world trade barriers, some revision in our trade legislation will be required. For more than a quarter century the basic legislation governing the determination of United States tariffs has been the Reciprocal Trade Agreements Act. This act provided a landmark in the history of world trade. Since it first came into force (1934) our average duty has been substantially reduced—perhaps as much as halved. Part of this decline was due to rising prices, which automatically cut the percentage impact of duties expressed in fixed dollar-and-cents amounts. But substantial reductions have also come through tariff bargaining between the United States and other countries.

What is not widely realized is that the process of effective tariff reduction has now largely halted. In the past decade duties paid on the average have dropped only one per cent, and again most of this small reduction has been the result of rising prices. Reductions through tariff bargaining have been confined chiefly to products bearing very high duties, and have been so limited as to have no real impact on trade. Meanwhile, the so-called "peril point" and "escape clause" provisions of the Trade Agreements Act have been strengthened.

These provisions, which are little understood by the general public, have the effect first of limiting any tariff cut to an amount which will continue to restrict imports to a relatively small proportion of the domestic market. Secondly, they empower the President to raise tariffs or other restrictions if imports are greater than expected and threaten injury to domestic producers. In effect they put a floor under reductions in tariffs—a floor which for the most part has now been reached.

To be effective in the Sixties, tariff legislation will require some modification of these "peril point" and "escape clause" provisions. At the same time, consideration should be given to developing a new technique for bargaining with other countries, one in which reciprocal concessions are not limited to a product-by-product basis. In recent years, tariffs between countries in Western Europe have been successfully cut back by agreement to make specific percentage reductions in particular *groups* of products, rather than in individual items themselves. This provides a necessary degree of flexibility, permitting each country to select the actual products on which tariff cuts will be made. Bargaining then comes to be focused on the most important aspect of national policy: the extent to which the over-all level of trade restrictions is to be reduced.

In making these changes Congress will naturally want to provide assurance that adjustments to tariff changes will not be so extreme as to cause substantial harm to industry and labor. Part of the answer here will lie in the technique of administration. Although ultimate goals may be agreed upon through bargaining, they can be reached through a series of small steps over a period of time. Many producers are spurred to make improvements, reflected in lower costs and increased productivity, and are able to continue to compete effectively.

There is merit, however, in providing special safeguards against any sudden disruption of domestic markets by a concerted concentration of foreign low-cost suppliers on the United States. The objective in such instances is not to bar such products on a permanent basis (except where they clearly have been produced under labor standards abnormal for the supplying country). Rather, it is to provide time for adjustments on the part of both industry and labor. Thus any safeguards initially applied should gradually be removed. Even then adjustments may not always be painless, and in these circumstances there is strong justification for the government to lend material assistance to both workers and employers.   The techniques and means for such assistance have already been given considerable study—they include such matters as re-training for workers, supplementary unemployment compensation benefits, allowances for relocation, special loans to individual businesses for conversion and modernization of facilities, and the like.   There is no reason why all these and other steps should not be employed.

Yet at the same time, the extent of the adjustments required by tariff changes should not be exaggerated.   If spread over a period of years, the annual dislocation is likely to be minute as compared with the adjustments that occur as a matter of course in an expanding economy operating under principles of free enterprise.   Moreover, the cost involved will be small as compared with the very real benefits to be derived.   A lowering of tariffs can make a considerable contribution to general economic expansion by bringing about a shift of resources from less efficient to more efficient industries.   Consumers as a whole are offered a wider range of goods at lower prices.   Export industries, which are among the more efficient, are stimulated.   In all, the benefits of freer trade are so large and pervasive that the nation can well afford the costs involved in achieving them.

It must also be remembered that we have become a creditor nation on a vast scale and that creditor nations require low tariffs.   For some years ahead the outflow of credits may exceed the inward flow of repayments.   But the balance may eventually swing the other way.   In the final analysis, other nations can repay us only if we are willing to accept goods and services; the alternative in the long run is a growing problem of transferring gold and dollar claims to the United States of the sort that developed in the late Twenties and early Thirties and which contributed to a world financial crisis.   It is for these reasons that a creditor nation must adopt liberal trade policies and promote the expansion of world trade.   Only in that way can such a nation derive real benefits from its international investments, and avoid measures which could precipitate serious financial difficulties on a world-wide front.

The bread of generous trade policies, cast on the troubled waters of the Sixties, will almost certainly return to the United States manyfold —in better living standards at home, as well as greater free world strength against the Communist challenge.

III

THE UNITED STATES AND REGIONAL GROUPS

The need for an expansive trade policy in the coming decade is given added emphasis by the emergence of new regional trading groups, particularly in Europe.   There is much to be said both for and against such regional economic groups. However, the significant fact today is that they actually are coming into being. The European Economic Community is off to a vigorous start and the European Free Trade Association has made a beginning. Likewise, the Central American Economic Association is being established, and a Latin American Free Trade Association is moving beyond the planning stage.

Policy towards the European Economic Community and the European Free Trade Association. In determining United States policy towards these regional groups, it is well to distinguish between groups in Europe and those in the less-developed areas. Insofar as the European Economic Community is concerned, there are strong political reasons for favoring its development. It provides a vehicle for increasing the ties among Western Germany, France, Italy and the Benelux nations. It promises to create a stronger economic entity on the Continent—one capable of sustaining rising living standards while contributing more effectively to mutual defense and economic development in other areas. All of this is in the interest of the United States and the free world as a whole.

At the same time, it is in the interests of the free world that the movement towards European unity include Great Britain as well as the principal countries on the Continent. The United States should use its good offices to prevent the development of a schism in Western Europe, such as is threatened by the existence of two separate trading blocs. Great Britain and such other members of the Free Trade Association as are free to do so should be encouraged to join or associate with the Six of the Common Market in an enlarged grouping. It is important that any arrangement for an enlarged group be framed in terms that contribute to the creation of political structures of wider and more responsible scope, as well as to the movement towards lower trade barriers.

Regional economic groupings of either the Common Market or Free Trade Area type discriminate against outsiders. They reduce and will eventually eliminate trade barriers among members, while maintaining barriers against other nations, including the United States. Thus, the United States must be in a position to bargain vigorously for reductions in the external trade restrictions of such groups and for full adherence to the principles of the General Agreement on Trade and Tariffs (GATT). In such bargaining, the Free Trade Area arrangement poses special problems in that the United States would have to bargain individually with each member, but would be required to extend to all members (under the most-favored-nation principle) the concessions it granted to each. On the other hand, concessions granted to the United States by any single member of the Free Trade Area would not be binding on the other members. In contrast, a Common Market, although bringing greater power to the bargaining table, can offer reductions in its external trade barriers which act to reduce the degree of discrimination for the area as a whole against outsiders, including the United States.

Fortunately, there is evidence that Europeans recognize that their long-run goal should be a liberal policy towards external trade. The European Economic Community has announced its willingness to reduce the level of external tariffs initially by 20 per cent in return for adequate concessions. Likewise, the Common Market and Free Trade Area groups are discussing mutual tariff reductions on products that are of key importance in trade between the two groups as well as with outsiders. The European countries, with a background of new vigour born of economic growth, should be well equipped to make these and other adjustments.

Policy toward regional groups in less-developed areas. Regional groups in areas like Central and South America, the Middle East and Africa pose additional problems and considerations. The political structure in some of these areas, with many small nations, together with their present economic environment, appears to be woefully inadequate in today's world with its wide aspirations for rapid development. Part of the problem in such areas, then, is to erect a new politico-economic structure which will permit the broadening of markets essential for economic development. The establishment of regional markets may be one necessary step in the working out of a solution.

In determining policy toward such groups, and indeed toward less-developed nations generally, one consideration not relevant to Western Europe needs to be taken into account. It may be necessary for the less-developed areas to maintain a special degree of tariff protection for infant industries until the latter can stand on their own feet. Industrialization can of course be stimulated by setting up tariffs to offer a protected market for local producers.

The test for the United States and the West in these circumstances is where to draw the line. The presumption is that infant industries will develop, become more efficient, and produce goods at less than the cost of imports. While this presumption must be recognized as being sound, care must also be taken that regional groups do not merely become an excuse for following a strictly protectionist path. The objective of the United States should be to help such groups evolve over a period of time into effective members of a world-wide multilateral trading system—a system which is in the ultimate interest of the free world as a whole.

It does not appear to be in the interests of the United States or the free world generally that the United States itself become a member of a regional trade group in the foreseeable future. Its greatest service, both in its own interest and to the free world, can be rendered through persistent efforts to create a world-wide system of multilateral trade, unhindered by artificial controls and with all nations and regions bound together by strong economic interests. These of course are the general principles which underlie the General Agreement on Tariffs and Trade (GATT)—an agreement which deserves continuing strong support from the United States.

IV

ECONOMIC ASSISTANCE TO THE LESS-DEVELOPED LANDS

As suggested earlier, the less-developed countries and their need for sustained economic growth pose one of the most difficult and important problems confronting the United States over the next decade. These lands comprise a third of the world's territory and contain two-fifths of its population. Many of the countries are relatively new, with economies ranging from the near-primitive to those like India and the Philippines which have made a start toward industrialization. A few like Argentina, Brazil, and Mexico are fairly well along the road toward modern industrial society. In all instances, however, people are stirring with a new knowledge of the potential for economic advance inherent in modern technology; they are dissatisfied with things as they are and seek to bring about changes designed to improve the lot of their people.

The interest of the United States in the less-developed lands is both economic and political. They are an important source of raw materials, even more so for our allies in Western Europe and Japan than for ourselves, and their significance in this respect is bound to grow over the years. Likewise, they provide natural markets for industrial products as well as opportunities for investment. But more important than these economic matters are the political and strategic aspects of a continuing relationship between the industrial nations and the less-developed lands. As already pointed out, they promise to be the principal battleground on which the forces of freedom and Communism compete—a battleground in which the future shape of society may finally be tested and determined.

Change in the less-developed lands is bound to unfold whether or not the United States and the West relate themselves to it. As matters now stand, incomes and living standards are exceedingly low for the great mass of the people—perhaps no more than an average of $125 per capita in some of the countries, and even less in a number of them. Moreover, the economic gap between most of these countries and the industrial nations, rather than narrowing, has continued to grow. In consequence we have what Sir Oliver Franks has called a "North-South problem," as well as that of the "East-West."

Nor in the end is there any real guarantee that these conditions can be overcome. Population in many countries is expanding rapidly and seems bound to continue to do so, if only because of a declining death rate. Many of the young nations lack political maturity, and in some cases outmoded social structures create additional problems. Indeed, these countries very often pose a strange paradox. As they take early steps toward development, and need outside help, their political behavior assumes a tinge of the irrational. They fall into the grip of emotional nationalism and not infrequently take action that acts to discourage outside assistance from both public and private sources.

Provocation in these latter instances is very often great, and there will be cases where the attitudes are such that the United States cannot in self respect lend assistance to the country involved. And yet such instances should be the exception. Notwithstanding all the uncertainties, and even apart from political considerations—which in themselves are compelling—the United States would fall short of its own values and tradition if it refused to do what it can to assist the less-developed countries. For close to two centuries our nation has nurtured the cause of freedom and liberty with persistence and often with sacrifice. We could hardly now deny other nations assistance in creating conditions necessary for a similar way of life. At the same time there is in the American character a broad streak of humanitarianism, an instinct of generosity toward those who are less fortunate. If for no other reason than that it is in keeping with our ingrained habits and values, we are bound to come to the aid of peoples in the less-developed lands.

The role of the United States in speeding economic growth. What part can the United States play in the process of speeding economic growth in the less-developed countries? Obviously the great bulk of the effort must be undertaken by the peoples themselves. Only they can shape their own destiny. They are the ones who must provide the major share of the saving and capital; it is they who must take the lead in preparing themselves to make use of modern technology; it is they who in the end must create stable governments, capable of enforcing contracts. All of these factors are necessary for economic growth in a free society.

Yet the outside world, including the United States, can also be helpful in a multitude of ways, and the margin provided might in some cases prove decisive. Such help may take the form of needed machinery, materials or foodstuffs; or it may entail the provision of technical know-how, or assistance in the education and training of managerial or worker personnel. Very often the process involves a net addition to the resources of the developing country—either in the form of a gift or a loan. But no less important is the ability of these countries to help themselves through an exchange of goods in trade with the industrial countries. Aid without trade would be unacceptable to any developing country, and it is essential that industrial nations, particularly those of Western Europe and the United States, open their doors to the products of these countries, including the products they come to manufacture.

It is very difficult to attach a measuring rod to the task confronting the United States and other industrial countries in assisting the less-developed lands. However, a few generalizations can be made which serve to outline the rough magnitude of the problem.

Broadly speaking, the less-developed countries now have a total Gross National Product on the order of $150 billion and they are growing at a rate on the average of 2 per cent per annum. (Some of course grow more rapidly and others more slowly.) With few exceptions the rate is such as to permit only a small advance in living standards after allowance for a rapidly increasing population—probably no more than ½ of 1 per cent a year. At such a pace the average per capita income in the year 2000 might rise to $150.

The current level of activity involves a rate of investment equal to about 13 per cent of Gross National Product. It is this investment which of course includes among other things the equipment, the machines and the buildings to house them in, which make for economic progress. It is a notable fact that countries which increase their rate of investment manage to speed economic growth; most countries today with investment equal to 20 per cent of Gross National Product realize a growth rate of 5-6 per cent per annum.

This does not mean that a ratio of investment to Gross National Product of 20 per cent will automatically produce 5-6 per cent growth. Much more is involved in accelerating economic growth. The 20 per cent ratio is set forth merely to illustrate the general dimensions of the financial problems that may be encountered in a program to support the agricultural and industrial development of the less-developed countries. Actually, one of the problems is how to use capital, the scarcest resource, in the most efficient manner. By working towards this end, the less-developed nations may be able to achieve more rapid economic growth with substantially less capital per unit of output than is used by the industrial nations.

The objective of the United States (and other industrial nations) should be to assist less-developed lands which desire to do so, to raise their rate of economic growth substantially—at least to 4 per cent per annum wherever possible. Not all countries of course would be able to achieve the same rate of progress. Nations only beginning the process of industrialization (like certain of those in Africa) would of necessity advance more slowly, while others might move ahead more expeditiously. To achieve a growth rate of 4 per cent or more might require an investment on the order of 20 per cent of Gross National Product. A necessary accompaniment to this would also be parallel advances in education and training, as well as a non-inflationary fiscal policy. In these circumstances a significant improvement in living conditions could be achieved over the course of a generation.

At present, outside sources, including the United States, account for about one-fourth of the investment in less-developed countries. It is doubtful if their *proportionate* amount could or should be raised beyond this as a permanent policy, although it might be higher for temporary periods. However, an increase in the absolute amount will be necessary as investment expands. If, for example, investment in all the developing countries were to be raised to 20 per cent of GNP within the next five years, the total investment expenditure might increase to approximately $35 billion, compared with some $20 billion today. In these circumstances, investment capital from outside sources might amount to $9 billion in 1965, as against $5 billion at the moment.

It bears emphasis that such calculations are merely rough estimates and are set forth here only to give some general idea of the magnitude of the task. It should be noted too that the external investment of $9 billion would include both public and private funds. Private funds in turn represent reinvestment of earnings by foreign owned enterprise, as well as new foreign capital that flows from abroad. These public and private funds might be expected to flow from many sources, although primarily from the United States, Western Europe and Japan. Placed in perspective, $9 billion of investment would represent about 1 per cent of the combined Gross National Product of the industrial countries of the West—hardly a forbidding sum. For the United States the amount of capital supplied would be about $5 to $5.5 billion a year, as compared with an average of $3.5 billion in the 1956-59 period ($1.9 billion of economic assistance and $1.6 billion of private investment).

Naturally an objective such as this can only be achieved if the developing countries themselves adopt it wholeheartedly, take the necessary steps internally to carry it out, and are willing to enlist outside cooperation. Fortunately, experience to date suggests that they will want to move in that direction—a number have already done so. The details of implementing such a policy will be many, and will require some of the best talent the Western world can muster. Here, however, special mention can be made of only a few related matters: the need to draw in Western Europe and Japan as major partners; the significant role of private investment and of technical assistance; and the problem of commodity price stabilization.

The place of Western Europe and Japan. The needs of the less-developed lands can only be met by cooperative action on the part of the industrial nations as a whole. The problem is much too vast and complex to be shouldered by the United States alone. The United States must therefore bend every effort to enlist the cooperation of Western Europe and Japan in a coordinated effort to assist the developing countries. To accomplish this, new forms and new techniques may be needed—a matter discussed in a subsequent section below.

Today Western Europe provides about $1.7 billion to the less-developed countries, including both public and private funds. Much of this is directed to areas with which individual European countries formerly had ties or still retain them. Moreover the flow varies greatly as between countries—France and Britain, for example, provide most of the funds, while West Germany, The Netherlands, and Italy provide proportionately less. The whole of Western Europe, with its immense power and technical skill, needs now to be harnessed to the task. Likewise, Japan is coming into a position to give greater assistance and the resources it can make available will require coordination with those of the West.

The role of private investment.   United States private investment can make a highly important contribution to the growth and modernization of the less-developed lands.   The capital needs of these countries for financing accelerated economic development substantially exceed the sum of local savings plus the amount that can realistically be expected in the form of aid, loans from foreign governments and funds from international institutions.   Private investment by American companies abroad offers a number of significant advantages.   It is the most effective mechanism for transferring the managerial and technical skills and the creative quality of private enterprise to the less-developed areas. American companies investing abroad train local citizens for both operative and managerial positions.   They frequently provide the technical and financial assistance needed to set up local concerns to supply parts or materials.   They provide a competitive spur to local business.   The private investor has an incentive to be more efficient and more conscious of costs than a government enterprise.

Despite these telling advantages, the flow of private investment into the less-developed areas has been small in relation to the potential need for capital, except in certain oil-producing nations. The problem is that private investment will flow into foreign fields only if there is the prospect of a return that will justify the assumption of the risks involved.

Foreign investment generally involves greater risks and uncertainties than does investment at home.   All too frequently, however, these risks are multiplied by policies and actions on the part of governments in the less-developed nations which, consciously or unconsciously, operate to discourage the inflow of foreign private investment capital. Inflation and controls over earnings remittances; expropriation without fair compensation; discriminatory taxes and regulations—all act to discourage foreign investment.   Often these and other unfavorable policies are induced by fierce nationalism, distrust of outsiders stemming from anti-colonialism, and the confusion attendant on rapid growth and inexperience.

While the major stimulus to enlarged private overseas investment must come from actions by foreign governments to provide a more hospitable climate, the United States government can itself take positive steps to emphasize private investment in the less-developed areas. The negotiation of Treaties of Friendship, Commerce, and Navigation helps assure non-discriminatory treatment of United States investments and focuses attention on the need for policies that will attract such investment.

In addition, tax treaties can make it possible for the less-developed nations to offer tax incentives to attract private investment from abroad. For instance, under such treaties any special tax reduction granted by the host government to a United States investor would not be offset— as it normally is—by additional corporate taxation by the United States government when the profits are remitted to the parent company.

Two other methods are available to increase the contribution of private investment. The imaginative application and expansion of guarantee programs can reduce the unusual risks incurred in foreign investment. Greater use can also be made of management contracts to develop, construct and operate projects in areas where the risks would preclude direct investment. Where possible, however, it is desirable for private participants to assume some share of the risks.

Granted favorable conditions, the role of private investment can be substantial. Total United States private investment in the less-developed countries increased in the years 1956-59 by an average of $1.6 billion a year (one industry, petroleum, accounted for a large amount, however). There is no way to estimate the potential advance in the outflow of private capital if a favorable investment climate were to exist throughout the less-developed areas. However, experience in recent years suggests that a doubling or possibly even a trebling of the recent rate would not be beyond the range of probability.

Finally, a far greater effort is needed to spread an understanding of the contributions United States private investment can make to local development. Careful studies have demonstrated that the great bulk of the sales proceeds of United States-financed private enterprises stays in the host country in the form of wages, salaries, taxes and purchases of local materials. In many cases remittances run to 7 per cent or less of sales, a small price to pay for activities that generate local income and employment while contributing to general economic development.

Technical assistance. Quite as important to the developing countries as resources for investment, and sometimes more so, is the provision of technical assistance. Perhaps no programs have yielded higher dividends to date than those directed primarily to this end. Indeed, in countries first freeing themselves from the pattern of traditional ways, a lack of trained manpower is frequently the paramount problem.

The United States should make every effort to assist such countries to overcome educational and technical deficiencies, both through opening its own facilities to them and by helping to organize training within their borders. At the same time we must recognize that our country needs to prepare itself more adequately for overseas work and technical assistance. The United States until recently has lacked any general tradition of overseas service. As a result our citizens, by and large, have been less well equipped to work with other peoples than the situation now demands. Moreover, in spite of much devoted service, those sent abroad under government programs have too often failed to be of the quality required.

Our universities and others are making a beginning to correct these shortcomings, but more will need to be done. Our aim should be the creation of a body of well-motivated, technically competent representatives who are knowledgeable in the language and customs of countries in which they will be located. Overseas service should become an added element to every profession, and men and women with a genuine aptitude for it should be trained from the ground up. The demand for this form of service, by business, government, and the international agencies, is certain to increase greatly in the decade ahead.

The problem of commodity price stabilization. Like the early United States, less-developed countries today depend mainly on the export of raw materials and agricultural commodities for needed foreign exchange. Moreover, provision of these commodities constitutes an important part of their internal economies. Unfortunately, the prices of such products tend to fluctuate more widely than those of imported manufactured goods, and this diversion in price movements sometimes becomes a source of friction and difficulty. In consequence, a variety of schemes to stabilize commodity prices have been put forward, many of which would require cooperation from consuming nations as well as producers.

The widest and most severe declines in primary commodity prices in the past have been associated with recessions and depressions in the industrial nations of the West. The less-developed lands have paid a price for these fluctuations as have the industrial nations themselves. Probably nothing could be more helpful in maintaining a stable demand for world commodities than successful control of the ups and downs of the business cycle. As suggested earlier, this should be one of the paramount objectives of United States policy.

A much more difficult, and more controversial matter, is the attempt to control prices of individual commodities. Price declines in these instances may reflect shifts in demand or even over-production. Efforts to stabilize prices under such circumstances are costly and postpone needed adjustments. The United States has seen to its grief the consequences of such a policy in its own domestic farm program.

Nevertheless, adjustments flowing from any basic change in supply or demand factors of a specific commodity can often be painful for the producing country. A number of proposals have been made in the hope of moderating the swings, but whether the remedy would contain defects worse than the effects they sought to cure is uncertain. Every seller would like to have maintained for him a uniformly high market. Perhaps the best of the methods is the concept of the creation of buffer stocks for certain products which might lend themselves to such a procedure.

In the case of nonferrous metals, particularly, it may be possible to work out internationally administered buffer stock programs. The buffer stock would buy or sell within a fairly wide price range, and the range would be automatically adjusted from year to year in line with the moving average of actual prices over the previous several years. A workable plan of this sort would not be easy to negotiate; yet it might meet a real need.

The case of farm products is much more difficult. Buffer stocks would be impracticable for such products as coffee and sugar. In coffee some short-term form of restriction on exports and imports might be worked out by producing and consuming nations to avoid sharp balance-of-payments crises in the next few years. Over the longer run, the remedy lies in shifting from coffee and other surplus products to more promising crops. The United States economic aid program could helpfully stress farm diversification. In any case, short-term actions to forestall crises should be accompanied by longer-term measures to deal with basic causes.

It should be emphasized that no panacea exists for the problem of commodity price instability. At best, international control schemes can merely ease the impact of adjustments. Such schemes are difficult to work out, and hard to operate. Under some conditions they may delay and magnify an inevitable readjustment. Nevertheless it appears the United States should assume leadership in joint efforts on the part of the industrialized and less-developed nations to deal with the problem of commodity prices as part of a general development program.

V

ECONOMIC RELATIONS WITH THE COMMUNIST BLOC

Economic relations with the Communist bloc promise to pose problems for the United States no less puzzling and difficult than those with the less-developed nations. Unlike free world countries, Communist lands make foreign trade a complete monopoly of the state, and the usual considerations of economic advantage are not necessarily dominant. Not infrequently trade is employed as a political weapon—a fact brought home dramatically to the United States by the current experience in Cuba. The Communists can at no more than a moment's notice, if it suits their purpose, disrupt world markets through dumping commodities or through pre-emptive buying. Likewise, they can attempt to tie the economies of smaller countries to their own through bilateral trade agreements—agreements which aim at a monopoly of trade in certain key commodities and may provide disguised subsidies if such action is in the Communist interest. In addition to all of this, however, the Communists also find it advantageous to carry on a more normal trade relationship with many free world countries, exchanging goods which they produce relatively cheaply for specialized materials and products from the other countries.

Consequently, two sets of problems are posed: countering the Soviet effort to achieve economic domination and political penetration of the less-developed nations; and preventing Soviet trade with industrial nations from disrupting world markets. The major answer to the threat of Soviet economic penetration lies in developing a workable structure within which the industrialized and the less-developed nations can cooperate in seeking mutual objectives. The industrial nations can offer markets that are far larger (and in the long run can trade on terms which are far more advantageous) than those likely to be offered by the Soviets. Even the record to date shows that the European satellites consistently receive less than world market prices for their exports to the Soviet Union, and do not receive compensating advantages on their imports.

Efforts to encourage economic development and to promote freer trade will act to reduce the Soviet's ability to use bilateral trading devices to achieve economic dominance of smaller nations. However, this will require that the industrial nations keep their markets open not only to the raw materials and foods from the less-developed areas but also, as industrialization proceeds, to manufactured products. This will necessitate adjustments within industrial nations as manufactured products produced in relatively low-wage countries become competitive. This is another reason for working towards a more liberal United States trade policy while simultaneously developing mechanisms to facilitate the adjustments involved.

Meanwhile, a mechanism is needed which will enable the industrial nations to deal with temporary surplus situations in commodities produced by less-developed nations. Soviet buyers moved in when Egypt had a surplus of cotton, when Iceland had its fish exports curtailed, when Burma had a rice surplus and when Uruguay and Argentina had difficulty selling wool and meat. Such situations offer ready targets for Soviet penetration and propaganda. It may be appropriate for members of the proposed Organization for Economic Cooperation and Development to work out arrangements by which alternatives to Soviet purchases can be provided where needed.

At the present time it is difficult to envisage anything approaching normal trading relationships between the industrial nations and the Soviet bloc. In fact, the Soviets have worked the trade rules and procedures of the free world to their own political advantage on numerous occasions. The Soviets have been given many advantages, such as freedom to establish banking facilities and trading offices in free world nations, without granting reciprocal rights. Experience would indicate that the free world should move very slowly in expanding trade with the Soviet bloc with its system of state trading monopolies whose activities are dominated by political as well as economic motives.

In the circumstances it is not in our interest, nor in that of other industrial nations, to provide a net addition to the resources available to the Communists by extending long-term credits to them. Moreover, it would appear appropriate to maintain the embargo against exports of products having direct military significance and to urge other industrial nations to do likewise.

If, in the years ahead, the Soviets should display an earnest of good intent to trade on the basis of pure economic advantage, free world nations should be ready to accommodate such trade. This will require the development of principles to govern such trade. Certainly the free world nations should not attempt to develop state trading mechanisms to deal with the Soviets. To do so would be to deny the principles of multilateral trade and non-discriminatory export pricing which underlie the trade of free nations. Instead, an attempt should be made through an appropriate organization (perhaps GATT) to work out a set of trading rules to which the Soviets would have to subscribe.

Soviet aid to the less-developed countries. From 1954 through 1959 the Soviet bloc offered about $2.5 billion in economic assistance to less-developed countries (exclusive of Eastern Europe and Communist China) of which a substantial part has been for future delivery. In the same period the economic aid actually given by the United States amounted to approximately $12.5 billion. Soviet assistance outside the Communist world has been concentrated on a relatively few areas which are judged to be of special importance, or offered where attractive political and propaganda opportunities present themselves. India and Egypt are examples of the former, while Guinea and Cuba fall in the latter category.

There is little reason to doubt that Communist bloc aid will be further expanded in the future. At the same time the ability of the developing countries to make effective use of such aid also should increase. In these circumstances there would be little point to the United States opposing such assistance, and in particular making non-acceptance of it a condition for United States aid. At the same time the United States should be alert to see that the Soviet Union does not gain a privileged position in any country as a result of economic assistance it renders. Broadly speaking we can make only one effective response to the Soviet challenge on aid: to demonstrate conclusively that Western methods and techniques for economic development hold infinitely more promise for the developing countries than do those of the Communists and at no cost to their freedom.

VI

THE UNITED STATES BALANCE OF PAYMENTS

Since 1958 any consideration of United States policy on world trade, economic aid or any other foreign economic matter has invariably entailed examination of the impact of such policy on the United States balance of payments with other nations. The reason for such scrutiny is that the United States recently has been running a substantial imbalance in its international payments. In 1958 and 1959 the imbalance consisted of a deficit of about $3.5 billion annually; again in 1960 the over-all deficit may not show great improvement. In 1958, moreover, the imbalance was accompanied by a substantial outflow of gold ($2.3 billion). Since then the gold outflow has persisted, although on a reduced scale for intermittent periods. In addition, foreigners during this time have chosen to add to their holdings of dollar assets in the United States (which themselves constitute a potential claim on gold).

Deficits in our payments with other nations on the order of those of recent years are too large to be tolerated much longer. They call into question the future stability of exchange rates and raise doubts about the ability of the United States in the end to pay off foreign liquid claims against the dollar. At present these claims amount to about $23 billion, of which approximately $15 billion represents dollar exchange reserves possessed by foreign central banks and international institutions. In general, the claims are held in the form of United States government securities, deposits with U. S. banks, and other short-term investments.

Against these liquid claims the United States carries a gold reserve of approximately $18 billion. Some $11.6 billion of this is required under present legislation to be retained as gold backing for Federal Reserve notes and deposits (25 per cent of total notes and deposits). However, this requirement can be waived if necessary and is subject to modification by Congress. The U. S. gold reserve represents about 45 per cent of the total gold stock held for monetary purposes by all free world nations. It should prove to be more than adequate so long as foreigners retain confidence in the value and integrity of the dollar.

The balance of payments and economic policy. It would be a tragic result if the United States balance of payments problem became so acute as to thwart fundamental objectives of the nation's foreign policy. Indeed, to permit it to do so would be a confusion of ends and means. Today the United States stands stronger than at any time in its history, with a Gross National Product exceeding $500 billion, and possessing more than two-fifths of the free world's industrial capacity. True, United

States foreign trade, while large in absolute terms, represents only a modest proportion of our total economic effort. Moreover, the nation has been called upon to accept a special responsibility as the repository for a sizable proportion of the world's currency reserves. Yet in no sense are the fundamentals governing our international economic position such as to warrant cutting back on badly needed commitments abroad of a political, military, and economic nature. On the contrary, the thing to do is to face the balance-of-payments problem squarely and take whatever action is necessary to resolve it.

The basic causes of the imbalance can be quickly summarized. It stems from the fact that in recent years United States exports have not displayed a strong upward trend. (While the estimated total of about $19 billion for 1960 represents a substantial recovery from the depressed level of 1958-59, it is not radically greater than the average for 1956-57.) At the same time imports have been considerably increased. Meanwhile, the nation has continued to undertake very heavy expenditures abroad for military purposes, economic aid, and foreign investment. The net result of these and other transactions is that the United States has been paying out to other countries on its international accounts considerably more than they have been paying into it. Moreover, this deficit at times can be further accentuated by a sizable outflow of short-term capital funds.

A number of lines of approach are open to right this maladjustment and the United States already is taking action on some of them. Certain of the major considerations are these:

(1) Central to any achievement of balance in international payments is the maintenance of sound health and competitive toughness in the American economy. What the United States does to keep its government finances in order, to prevent inflation, to increase productivity, and to hold wage advances in line with rising productivity—all these will have a significant impact on the balance of payments.

(2) The United States in the end must export considerably more than it imports if it is to fulfill its world commitments. Moreover, a good part of this surplus must be achieved through private trade, and it will have to be earned. To achieve a surplus artificially, through cutting back on imports by tariffs, quotas or other restrictions, would be self-defeating. It would merely add a host of new problems to old ones, while forsaking a type of trade policy that is essential to the good health of the free world. While it is true that competition is becoming tougher (particularly from Western Europe), this acts to place a greater premium on the development of new products and of new and cheaper ways of doing things, in both of which the United States excels.

(3) It is extremely important that other countries, particularly those in Western Europe, remove whatever quotas and other quantitative restrictions still hang on against U. S. imports. These restrictions are a holdover from the days of the so-called dollar shortage. There is absolutely no justification for their retention in most industrial countries today.

(4) It is equally important that other countries, particularly those of Western Europe as well as Japan, assume a greater share of the burden of economic aid. Some should also assume a larger share of military expenditures. Both of these factors have weighed too heavily on the United States in light of the increased strength of Europe. Arrangements with regard to them were developed in an era of post-war reconstruction and dollar shortages. These conditions have long since passed and it is to the mutual interest of the United States and its allies to review and deal with the proper sharing of these necessary obligations.

(5) Talk is occasionally heard of a possible need to devalue the United States dollar. There is no necessity for such action if we manage our affairs prudently and others perform their rightful share. The dollar today is a key currency of the free world—the only one which is fully acceptable in lieu of gold and fully exchangeable into gold. Its devaluation relative to other currencies would be manifestly unfair to those countries which hold a sizable portion of their exchange reserves in the form of dollar assets; it would destroy the international financial mechanism as it now stands; and it would shatter confidence in the country and its ability to help manage world affairs to a degree which could affect the security of the whole free world. This is not to say that the present pattern of world exchange rates in all its details should be expected to remain unchanged forever. No decade in the twentieth century has passed without adjustments in certain rates. It should be the objective of the United States to cooperate with other nations through the International Monetary Fund in maintaining a continuous scrutiny over the pattern of world exchange rates. If changes become needed to correct fundamental maladjustments, they should be undertaken.

(6) Since it is important that the United States continue to be a major center for foreign currency reserves, steps should be taken in advance to strengthen the hand of the government (and other nations) to deal with emergencies or periods of adversity that could conceivably arise. For one thing, the earmarking of gold as backing for Federal Reserve notes and deposits is of questionable necessity and ties up scarce gold that might be available, if needed, for international purposes. Congress should give early consideration to changing the law so as to free such gold completely.

At the same time, careful study should be undertaken of the various proposals which have been made to meet the demand for liquidity on the part of the rest of the world without imposing undue strains on the dollar and the United States gold reserve. This is a most complex question involving such matters as techniques for cooperation among Central Banks, means for further strengthening the International Monetary Fund, and the like. Our broad objective must be to develop the measures needed to finance a broad expansion of international trade and services without imposing unusual or unnecessary stress on individual nations.

(7) It would be most unwise to reduce economic assistance to developing countries because of an imbalance in the international payments of the United States. Aid could be given directly and in kind in the form of machinery, foodstuffs, supplies and services, rather than in dollars. In some respects it would be more consistent with a liberal trade policy not to proceed in this manner, but instead to grant assistance for projects in the form of dollars, with authority to use them wherever equipment and supplies can be obtained most reasonably. Until other countries are prepared to do likewise, however, it would appear that the United States in the circumstances now existing would do better to tie the bulk of economic aid directly to exports, if only as a matter of leverage.

The present imbalance in United States international payments is a serious matter. However, the imbalance arises from the strength of the United States rather than its weakness; from its success in the rehabilitation of other economies rather than its failure. Programs of economic aid, United States military aid (which is provided directly in the form of military equipment and supplies), and the operation of overseas military facilities for common defense are all interrelated. It is possible to plan and coordinate these various programs, in cooperation with our allies, so that they will not place undue strain on the balance of payments of the United States or any other nation. This should be our objective and our policy.

VII

NEW FORMS FOR COOPERATION

Throughout this entire survey of the objectives of United States foreign economic policy one fact has stood out consistently—the United States cannot act alone. It must plan and carry out its policies in harmony with other nations. U. S. trade policy must of necessity be coordinated with that of other countries; the provision of economic assistance to developing nations has become a multi-national responsibility; balance of payments problems can only be overcome with the cooperation of others. More than ever the United States lives in an interdependent world—a world in which it is a leader, perhaps the principal leader, but not a dominant force, a world in which all nations must take heed of the desires and policies of others.

Such a world may stand or fall on its ability to devise means and methods for essential coordination and cooperation. One of the most difficult problems confronting the United States and the rest of the free world in the years ahead may well be the fashioning of adequate machinery for this purpose. One thing seems clear: new forms and new approaches will be needed, in addition to strengthening existing international institutions.

It is evident particularly that the United States must work in ever closer cooperation with Western Europe. Even today few Americans (or Europeans for that matter) appreciate the immense strength and promise of our Western European allies. Here is an area composed of about 260 million people; it has enormous resources when they are all put together; it has a steel capacity greater than that of the Soviet Union; a magnificent communications system; it is the repository of much of the best managerial and technical skills the world possesses, not to mention the greatest cultural reserves. To treat such an area and potential in our thinking as having no more than a trip-wire or shield function in the security of the West is both defeatist and unimaginative.

The time has come to take an entirely new measure of Europe's strength. It needs to be stimulated and energized, for it can be made a major element of the counterforce to the Sino-Soviet mass of which we stand in need. By itself, with all its potential, it may still not be enough to cope with the weight and pressure from the East or with the demands of the nuclear age. But when joined with the might of the Western Atlantic world and the British Commonwealth we have a strength and potential which, if it does not dwarf all opposing forces, certainly reduces to much more manageable size and to a proper perspective the menace of Sino-Soviet world domination.

The Organization for Economic Cooperation and Development. A start has been made in fashioning these new forms, but only a start. The newly proposed Organization for Economic Cooperation and Development (OECD), is one step in this direction, with its aim of joining the Western European nations with the United States and Canada for coordinated planning and action. If such an organization is properly conceived and managed it could become a key instrument for tackling many of the economic problems which confront the free world: foreign aid and the sharing of burdens, stability of prices, ironing out of economic fluctuations, and the like. Under such conditions, balance of payments matters could be viewed as a general problem of all countries and not something which falls primarily in the province of an individual nation, even the United States.

Again care should be taken that such a group does not merely become an exclusive club of industrial nations. A better form of representation of the less-developed countries of South America, Asia and Africa must also be explored. New regional groups now being formed may provide one aspect of such representation. It is possible, for example, that regional groups might form special missions to deal with the OECD with regard to economic assistance and other matters. In some instances individual countries might also establish such missions with OECD.

One cannot lay out any precise blueprint today of the organization and functioning of these new forms; nor of the details of their relationships with existing institutions. However, one of the prime functions of OECD, or of a Development Assistance Group within it, would undoubtedly be that of allocating the burden of global aid among its various members. The actual administration of aid, and even the determination of which countries and agencies should deal with specific projects, might be left to existing institutions.

Increased role of the international institutions. At the same time, the international institutions should also be expected to play an expanding role in world economic affairs—institutions like the International Bank for Reconstruction and Development (including its affiliates, the International Finance Corporation and the International Development Association), the International Monetary Fund, the United Nations Special Fund, and the GATT organization. These agencies have long demonstrated their competence and usefulness. They serve as a meeting ground for both the industrial and less-developed lands (almost all of whom are members), and they are staffed by able officers with detailed knowledge of the plans and problems in various countries. It is clearly desirable that these international institutions (including regional institutions like the Inter-American Development Bank) be accorded an even more important role in administering and coordinating free world economic programs in the future.

All this is not to say that bilateral contacts and national agencies will be outmoded. The problems are so vast and complicated that activity will be necessary at many levels. At present within the United States, for example, the International Cooperation Administration, the Development Loan Fund, The Export-Import Bank and the Department of Agriculture (through its surplus commodity disposal program) all play major roles in economic assistance to less-developed lands. Here the need is not for new organizations, but rather for a more effective framework for directing and coordinating the over-all effort of the United States.

There is no question but that the proper grouping of the forces of the free world, both on the side of the developed nations and those that are less-developed with common objectives and common obligations, can be the answer to many of our world problems, economic and political. It could be the chief stabilizing factor to a nuclear age. It might eliminate the threats and fears which plague the world today. It could remove the element of miscalculation or so reduce the possibility of it that the cause of peace could be immeasurably advanced. It could open to all nations the possibility of growth and increased well-being in the context of a free society.

The whole project is deeply challenging and it might with justice be said that this grouping constitutes the greatest imperative upon the statesmen of the United States and the free world today.

16

A LOOK FURTHER AHEAD

WILLIAM P. BUNDY

16

THIS CHAPTER, *written by the Commission's Staff Director, William P. Bundy, focuses on issues that will challenge us for decades to come: world population increase, and the continuing gap between the prosperity of the industrial and the poverty of the underdeveloped portions of the world.*

Mr. Bundy is on leave from the Board of National Estimates of the Central Intelligence Agency. The views expressed in the chapter are entirely his responsibility and do not reflect any official government position.

A LOOK FURTHER AHEAD

WILLIAM P. BUNDY

In the conduct of our national affairs over the next decade, we must
have in the back of our minds some picture of the problems that lie over
the brow of the hill—problems likely to arise for the first time or become
vastly more serious, possibly in the next decade, more probably beyond
that time. For those problems that may be totally new, we must start
preparing our minds; for present problems that appear likely to become
more acute, our efforts must build up momentum.

The perils of prophecy are obvious. Economists, politicians, experts
in foreign affairs are confounded at every turn. We cannot predict
even our own behavior in basic matters. To the American of the
Twenties and Thirties few things appeared more certain than that the
U.S. birth rate had leveled off and would continue to decline slowly,
so that our population would stabilize at about 160 million. Our postwar "baby boom" completely belied these predictions, creating a landmark in population study.

The failures of prophecy may cut both ways. The speculative dark
cloud may not materialize, but a storm come from another direction.
Events may come much more slowly than we anticipate, but equally
they may come much more rapidly. To take one of the other central
events of today, we all knew at the close of World War II that the
underdeveloped areas of Asia and Africa would in time assert their
independence. But very few would have expected this process to be
more than about halfway along by 1960. Instead it has gone 90 per cent
of the way, and the remaining 10 per cent seems imminent.

Both examples suggest that the risks of prophecy today, at least for
most of the world, run in the direction of underestimating rather than
overestimating the pace and degree of change.

To look usefully beyond the next decade, we must assume that there
will be no major war, that violence will be kept under some sort of
control, and that the course of the cold war will not turn drastically
in favor of the Sino-Soviet powers. International tension and arms
burdens seem likely to persist, however, and the balance of real or
assumed military strength to remain a major factor in the relationship of
the great powers.

This chapter is concerned with two other elements that lend themselves to prediction in some degree, and that will crucially affect the
ultimate questions: whether most nations of the world will choose the
methods of freedom, and whether men can learn to live together constructively in a world of developing justice and order. These elements
are:

- The increase of population, and its attendant political, economic, and technological problems.

- Changes in the relative economic stature of nations, first as between the Sino-Soviet powers and the developed countries of the free world, and second as between the developed countries, both free and Communist, and the countries now less developed.

I

POPULATION GROWTH AND ITS IMPACT

After the pace of changes in technology, and in large part because of those changes, the growth of the world's population stands as the second great characteristic of the present period in world history. From a level of about ½ billion in 1650, world population grew to a billion in 1850, and doubled again in the 80 years to 1930. The next doubling, to 4 billion, is almost certain to be complete by 1980, and after that the next might come within 35 years.

Concurrently, the relative rates of population growth in different world areas have shifted markedly. The areas we now consider developed— Europe, Russia, the United States—generally had their greatest rates of internal population growth in the eighteenth and nineteenth centuries. In most of the less developed areas such as India, rapid growth began toward the middle of the nineteenth century, and has not yet reached its peak. But it is not possible to draw the line between developed and less developed too firmly, either historically or at present. China had a rapid growth from 1750 to 1850 and then apparently slowed down for a century, resuming speed only as order and mainland unity were restored. Conversely the United States and Soviet Russia have not followed the pattern of Western Europe, but stand today in middle positions somewhat similar to each other in their patterns and rates of growth.

World population growth over the next forty years cannot, of course, be predicted with certainty. In most of the less developed areas, census methods and analysis are rudimentary; a few, however, such as India, Nationalist China and Singapore, provide excellent benchmarks. Most of the projected increases are based on falling death rates, and this trend is almost certain to continue, barring major calamity. Some decline in birth rates can be assumed, but this would have to be on an extraordinary scale to slow the rate of growth appreciably. Thus there can be little doubt of the main trends, and for a period as short as forty years the percentile range of probable error is not large.

Estimating the population of selected world areas at 25-year intervals for the period 1950-2000, on "medium" assumptions of future changes in birth and death rates, the careful studies of the UN—from which independent population experts do not differ materially—produce the results shown in Table I below. The U.S. figures for the table are derived from U.S. Census Bureau projections.

TABLE I

Estimated Population of Selected World Regions—1950-2000
(Medium Assumption) [a]

| | Population nearest million | | | Increase (per cent) | | Population in 2000 per 100 population |
	1950	1975	2000	1950–75	1975–2000	in 1950
Central America and Tropical South America...........	119	235	489	97%	108%	411
South-West Asia (incl. Near East)....................	63	116	206	84	78	327
South-East Asia............	171	280	498	64	78	291
East Asia minus Japan (mostly China)..........	595	958	1700	61	77	286
Central South Asia (mostly India).................	466	737	1310	58	78	281
Africa....................	199	303	517	52	71	260
U.S.S.R..................	181	275	379	52	38	209
Temperate South America...	27	42	56	56	33	207
U.S.[b]....................	152	235	310	55	32	204
Japan and Ryukyus........	84	117	153	39	31	182
Europe (excl. European part of Soviet Union).........	393	476	568	21	19	145

[a] "The Future Growth of World Population" (UN, 1960). See especially Appendix C, Table I (A) and I (B), and Table 9 in the text.
[b] U.S. Census Bureau, Series II projections for 1975, with the assumptions of Series II carried forward to 2000. The U.S. Department of Labor uses the Series III projections, which are slightly lower.

From these calculations (supplemented of course for the other areas not included in the Table), the UN projections conclude that total world population, estimated at 2.5 billion in 1950 and about 2.9 billion in 1960, should rise at an increasingly rapid rate each decade, with a total of 6-7 billion in 2000 "almost a matter of practical certainty."

Table I is designed, however, not so much to highlight total world growth as to bring out two more immediately crucial points: (a) the generally more rapid rise of population in the less developed areas; (b) the fact that while the rate of increase in 1975-2000 becomes *greater* than in 1950-75 for the less developed areas (except South-West Asia), it drops or remains about the same for the developed areas (and for Argentina and Chile, which are of course developed nations in many respects).

These two points are more significant than the world totals, whi tend to focus attention on the question of whether the total resour of the world in food and energy will be adequate. The problem is really not one of technological capacity, at least for this time period. We must of course make the proper effort to find new solutions to such immediate problems as water supply, to advance the sciences of agriculture and nutrition as rapidly as possible, and to develop energy sources, notably in the new atomic and solar fields. With such measures, *aggregate* world-wide supplies of food and energy can go far to reduce present mass poverty and malnutrition, and can prove equal to probable population increases over the next 10-30 years at least—*if the available and expected resources can be brought to bear.*

In short, the immediate problem—as so often happens—is much less one of technological capacity than of economic, and ultimately political, strains. These will come to a head far sooner than any theoretical imbalance of resources and population.

The economic side. The necessary effort requires, clearly, a major outflow of men, material, and techniques from the developed to the less developed nations. Most advances in technique must continue to come in the first instance from the developed countries. Their spread to the less developed nations, and instruction in how to apply them within a framework of effective over-all programs, will be a task of growing dimensions. The most difficult factor of all may be the process of learning and adaptation, which must take place at rates unprecedented in human history and in ways that affect the deepest social beliefs and practices.

During this process, population growth is bound to have a heavy and continuing impact on the costs and growth plans of the less developed nations. Whereas the United States, Western Europe, and even the USSR started the process of industrial advance with relatively small populations, the less developed nations (including Communist China) are attempting the same process at a time when their populations are already large and are expanding rapidly. The result is twofold: (1) a large proportion of the products of economic advance must go simply to maintain existing standards of living for a larger population; (2) the development of productive methods on the most efficient labor-saving lines leads to serious short-run unemployment and dislocation, and for this reason often cannot be undertaken fully in a free society.

These two differences alone make difficult any comparison between the economic history of the developed nations and the situation now faced by the less developed nations. Moreover, they sharpen the choice between free methods—recognizing human costs and seeking to meet the wants of people for higher standards of living—and methods of compulsion able, at least for a time, to deny these desires in the interest of future expansion.

How difficult the effort may become can be seen most clearly, perhaps, in the case of India, now about to embark on its third Five

Year Plan. The key feature of this Plan is a ratio of investment to total output of about 16-20 per cent per year, from which India hopes to achieve an annual growth rate of about 5 per cent.

Under its first Five Year Plan, from 1951 to 1956, India had estimated that its population was increasing by about 1.25 per cent per year, which would draw off relatively little investment. The validity of these calculations began to be questioned about 1956 as spot population checks were made. It now appears, according to present Indian estimates, that population actually was increasing at 1.6 per cent per year in 1951-56 and at 1.9 per cent per year in 1956-61, and is almost certain to increase at more than 2 per cent per year in the period of the Third Plan.

If India had not succeeded, with much foreign help, in raising the investment ratio from 9 percent at the beginning of the First Plan to the present 16 percent, virtually all new investment would have been required to meet population increase alone. As it is, nearly half will be so diverted. Yet the annual investment ratio India is now achieving with foreign help is a remarkable performance.

By contrast, the methods of Communist China illustrate the approach of compulsion in the face of a similar rate of population increase, now estimated at 2-2½ per cent per year. To increase food production is more difficult for China than for India, and more than 10 per cent of Communist China's output is now being devoted to agricultural investment. Agriculture is without doubt the weak point of the Chinese economy. But by holding down consumption and permitting, if not forcing, near-starvation in certain areas—in short by methods unbearable to a free society—China is nonetheless attaining a total investment ratio of 30 per cent or more a year. The proportion of investment effectively devoted to economic growth (after providing for the population increase) is thus much more than double that of India.

India and, in a different sense, Communist China are dramatic examples, but the problem is essentially the same in almost all the less developed countries. Some of the Latin American countries, notably Mexico with private American technical aid, have made remarkable strides in developing food production. On the other hand, the difficulty of applying even known and inexpensive techniques has been illustrated in Southeast Asia by the slow spread of Japanese methods of rice culture.

From an economic standpoint, in sum, population increase is a major drag on the progress of the underdeveloped countries, preventing any real rise in individual standards of living in some countries, dividing that increase by half or more even where development is proceeding at nearly the maximum attainable rates, and above all deferring the date when those nations can attain economic momentum on their own. It is of course by no means the only factor. But whereas others—leadership, capital supply, the spread of economic skills, adaptation to needed social change—may move cumulatively in a more favorable direction, the factor of population increase will remain for the next 10-30 years at least as burdensome as at present and probably more so.

Political consequences. Conditions of life in the less developed nations are not, to begin with, at levels that foster political stability. Indeed it is quite probable that, in the face of the population increases of the 1930's and 1940's, living standards have actually been going down until recently in much of the less developed world. *Per capita* food production in large parts of Asia and Latin America is almost certainly less than it was before World War II.

Thus, dissatisfaction would be natural in any event. With the spread of nationalism and the increasing visibility of living standards in the advanced nations, most notably in the U.S. itself, the result is a level of expectation throughout the world that places tremendous pressure on unsteady political structures.

Even if some progress is being attained, it may not be enough to resist this pressure. Indeed the history of past revolutions suggests strongly that the greatest danger period is not when living standards are actually lowest, but rather when they have started to rise, but not enough to satisfy aroused hopes.

Economic advance to meet rising expectations is by no means the only essential of stable government. There is no easy answer to a Castro or a Lumumba. Education, the training of leadership, the legacy of the past, and many other factors can be equally crucial. But without economic progress felt by the mass of the population in their own lives, the hope for political stability becomes dim indeed. Failure on any count means in the end either a turning to aggression abroad, or to methods of compulsion at home, or often to both at once and usually with Communist influence and tutelage. The U.S. and the rest of the free world can stand a few such calamities, but any large number would seriously imperil the open world order we are seeking to help build.

Issues for United States policy. World population increases, and especially those of the less developed countries, pose three issues for U.S. policy.

The first and simplest of these is at the technological level: to improve the supply of food, energy, and other resources, to reduce their cost, and to bring them increasingly within the reach of less developed nations. Whatever the trends of population may become, this will remain a first priority task.

The second issue concerns U.S. aid policy. Where food shortages develop, U.S. and other surpluses may help temporarily, but they cannot possibly be the permanent answer. For the long run we must anticipate the difficulties and give agricultural production special emphasis in planning our aid program. This, too, must be a first priority task under any circumstances.

What we clearly must not do in our aid program is to make any aspect of it conditional on a nation's handling of its population problem. Under no conditions should the U.S. government interfere in or attempt to influence local policy or desires regarding population. Birth rates are the result of choices that lie at the heart of human freedom and often of religious belief. Any government, even a totalitarian one, must weigh carefully the degree to which its influence should be exerted in this area among its own people. Overt influence by a foreign government should be out of the question.

Yet this basic principle leaves a third issue, one already troubling many Americans and almost certain to become more serious in the coming decade. The free choices that add up to our own birth rate are taken with knowledge and widespread use of available methods of control. Other nations are already seeking to make such knowledge and methods widely available to their people, and one major ambassador has suggested that the U.S. government should assist in this effort. If the need goes beyond the capacity of private groups, as seems likely, and if the methods used are similar to those legally practiced in the United States, a most critical issue of public policy will be posed.

The arguments for and against rendering such assistance—making it abhorrent to some Americans, and of the highest importance to others—need not be reviewed here. It is as difficult an issue as any democracy can face.

But however we may view this issue, it must not, at all costs, distract us from going ahead with our share of the technological and economic measures necessary to meet the basic needs of the world.

II

THE ECONOMIC STATURE OF MAJOR NATIONS AND AREAS

The decade of the 1950's will be remembered for a series of major changes in the relative economic stature of nations, notably the rapid industrial growth of the Soviet Union and of Communist China, and the re-emergence of Western Europe and Japan—greatly helped at the outset by the United States—as great centers of economic strength.

Considerable progress has been made in analysis of these developments, and of the condition of the less advanced areas, but such analysis is still far from exact. The principal tools, estimates of gross national product and capital accumulation, have considerable validity for individual nations, particularly those now in the advanced category. But comparisons among even the advanced nations can only be done with a rough measure of accuracy, and comparisons between the advanced and less advanced nations are even less subject to numerical expression.

Thus, any estimate of the present situation and any projection of the future even for a decade must be done with a broad brush and with a recognition that the margins of error are considerable.

Yet, with all these reservations, it remains essential to form some picture of the situation as it seems likely to develop over the next decade, and to see where the U.S. and the world might be found if a Commission of this sort should sit down to the same task in 1970.

Projections for the *U.S.* itself have been given in an earlier chapter (see p. 171).   Since ours is the most advanced economy in the world, the analysis is probably the most reliable.   Whether the U.S. economy grows at a rate of 35-40 per cent for the decade, as the earlier chapter predicts, or at the higher rate predicted or urged by some, we know what general level we may achieve.

The same is true for *Western Europe,* for the advanced nations of the *British Commonwealth,* and for *Japan* (subject to concern for the availability of its essential international markets).   If the affairs of these areas are handled competently, and political stability maintained or improved, the progress of the 1950's can continue.   This would give their people a rising standard of living, and would also provide the resources for Western Europe at least to become an increasingly major partner in the export of capital to other areas.

Continued economic growth by the *USSR,* and to a lesser degree by the *European Satellites,* is also probable.   In essence, these areas have now arrived as advanced nations.   Under totalitarian controls, they have a great and growing economic capacity to implement their policies (including the military side).   By continuing to devote to investment substantially higher proportions of their total product than the U.S. and Western Europe, they can probably continue to grow at rates on the order of 6 per cent per year.   Even on the consumption side, the condition of the Soviet and Satellite people should improve markedly; showcase achievements will not, however, obscure the continuing difference in the true standard of living, and it must be borne in mind that aggregate figures cannot take adequate account of the inferior quality of consumer goods noted by observers of the USSR.

The growth policies of *Communist China,* with their incalculable human costs, appear to have produced extraordinary material results over the past decade.   Even if growth has been short of the claims made, particularly in the 1958-59 period, it seems clear that the rate has been extremely high.   With forced investment running at 30-40 per cent of total output, continued industrial and aggregate growth seems likely. Any prediction, however, is subject to a major question mark of political stability, affected especially by progress in the crucial area of agriculture. The Chinese peasant may rebel, but it is wiser to assume that he will not.

Finally, for *the less advanced nations of the free world,* estimates of aggregate output are least accurate and meaningful.   But what is clear beyond the slightest doubt is that they start at such a low point, both in total and *per capita* output, that even rapid progress in the next decade will still leave these nations far behind. Nonetheless total growth rates at a fairly high level—much higher than those of the 1950's—are attainable in most countries *if* the necessary internal steps are taken and if substantial foreign capital and technical assistance are provided by a concerted effort in which the U.S. and at least the major nations of Western Europe join. These are the assumptions underlying the projections of Table II.

TABLE II

Selected Projections of Gross National Product

	ORDERS OF MAGNITUDE ONLY				
	Estimated 1960 Total (billion $)	Assumed 1960–70 Rate of Increase %	Estimated 1970 Total* (billion $)	Resulting 1960 Per Capita ($)	Resulting 1970 Per Capita ($)
Advanced Free Nations					
U.S.	$500	40%	$700	$2,800	$3,400
Great Britain, France, W. Germany.	175	40	250	1,200	1,600
Rest of Western Europe.	115	40	160	650	850
Canada/Aus/NZ.	55	50	80	1,800	2,200
Japan.	35	55	55	350	500
Sino-Soviet Bloc					
USSR	225	70	380	1,000	1,500
European Satellites. . . .	80	60	130	800	1,200
Communist China.	90	100	180	130	210
Less Advanced Free Nations					
Near East (incl. Greece, Turkey and Egyptian part of UAR).	22	60	35	185	225
South Asia	40	60	65	75	100
Free Far East (excluding Japan).	25	60	40	100	130
Africa.	30	60	50	135	170
Latin America	50	60	80	250	300

Sources: 1960 data derived from best available published estimates, principally from Congressional hearings. All estimates in 1958 U.S. dollars.

Table II uses these general estimates as a basis for projections of the possible situation in 1970. The data for 1960 are derived from published estimates, principally as presented to committees of the U.S. Congress by responsible Administration officials. To derive *per capita* output figures from the projected totals, UN population projections (on the "medium" basis) have been used.

The result is *not* to be interpreted as a precise forecast. This is particularly so for comparisons between the U.S. and USSR; even if the GNP projections were numerically accurate, a realistic comparison would focus rather on the allocation of resources for key national uses, where the gap is much narrower, and on living standards, where the gap is wider.

But there are three important conclusions concerning the coming decade to be drawn from Table II. These conclusions are "broad brush" but nonetheless so clear as to withstand any reasonable adjustments that might be required in particular figures.

1. In terms of total production and *per capita* income, the U.S. and the major advanced free nations will continue to have the capacity for rising living standards and adequate defense, and will have increased capacity for assistance to the less advanced nations. Total product will be substantially greater than that of the Sino-Soviet Bloc.

2. By 1970 the Soviet Union will have further consolidated its status as an advanced nation, with the capacity to support a major military effort, to increase the living standards of its people, and also to engage in far more extensive foreign economic activity. The same is true of the European satellites, which must be considered instruments of Soviet policy. Communist China presents a different and unique picture, with strong and growing elements of contrast. Rapid industrialization may well bring output in key areas, such as steel and electric power, within reach of the stated goal of surpassing Great Britain; though its technology will not be up to Japanese levels, Communist China may be well on the way to becoming the dominant industrial power of all Asia, surpassing both Japan and India.

On the other hand, low *per capita* output will still require Peiping to concentrate heavily on internal development; in effect, Chinese leaders themselves concede this when they speak of the many more years, after this decade, needed for "building socialism." This does not diminish one whit the psychological and practical effect on Asia of Communist China's material advance, but it does define limits to what Communist China will have achieved. It will be a nation "advanced" in a few formidable respects, but with over-all rounded development still distant.

3. The nations included in the "less advanced" category, both individually and in any conceivable grouping of common economic and political purpose, will remain well behind the advanced nations. The average *per capita* figures are a general indication of their continuing need for capital. This will be true to some degree even in the exceptional cases of Israel and Venezuela; it will most assuredly be the case for such major nations as India and Brazil, which will have *per capita* products on the order of $100 and $250 respectively.

III

CONCLUSIONS

What is clear beyond any doubt is that the path beyond 1970 will still be uphill. With continuing economic stresses, the problems of political stability and of the growth of freedom are bound to remain acute. The population problem in particular will become more, rather than less, difficult beyond the next decade.

The trends described above point up two major dangers that will confront us both in the coming decade and beyond. One is the effect of Sino-Soviet Bloc economic activity. Unlike the early years of the Soviet "economic offensive" (roughly 1954-57), the future will see the USSR increasingly recognized for what it is—a major advanced nation in position to furnish not merely spectacular "one-shot" assistance but continuing large-scale help. Soviet political gains can no longer be totally disproportionate, as they have been in a few cases, to the aid actually rendered.

By adroit action, however, the Soviets or Chinese will still be able to take advantage of political ferment, particularly in the first years of emerging nations. Guinea, the Congo, Cuba, will probably be multiplied.

The second great danger is more general. It lies in the excessive expectations of the newer nations, and their envy of the standards of the advanced nations—which will inevitably be increasingly visible to them, and increasingly far ahead of their own condition. Unmixed with realism and unmitigated by some signs of progress, such expectations can only strengthen those forces, internal and external, that would discard the help of the free advanced nations and turn to the Bloc and to methods of internal compulsion.

These dangers are formidable. They will certainly make our task painful and filled with setbacks.

Yet as the story unfolds there will also be great opportunities. One of them is to strengthen the bonds between the United States and the other free and advanced nations. The frictions of the last fifteen years over the U.S. position on "colonialism" may shortly begin to drop astern, and leave the way open to realize fully the broad community of interest that should exist in aiding the less advanced nations. Much has happened in the last two years to develop effective working machinery; this could be only the beginning. Properly applied, the assets of the free advanced nations can vastly outweigh those of the hostile Communist powers; by behaving constructively it is not wholly impossible that we could bring sufficient pressure to induce the Soviet Union to join the effort on a truly constructive basis. If so, we and the world should only welcome it.

Lastly, there is real hope that the less advanced nations themselves will see more clearly the logic of the situation, and the interdependence of their long-term interests and those of the more advanced nations.

Already many of the nations that came first to independence after the War are showing such understanding, setting their expectations at realistic levels, and discarding showcase projects (usually first offered by the Bloc) in favor of more fundamental economic efforts. If this trend should flourish, the task would be more and more what it should be—a common enterprise in which helped and helper have the same goal.

Essentially, the difficulties are such that a policy of maximum assistance by the United States and other advanced nations will remain a gamble. In the case of the Marshall Plan for Europe, the results were anticipated by many far-sighted men on both sides of the Atlantic, and began to be realized within five years. The present world-wide problem has no such predictable solution. The necessary pace of improvement will not have been reached by 1970, or for a long time after that. But to shirk the effort would be unthinkable.